Generative AI for Game Development

Crafting Narrative Worlds with Machines

Shesh Narayan Gupta

Apress®

Generative AI for Game Development: Crafting Narrative Worlds with Machines

Shesh Narayan Gupta
Varanasi, Uttar Pradesh, India

ISBN-13 (pbk): 979-8-8688-2438-8 ISBN-13 (electronic): 979-8-8688-2439-5
https://doi.org/10.1007/979-8-8688-2439-5

Managing Director, Apress Media LLC: Welmoed Spahr
Acquisitions Editor: Spandana Chatterjee
Coordinating Editor: Gryffin Winkler

Cover image by Freepik (www.freepik.com)

Distributed to the book trade worldwide by Springer Science+Business Media New York, 1 New York Plaza, New York, NY 10004. Phone 1-800-SPRINGER, fax (201) 348-4505, e-mail orders-ny@springer-sbm.com, or visit www.springeronline.com. Apress Media, LLC is a Delaware LLC and the sole member (owner) is Springer Science + Business Media Finance Inc (SSBM Finance Inc). SSBM Finance Inc is a **Delaware** corporation.

For information on translations, please e-mail booktranslations@springernature.com; for reprint, paperback, or audio rights, please e-mail bookpermissions@springernature.com.

Apress titles may be purchased in bulk for academic, corporate, or promotional use. eBook versions and licenses are also available for most titles. For more information, reference our Print and eBook Bulk Sales web page at http://www.apress.com/bulk-sales.

Any source code or other supplementary material referenced by the author in this book is available to readers on GitHub (https://github.com/Apress). For more detailed information, please visit https://www.apress.com/gp/services/source-code.

If disposing of this product, please recycle the paper

To my family, past and present, for their endless love, support, and encouragement.

Table of Contents

About the Author

Shesh Narayan Gupta is a Senior Manager in a financial service organization and holds a master's degree in data science. With a strong foundation in artificial intelligence and years of professional experience in data-driven problem-solving, he brings a unique perspective to the intersection of technology, creativity, and storytelling. His expertise spans machine learning, generative AI, and the practical application of AI in various industries, including finance, marketing, and education.

Shesh's expertise and contributions in AI have earned him recognition beyond the workplace, including being featured in *Times New Square* for his mentorship and contributions in data science. As a seasoned data science leader, Shesh Narayan has been at the forefront of leveraging AI technologies to drive innovation and efficiency in real-world scenarios. His hands-on experience guiding AI teams and building production-ready solutions gives him a grounded understanding of how emerging technologies can be applied responsibly and effectively. Beyond his corporate career, he has a deep passion for storytelling and game design, which has led him to explore how generative AI can revolutionize narrative creation, game development, and interactive media.

Acknowledgments

Writing this book has been a journey shaped by the insight, encouragement, and support of many remarkable individuals. I am deeply grateful to everyone who contributed their time, expertise, and inspiration along the way.

My sincere thanks go to Professor Nik Bear Brown for sharing his knowledge and thoughtful perspectives, which added depth to the discussion of AI and interactive systems. I am also thankful to Shubhi Saxena, Raghav Kandarpa, and Shivangi Saxena for participating in the interview process. Their experiences and ideas helped ground the book in real-world practice and strengthened several key sections.

To my wife, thank you for your patience, encouragement, and constant belief in this project. Your support made the long hours of writing possible.

A special acknowledgment goes to my son. His curiosity, laughter, and boundless imagination give my work meaning and inspire me every single day. Your favorite expression, "easy peeze, lemon squezee," stayed with me throughout this journey and reminded me that even the hardest tasks can feel lighter with the right mindset.

I am deeply grateful to my parents for their lifelong support, their guidance, and the values they instilled in me. Their encouragement has shaped who I am and made this work possible.

To all of you, and to everyone who has supported this work in ways big and small, thank you. Your kindness and belief in this project helped bring this book to life.

This work was created for the joy of sharing knowledge and ideas, with the hope that it helps others explore, learn, and create, rather than for any monetary benefit.

Introduction

Games have always been stories waiting to be played. From branching dialogue and emergent worlds to emotionally responsive characters, the drive to create living, reactive experiences has shaped game development for decades. Generative AI marks a turning point in that evolution. What was once static, scripted, and labor-intensive can now become adaptive, personalized, and endlessly expressive.

Generative AI for game development explores how modern AI systems can be used as creative collaborators across interactive experiences. While games remain the primary lens of this book, the techniques, patterns, and design principles extend naturally to related domains such as marketing, education, training simulations, and therapeutic storytelling. Wherever interaction, narrative, and personalization matter, generative AI has a role to play.

This book focuses on practical, system-level thinking rather than short-lived tools. Readers will learn how to integrate generative models into storytelling, character behavior, procedural worldbuilding, and adaptive experiences while maintaining narrative coherence, ethical responsibility, and authorial control. Through hands-on examples and progressively built projects, the book demonstrates how AI-driven systems can scale beyond entertainment into real-world applications.

As generative AI capabilities accelerate and new tools emerge at an unprecedented pace, understanding foundational concepts becomes essential. This book equips developers, designers, and technologists with the frameworks needed to evaluate evolving AI services, compare capabilities, and apply them confidently across games and other interactive experiences.

Introduction

CHAPTER 1

What Is Generative AI?

The rapid evolution of artificial intelligence (AI) has reshaped various industries, from software and finance to marketing and game development. Among the most transformative branches of AI is **generative AI**, a subset of machine learning designed to create original content, such as text, images, music, and even game narratives.

For game developers, generative AI presents a new frontier, offering tools to automate worldbuilding, generate dynamic stories, and create adaptive gameplay experiences. The ability to **generate**, rather than simply analyze, data makes this technology a powerful creative ally for designers, writers, and artists in the gaming industry.

This chapter introduces the concept of generative AI, its evolution from simple text-based models to sophisticated multimodal systems, and its applications in game development. By the end of this chapter, readers will have a solid foundational understanding of generative AI and its impact on the future of gaming.

Definition of Generative AI

Generative AI refers to a class of **machine learning models** designed to generate new content based on patterns learned from vast datasets. Unlike traditional AI, which primarily focuses on **recognition and classification**, generative AI excels in **creation and innovation**.

S. N. Gupta, *Generative AI for Game Development*, https://doi.org/10.1007/979-8-8688-2439-5_1

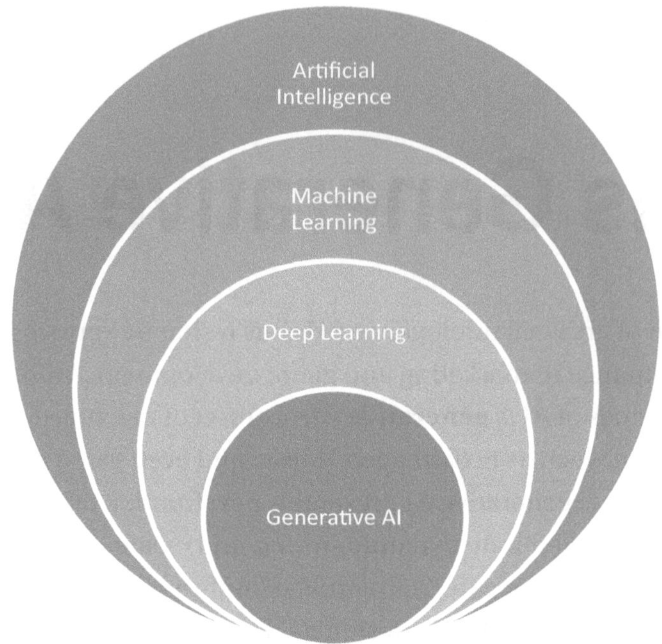

Figure 1-1. *GenAI is a subset of all*

For example, traditional AI in games might recognize a player's movement patterns and adjust enemy difficulty accordingly. In contrast, generative AI can create entirely new levels, write dynamic story elements, or generate unique character dialogues that adapt to the player's choices.

How Does Generative AI Work?

Generative AI relies on sophisticated **machine learning models** to create new content based on patterns learned from large datasets. These models use statistical probabilities and deep learning architectures to simulate creativity and generate realistic outputs across text, images, and other media.

Core Machine Learning Techniques in Generative AI

Several key models drive generative AI's capabilities, each using different mathematical and algorithmic approaches. I'll explain some core models and techniques in generative AI.

Neural Networks: The Building Blocks of AI Creativity

Neural networks are the fundamental architecture behind deep learning. They are inspired by the **human brain**, consisting of interconnected layers of artificial neurons that process and transform data. The ability of neural network models to understand complex connections and identify patterns and correlations makes them a top choice to use for adaptive responses to scenarios in gaming.

Basic Mechanics of Neural Networks

1. **Input Layer**: Receives raw data (e.g., text, images, or sound).
2. **Hidden Layers**: Process data through weighted connections, adjusting parameters to recognize complex patterns.
3. **Activation Functions**: Decide how neurons respond to inputs (e.g., ReLU, Sigmoid).
4. **Output Layer**: Generates the final result, such as a predicted word, an image, or a sound.

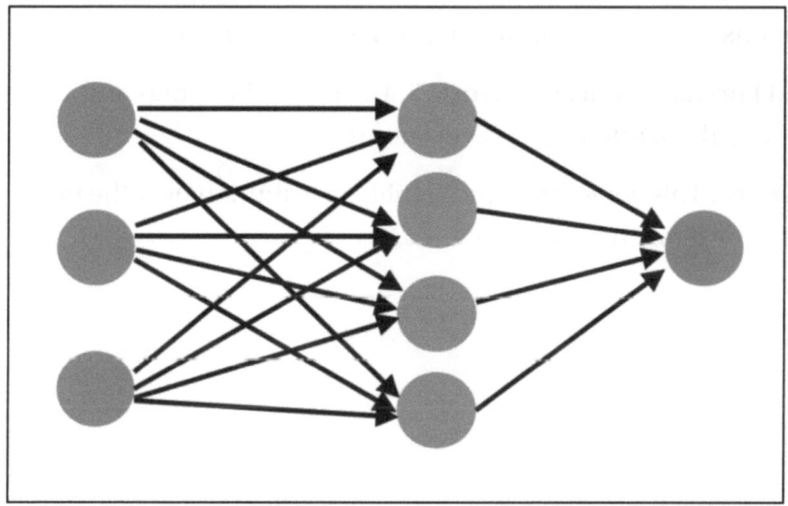

Figure 1-2. *A simple neural network, with input, hidden, and output layers*

Example in Game Development

1. **AI-Generated NPC Behavior**: Neural networks analyze player actions and generate **adaptive AI responses** in open-world games.

Transformer Models: Powering Advanced Text and Image Generation

Transformers are a breakthrough in deep learning that significantly improved AI's ability to understand and generate text, images, and code. The most famous example is GPT (Generative Pre-trained Transformer), used in AI-driven storytelling, and this feature of the transformer models makes them well suited for use in game development.

How Do Transformer Models Work?

1. **Self-Attention Mechanism**: Transformers evaluate all words in a sequence **simultaneously**, unlike previous models that processed words sequentially. This allows AI to **understand context and relationships between words.**

2. **Positional Encoding**: Unlike recurrent models, transformers don't rely on sequential memory but instead use **mathematical position embeddings** to track word order.

3. **Multi-head Attention**: The model processes multiple contextual relationships at once, improving coherence in generated content.

4. **Feed Forward Neural Network**: Takes the embeddings and converts them into higher-level features.

5. **Decoder**: This generates a probability distribution over the input for the next token in sequence.

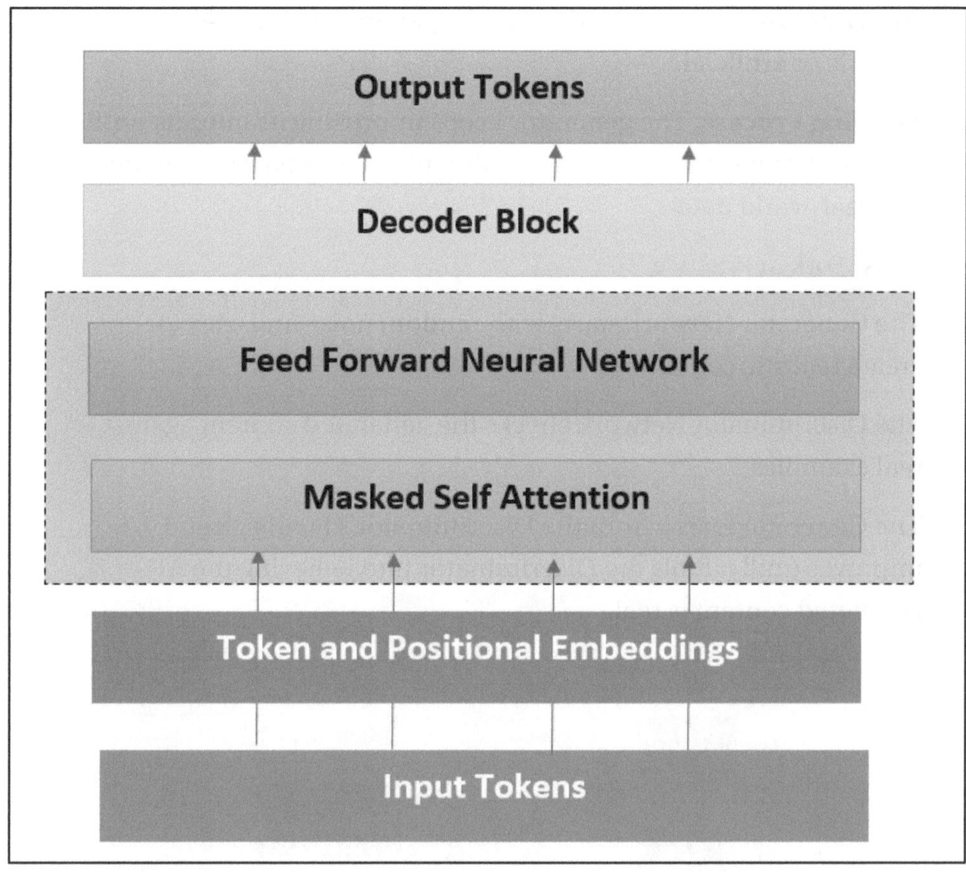

Figure 1-3. *A simple GPT (transformer model)*

Example in Game Development

1. **AI-Generated Quest Dialogues**: Transformer models can create **realistic, branching narratives** for RPG games based on player choices.

Generative Adversarial Networks (GANs): AI's Creativity Engine

GANs are a **unique AI approach** where two neural networks work **against each other** in a creative competition:

1. **Generator**: Creates new content (e.g., an image, texture, or 3D model).

2. **Discriminator**: Evaluates whether the generated content is realistic or artificial.
3. **Training Process**: The generator keeps improving its outputs until the discriminator can no longer distinguish between AI-generated and real-world data.

How GANs Work in Practice

1. The Generator Network starts with random noise and tries to create realistic content.
2. The Discriminator Network checks the generated content against real examples.
3. The Generator learns from the Discriminator's feedback and improves until it fools the Discriminator into believing the AI-generated content is real.

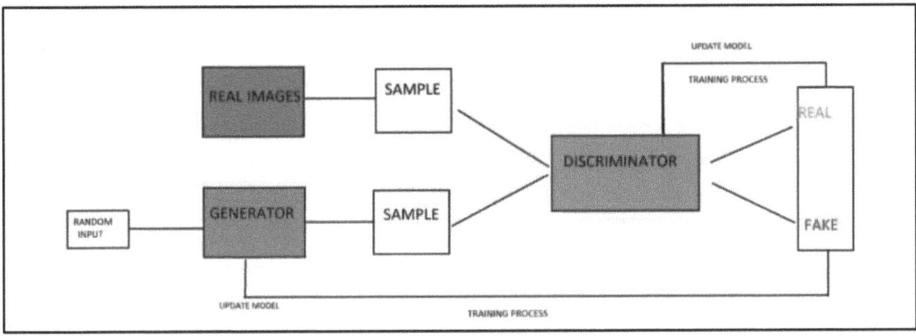

***Figure 1-4.** A simple GAN model*

Example in Game Development

1. **AI-Generated Game Assets**: GANs create realistic character faces, environments, and textures for game worlds.
2. **Procedural Game Art**: Tools like NVIDIA's GauGAN allow developers to generate landscapes and textures instantly.

Variational Autoencoders (VAEs): Learning Creativity from Data

VAEs are another type of generative AI model, used primarily for encoding complex data into a lower-dimensional space and reconstructing it creatively. They are especially useful for designing new game assets based on learned patterns.

How VAEs Work

1. **Encoding Phase**: The AI **compresses real-world data** (e.g., images, characters, levels) into a smaller representation.
2. **Latent Space Representation**: The compressed data is stored as a "blueprint" that AI can modify or mix.
3. **Decoding Phase**: The AI reconstructs the compressed data, **but with added variations**, generating new content that shares characteristics with the original dataset.

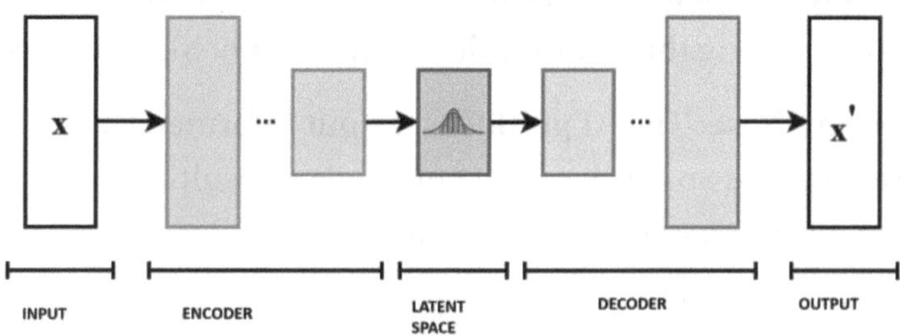

Figure 1-5. *A simple VAE model*

Example in Game Development

1. **AI-Designed Game Levels**: VAEs are used to **generate diverse game levels** that mix features from existing ones while introducing fresh variations.
2. **Character Style Transfer**: VAEs can morph character designs to create **unique art styles or blend different character traits.**

Retrieval-Augmented Generation (RAG): Guiding AI with Game-Specific Knowledge

RAG is a hybrid AI approach that improves generative models by grounding them in external information. Instead of relying solely on what the model has learned during training, RAG retrieves relevant data such as game lore, world rules, character backstories, or asset descriptions and uses it to create more accurate, consistent, and purposeful outputs. This makes it especially valuable in game development, where narrative coherence and design constraints matter.

How RAG Works

1. **Retrieval Phase**: The system searches a knowledge base (e.g., lore documents, design rules, item metadata) to extract information relevant to the prompt.
2. **Augmentation Phase**: The retrieved text is combined with the user's query, giving the AI grounded, context-specific guidance.
3. **Generation Phase**: The AI produces output informed by both the retrieved data and its internal knowledge, resulting in more coherent, accurate, and tailored content.

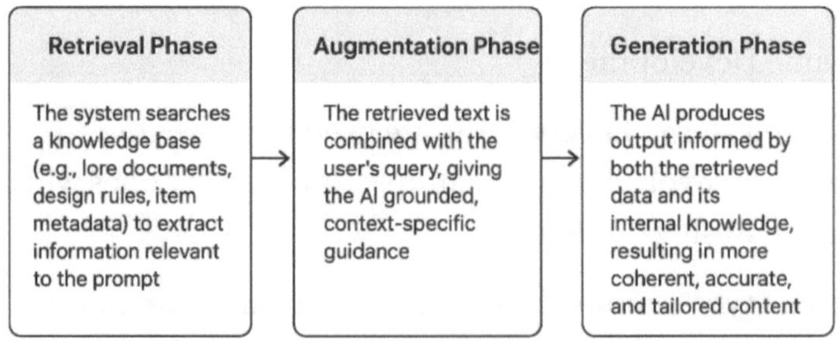

Figure 1-6. *Retrieval-Augmented Generation (RAG) workflow*

Example in Game Development

1. **Lore-Consistent NPC Dialogue**: RAG ensures NPCs reference the correct history, factions, events, or character relationships from the game world.

2. **Controlled Procedural Storytelling**: Designers can anchor procedural quests or branching narratives in curated databases, preventing contradictions or hallucinated details.

3. **Dynamic Game Documentation**: Game assets, crafting systems, or item properties can be updated in the knowledge base that gets instantly reflected in AI-generated content without retraining models.

Table 1-1. *Key Differences Between These AI Techniques*

AI Model	Primary Function	Strengths	Common Use in Game Development
Neural networks	Learning and recognizing patterns	Flexible, general-purpose	AI-powered NPCs and adaptive difficulty
Transformers (GPT, BERT)	Understanding and generating text	Context-aware, scalable	AI-driven storytelling and dynamic dialogues
GANs (Generative Adversarial Networks)	Creating realistic content	High-quality image and texture generation	AI-generated game assets and environments
VAEs (Variational Autoencoders)	Learning compressed data representations	Efficient, customizable	Procedural worldbuilding and art generation
RAG (Retrieval-Augmented Generation)	Grounding AI generation in external knowledge sources	Accurate, consistent, reduces hallucinations	Lore-consistent NPC dialogue, structured quest generation, controlled narrative design

How These Models Work Together in Game Development

Generative AI models are often combined to maximize creativity and automation in game design.

For example, a game studio developing an open-world RPG might use

1. **Transformers (GPT-4)**: For generating dynamic NPC dialogues and evolving quests
2. **GANs**: For auto-generating diverse character faces and textures
3. **VAEs**: To create new game levels that resemble hand-designed maps
4. **Neural Networks**: To enhance NPC behavior based on player actions

Generative AI is not just about automating content creation; it is a powerful tool that enhances creativity, innovation, and player immersion. By understanding how these models work, game developers can harness AI's potential to build smarter, more adaptive, and visually stunning game worlds. Each of these models contributes to how AI can generate art, music, text, and even entire game environments. I'll briefly describe where these generative AI models could be of use in gaming below.

Applications of Generative AI in Gaming

1. **Procedural World Generation**: AI-generated landscapes, cities, and ecosystems
2. **Dynamic Storytelling**: AI-driven plotlines that adapt to player actions
3. **AI-Generated Characters**: NPCs with unique dialogues and personalities
4. **Adaptive Sound and Music**: AI-composed soundtracks that shift with gameplay
5. **AI Coding and Development Assistance**: Generative AI tools that help developers write code, debug scripts, generate assets, and accelerate prototyping throughout the game development lifecycle

Evolution: From Simple Text Generation to Multimodal AI

The generative AI era, what we know now, was not always like this. The journey of generative AI spans several decades, beginning with simple text generation models and evolving into today's sophisticated multimodal AI, capable of handling text, images, video, and sound.

Early Stages: Rule-Based and Statistical AI

Before deep learning, AI-generated content was primarily **rule-based**, following predefined templates with limited flexibility, and below are some of the examples:

1. **Markov Chains (1950s–1970s)**: Early AI models for predictive text generation, often used in simple chatbots.
2. **Statistical Language Models (1980s–1990s)**: Introduced probability-based text prediction.
3. **PCG (Procedural Content Generation) in Games (1990s–2000s)**: Titles like *Diablo* and *Dwarf Fortress* used basic AI rules to generate random dungeons.

Rise of Deep Learning and Transformer Models

The advent of **deep learning (2010s)** revolutionized AI content generation. The following are the two most commonly used deep learning models in several different areas and industries:

1. **Recurrent Neural Networks (RNNs) and LSTMs (2014–2016)**: Enabled longer, more coherent text sequences for chatbots and procedural storytelling.
2. **Transformer Models (2017–Present)**: With the introduction of OpenAI's GPT (Generative Pre-trained Transformer), AI became capable of understanding context and generating humanlike text.

The Age of Multimodal AI

Modern generative AI models now work across **multiple media** types:

1. **Text-to-Image (DALL·E, Stable Diffusion, Midjourney)**: AI-generated game assets and textures
2. **Text-to-Video (Runway, Pika Labs)**: AI-generated cutscenes and cinematics
3. **Text-to-Audio (Jukebox, Riffusion)**: AI-composed adaptive game music
4. **Text-to-3D (Meshy, OpenAI Shap-E, Tripo AI)**: Tools that convert text or images into 3D models for characters, props, and environments

These advancements are blurring the lines between AI and human creativity—in a good sense, empowering developers with powerful co-creation tools.

Note The multimodal AI landscape is expanding rapidly. New tools, models, and platforms appear almost every week. Rather than relying on a single solution, creators should understand the core concepts so they can evaluate and "shop around" for tools that best fit their game design needs, art style, and workflow.

Key Tools for Generative AI in Game Development

The rise of generative AI in game development has introduced a wide range of powerful tools designed to enhance creativity, streamline production, and push the boundaries of interactive storytelling. From generating vast open worlds to crafting dynamic narratives and lifelike NPCs, AI-driven tools have become integral to modern game design. Developers now have access to models that can generate realistic dialogues, produce high-quality textures, and even design entire game levels with minimal manual intervention. These tools not only accelerate development workflows but also provide endless possibilities for creating immersive and adaptive gaming experiences. This section explores some of the most influential AI-powered frameworks and models currently shaping the future of game development.

GPT (Generative Pre-trained Transformer)

Generative Pre-trained Transformer (GPT) has emerged as one of the most powerful AI models for text generation, redefining how narratives and dialogues are crafted in modern games. Unlike traditional rule-based systems, GPT leverages deep learning to understand context, generate coherent text, and adapt dynamically to player choices. This capability makes it an invaluable tool for creating **interactive NPC conversations, branching storylines, and adaptive quest systems**. By analyzing vast amounts of text data, GPT can generate responses that feel natural and immersive, allowing game developers to build richer, more engaging worlds. Whether used to power text-based adventure games, procedural quest dialogues, or AI-driven lore generation, GPT is transforming the way stories are told in the gaming industry.

Application: Dynamic NPC dialogue, AI-assisted storytelling, quest generation

Example: *AI Dungeon*, which creates interactive stories based on user input

DALL·E and Stable Diffusion

Visual design plays a crucial role in shaping the aesthetic and immersive quality of a game, and AI-driven tools like DALL·E and Stable Diffusion are revolutionizing how game assets are created. These advanced models use deep learning to generate high-quality images from text prompts, enabling developers to rapidly produce **concept art, character designs, textures, and environment assets** without the need for extensive manual work. Unlike traditional asset creation, which demands hours of artistic effort, these AI models allow for rapid iteration and creative exploration, helping teams visualize ideas instantly. DALL·E, developed by OpenAI, excels in generating detailed and diverse images, while Stable Diffusion offers an open-source alternative that gives developers greater flexibility and customization options. Whether used to inspire new artistic directions or to supplement traditional workflows, these AI-powered tools are reshaping the way visual content is developed in modern game production.

Application: AI-generated game assets, concept art, character designs

Example: Automating 2D/3D character design in *Cyberpunk 2077* mods

Unity ML-Agents, Unity Sentis, and Unreal Engine AI

AI is no longer just a background component in game development; it is actively shaping how games respond to players in real time. Unity ML-Agents and Unreal Engine AI tools provide developers with powerful frameworks to integrate machine learning into gameplay, creating **smarter NPCs, adaptive enemy behaviors, and dynamic game environments**. Unity's ML-Agents Toolkit allows developers to train AI using reinforcement learning, enabling characters to learn from player interactions and improve their responses over time. This is particularly useful for **AI-driven opponents, procedural level generation, and real-time strategy game simulations**.

Unity Sentis, a more recent addition, allows developers to run advanced neural networks directly on-device within a Unity game. This means creators can integrate LLM-based behaviors, vision models, or custom inference pipelines *without relying on cloud calls*. Sentis opens doors for real-time NPC reasoning, on-device personalization, and lightweight generative systems built directly into gameplay.

On the other hand, Unreal Engine AI offers built-in behavior trees, navigation systems, and AI perception tools, making it easier to design NPCs that exhibit realistic decision-making and situational awareness. These tools not only improve gameplay realism but also enable **more complex and engaging AI-driven experiences**, allowing developers to craft immersive worlds that feel truly alive.

> **Application:** AI-driven procedural generation and behavior modeling
>
> **Example:** AI-generated dungeons in *Spelunky* using machine learning

AI Dungeon and Twine

Storytelling in games has evolved from linear narratives to highly interactive experiences where players shape the unfolding events. Although there are many AI tools, AI Dungeon and Twine stand at the forefront of this transformation, offering developers and writers tools to craft **dynamic, branching narratives with limitless possibilities**. AI Dungeon, powered by advanced language models like GPT, generates real-time, adaptive storytelling where every player input influences the direction of the plot. This makes it ideal for **text-based RPGs, procedurally generated quests, and emergent storytelling**, allowing for unpredictable and highly immersive narratives. Meanwhile, Twine provides a visual framework for creating **branching dialogues, nonlinear stories, and choice-driven adventures**, making it a favorite among indie developers and interactive fiction creators. These tools enable storytellers to break free from rigid scripting, offering game worlds that **react organically to player decisions**, ensuring a fresh and personalized experience with every playthrough.

Application: AI-driven branching narratives and text-based RPGs

Example: Creating nonlinear quests with AI-generated variations

Real-World Applications in Gaming

Generative AI is no longer a futuristic concept; it is actively transforming how games are designed, played, and experienced. From procedural content generation to AI-driven storytelling, developers are leveraging AI to create vast, dynamic worlds and more immersive player interactions. Open-world games like *Oasis* use AI algorithms to generate **entire ecosystems**, ensuring that no two players explore the same environment. Narrative-driven games benefit from AI-powered dialogue systems, as seen in *AI Dungeon*, where generative models craft adaptive, player-driven stories in real time. Even character development has evolved, with AI tools helping to **generate realistic NPCs, unique questlines, and lifelike animations**. Beyond traditional gaming, AI-driven simulations are being used in VR training, educational storytelling, and AI-assisted game testing, making development more efficient and interactive experiences more engaging. As AI continues to advance, its role in gaming will only expand, blurring the line between human-crafted design and AI-generated creativity. Here are some good examples which exist till date.

AI-Generated Game Narratives

AI Dungeon: Uses GPT to generate real-time, interactive stories

Project December: AI-driven chatbot narratives with unique personalities

Procedural World Generation

Oasis: Uses AI-assisted algorithms for terrain generation

AI-Enhanced NPC Behavior

Cyberpunk 2077: AI-driven NPC routines and dialogue generation

The Elder Scrolls V: Skyrim (Modding Community): AI-generated voice synthesis for unique character interactions

Conclusion

Generative AI is rapidly reshaping the gaming industry, enabling richer storytelling, intelligent worldbuilding, and deeply immersive player experiences. What once required large teams and long production cycles can now be prototyped or automated with AI tools, but more importantly, this transformation is accelerating. New models, multimodal systems, and specialized game-development tools are emerging at a pace that grows faster each year.

For developers, this means two things:

1. **The opportunity space is expanding quickly**, with AI tools becoming more powerful, accessible, and tightly integrated into mainstream engines and workflows.
2. **Understanding the fundamentals is essential** not just to use today's tools, but to evaluate the capabilities of tomorrow's. As new services, APIs, and creative models appear almost weekly, developers who grasp the underlying concepts will be far better prepared to "shop around," compare features, and choose the technologies that best fit their projects.

Embracing AI as a creative partner will unlock new possibilities, allowing game developers to build experiences that are faster to produce, smarter in their behavior, and more interactive than ever before. Those who build a solid foundation now will be best positioned to harness the next wave of innovation in generative AI.

CHAPTER 2

Why Generative AI Matters in Game Development

The gaming industry has always thrived on innovation, constantly pushing the boundaries of storytelling, graphics, and interactivity. With the rise of generative AI, game development is undergoing a transformative shift, enabling the creation of adaptive gameplay, procedural content, and personalized player experiences at an unprecedented scale. No longer limited to pre-scripted dialogues, handcrafted levels, or static narratives, modern games can now dynamically evolve, offering unique experiences tailored to each player.

This chapter explores why generative AI is a game-changer, provide more details about how it enhances creativity, improves scalability, and redefines personalization in gaming. Through real-world examples and industry insights, we'll examine how AI is shaping the future of game development and what this means for developers, designers, and players alike.

The Rise of Adaptive and Dynamic Gameplay

One of the most significant contributions of generative AI to game development is the ability to create adaptive gameplay where a game reacts intelligently to player actions, offering a unique and immersive experience every time it is played. Unlike traditional scripted logic, which follows predefined branching paths, AI-driven systems can adjust in real time, generate new challenges, and personalize interactions dynamically.

AI-Driven Game Mechanics

Generative AI enhances gameplay mechanics by introducing elements that learn, evolve, and respond based on player behavior:

S. N. Gupta, *Generative AI for Game Development*, https://doi.org/10.1007/979-8-8688-2439-5_2

1. **Procedural Storytelling**: Games like *AI Dungeon* use language models (such as GPT) to generate real-time, evolving storylines, making each playthrough unique.
2. **Intelligent Enemy Behavior**: AI-powered opponents in *Alien: Isolation* dynamically adjust strategies based on player movement, creating suspenseful and unpredictable encounters.
3. **Adaptive Difficulty Scaling**: Games like *Left 4 Dead* use an **AI Director** to alter enemy spawn rates, supply distribution, and intensity based on the player's skill level and performance.

Example: *Left 4 Dead*'s AI Director

In *Left 4 Dead,* the AI Director dynamically controls zombie spawns, item placements, and difficulty based on real-time player performance. If a team is struggling, the AI eases enemy waves and provides extra health pickups. If players are dominating, it ramps up the difficulty by spawning more aggressive enemies and reducing resources. This ensures that each playthrough is unpredictable, challenging, and immersive.

AI-Driven Personalization and Player Engagement

The modern gaming audience demands experiences that feel tailored to their preferences and playstyles. Generative AI allows developers to create hyper-personalized content, ensuring that every player feels engaged in a game world that adapts to their choices and behaviors.

How AI Personalizes Gaming Experiences

1. **AI-Generated NPC Dialogues**: Instead of relying on pre-recorded responses, AI-generated conversations, which are carefully generated with appropriate guardrails and testing, allow NPCs to adapt to player interactions, tone, and past actions.

2. **Personalized Quests and Missions**: AI can dynamically create side quests that are customized based on a player's in-game history.

3. **Emotionally Responsive Characters**: Sentiment analysis tools (like VADER or GPT-based dialogue systems) enable NPCs to react to player emotions, making interactions feel natural and engaging.

Example: AI-Powered NPCs in Roleplaying Games (RPGs)

Games like *The Elder Scrolls V: Skyrim* have seen AI-driven mods that allow NPCs to generate unique responses based on in-game events. Imagine an NPC that remembers your past actions, references your decisions, and adapts its dialogue accordingly; this is the future that generative AI enables.

Generative AI in Procedural Content and Narrative Design

Procedural content generation (PCG) has been a staple in gaming for decades, allowing developers to create vast, replay able environments with minimal manual work. However, traditional PCG relied on static algorithms, while generative AI introduces dynamic, evolving, and context-aware content creation.

How AI Enhances Procedural Content Generation

1. **Level Design**: AI-generated terrain and dungeon layouts ensure infinite exploration possibilities (e.g., AI *Minecraft*).

2. **Dynamic Storytelling**: AI-driven narrative engines craft real-time, player-driven story arcs rather than following pre-written scripts.

3. **Item and Enemy Generation**: AI balances loot drops, NPC placement, and enemy behavior dynamically, ensuring a fair and engaging experience.

Example: *Oasis*—AI-Generated Universes

One of the most ambitious uses of AI-driven procedural generation, Oasis (AI Minecraft) leverages AI to generate almost infinite unique landscapes, each with distinct ecosystems, environment conditions, flora, and fauna. Every player's journey is different, making navigation feel endless and unpredictable.

Why AI Tools Are Essential: A Comparison of Traditional vs. AI-Driven Game Development

Generative AI is revolutionizing game development, but why is it necessary? Couldn't developers achieve the same results using traditional methods? While technically possible, the difference lies in time, scalability, efficiency, and creative flexibility. Below, I'll provide a detailed comparison of how AI tools accelerate and enhance the game development process compared to traditional methods.

Game World Creation: Traditional vs. AI-Driven

Creating expansive and immersive game worlds has always been one of the most challenging aspects of game development. Traditionally, designers and artists have spent years meticulously crafting landscapes, structures, and environmental details by hand, ensuring every element feels unique and engaging. While this approach allows for high levels of artistic control, it is also incredibly time-consuming and resource-intensive, often requiring large development teams. With the advent of AI-powered procedural generation, developers can now create vast, dynamic environments in a fraction of the time, enabling richer worlds that adapt to player exploration while maintaining artistic quality and design coherence. This shift is not about replacing human creativity but enhancing it, allowing developers to focus on fine-tuning and storytelling rather than manually placing every rock and tree. The following are some major advantages of AI-powered methods over traditional methods in gaming world creation.

Traditional Method (Handcrafted Environments)

1. **Time-Consuming**: Creating detailed game worlds manually requires thousands of hours from level designers, artists, and modelers.
2. **Repetitive Work**: Developers must handcraft terrain, buildings, landscapes, and textures, limiting the scale of game environments.
3. **Static Worlds**: Pre-designed worlds remain unchanging, requiring separate scripting for variations or expansions.

AI-Powered Method (Procedural Generation and AI-Enhanced Level Design)

1. **Rule-Based**: AI generates entire game worlds based on rules set by developers, dramatically reducing design time.
2. **Scalability**: Instead of handcrafting hundreds of levels, AI can dynamically create infinite environments (as seen in *Oasis*).
3. **Adaptable**: AI-driven terrain generation adapts to gameplay, meaning no two players experience the exact same world.

Example: *Oasis* vs. Handcrafted Open Worlds

Oasis used transformer AI procedural generation to create endless landscapes, something impossible to achieve manually, as compared to *The Witcher 3* (handcrafted world) that took over three years and 1,500 developers[1] to complete, with every detail placed manually.

Note Without AI, large-scale open worlds are extremely expensive and time-consuming to develop.

---

[1] Reference taken from Wikipedia.

Storytelling and Dialogue: Traditional vs. AI-Generated

Storytelling has always been the heart of immersive gaming, shaping player experiences through well-crafted narratives and engaging dialogues. Traditionally, writers meticulously script every interaction, designing branching dialogue trees and multiple story paths to account for player choices. While this method ensures narrative depth, it is inherently limited by time, scope, and manpower, often resulting in rigid, repetitive conversations and a finite number of outcomes. AI-generated storytelling, on the other hand, introduces dynamic, real-time dialogue generation, allowing NPCs to respond intelligently to player actions, emotions, and choices.

Instead of following pre-written lines, AI-powered narratives can evolve organically, making interactions feel more natural, unpredictable, and immersive. By combining AI-assisted storytelling with human creativity, developers can create more expansive, player-driven narratives without the constraints of traditional scripting. Below are some of the notable advantages of AI-powered methods over traditional storytelling.

Traditional Method (Scripted Storylines and Predefined NPC Dialogues)

1. **Requires human writers** to script every possible dialogue tree and branching path.

2. **Static Conversations**: NPCs repeat the same dialogue every time, reducing immersion.

3. **Limited Replay Ability**: Players exhaust dialogue options, making character interactions feel repetitive.

AI-Powered Method (Adaptive, Player-Driven Narratives)

1. **Dynamic**: AI generates dynamic NPC responses, making conversations feel natural and evolving.

2. **Real Time**: AI-powered storytelling tools (like GPT-based systems) can generate real-time, unique questlines instead of relying on pre-written ones.

3. **Adaptable**: AI adapts narratives to player actions, ensuring each player's experience is unique.

Example: AI Dungeon vs. Traditional RPGs

AI Dungeon uses GPT models to create infinite, unpredictable stories, compared to traditional RPGs, which rely on fixed quest trees. A good example is *Mass Effect* which required over 1.2 million[2] words of pre-scripted dialogue, limiting its ability to evolve dynamically based on choices.

Note Without AI, game stories are limited by human scripting capacity, reducing narrative flexibility.

NPC Behavior: Traditional vs. AI-Enhanced

Non-playable characters (NPCs) are essential to creating immersive game worlds, but their behavior has traditionally been limited by predefined scripts and behavior trees. In classic game design, NPCs follow fixed movement patterns, predictable responses, and scripted routines, making their interactions feel repetitive and mechanical over time. While developers can design complex AI systems manually, these require extensive coding, significant development time, and constant fine-tuning. AI-enhanced NPCs, however, bring a new level of realism by utilizing machine learning and adaptive behavior models. These AI-driven characters can learn from player interactions, react dynamically to in-game events, and adjust their strategies in real time.

Whether it's an enemy that adapts to combat tactics or a shopkeeper that remembers previous conversations, AI-powered NPCs create a more immersive, lifelike, and unpredictable gaming experience. Instead of feeling like static background elements, they become reactive and intelligent participants in the game world, enhancing both storytelling and gameplay depth. Below, we can see the core differences of AI-powered vs. traditional methods in NPC behavior.

[2] Reference taken from GameFAQs.

Traditional Method (Pre-scripted AI and Fixed Behavior Trees)

1. NPC actions are **pre-programmed**, meaning they react the same way every time.
2. Complex AI behavior requires **thousands of lines of code**, making NPCs rigid and predictable.
3. **No adaptive learning since** NPCs don't adjust to player strategies, leading to repetitive enemy encounters.

AI-Powered Method (Machine Learning for Smarter NPCs)

1. **Smarter NPC**: AI-powered NPCs learn from player behavior and adapt their responses dynamically.
2. **Self-Learning**: Reinforcement learning enables AI to train itself to behave intelligently, rather than following scripted actions.
3. **Dynamic**: AI-enhanced NPCs can create unscripted, emergent gameplay, making interactions feel more organic.

Example: *Alien: Isolation* vs. Older Stealth Games

Alien: Isolation uses AI-driven enemy behavior, allowing the alien to learn and evolve rather than follow predictable patterns, as compared to *Metal Gear Solid 2* that relied on fixed enemy patrols and pre-scripted reactions, making them easier to exploit.

Note Without AI, NPCs lack unpredictability, making enemy encounters repetitive and less immersive.

Game Asset Creation: Traditional vs. AI-Assisted

Creating high-quality game assets such as character models, textures, environments, and animations has traditionally been a labor-intensive process, requiring skilled artists to meticulously design each element by hand. From concept art to final rendering, every stage demands significant time and effort, especially for large-scale games with expansive worlds. While this approach ensures artistic precision, it also limits scalability and can significantly extend development timelines. AI-assisted tools, such as DALL·E and Stable Diffusion for concept art or GAN-based texture generation, are transforming asset creation by enabling rapid prototyping, automatic texture generation, and real-time asset enhancements.

With AI, artists can iterate faster, generate variations instantly, and focus on refining details rather than starting from scratch. **This does not replace human creativity but enhances it, allowing developers to maintain artistic vision while significantly reducing production time and resource constraints**. The following are the key differences in traditional asset creation vs. AI-assisted asset creation.

Traditional Method (Handcrafted Game Assets and Textures)

1. **Manual**: Artists manually draw, sculpt, and texture characters, environments, and objects.
2. **Effort**: Each iteration requires significant time and effort, especially for high-resolution assets.
3. **Size Limitation**: Game assets must be painstakingly optimized for performance across platforms.

AI-Powered Method (DALL·E and Stable Diffusion for Instant Asset Generation)

1. **Fast**: AI generates concept art, character designs, and textures in seconds, reducing the need for manual work.
2. **Optimized**: AI enhances and optimizes textures automatically, ensuring high-quality graphics without bloating file sizes.
3. **Efficient**: AI tools allow for rapid prototyping, helping designers iterate faster and refine ideas more efficiently.

Example: *Cyberpunk 2077* (Handcrafted) vs. AI-Assisted Art Generation

Cyberpunk 2077 required thousands of artists to manually create characters and city environments as compared to AI-driven tools like Stable Diffusion that could have automated texture and environment generation, significantly reducing production time.

Note Without AI, game asset creation remains an expensive, time-consuming process requiring large teams.

Table 2-1. *Final Comparison: Traditional vs. AI-Driven Game Development*

Aspect	Traditional Method	AI-Powered Method
Game World Creation	Handcrafted environments, time-consuming	AI-generated landscapes, infinite scalability
Storytelling and NPC Dialogue	Pre-written scripts, limited flexibility	Adaptive, dynamic conversations and quests
NPC Behavior	Fixed enemy actions, no learning	AI-driven, unpredictable, and evolving behaviors
Game Asset Design	Manual character and texture creation	AI-assisted art generation, faster iterations

EXERCISE: GENERATE AN AI-ASSISTED ART

Use the below prompt to generate an AI-assisted art using DALL·E, Stable Diffusion, or any other image generation AI tool, and see for yourself how powerful and fast these tools can be.

Prompt: A formidable evil character engulfed in a mesmerizing aura of plasma energy, rendered in a unique blend of traditional illustration and fluid illustration techniques. Bold uniform strokes capture the character's malevolent essence, while intricate details highlight the flames that dance around their form, creating a striking contrast against the epic sci-fi environment made of fire and flames. The dramatic viewpoint enhances the character's imposing presence, as they wield an ominous weapon forged from fire and flames, exuding an air of enchanting enigma.

Figure 2-1. *Output image from CGdream.ai using the exercise prompt*

Why AI Is a Game-Changer

While traditional methods have produced some of the most iconic games in history, generative AI is redefining how games are built, played, and experienced. AI-powered tools drastically reduce development time, increase scalability, and enhance immersion by allowing for dynamic, evolving game worlds. Without AI, developers face longer production cycles, higher costs, and limitations in content generation.

However, **AI should not be seen as a replacement for human creativity but as a collaborative tool** that empowers game designers, artists, and storytellers. The future of game development will be a blend of human-driven creativity and AI-enhanced innovation, paving the way for **games that are more immersive, intelligent, and limitless than ever before.**

The Future of Generative AI in Game Development: What's Next?

Generative AI is still evolving, but its impact on gaming will only grow in the coming years. Some exciting possibilities include

1. **Fully AI-Generated Games**: Imagine a game where every environment, character, and storyline are uniquely generated for each player.
2. **AI As a Co-developer**: AI-driven game engines could assist developers in coding, asset generation, and debugging.
3. **Smarter AI Opponents**: Future AI models will create opponents that learn and evolve, mimicking humanlike behavior.

While generative AI offers incredible benefits, it also raises important challenges:

1. **AI Bias in Storytelling and Character Design**: Ensuring fairness and inclusivity in AI-generated content
2. **Player Data and Privacy**: Managing how AI tracks and adapts to player behaviors without invading privacy
3. **Game Balance and AI Dependency**: Preventing AI from making games too unpredictable or unmanageable

---

Note We will cover more on ethical considerations and challenges in Chapter 8.

Conclusion

Generative AI is reshaping the gaming landscape, allowing developers to create richer, more dynamic experiences than ever before. From adaptive storytelling and intelligent NPCs to procedural worlds and personalized quests, AI is unlocking new levels of immersion and interactivity.

For game developers, embracing AI as a creative tool rather than a replacement is key. By combining human ingenuity with AI-driven innovation, the future of gaming will be more expansive, personalized, and engaging than ever before.

CHAPTER 3

Purpose and Audience of the Book

Generative AI is no longer a futuristic concept. It is actively reshaping how games are imagined, developed, and experienced. However, the rapid growth of this field has created a gap between the potential of these technologies and the practical understanding needed to apply them effectively in creative domains like game development. This book aims to bridge that gap. Whether you're a developer looking to integrate AI into your workflow, a writer interested in building dynamic narratives, or a designer experimenting with procedural generation, this book provides a clear, structured path to understanding and leveraging generative AI tools.

In this chapter, we'll define who this book is for, outline the skills and knowledge it imparts, and explain how the chapters are organized to guide readers from foundational concepts to advanced applications.

Who This Book Is For

This book is written for readers who are ready to move beyond the theoretical and start practically applying generative AI in the context of game development and interactive storytelling. While prior experience in AI or machine learning is not mandatory, readers should have a basic understanding of game design principles and interactivity in digital media.

S. N. Gupta, *Generative AI for Game Development*, https://doi.org/10.1007/979-8-8688-2439-5_3

Target Audience

1. **Game developers** interested in incorporating AI into level design, character creation, or procedural worldbuilding.
2. **Narrative designers and writers** seeking to craft dynamic, branching stories using AI-driven tools.
3. **AI enthusiasts and technical artists** looking to understand how generative models like GPT or Stable Diffusion can be adapted for creative applications.
4. **Educators and students** working on game development, digital storytelling, or interactive design projects.
5. **Indie developers and solo creators** exploring efficient ways to scale content generation without large teams.

The book is tailored for **intermediate users** who have a foundation in either game development or creative coding and are now looking to integrate emerging technologies like generative AI into their work.

Key Takeaways: What You Will Gain

By the end of this book, readers will have developed practical, hands-on knowledge of using generative AI to enhance creative workflows, along with the conceptual tools to think critically about the role of AI in interactive media.

What You Will Learn

1. Understanding the core mechanics of GPT, DALL·E, Stable Diffusion, VAE, GANs, and other foundational AI models
2. Using AI to generate interactive narratives, design emotionally responsive NPCs, and build adaptive dialogue systems
3. Applying sentiment analysis and other natural language processing techniques to enhance player immersion

4. Building projects such as procedural story generators, emotionally intelligent characters, and branching dialogue games using tools like Twine, Python, and Unity

5. Evaluating the ethical implications and creative opportunities of AI-generated content

These outcomes are not just theoretical. Each concept is paired with real-world examples, industry case studies, and step-by-step projects to reinforce understanding and provide inspiration for your own work.

How This Book Is Structured

The book is designed to guide readers progressively, starting with a foundation in generative AI, followed by applications in storytelling, and culminating in implementation, industry-specific use cases, and practical projects.

Part 1: Foundations of AI Storytelling

Covers the building blocks of storytelling, interactive narratives, and how AI can augment traditional narrative structures. It introduces tools such as GPT and Twine and explains how to apply them creatively.

Part 2: Designing Interactive Narratives

Focuses on the design and structure of branching storylines, emotionally engaging content, and sentiment-driven storytelling. This part introduces key techniques for building reactive narratives.

Part 3: Implementing AI-Driven Storytelling

Provides a technical deep dive into integrating AI tools with development environments like Python, Flask, and Unity. Readers will walk through projects such as AI-generated dialogue systems and procedural worldbuilding.

Part 4: Advanced Techniques Across Industries

Explores the application of generative AI beyond entertainment such as in education, marketing, and mental health, showcasing how the same tools can be adapted across domains.

Part 5: Challenges, Best Practices, and Future Trends

Looks at the ethical, technical, and creative challenges of working with AI while also providing best practices for sustainable, inclusive, and responsible development.

Part 6: Practical Projects and Templates

Offers ready-to-use frameworks, reusable code snippets, and project ideas that can be customized for different applications. This part is hands-on and ideal for readers ready to prototype and build.

Why This Book Matters Now

The integration of AI into creative workflows is not a distant innovation; it's happening right now. Studios are experimenting with AI-generated scripts, indie developers are using AI to scale content, and educators are introducing AI tools in classrooms. Yet, many creators feel overwhelmed by the pace of change or unsure of where to begin.

This book offers a clear, grounded entry point rooted in real tools, actual use cases, and tangible outcomes. It's not about hype; it's about equipping creators with the practical knowledge and ethical frameworks to harness AI as a collaborative partner in game development and storytelling.

Conclusion

This book is for creators, thinkers, and builders who see the potential of AI not as a replacement for human creativity but as a tool for enhancing it. Whether you're a developer designing your first AI-enhanced game or a writer exploring new ways to tell stories, this book will give you the skills, insight, and inspiration to make it happen.

PART I

Foundations of AI Storytelling

CHAPTER 4

What Is Storytelling?

Storytelling is one of the most powerful and enduring forms of human expression. It predates the written word and has evolved alongside every cultural and technological advancement throughout history. From oral myths passed down through generations to cinematic masterpieces and interactive games, storytelling remains central to how we understand the world, build empathy, and share ideas.

In the realm of game development, storytelling is not just an aesthetic element; it is a core pillar of design. A well-told story can elevate gameplay, deepen immersion, and create emotional experiences that players carry long after the game ends. Whether you're crafting a AAA cinematic experience or a text-based indie adventure, understanding how stories work, what they're made of, how they're structured, and why they matter is essential.

This chapter explores the role of storytelling in games, dissects its core components, and tracks its evolution from ancient tradition to AI-enhanced narratives, preparing the groundwork for the chapters ahead.

As we move into AI-driven storytelling systems, understanding these foundational narrative elements becomes essential. Generative AI models such as GPT, narrative engines, and procedural story generators operate on these same structures: plot, character, setting, conflict, and resolution. This chapter provides the narrative fundamentals that AI tools rely on, enabling developers to guide, refine, and evaluate the stories AI produces.

The Role of Storytelling in Games

Storytelling in games performs a unique function. Unlike books or films, where the audience passively absorbs the story, games invite players to become participants in the narrative. This interactivity demands that the story be more than just background; it must respond, adapt, and sometimes even emerge from the player's actions.

S. N. Gupta, *Generative AI for Game Development*, https://doi.org/10.1007/979-8-8688-2439-5_4

Why Narrative Matters in Games

Storytelling in games serves more than just entertainment. It offers context, purpose, and emotional weight to the actions players take. A well-crafted narrative turns a mission from a checklist into a cause worth fighting for. It creates tension, reveals character motivations, and makes victories feel earned rather than arbitrary. It's the game narrative that does the following:

Contextualizing Gameplay

A compelling story gives meaning to actions. Without narrative context, collecting items or defeating enemies can feel hollow. With a story, the same actions can feel purposeful and emotionally resonant.

Example: In *The Last of Us*, sneaking past enemies or scavenging for supplies is made meaningful by Joel and Ellie's journey and the bond between them.

Driving Emotional Engagement

Stories allow players to connect with characters, feel the weight of their decisions, and care about outcomes.

Example: *Red Dead Redemption 2* leverages story arcs and character development to deliver emotional impact rarely seen in games.

Immersion and Worldbuilding

Narrative gives depth to the game world. Lore, histories, cultures, and motivations make virtual environments feel authentic.

Example: *Elder Scrolls V: Skyrim* immerses players through books, dialogue, and environmental cues that hint at a rich and ancient world.

Nonlinear Exploration and Replay Ability

Games that offer narrative choices or emergent storytelling provide multiple paths, encouraging players to return and explore different outcomes.

Example: *Detroit: Become Human* allows branching storylines where every choice leads to different consequences, unlocking a variety of endings.

WHY GENERATIVE AI NEEDS NARRATIVE STRUCTURE

Generative AI doesn't invent story logic from scratch; it builds upon patterns learned from millions of story examples. When developers understand narrative principles, they can

a. Prompt AI more effectively.

b. Reduce inconsistent or incoherent outputs.

c. Design branching or adaptive narratives that AI can expand.

d. Use tools like GPT to generate side quests, character backstories, or dialogue that fit the overall story.

The stronger the narrative foundation, the better AI can support and enhance storytelling.

Core Elements of a Story

Even the most complex narratives are built upon a few foundational elements. These elements shape how the story unfolds and how players emotionally engage with it.

When working with generative AI, these story elements become the "building blocks" AI uses to construct or adapt narrative content. Many AI systems generate plot outlines, write character dialogue, or produce setting descriptions by analyzing patterns in these components. Understanding them helps developers prompt AI with clarity and evaluate whether AI-generated content fits the intended narrative design.

Plot: The Sequence of Meaningful Events

Plot refers to the structured series of events that drive the story from beginning to end. It includes the central conflict and how it develops over time. In games, the plot can be linear, branching, or fully dynamic, but its core function remains the same: to move the story forward with purpose and consequence.

Classical Structure

- **Exposition**: Introduces setting, characters, and premise.

  In *BioShock*, the player's arrival in Rapture immediately establishes mystery, tone, and location.

- **Rising Action**: Challenges emerge, and stakes increase.

  In *Mass Effect*, missions uncover layers of intergalactic conflict and personal stakes.

- **Climax**: The turning point of maximum tension.

  In *The Witcher 3*, key choices during the main questline led to moments of irreversible consequence.

- **Falling Action and Resolution**: Loose ends are tied, and outcomes are revealed.

  In *Life is Strange*, the story ends based on moral choices that reflect your emotional journey.

While plots can vary widely, most narratives fall into a set of **recurring archetypes** and time-tested structures that resonate across cultures and mediums. In game development, recognizing these types of plots helps writers and designers craft stories that align with gameplay goals while connecting with players on a deeper level.

Let's explore the most common **types of plots**, how they function, and how they appear in both games and traditional storytelling.

i. The Hero's Journey (The Quest)

Structure: A protagonist leaves the familiar world, faces trials, undergoes transformation, and returns changed.

Core Themes: Growth, transformation, discovery.

Example: *The Legend of Zelda: Ocarina of Time* features Link stepping into a destiny greater than himself, overcoming internal and external challenges to restore balance.

Why It Works: This structure taps into the universal experience of growth through adversity. In games, it pairs well with leveling mechanics, exploration, and skill progression.

ii. Rags to Riches

Structure: The protagonist rises from humble beginnings to greatness, often facing setbacks before achieving success.

Core Themes: Ambition, perseverance, identity.

Example: *Stardew Valley* begins with the player inheriting a run-down farm and, through hard work, transforming it into a thriving homestead.

Why It Works: This plot aligns well with games that emphasize building, upgrading, or reputation growth. It gives the player a clear sense of progression and reward.

iii. Overcoming the Monster

Structure: A hero faces and defeats a powerful evil, whether literal or metaphorical.

Core Themes: Courage, survival, resistance.

Example: *Dark Souls* centers entirely around overcoming massive, near-impossible foes in a grim and mysterious world.

Why It Works: This plot suits combat-driven games or horror narratives where the player is at a disadvantage and must use strategy, persistence, or growth to triumph.

iv. The Tragedy

Structure: A central character falls from grace due to a fatal flaw, moral failing, or external forces, often leading to loss or death.

Core Themes: Hubris, fate, regret.

Example: *Red Dead Redemption* and its sequel both follow characters haunted by their pasts, ultimately consumed by their choices.

Why It Works: Though less common in gameplay-first titles, tragic plots are powerful in story-driven games where character arcs are central. They provoke reflection and emotional investment.

v. The Voyage and Return

Structure: A protagonist enters a strange world, confronts challenges, and returns home wiser or changed.

Core Themes: Self-discovery, adaptation, transformation.

Example: *BioShock Infinite* sends players into a visually stunning and ideologically extreme city in the sky, only to return to the beginning with a new understanding of identity and choice.

Why It Works: This plot supports games with strong exploration elements or settings that contrast with the player's starting environment, creating visual and emotional arcs.

vi. The Rebirth

Structure: The protagonist faces a form of death (literal or figurative), undergoes change, and is "reborn" with a new perspective or purpose.

Core Themes: Redemption, renewal, awakening.

Example: *Shadow of the Colossus* tells a quiet story of sacrifice and transformation, where the protagonist's journey leads to a mysterious form of rebirth.

Why It Works: This plot fits games that explore morality, consequence, or the human condition. It's also common in games with multiple endings based on player decisions.

vii. The Mystery

Structure: A problem or crime is introduced; the protagonist investigates clues and uncovers the truth.

Core Themes: Truth, deception, justice.

Example: *L.A. Noire* and *The Return of the Obra Dinn* challenge players to piece together events through evidence and observation.

Why It Works: Games that involve investigation, deduction, or piecing together fragmented narratives are natural fits for this plot. They rely on the player's cognitive engagement and sense of curiosity.

viii. The Transformation (Internal Journey)

Structure: Focused more on character development than external conflict, this plot follows a personal evolution, often catalyzed by life-changing events.

Core Themes: Self-awareness, inner conflict, emotional growth.

Example: *Celeste* follows Madeline's physical and emotional journey as she climbs a mountain while confronting her own anxieties and fears.

Why It Works: Emotional resonance and character-driven storytelling work especially well in indie games or visual novels, where subtlety and introspection are central.

Plot structures help generative models produce coherent long-form narratives, ensuring AI-generated quests or story arcs follow meaningful progression.

Characters: The Emotional Anchor of the Narrative

Characters provide the heart and soul of a story. Whether playable or non-playable, they serve as the player's point of emotional investment. They serve as the **emotional anchor** of any story. In games, they can be player-controlled protagonists, allies, antagonists, or neutral NPCs. Strong character development helps players form **emotional bonds** with the narrative.

Key Traits of Effective Characters

Relatable or Compelling Motives: What does the character want, and why?

Growth or Change: How do they evolve in response to conflict?

Flaws and Complexity: Realism comes from imperfection.

In narrative design, even NPCs can carry depth through subtle writing and player interaction. Games like *Disco Elysium* thrive on character dialogue that feels authentic, layered, and surprising.

Characters are more than just avatars or vessels for gameplay; they are often the emotional core of the experience. Whether a player controls them, fights alongside them, or learns about them through the environment, characters provide context, motivation, and emotional depth. Strong characters help transform a game from a series of mechanics into a living narrative, and understanding the types of characters commonly found in interactive media is essential for designing memorable, believable, and purpose-driven roles.

Below is a breakdown of the most common character types in games, their narrative functions, and real-world examples.

i. The Protagonist (Player Character)

The protagonist is the central figure in the story, often serving as the player's point of view. In many games, this is the character controlled by the player. Their goals, choices, and arc are typically what drive the plot forward.

Types of Protagonists

1. **Silent Protagonist**: Character with no spoken dialogue, allowing players to project their own identity

   Example: Link from *The Legend of Zelda* series

2. **Defined Personality Protagonist**: Character with established traits, voice, and backstory

   Example: Joel and Ellie in *The Last of Us*

3. **Customizable Protagonist**: Created and shaped by the player, often in RPGs

   Example: Commander Shepard in *Mass Effect*

Narrative Role

The protagonist often undergoes transformation, wrestles with internal or external conflict, and is central to moral decisions. In AI-driven storytelling, protagonists can also be dynamically shaped by player behavior, adding layers of complexity to how their character evolves.

ii. The Antagonist

The antagonist opposes the protagonist, creating conflict and tension that drive the plot. Antagonists can be villains, natural forces, institutions, or even the protagonist's inner self.

Types of Antagonists

1. **Classic Villain**: Evil or corrupt character with destructive motives

   Example: Ganon in *The Legend of Zelda* or Sephiroth in *Final Fantasy VII*

2. **Moral Mirror or Foil**: Antagonist with similar goals or traits as the protagonist but a different ideology

   Example: Dutch van der Linde in *Red Dead Redemption 2*

3. **Systemic Antagonist**: Society, government, or rules that suppress the character

   Example: The oppressive regime in *Papers, Please*

Narrative Role

A well-written antagonist adds depth to the story. Instead of being purely evil, compelling antagonists challenge the player's worldview and force difficult choices, which can be mirrored or evolved through generative AI systems.

iii. Companion Characters (Allies and Sidekicks)

These are characters who assist the protagonist, either narratively or mechanically. They often offer insight into the game world, contribute to emotional depth, and influence the protagonist's development.

Examples

1. **Ellie** in *The Last of Us*, whose relationship with Joel becomes the emotional spine of the game
2. **Atreus** in *God of War (2018)*, who matures alongside his father while also shaping the story's mythology
3. **Cortana** in *Halo*, who provides mission support and increasingly complex emotional interactions

Narrative Role

Companions allow for exposition without breaking immersion. They also help express emotional stakes, offer moral guidance, or act as foils to the protagonist. In AI-enhanced storytelling, companions can evolve based on sentiment analysis and dialogue generation to become adaptive emotional partners.

iv. Non-playable Characters (NPCs)

NPCs populate the game world and often play a crucial role in building immersion. They can be quest givers, background figures, vendors, or narratively significant characters.

Types of NPCs

1. **Functional NPCs**: Deliver quests, tutorials, or trade goods.

   Example: Shopkeepers in *Skyrim* or *Zelda: Breath of the Wild*

2. **Narrative NPCs**: Contribute to story arcs and lore.

   Example: NPCs in *Disco Elysium* who drive philosophical and political conversations

3. **Ambient NPCs**: Populate the environment to make it feel alive.

   Example: Citizens in *Assassin's Creed* games who react to player actions

Narrative Role

Though often overlooked, well-written NPCs enrich the world and add realism. With generative AI, NPCs can now respond to the player's history, make small talk that changes over time, or even develop their own goals, radically transforming how background characters contribute to the narrative.

v. The Mentor or Guide

Mentors provide wisdom, tools, or moral guidance to the protagonist. Often older or more experienced, they can represent a prior generation or ideological path.

Examples

1. **Master Roshi** in *Dragon Ball Z* games
2. **The Gatekeeper** in *Hades*, offering guidance and lore before every attempt
3. **Yoda** in *Star Wars* games, embodying the ancient, mystical guide archetype

Narrative Role

Mentors help orient players early in the game, especially during tutorials or story introductions. In some narratives, mentors are lost or corrupted, driving the protagonist forward. Generative AI can allow for dynamic mentorship where the guide reacts to the player's choices, adapting their advice or warnings.

vi. The Trickster or Wildcard

These characters often serve as agents of chaos or unpredictability. They may help or hinder the protagonist at different times and often blur the line between ally and enemy.

Examples

1. **The Joker** in *Batman: Arkham Asylum*
2. **Varric** in *Dragon Age II*, who narrates the story with unreliable memory
3. **Sheogorath** in *The Elder Scrolls IV: Oblivion*, the Daedric Prince of Madness

Narrative Role

Tricksters add depth and unpredictability to narratives. They can challenge the protagonist's assumptions, insert humor or irony, and introduce subversion. In AI-driven games, these roles could be fully adaptive, constantly shifting alliances based on complex player interactions.

vii. The Player-Created Character (Avatar)

In many roleplaying games, players design their own characters, shaping their appearance, background, and sometimes personality. These characters serve as both extensions of the player and vessels for storytelling.

Examples

1. The custom protagonist in *Elden Ring*
2. Shepard in *Mass Effect,* where dialogue and choices shape identity
3. The Vault Dweller in *Fallout*

Narrative Role

Player-created characters offer agency, encouraging immersion and ownership. They often lack fixed personalities but evolve based on decisions, relationships, and game consequences. AI-enhanced storytelling can deepen this experience by tracking long-term player behavior to generate reflective dialogue or story arcs.

Character attributes and motivations guide AI-generated dialogue and behavior, enabling NPCs to respond consistently within their personalities.

Setting: The World Where the Story Unfolds

The setting shapes the tone, genre, and boundaries of the narrative. It can be a character in its own right. Remember, it isn't just a backdrop; it actively influences the tone, themes, and plot of a story. In games, settings are **interactive environments** that reveal narrative through exploration, architecture, weather, and ambient storytelling.

In Games, Setting Is Multifaceted

- **Visual and Environmental Design**: Architecture, geography, color, and lighting convey mood.
- **Cultural and Historical Context**: Societies, factions, and backstory enhance immersion.
- **Interactivity**: Players can explore, discover lore, and piece together story fragments.

Just as literature and film use setting to support narrative, games expand the concept by making it immersive and responsive. Players don't just witness a setting; they inhabit it, navigate it, and uncover its secrets. Understanding the varieties of settings commonly used in games can help writers and designers craft environments that not only support the narrative but amplify its impact.

i. Fantasy Worlds

Imaginary worlds grounded in magic, myth, or supernatural elements, often inspired by medieval or folkloric traditions.

Key Characteristics

- Presence of mythical creatures, magical systems, and ancient lore.
- Kingdoms, castles, forests, and ruins are common architectural motifs.
- A deep sense of history and otherworldliness.

Example

The Elder Scrolls V: Skyrim offers an expansive fantasy setting filled with dragons, ancient civilizations, and magical guilds. Players not only explore a massive world but also engage with different cultures, religious systems, and historical conflicts that shape the narrative.

Narrative Function

Fantasy settings allow for high-stakes heroism, morality tales, and richly layered lore. They support quest-driven narratives and exploration-based gameplay. These settings are often ideal for open-world storytelling or AI-enhanced procedural narratives due to their scale and variety.

ii. Science Fiction and Futuristic Settings

Settings based on speculative futures, space exploration, advanced technology, or alternate timelines.

Key Characteristics

- Spaceships, alien civilizations, AI systems, cybernetics, and dystopian societies
- Exploration of themes like identity, humanity, ethics of technology, and existentialism
- Complex political structures and advanced weaponry or systems

Example

Mass Effect transports players into a galaxy filled with alien species, political intrigue, and moral dilemmas. The setting drives the narrative by constantly challenging the player's ethical decisions, beliefs, and loyalties.

Narrative Function

Sci-fi settings are ideal for exploring moral ambiguity, societal questions, and technological consequences. They also support rich worldbuilding and adaptive systems, making them a natural fit for games powered by AI-generated environments and branching dialogue.

iii. Post-Apocalyptic Worlds

Settings that take place after a major catastrophe, natural, nuclear, or societal, often depicting the collapse of civilization.

Key Characteristics

- Scarcity, survival mechanics, lawlessness, and moral decay
- Emphasis on ruins, decay, and desolate landscapes
- Themes of resilience, loss, and hope amid ruin

Example

The Last of Us features a post-pandemic United States where humanity clings to survival. The decaying cities, overgrown nature, and fragmented society create a tone that is intimate, haunting, and deeply emotional.

Narrative Function

Post-apocalyptic settings allow for stories that examine human nature under pressure, as well as complex character arcs driven by survival. These environments naturally support dynamic storytelling, especially in AI-powered games that simulate emergent behavior or resource scarcity.

vi. Historical Settings

Settings grounded in real-world historical periods, often with cultural or political accuracy.

Key Characteristics

- Authentic architecture, customs, clothing, and social systems
- Interactions with real historical figures or events
- Emphasis on immersion and historical detail

Example

Assassin's Creed II places players in Renaissance-era Italy, allowing them to experience historical locations and interact with figures like Leonardo da Vinci and the Medici family. The setting offers narrative depth by blending real history with fictional intrigue.

Narrative Function

Historical settings provide a sense of realism and educational value while supporting stories of politics, rebellion, discovery, and war. They are particularly effective for games with investigative, stealth, or diplomacy-based mechanics.

v. Urban and Modern-Day Settings

Stories that take place in contemporary or near-contemporary urban environments, often mirroring the player's real world.

Key Characteristics

- Familiar settings like cities, schools, offices, or suburbs
- Realistic social dynamics and dialogue
- Exploration of current issues such as identity, inequality, and technology

Example

Watch Dogs 2 takes place in a stylized version of San Francisco and focuses on surveillance, hacking, and digital activism. The setting becomes a tool for both gameplay and narrative, enabling commentary on data privacy and social control.

Narrative Function

Modern-day settings are perfect for grounded, character-driven narratives or satirical commentary. They also provide a familiar canvas for storytelling, making them accessible and relatable for players.

vi. Horror and Psychological Settings

Environments designed to evoke fear, anxiety, or unease, often supernatural or psychologically disturbing.

Key Characteristics

- Abandoned places, darkness, tight spaces, visual distortion.
- Sound design and atmosphere are central.
- Use of symbolism and surrealism.

Example

Silent Hill 2 uses setting as a reflection of the protagonist's guilt and trauma. The town changes based on the character's mental state, turning the setting into a psychological map.

Narrative Function

These settings enable internal storytelling emotions and mental states externalized through the environment. With AI-driven environmental shifts based on player behavior or emotional input, horror settings can evolve in real time, enhancing psychological tension.

vii. Mythical or Surreal Settings

Dreamlike, symbolic, or abstract environments that operate by their own logic and defy realism.

Key Characteristics

- Visual abstraction, floating islands, surreal architecture.
- Symbolism replaces literal storytelling.
- Often tied to themes like memory, death, or spirituality.

Example

Journey offers a minimalistic desert world that feels ancient, mythic, and symbolic. The lack of dialogue forces players to interpret meaning through movement, music, and imagery.

Narrative Function

These settings invite interpretation and emotional resonance rather than exposition. They are often used in games with minimal mechanics but deep narrative symbolism and work well with AI-generated visuals or audio design to create unique experiences.

viii. Hybrid and Multiverse Settings

Settings that combine multiple genres, time periods, or realities, allowing players to shift between them.

Key Characteristics

- Parallel worlds, time travel, or blending of fantasy with sci-fi.
- Shifting aesthetics and rules based on setting transitions.
- Often used for experimental or metafictional storytelling.

Example

Control merges reality with supernatural and interdimensional spaces. As the player navigates shifting environments, they uncover a world that obeys dreamlike rules, constantly challenging perception.

Narrative Function

Hybrid settings allow developers to break narrative conventions, introduce nonlinear timelines, or contrast different emotional tones. When paired with AI, these settings offer immense creative flexibility in procedural generation or adaptive storytelling.

Setting descriptions allow AI to generate worldbuilding content such as lore entries, environmental narratives, or procedural world details aligned with the game's tone.

Conflict: The Engine of the Story

Conflict is the narrative engine that drives every story forward. Without conflict, there is no challenge, no growth, and no reason for the player to act. In storytelling, conflict introduces tension and raises stakes. In games, conflict becomes even more essential, as it directly shapes the core gameplay experience, whether it's combat, decision-making, exploration, or survival. Understanding the types of conflict that can exist within a game narrative allows developers and writers to design stories that are not only engaging but also emotionally and mechanically compelling.

Unlike passive storytelling mediums, games allow players to confront conflict directly through their actions. Whether they're solving puzzles, making ethical choices, or battling enemies, conflict in games is interactive, and its resolution often depends on the player's decisions and skill.

i. Character vs. Self (Internal Conflict)

This is a psychological or emotional struggle within a character. The player's avatar may be torn between two values, haunted by past decisions, or grappling with identity and purpose.

Example

In *Celeste*, the main character, Madeline, battles her own anxiety and self-doubt as she climbs the mountain. Her internal conflict is visualized through the "dark version" of herself, forcing players to face her emotional struggles both narratively and mechanically.

Narrative Function

Internal conflict provides emotional depth and character development. It allows players to explore vulnerability, choice, and identity. Games with branching dialogue or morality systems often rely on internal conflict to drive decision-making.

ii. Character vs. Character

A protagonist is opposed by another individual or group with clashing goals or beliefs. This is one of the most recognizable and direct forms of conflict.

Example

Metal Gear Solid features deep interpersonal rivalries, especially between Snake and Liquid, where ideological conflict enhances the stakes of physical confrontation.

Narrative Function

Character-based conflict gives the story a personal dimension. Whether it's a villain seeking control or a former ally turned enemy, these conflicts allow for emotional investment, especially when enhanced through dynamic interactions or evolving relationships.

iii. Character vs. Society

The protagonist is at odds with societal norms, institutions, or power structures. This conflict often revolves around issues of justice, oppression, or rebellion.

Example

In *Papers, Please,* the player assumes the role of a border agent in a dystopian regime, constantly torn between enforcing unjust laws and preserving one's humanity and family. The game explores systemic oppression through mechanical repetition and moral choices.

Narrative Function

This type of conflict is ideal for exploring themes of conformity, resistance, and moral ambiguity. It often appears in games that include politics, surveillance, or ethical dilemmas and can be particularly powerful when player choices affect the balance between self-interest and collective welfare.

iv. Character vs. Nature

The player struggles against natural forces, such as climate, wildlife, disease, or survival in harsh environments.

Example

In *The Long Dark,* players must survive in the Canadian wilderness after a geomagnetic disaster. There are no monsters, only the cold, hunger, and isolation.

Narrative Function

This form of conflict focuses on resilience, survival, and vulnerability, often emphasizing player resourcefulness and long-term planning. AI can enhance this conflict by generating unpredictable weather systems or adaptive ecosystems that react to player actions.

v. Character vs. Technology

A modern evolution of conflict, this pits the player against machines, artificial intelligence, or the unintended consequences of technological advancement.

Example

Detroit: Become Human centers on androids gaining consciousness, exploring ethical questions about freedom, control, and what it means to be human. The player's choices shape the outcome of this technological uprising.

Narrative Function

This conflict allows developers to examine themes like automation, surveillance, AI ethics, and human dependence on technology. It also opens the door to gameplay mechanics involving hacking, manipulation, or identity crisis.

vi. Character vs. Supernatural

The protagonist faces forces beyond natural understanding, ghosts, gods, curses, or mythical beings.

Example

Bloodborne plunges players into a gothic nightmare filled with eldritch creatures and cosmic horror. The supernatural setting is steeped in mystery and symbolism, and the protagonist's journey is as much psychological as it is physical.

Narrative Function

This conflict creates a sense of awe, fear, or existential dread. It is effective for horror, fantasy, and surreal narratives. AI tools can add unpredictable or procedural supernatural elements, such as enemies that adapt, morph, or rewrite reality.

vii. Character vs. Time

Here, the primary obstacle is time itself, whether through countdowns, aging, temporal manipulation, or fate.

Example

In *Majora's Mask*, players repeat the same three days, racing against time to prevent the moon from destroying the world. Every decision must be made with the clock ticking, which creates constant urgency and tension.

Narrative Function

Time-based conflict creates pressure, repetition, and emotional weight. It's especially powerful in games where timing, planning, and loss play a central role. With AI systems, time loops or evolving consequences can be procedurally generated for infinite variations.

viii. Character vs. The Unknown (Existential or Metaphysical Conflict)

This abstract conflict challenges the character's understanding of reality, identity, or the nature of existence.

Example

Inside never explicitly explains the world or the protagonist's role, but the oppressive, haunting atmosphere forces players to question what they're doing and why. Similarly, *The Stanley Parable* dissects the concept of free will through meta-narrative design.

Narrative Function

This type of conflict is ideal for philosophical or introspective stories. It often appears in narrative-driven indie games or titles that blur the line between player and protagonist. It also complements AI storytelling systems that adjust meaning, tone, or world logic in response to the player's behavior.

Generative models use conflict patterns to create quests, dilemmas, and branching decision points that feel meaningful to players.

Resolution: The Payoff or Aftermath

A story's resolution offers closure, though in interactive narratives, it may vary. The resolution doesn't always provide answers; it can be tragic, open-ended, or cyclical. In interactive stories, resolution may vary based on choices made, making it even more impactful and personal for the player. These resolutions can provide satisfaction, provoke reflection, or even challenge players by denying closure altogether. Understanding the different types of resolutions can help writers and designers craft endings that align with the game's tone, reinforce its themes, and enhance emotional impact.

i. Closed or Definitive Resolution

The story ties up all major plot points and character arcs with a clear, final outcome.

Example

In *Uncharted 4: A Thief's End*, Nathan Drake retires from adventuring to settle down with his family. The story concludes with peace and legacy, offering satisfying closure to a long-running character arc.

Narrative Function

A closed resolution provides a sense of completion and emotional payoff. It reassures players that their journey has a purpose and an endpoint. This type is especially effective for story-heavy, linear games that emphasize character development and thematic resolution.

ii. Open-Ended Resolution

The narrative ends with ambiguity, leaving certain questions unresolved or inviting interpretation.

Example

Inside concludes without dialogue or explanation, leaving players to wonder about the meaning of its haunting final scene. Similarly, *Limbo* ends in a mysterious moment that reframes the entire experience.

Narrative Function

Open-ended resolutions encourage post-game reflection and discussion. They work well in games that aim to evoke emotion, mystery, or philosophical inquiry, especially in indie or experimental titles. These endings also complement AI-generated stories, where procedural content might vary in meaning each time.

iii. Branching or Multiple Endings

The game features several different endings, determined by player choices throughout the narrative.

Example

Detroit: Become Human offers dozens of ending combinations based on moral choices, character survival, and dialogue decisions. *The Witcher 3* uses nuanced variables to determine not just who wins, but how the world remembers the protagonist.

Narrative Function

Branching resolutions empower players by validating their agency and investment. They reinforce the idea that actions matter and that narrative is not fixed but collaboratively authored. These resolutions pair perfectly with AI-driven storytelling, where adaptive narratives can produce new outcomes each time.

iv. Circular or Looping Resolution

The story appears to reset, returning the player or world to its starting point, sometimes literally, sometimes metaphorically.

Example

In *The Legend of Zelda: Majora's Mask*, the player relives the same three days repeatedly. Though progress is made, the resolution is **cyclical**, reflecting themes of time, inevitability, and repetition. *Hades* similarly uses the concept of death and rebirth as part of its narrative rhythm.

Narrative Function

Circular resolutions are effective for games exploring themes of fate, time, or personal growth. They also align with roguelike mechanics, where repeated attempts are part of the player's journey. These endings may offer closure in the form of acceptance rather than change.

v. Tragic or Bittersweet Resolution

The protagonist achieves some form of resolution, but at a significant cost, personal, emotional, or moral.

Example

In *Red Dead Redemption 2*, Arthur Morgan's path leads to redemption, but also death. The ending offers closure, but not comfort. The player is left to reflect on sacrifice, loyalty, and the weight of choices.

Narrative Function

Bittersweet or tragic resolutions create lasting emotional resonance. They work well for mature narratives that explore morality, sacrifice, or realism. These endings often remain with players long after the game ends, precisely because they resist tidy conclusions.

vi. Player-Defined or Emergent Resolution

The story's end is not scripted in a traditional sense but emerges from how the player interacts with the game world and systems.

Example

In *Minecraft* or *Mount & Blade*, there is no set ending. Instead, resolution is defined by player goals, whether building a castle, conquering a region, or simply surviving. The "ending" occurs when the player decides it does.

Narrative Function

Player-defined resolutions emphasize freedom, sandbox design, and self-authored stories. These games often use procedural generation or systems-driven storytelling, where players create meaning through interaction. In AI-enhanced games, emergent resolutions can be shaped dynamically by player behavior, making each experience uniquely personal.

vii. False or Deceptive Resolution

The game presents what appears to be a resolution, only to subvert it later through a twist, betrayal, or continued narrative.

Example

NieR: Automata has multiple endings that seem final but are later revealed to be incomplete. Only by replaying from different perspectives does the full truth emerge. The player is led to believe closure has been achieved, only to be pulled deeper into the story.

Narrative Function

False resolutions challenge the player's expectations and assumptions. They are effective in games with layered storytelling, unreliable narrators, or meta-narrative twists. When powered by AI, these resolutions can be procedurally timed or triggered based on subtle variables, creating genuine surprise.

Understanding resolution types helps developers shape AI-generated endings or outcome variations that remain thematically consistent.

As storytelling has evolved through history, the structure and delivery of narratives have always reflected the technologies of the time. Generative AI represents the next major leap, one that not only supports storytelling but actively participates in creating and shaping it.

The Evolution of Storytelling: From Oral Tales to AI Narratives

Storytelling has always evolved alongside the tools and technologies of each era. What began as spoken myths around firelight eventually transformed into written epics, theatrical performances, printed novels, and cinematic experiences. With each progression, the storyteller's reach expanded, and so did the ways in which stories could be told and experienced. Today, storytelling is entering a new phase, one shaped not solely by human imagination but by intelligent systems capable of generating, adapting, and personalizing narratives in real time. From oral traditions to artificial intelligence, the journey of storytelling reflects both our changing culture and our enduring need to make sense of the world through stories. Here is a small glimpse of how storytelling evolved over time.

Early Storytelling

Myths, legends, and moral lessons passed down verbally or structured narratives in literature and theater.

1. **Oral Traditions**: Myths, folktales, and legends passed down to teach values and explain natural phenomena.
2. **Written Epics**: Texts like *The Iliad* and *The Ramayana* formalized structure and hero archetypes.
3. **Theatre and Literature**: Focused on dialogue, symbolism, and audience connection.

Film and Television

Stories enhanced through visuals, editing, and sound.

1. Emphasized visual storytelling, sound, performance, and pacing
2. Used editing, framing, and music to guide emotion and focus

Generative AI builds on the principles of interactive storytelling but adds scalability and adaptiveness that traditional systems could not achieve. While earlier games relied on manually authored branches, AI can analyze player intent, sentiment, or behavior to generate content dynamically, making the narrative more personal and responsive.

Interactive Storytelling

Interactive storytelling with player agency and real-time consequences.

1. **Text adventures and visual novels** introduced branching narratives (e.g., *Zork, Fate/stay night*).
2. **Modern games** blend mechanics and story (e.g., *God of War, Celeste, Firewatch*).
3. Story can be **player-authored**, meaning every playthrough is a co-creation between game and player.

AI-Enhanced Storytelling: A New Frontier

Generative AI introduces nonlinear, procedurally generated, and emotion-sensitive storytelling.

1. **AI Dungeon** uses language models to create endless story paths based on player prompts.
2. **Project December** simulates conversations with emotionally nuanced AI characters.
3. **Modding communities** are already integrating GPT-powered NPC dialogue systems into games like *Skyrim*, creating NPCs who remember and respond to prior events.

How AI Is Changing Storytelling

While traditional narratives are authored and fixed, AI-enhanced storytelling allows for living, evolving narratives. Using tools like GPT, developers can build games where no two playthroughs are the same, and characters react dynamically to player input. AI doesn't replace the storyteller; it expands what's possible by making stories responsive and adaptive at a scale previously unimaginable.

Note In an AI-powered RPG, the storyline can shift entirely based on subtle player actions, allowing for emergent storytelling that feels authored but is generated in real time.

As we move deeper into generative AI, these narrative fundamentals will guide how we design prompts, evaluate AI-generated content, and build systems that collaborate with human creativity. AI can automate parts of storytelling, but it relies on developers and designers to shape its direction through structure, constraints, and narrative understanding.

Conclusion

Storytelling is the soul of interactive media including games. Its principles, plot, character, setting, conflict, and resolution remain constant, even as technologies change. In games, storytelling takes on a new dimension, allowing players to shape the story through their choices and actions.

As we look ahead to AI-driven storytelling, these narrative fundamentals will become even more critical. The tools may evolve, but the goal remains timeless: to create stories that move us, challenge us, and connect us, whether written by humans, machines, or both.

CHAPTER 5

Understanding Narrative Structures

Every story, whether it's a tightly written novel or a massive open-world game, follows a structure. It may not always be obvious to the audience, but behind every compelling narrative is an underlying framework that gives it rhythm, emotional pacing, and a sense of direction. In games, structure is more than just a storytelling device; it's a design principle. It affects how players engage with the world, how they experience conflict and resolution, and how their choices shape outcomes.

This chapter explores the key narrative structures used in both traditional and interactive storytelling, showing how they influence player experience and how they can be adapted to fit different types of games. We will also be highlighting their strengths, limitations, and how they align with different gameplay goals.

Whether your game is tightly scripted or entirely emergent, the right structure helps translate story into player experience.

Modern generative AI systems such as GPT-based narrative engines use these narrative structures to generate plotlines, quests, dialogue, and branching story paths. Understanding these structures helps developers prompt AI effectively, evaluate AI-generated content, and design systems where AI can extend or adapt narrative elements.

Linear Narrative: Structure with Purpose

A linear narrative follows a predefined sequence. The player experiences events in the order designed by the creators, moving from point A to B to C, without deviating from the intended path.

S. N. Gupta, *Generative AI for Game Development*, https://doi.org/10.1007/979-8-8688-2439-5_5

This structure is common in story-driven action-adventures, platformers, and cinematic games where storytelling and emotional pacing take center stage.

Linear narratives are particularly effective when the writer wants to control tone, pacing, and character development. Since all players experience the same events in the same order, developers can focus on refining emotional moments, visual storytelling, and thematic consistency.

However, linear stories do have limitations in replay ability. Once the narrative arc is experienced, there's often little variation on a second playthrough unless difficulty levels, collectibles, or hidden lore offer additional engagement.

Example

In *God of War (2018)*, players accompany Kratos and Atreus on a tightly guided journey. Each event builds on the last, gradually revealing their relationship and the deeper world around them. The story unfolds like a novel or film, deliberate, dramatic, and emotionally choreographed.

What It's Good For

- Cinematic storytelling
- Emotional character arcs
- Focused gameplay experiences

Key Benefits

- Complete control over pacing, tone, and plot development
- Easier to write, test, and polish
- Ideal for storytelling that relies on strong character-driven narratives or plot twists

Challenges

- Requires excellent pacing to keep players engaged
- Player choices typically don't affect the outcome, which may reduce replay ability

Potential Downsides

- Limited agency may leave some players feeling passive.
- Can feel restrictive if not well-integrated with gameplay.

Linear structures are easiest for GenAI models to follow and reproduce, making them ideal for AI-generated cutscenes, quests, or tightly paced narrative beats.

Nonlinear Narrative: Freedom and Discovery

Nonlinear storytelling abandons the strict chronological flow, allowing players to uncover the story in pieces or out of order. Events may occur across multiple timelines, or the player may have freedom to choose which missions or dialogues to explore first.

This approach increases replay value and player engagement, as players uncover different details or outcomes on subsequent playthroughs. The trade-off is that nonlinear structures require more complex writing and worldbuilding, since each branch must be coherent, meaningful, and rewarding on its own.

Example

Disco Elysium is a nonlinear detective RPG that drops players into a world full of possibilities. The player determines which leads to follow, which characters to interrogate, and in what order. Each decision uncovers new pieces of the narrative puzzle, and no two players experience the story the same way.

What It's Good For

- Exploration-based games
- Detective/investigative gameplay
- Stories about memory, identity, or mystery

Key Benefits

- Promotes discovery and recontextualization
- Encourages player agency and curiosity
- Enhances replay ability by supporting different narrative orders

Challenges

- Difficult to maintain narrative clarity and emotional pacing
- Requires extra work to ensure each segment makes sense in any order

Potential Downsides

- Some players may miss key plot points or become confused.
- Difficult to manage narrative escalation and climax without a linear flow.

Decision Trees and Consequence Mapping

As soon as you give players the ability to choose, your story begins to branch. These branching narratives are structured around player decisions, each leading to different consequences, storylines, or endings.

A decision tree maps out every possible choice and its resulting outcome. Some trees are shallow (with branches that quickly converge again), while others are deep and wide, allowing for dramatically different experiences.

Example

In *The Witcher 3: Wild Hunt,* major decisions like whether to spare a character or support a faction lead to different outcomes later in the story. These choices feel impactful because the consequences are not immediate but unfold naturally over time, affecting the game's world and ending.

Some games give the illusion of branching but eventually funnel all choices back to a common narrative point. This is known as a "foldback" structure. It's efficient for development, as it reduces the number of unique assets needed while still offering the appearance of choice.

Games like *Mass Effect* use a mix of deep and shallow branching. While many side quests and relationship arcs are highly variable, the central plot beats are consistent. This allows for player expression while preserving a core narrative framework.

What It's Good For

- RPGs and narrative-driven games
- Moral and ethical dilemmas
- Games where player agency is core to the experience

Key Benefits

- Gives players a sense of ownership over the story
- Increases replay value with different outcomes
- Supports moral complexity and consequence-driven storytelling

Challenges

- High content production cost (each branch needs writing, assets, testing)
- Difficult to maintain narrative cohesion across multiple paths

Potential Downsides

- Some choices may feel shallow or inconsequential if not well-designed.
- Players might never see large portions of the story.

Modular and Episodic Structures

Modular structures break a story into discrete narrative units that can be experienced in different orders or independently. This approach is common in open-world, sandbox, or mission-based games, where players choose their own path through the content.

Episodic Games

In episodic storytelling, each "episode" acts like a chapter of a TV series, part of a larger arc, but self-contained enough to be enjoyed on its own. A good example of an episodic game is *Life is Strange* which unfolds across five episodes. Each one builds on the last, but introduces new conflicts, decisions, and character developments. The episodic format allows time between releases for community discussion, speculation, and emotional digestion.

Modular Game Design

In open-world games like *Skyrim* or *Cyberpunk 2077*, players choose which quests to pursue, in what order, and often with multiple possible resolutions. Some missions are part of the main story; others simply add color and depth to the world.

The modular structure allows for high replay ability and personalization. However, designers must ensure that the **core** emotional or thematic threads remain coherent, even when experienced out of sequence.

What It's Good For

- Open-world and sandbox games
- Episodic releases
- Side quests and modular storytelling

Key Benefits

- Supports player freedom and flexible pacing
- Easier to build and test in parts
- Ideal for large, content-rich games with multiple activities

Challenges

- Risk of disconnection between modules if not narratively linked
- Harder to build emotional momentum across a fragmented story

Potential Downsides

- The main story may feel diluted if side content overwhelms the core narrative.
- In episodic formats, players may lose engagement between releases.

Nested and Layered Narratives

Nested narratives are stories within stories. This structure allows a game to build complexity, surprise, and recontextualization. Players might begin with one understanding of the story, only to have that understanding **challenged or reframed** later.

The key to effective layered narratives is clarity in complexity, ensuring players can follow the thread even as the layers deepen.

Example

In *BioShock Infinite*, the player slowly uncovers the truth about the multiverse, identity, and memory. Early scenes gain new meaning as the player uncovers deeper layers of the narrative. What begins as a rescue mission evolves into a story about fate, control, and personal reckoning.

What It's Good For

- Psychological thrillers or mystery games
- Themes of identity, memory, or perception
- Revealing plot twists over time

Key Benefits

- Adds narrative depth and complexity
- Encourages re-evaluation of earlier story moments
- Creates strong emotional and philosophical engagement

Challenges

- Difficult to balance clarity and complexity
- Risk of confusing the player if layers aren't clearly distinguished

Potential Downsides

- Can alienate players who prefer straightforward storytelling
- Requires high-quality writing and direction to maintain cohesion

Branching structures align naturally with generative AI, which can produce multiple variations of dialogue or outcomes based on player choices.

Emergent Narratives

Emergent storytelling happens when the systems of a game interact in ways that produce unique, unscripted events. These narratives are not pre-written; they are discovered through play.

It relies on the player's imagination and decision-making to form a meaningful arc. While these stories may lack traditional structure, they can feel more personal and memorable because the player shaped them entirely.

Example

In *Mount & Blade*, players create their own story by building armies, forging alliances, and managing political relationships. There's no scripted path, just systems, and the player's ability to navigate them.

What It's Good For

- Simulation and sandbox games
- AI-driven or procedural storytelling
- Player-driven narratives

Key Benefits

- Each player's story is unique and unscripted.
- Offers high replay ability and personalization.
- Can create moments of surprise, tension, and humor that feel organic.

Challenges

- Lack of authorial control over story direction
- Requires robust game systems that interact in meaningful ways

Potential Downsides

- Stories may lack emotional weight or narrative structure.
- Some players may struggle to create their own goals or meaning.

Emergent systems pair exceptionally well with AI agents and procedural text generation, enabling narratives that adapt dynamically to player behavior.

Blended Structures in Modern Game Design

Most games today use a combination of the above structures. For instance, a game might follow a linear main story while offering nonlinear side content and emergent world interactions.

Example

Red Dead Redemption 2 uses a primarily linear main narrative. But within that structure, players encounter modular missions, emergent events, and layered subplots, all of which contribute to the story's emotional weight and realism.

What It's Good For

- Complex or large-scale narratives
- Balancing story depth with gameplay freedom
- Layering player agency into curated experiences

Key Benefits

- Flexibility to engage different player types
- Allows developers to focus on polishing where it matters (e.g., main story)
- Supports both emotional arcs and sandbox freedom

Challenges

- Can result in inconsistent tone or pacing
- Requires careful integration to avoid disjointed experiences

Potential Downsides

- Players may focus only on parts of the structure and miss core story beats.
- More complex to manage during development and QA.

Comparing Narrative Structures in Games

Narrative structures shape not only how a story unfolds but also how players engage with it. Each structure, linear, nonlinear, branching, modular, nested, or emergent, represents a different balance between authorial intent and player freedom. A linear structure gives developers full control over pacing and emotion, while nonlinear and branching structures open the door for player choice. Modular structures support open-world exploration, and emergent structures allow stories to arise naturally from gameplay systems. Understanding these differences is crucial because the narrative framework determines how players interpret their actions, how much agency they feel, and how the story delivers meaning.

In the context of generative AI, these structures become even more important. AI systems generate text, quests, dialogue, and narrative content based on underlying patterns, and each structure creates different constraints for the AI to work within. For example, linear narratives help AI produce coherent sequences without drifting off-topic, while branching structures leverage AI's strength in generating multiple variations of the same scene. Emergent structures align well with AI agents and procedural generation, where the AI adapts content in real time based on player behavior. By comparing these structures, developers can better decide how and where AI tools can meaningfully enhance narrative design.

The table below summarizes the trade-offs between player agency, replay ability, and narrative control across different structures. This comparison helps designers and AI systems select the narrative framework that best matches their game's storytelling goals.

Table 5-1. *Key Differences Between Narrative Structures*

Structure	Player Agency	Replay Ability	Narrative Control	Ideal For
Linear	Low	Moderate	High	Cinematic games, emotional arcs
Nonlinear	Moderate	High	Medium	Exploration, puzzle, mystery games
Branching	High	Very high	Shared (player + dev)	RPGs, choice-driven narratives
Modular/Episodic	Moderate	Moderate–high	Medium	Open world, story chapters
Nested	Moderate	High	High	Psychological, mystery, experimental
Emergent	Very high	Infinite	Low	Sandbox, simulation, AI-generated

Real-World Examples: AI Dungeon and Bandersnatch

To truly understand how narrative structures function in interactive storytelling, it helps to look at real-world examples that push the boundaries of form and player agency. Both AI Dungeon and Black Mirror: Bandersnatch represent innovative approaches to narrative design, one through emergent, AI-generated storytelling and the other through a carefully orchestrated branching structure. While their tools and techniques differ, both showcase how narrative structure can define the player's role in shaping the story.

AI Dungeon: Narrative Without a Script

AI Dungeon is a groundbreaking experiment in emergent storytelling, built on natural language generation technology. Instead of following a fixed narrative, it creates stories on the fly based on player input, generating unique scenarios, dialogue, and outcomes in real time.

At its core, AI Dungeon doesn't follow a traditional structure. There are no pre-written scenes, no fixed plot beats, and no decision trees. Instead, it leans entirely on player interaction and machine learning to generate a continuous flow of storytelling.

Narrative Structure: Emergent and Dynamic

Unlike games that use branching or modular structures, AI Dungeon allows stories to evolve organically, often in unpredictable directions. The AI responds to what the player types, adapting its tone, characters, and plot developments accordingly.

For example, a player might begin in a medieval fantasy village and, within minutes, find themselves negotiating peace between alien civilizations or battling sentient shadows in an enchanted forest, all shaped by the player's imagination and the AI's interpretation.

What It's Good For

- Storytelling sandbox experiences
- Roleplaying without narrative constraints
- Testing the boundaries of procedural creativity

Benefits

- Infinitely replay able, since no two stories are the same
- Encourages creativity and improvisation
- Gives players full control over direction, tone, and pacing

Challenges

- Lack of narrative cohesion or emotional arc
- Inconsistencies in character behavior or plot logic
- Requires players to take a more active storytelling role

Why It Matters

AI Dungeon demonstrates the potential of emergent structure in interactive narratives. It shifts the focus from fixed stories to collaborative storytelling between human and machine, opening up new creative possibilities, especially as generative AI continues to evolve.

Bandersnatch: Branching Narratives in Cinematic Form

Released as part of Netflix's *Black Mirror* anthology, Bandersnatch offers a different kind of interactivity. Rather than procedurally generating content, it presents a carefully crafted branching narrative, where the viewer's decisions affect the direction and outcome of the story.

Set in the 1980s, Bandersnatch follows a young programmer named Stefan as he attempts to adapt a choose-your-own-adventure book into a video game while slowly losing his grip on reality. The viewer is prompted at key moments to make decisions on Stefan's behalf, such as what cereal he eats, which music he listens to, or how he reacts to conflict.

Narrative Structure: Deeply Branching Decision Tree

Behind the scenes, Bandersnatch uses a complex decision tree structure with multiple branching paths and five major endings. Some choices quickly loop back into the main storyline, while others open entirely new scenes or outcomes.

What makes Bandersnatch notable is how it plays with the structure itself. In certain branches, Stefan becomes aware that his actions are being controlled. The narrative breaks the fourth wall and begins to comment on the illusion of choice, making the structure of the story a central narrative device.

What It's Good For

- Cinematic storytelling with meaningful player input
- Exploring themes of free will, control, and recursion
- Designing fixed branching narratives that still feel organic

Benefits

- Highly polished, cohesive storytelling
- Allows viewers to reflect on their choices
- Offers multiple rewatchable paths with different outcomes

Challenges

- Expensive and labor-intensive to produce each branch
- Risk of players feeling limited if branches converge too often
- Requires careful balancing between freedom and narrative coherence

Why It Matters

Bandersnatch represents a mature use of branching structure, not just as a storytelling mechanic but as part of the narrative's core theme. It shows how interactive storytelling can be tightly scripted and still feel dynamic, especially when the structure itself becomes part of the story.

***Table 5-2.** AI Dungeon vs. Bandersnatch*

Feature	AI Dungeon	Bandersnatch
Structure Type	Emergent (AI-generated, freeform)	Branching (predefined decision trees)
Replay Ability	Infinite variations	Multiple paths, finite permutations
Player Role	Co-author of the story	Participant making narrative decisions
Narrative Control	Low control from creators	High authorial intent from designers
Best For	Improvisational play, worldbuilding	Structured exploration, ethical dilemmas

Both AI Dungeon and Bandersnatch highlight how narrative structure defines player experience in interactive media. One leans into chaos and creativity, while the other tightly choreographs every possible choice. Yet both succeed in giving the player a sense of authorship, one by responding in real time and the other by offering meaningful branches within a crafted narrative.

These examples remind us that the future of storytelling is not about choosing one structure over another. It's about understanding what each structure enables and how best to use it to deliver powerful, memorable, and player-driven stories.

These structures form the narrative vocabulary that generative AI uses when creating or adapting stories. Whether a model is generating a linear quest, improvising an emergent event, or expanding a branching dialogue, it relies on these foundational structures. Understanding them prepares us for the next chapters, where we integrate AI tools directly into narrative design.

How Generative AI Uses Narrative Structures

Generative AI does not create stories at random; it builds on patterns learned from narrative structures like the ones explored in this chapter. When developers understand these structures, they can guide AI systems to produce more coherent, meaningful, and game-ready content.

- **Linear structures** help AI maintain clarity and pacing when generating quests, cutscenes, or scripted sequences.
- **Nonlinear and branching structures** allow AI to produce multiple dialogue variations, alternative outcomes, and player-dependent story paths.

- **Modular and episodic structures** align with how AI generates content in reusable segments such as missions, encounters, lore entries, or character arcs.
- **Nested structures** help AI create layered mysteries, plot twists, or recontextualized story moments.
- **Emergent structures** pair naturally with AI agents and procedural generation, allowing narrative to evolve in real time based on player actions.

By understanding these narrative frameworks, developers can prompt AI tools more effectively, constrain them where necessary, and ensure that AI-generated content supports the game's broader thematic and emotional goals. These structures form the narrative foundation upon which AI-driven storytelling and the rest of this book builds.

Conclusion

Narrative structure is the foundation on which a game's story is built. It influences how players understand events, connect with characters, and interpret their own role in the game world. For developers and writers, structure is a tool, not a restriction. It offers a way to shape emotion, engagement, and meaning.

As games become more interactive, personalized, and AI-enhanced, the boundaries of narrative structure are continuing to evolve. But at their core, all structures serve the same purpose: to help us tell stories that matter and to make those stories feel alive in the hands of the player.

CHAPTER 6

Types of Interactive Narratives

In the previous chapter, we looked at the architecture of interactive storytelling, the frameworks that shape how a narrative is structured behind the scenes. We explored linear, nonlinear, branching, modular, and emergent structures, focusing on how stories are organized and paced from a storyteller's point of view. That chapter was about the blueprint, the bones of the story.

This chapter shifts perspective. Now, we turn our attention to how players actually experience those stories through gameplay. It's not just about how a story is built, but how it's delivered, explored, and influenced by player interaction. This includes the tools and techniques developers use to present the narrative: dialogue systems, exploration mechanics, procedural content, environmental clues, and more.

So, while Chapter 5 asked,

"How is this story structured?"

Chapter 6 asks,

"How does the player engage with the story moment to moment, choice by choice?"

In this chapter, we'll explore the types of interactive narratives that emerge when story and gameplay collide. We'll examine different methods of narrative delivery like branching choices, open-world discovery, AI-generated storytelling, and dialogue systems and how each one creates a unique kind of experience for the player.

By the end of this chapter, you'll have a clearer understanding of the narrative formats available to game designers, what each is best suited for, and how to match the right narrative style to your game's mechanics, world, and audience.

S. N. Gupta, *Generative AI for Game Development*, https://doi.org/10.1007/979-8-8688-2439-5_6

Interactive Narratives

Interactive storytelling goes beyond traditional narrative by placing the audience in the role of an active participant. In games, stories are not just told; they're discovered, influenced, and sometimes written by the players themselves. The term "interactive narrative" covers a wide range of structures and mechanics, from simple dialogue choices to complex, branching worlds with emergent storylines.

Each type of interactive narrative serves a different purpose and suits different styles of gameplay. Understanding these variations is essential for designing experiences that feel **engaging, responsive, and meaningful**. In the below sections, we will explore the primary types of interactive narratives, examining how each works, what they're best suited for, and what challenges developers may encounter when implementing them.

Branching Narratives

A branching narrative gives the player meaningful choices that split the story into different paths. Each choice leads to consequences that affect future events, character relationships, or the overall outcome.

How It Works

At key decision points, players are offered choices such as how to respond in a conversation, what direction to take, or whether to support one character over another. These decisions create **divergent story branches**, some of which may rejoin the main plotline, while others may lead to entirely different conclusions.

Best For

- Narrative-driven RPGs
- Moral and ethical dilemmas
- Games with strong character development

Benefits

- High replay value.
- Strong emotional engagement.
- Player agency is front and center.

Challenges

- Requires extensive writing and asset creation
- Hard to maintain consistent pacing across branches
- Risk of overwhelming complexity as branches multiply

Example: *The Walking Dead* (Telltale Games)

In this episodic game, players shape the story through a series of moral and emotional choices. Whether you choose to lie, tell the truth, spare a character, or leave them behind, your actions carry weight. The game constantly tracks these decisions and references them in later episodes, making the player feel **personally responsible** for the story's direction.

Generative AI is particularly effective in branching narratives because it can produce multiple variations of dialogue, consequences, and scene descriptions. AI can also help fill content gaps by generating alternate branches or rewriting scenes to maintain consistency across divergent paths.

Open-Ended Narratives

Open-ended narratives give players the freedom to shape the story through exploration, discovery, and interaction without guiding them through a fixed plot. Instead of linear missions or clearly defined chapters, the story unfolds gradually based on how the player chooses to engage with the world.

How It Works

In these games, the narrative emerges through **player-driven interaction with the environment, systems, and characters**. Story elements are often revealed in fragments through dialogue, environmental clues, item descriptions, or player-triggered events.

Best For

- Open-world RPGs
- Exploration-based games
- Games that prioritize player freedom

Benefits

- Strong sense of immersion and discovery
- Supports multiple playstyles and pacing preferences
- Encourages roleplaying and creative choices

Challenges

- Lack of structure can lead to narrative disconnection.
- Hard to create a strong emotional arc.
- Players may miss important content without guidance.

Example: *The Elder Scrolls V: Skyrim*

While there is a central storyline about dragons and ancient prophecies, players are not required to follow it. They can ignore the main quest entirely, choosing instead to join a thieves' guild, build a house, become a vampire, or explore distant mountain ranges. The narrative is shaped by what the player chooses to focus on.

In open-ended worlds, GenAI can generate contextual lore, side quests, ambient dialogue, and world events based on player exploration patterns. AI tools can create dynamic responses that make a large world feel more reactive and alive, even with minimal pre-scripted content.

Procedural or Generated Narratives

Procedural narratives are not pre-written. Instead, they are generated by algorithms and systems, often using AI or logic-based engines to create unique storylines on the fly. These stories evolve dynamically as the game is played.

How It Works

Narrative fragments, character traits, world events, and interactions are procedurally generated using predefined parameters. The player's actions influence how these elements come together, creating a **personalized, emergent narrative**.

Best For

- Sandbox games
- Creative tools and AI-assisted storytelling
- Replay able, improvisational experiences

Benefits

- Infinite variety and uniqueness
- Highly personalized experiences
- Allows small teams to build vast content

Challenges

- Risk of incoherent or inconsistent storytelling.
- Difficult to create strong character arcs or plot structure.
- Narrative quality can vary dramatically.

Example: AI Dungeon

Built on GPT-based technology, AI Dungeon creates text-based adventures that respond dynamically to player input. There are no predetermined branches or storylines. Every time a player inputs a command or makes a decision, the AI generates a new response, continuing the story in real time. The result is a limitless and personalized narrative sandbox.

This narrative type aligns directly with GenAI. Models like GPT can generate story fragments, world events, item descriptions, and NPC dialogue on the fly, making each playthrough unique. AI can also help maintain coherence by anchoring procedural content to character goals or world themes.

Dialogue-Driven Narratives

Dialogue-driven narratives use conversation as the primary mechanic through which the story unfolds. Players choose from dialogue options that affect character relationships, reveal worldbuilding details, or influence the plot.

How It Works

Players interact with other characters via conversation menus. Choices often include multiple emotional tones, aggressive, diplomatic, curious, sarcastic, and each one can trigger different responses, shift character attitudes, or alter the narrative's direction.

Best For

- Character-driven RPGs
- Relationship-focused narratives
- Interactive dramas

Benefits

- High emotional immersion
- Rich character interaction
- Encourages replay with different personality choices

Challenges

- Dialogue must feel natural and reactive.
- Branching responses require significant writing.
- Risk of choice fatigue if options are too frequent or repetitive.

Example: *Mass Effect* Series

The dialogue wheel allows players to shape protagonist Commander Shepard's personality and relationships. Whether you play as a compassionate diplomat or a ruthless soldier, the way you engage in conversations affects both immediate responses and long-term consequences, including character loyalty and romantic outcomes.

GenAI excels at producing conversational content, branching dialogue variations, emotional tone shifts, and reactive responses to player choices. AI can also automatically adapt NPC personalities, generate contextual dialogue, and reduce writing workload.

Environmental and Embedded Narratives

Environmental storytelling conveys narrative through the **physical world and player surroundings** rather than dialogue or cutscenes. It involves details like architecture, objects, sound design, lighting, and written clues embedded in the environment.

How It Works

Players uncover the story by observing and interacting with the world. A bloodstain on a wall, a broken photo frame, or graffiti in an alley may all suggest pieces of a larger narrative. These clues are rarely spelled out, encouraging interpretation.

Best For

- Mystery and exploration games
- Horror or psychological storytelling
- Games with minimalist design

Benefits

- Deep immersion without exposition
- Encourages curiosity and close observation
- Enables nonlinear storytelling without branching

Challenges

- Requires careful design and detail.
- Risk that players overlook or misinterpret story elements.
- Narrative pacing is entirely controlled by the player.

Example: *Gone Home*

Set entirely in a single abandoned house, the player learns about a family's history and a young girl's coming-of-age story by exploring rooms and inspecting objects. There are no enemies, objectives, or dialogue trees, just environmental storytelling and subtle clues.

AI can generate environmental details such as notes, logs, graffiti, item descriptions, and ambient lore based on player actions or world states. It can also analyze player behavior to embed clues or story fragments that are tailored to their exploration patterns.

Hybrid Narratives

Hybrid narratives combine multiple storytelling methods, branching choices, environmental clues, procedural events, and dialogue interactions, into a **layered and flexible narrative structure**.

How It Works

The core story may follow a linear or branching path, while side content and worldbuilding emerge through environmental storytelling or player-driven choices. The narrative adapts based on how players engage with different aspects of the game.

Best For

- AAA open-world games
- Games focused on immersion and realism
- Narratives with emotional and systemic depth

Benefits

- Appeals to diverse playstyles
- Supports both guided storytelling and freedom
- Balances structure with organic discovery

Challenges

- Requires extensive development time and resources.
- Maintaining consistency across narrative types can be difficult.
- Player experiences may vary widely, making it hard to control narrative impact.

Example: *Red Dead Redemption 2*

While the main story is largely linear, players encounter a wide range of narrative styles: dialogue-based missions, emergent events in the open world, random encounters, and richly detailed environments that tell their own stories. These elements work together to create a cohesive and living world.

Hybrid systems benefit from GenAI's flexibility. AI can support linear missions with dynamic dialogue, populate open worlds with emergent events, generate procedural side quests, or enrich environmental storytelling with adaptive lore. It serves as a narrative "glue" between multiple formats.

Comparison of Interactive Narrative Types

Interactive narratives differ not only in how they present story content but also in how they shape player agency, pacing, and emotional engagement. Linear narratives emphasize tight control and predictable pacing, while branching stories offer meaningful choice and replay ability. Modular narratives support open-world exploration, and emergent storytelling relies on systems that generate surprising or unscripted moments during play. Each structure comes with unique design strengths and trade-offs, influencing the overall player experience and the complexity of authoring content.

By comparing these structures side-by-side, developers can better understand how narrative format affects workload, player expectations, and the degree of control designers retain over tone and pacing. This comparison also helps identify how different structures align with modern workflows, particularly when integrating generative

AI. Because AI models generate text, dialogue, quests, and dynamic responses more effectively when guided by a clear narrative framework, understanding these distinctions becomes essential before applying AI to interactive storytelling.

***Table 6-1.** Key Differences Between Narrative Structures*

Narrative Type	Core Mechanic	Best For	Key Benefits	Common Challenges	Example Game
Branching Narrative	Player choices create divergent storylines	Choice-based RPGs, moral dilemmas	High replay ability, emotional investment	Content-intensive, complex to manage narrative cohesion	*The Walking Dead* (Telltale)
Open-Ended Narrative	Freeform exploration and player-driven pacing	Open-world, sandbox, and roleplaying games	High freedom, immersive discovery	Risk of narrative dilution, uneven pacing	*Skyrim*
Procedural/ Generated	Systems or AI generate narrative dynamically	Sandbox, roguelike, and experimental games	Infinite variety, unique playthroughs	Inconsistencies, lack of emotional structure	*AI Dungeon*
Dialogue-Driven	Player influences the story through conversations	Character-driven RPGs, relationship-focused games	Strong character depth, roleplaying variety	Writing-intensive, branching dialogue is hard to balance	*Mass Effect* series
Environmental/ Embedded	Story revealed through world details and exploration	Horror, mystery, atmospheric exploration	Subtle storytelling, immersive worldbuilding	Requires attentive players, can be missed or misinterpreted	*Gone Home*
Hybrid Narrative	Mix of multiple narrative systems	Large-scale games aiming for realism or flexibility	Appeals to many playstyles, rich and layered experience	Risk of tonal inconsistency, complex to execute	*Red Dead Redemption 2*

Understanding how these narrative types differ is only the first step. Each structure also varies in how well it aligns with generative AI tools. Some formats such as branching and procedural narratives naturally benefit from AI's ability to generate variations, fill content gaps, or adapt story elements to player behavior. Others, like tightly authored linear narratives, require more control and careful prompting to maintain tone and coherence. The following **AI Suitability Matrix** provides a clearer view of how effectively GenAI tools support each narrative type and what kinds of tasks developers can offload to AI within those structures.

Table 6-2. *AI Suitability Matrix of Narrative Structures*

Narrative Type	AI Suitability	Why/How AI Helps	Example GenAI Use Cases
Linear Narrative	Moderate	AI can assist with drafting scenes, dialogue, and lore, but developers must tightly control pacing and tone.	Generate cutscene scripts, expand narrative beats, create descriptive passages, polish dialogue.
Branching Narrative	High	LLMs excel at generating multiple variations of the same scene, offering alternate choices, consequences, and character responses.	Auto-generate dialogue branches, alternative quest outcomes, emotional variants, choice-driven scenes.
Modular/ Episodic Narrative	High	AI generates reusable content blocks (quests, encounters, lore entries) that fit into modular frameworks.	Generate side missions, item lore, NPC backstories, episodic story beats.
Nonlinear Narrative	Moderate–High	AI can assist with worldbuilding and creating story fragments players uncover in any order.	Generate collectibles, scattered lore, environmental storytelling content.
Open-Ended Narrative	High	AI dynamically generates descriptions, lore, and reactive content based on player exploration.	AI-generated exploration logs, procedural lore, adaptive world events.

(*continued*)

Table 6-2. *(continued)*

Narrative Type	AI Suitability	Why/How AI Helps	Example GenAI Use Cases
Procedural Narrative	Very High	Perfect fit for AI: LLMs generate story seeds, encounters, and events that evolve with world state.	Procedural quests, faction events, random encounters, location descriptions.
Dialogue-Driven Narrative	Very High	AI excels at producing conversational text, emotional tone shifts, and reactive responses.	NPC personality engines, reactive dialogue, emotional adaptation, dynamic banter.
Environmental/ Embedded Narrative	High	AI generates in-world artifacts such as notes, logs, graffiti, and item descriptions.	AI-generated journals, terminal logs, collectibles, environmental clues.
Emergent Narrative	Moderate–High	AI agents generate behaviors, motivations, and unscripted reactions that form story events.	Dynamic NPC behavior, faction systems, real-time AI story events.
Hybrid Narrative	Very High	AI fills gaps between systems and supports mixing of linear, branching, and procedural forms.	Mixed narrative generation: main plot + AI side quests + dynamic dialogue.

Generative AI plays a significant role in shaping how these narrative types can be implemented in modern games. Each structure presents different opportunities for AI-powered content generation: branching narratives benefit from AI's ability to produce alternate paths quickly; procedural narratives leverage AI for on-the-fly story creation; open-ended and hybrid narratives use AI to fill worlds with contextually appropriate lore, dialogue, and events. Understanding these structures is essential for identifying where AI can enhance, automate, or intelligently adapt narrative systems.

As developers integrate generative AI into their workflows, the narrative type becomes a key design decision that determines how AI models generate, adapt, and deliver story content. This chapter lays the groundwork for the practical AI implementation covered in later chapters, ensuring that readers can match the right AI tools to the right narrative format.

Interactive narratives are not defined by a single structure; they are defined by the relationship between **player and story**. Whether through tightly scripted choices or open-ended exploration, the goal is the same: to create a story that feels alive, responsive, and meaningful.

Each narrative type has its strengths and trade-offs. Some prioritize **emotional immersion**, while others focus on **freedom and player creativity**. The most impactful games often blend these approaches, tailoring structure to gameplay and theme.

How Developers Use Generative AI Within These Narrative Structures

Generative AI plays a different role depending on the narrative structure chosen for a game. In branching narratives, developers often use LLMs such as GPT-4, Claude, or Llama to produce multiple dialogue variations or alternative outcomes quickly. By feeding the model key story beats or decision points, writers can generate new branches, rewrite existing ones, or explore subtle emotional differences that add depth without dramatically increasing labor.

In open-ended or exploratory narratives, developers use AI to populate worlds with contextual content, lore fragments, item descriptions, NPC chatter, environmental notes, or dynamic world responses. Tools like RAG help ensure the generated content remains consistent with established lore, while AI-assisted content pipelines allow designers to add large amounts of flavor text rapidly.

Procedural and emergent narrative systems benefit heavily from GenAI because AI can generate story seeds, world events, or adaptive narrative elements that respond to player actions. Developers can integrate LLM outputs with procedural generation systems in Unity or Unreal so encounters, quests, and NPC motivations evolve in real time. Dialogue-driven narratives, on the other hand, use GenAI to create character speech patterns, rewrite dialogue to match personality traits, or generate reactive responses based on sentiment or player choices.

By aligning the chosen narrative structure with the capabilities of modern AI tools, developers can determine where and how AI will provide the most value, whether that means speeding up content creation, expanding player agency, or enabling dynamic storytelling that would be impractical to build manually.

Conclusion

As technology advances and AI becomes more integrated into storytelling, the possibilities for interactive narratives will continue to expand. The key for developers and writers is not to chase complexity for its own sake, but to choose the structure that best supports the story they want to tell and the experience they want the player to have.

EXERCISE: CREATE A FLOWCHART FOR BRANCHING STORY

Understanding branching narratives conceptually is one thing, but designing them puts theory into practice. This exercise challenges you to sketch your own branching narrative flow, using a simple story structure that demonstrates how player decisions can shape outcomes.

Objective

Design a basic branching narrative flowchart with

- At least three decision points
- At least two distinct endings
- Logical connections between choices and consequences

This exercise will help you

- Think like a narrative designer.
- Visualize cause and effect in storytelling.
- Practice organizing player-driven story paths.

Instructions

1. Choose a simple story premise (e.g., escaping a forest, solving a mystery, navigating a conversation, etc.).
2. Identify the key decision points where the player can make choices.
3. For each decision, map out the resulting outcomes.
4. Use basic shapes (boxes and arrows) to show how paths branch and reconnect or diverge completely.

5. Label each node clearly: decision, event, or ending.

You can do this on paper, in a digital drawing tool, or with free flowchart software (like draw.io or Lucidchart).

Sample Scenario: "The Abandoned House"

You, the player, come across a mysterious abandoned house during a storm. Do you enter? What do you find? Will you make it out?

Figure 6-1. *Sample flowchart for "The Abandoned House" scenario*

Reflection Questions

- Which decision had the biggest impact on the outcome?
- Were any paths more narratively satisfying than others?
- How could you reuse or reconnect branches to reduce narrative complexity?

Tip When designing branching stories for actual games, always consider: how much content is hidden behind each path, how to balance player freedom with narrative focus, and when to let branches converge back to streamline development.

CHAPTER 7

AI Tools and Technologies for Storytelling

As the boundaries between narrative design and artificial intelligence continue to blur, the role of the storyteller is evolving. Writers and game developers are no longer limited to crafting every line of dialogue or every narrative branch by hand. Today, a new generation of AI-powered tools can support, accelerate, and even co-author aspects of storytelling, generating dynamic dialogue, analyzing emotional tone, and adapting narratives in real time.

This chapter offers a practical look at some of the most relevant and accessible AI tools used in narrative development. From lightweight scripting utilities to advanced machine learning models, we'll explore how each tool can contribute to different aspects of the storytelling process. Whether you're building interactive fiction, procedurally generated quests, or emotion-sensitive dialogue systems, these technologies are opening doors to narrative possibilities that were once impractical or impossible.

Lightweight Tools vs. Advanced AI Systems

Before diving into specific technologies, it's helpful to understand the distinction between two broad categories of storytelling tools: **lightweight tools** and **advanced AI systems**. Each offers different strengths depending on the complexity, scope, and goals of your narrative project.

S. N. Gupta, *Generative AI for Game Development*, https://doi.org/10.1007/979-8-8688-2439-5_7

Lightweight Tools

Lightweight tools are rule-based systems designed for ease of use, clarity, and fast iteration. They are typically driven by simple scripting logic, decision trees, or visual nodes, and they require little to no background in machine learning or programming. These tools are widely used in early-stage development, rapid prototyping, and by narrative designers who want full control over branching logic.

Key Features

- Easy to learn and use
- Visual or text-based interfaces
- Deterministic (outcomes are predictable and testable)

Common Examples

- **Twine**: A visual tool for writing branching narratives
- **Ink** (by Inkle Studios): A scripting language used in *80 Days* and *Heaven's Vault*
- **Yarn Spinner**: Dialogue-focused scripting tool used in *Night in the Woods*
- **Ren'Py**: A popular engine for visual novels, supporting character dialogue, choice paths, and images

Advanced AI Systems

Advanced AI systems use machine learning and large-scale language models to create dynamic, context-aware content. These tools rely on training data, neural networks, and complex algorithms to generate text, analyze tone, or simulate decision-making. They are more computationally intensive and require technical understanding to integrate effectively, but they unlock narrative possibilities that static systems can't match.

Key Features

- Capable of generating original, adaptive content
- Can interpret player input in natural language
- Able to learn or change over time (in some implementations)

Common Examples

- **GPT (OpenAI)**: Generates humanlike text for dialogue, quests, or lore
- **DALL·E/Stable Diffusion**: Text-to-image models for visual storytelling
- **VADER**: A sentiment analysis tool for evaluating emotional tone in text
- **Unity ML-Agents**: A reinforcement learning toolkit for intelligent character behavior
- **Charisma.ai**: A narrative AI platform for real-time, conversational storytelling
- **Promethean AI**: Assists in worldbuilding and level design with context-aware suggestions

Lightweight Tools vs. Advanced AI Systems: A Comparison

Table 7-1. *Key Differences Between Lightweight Tools and Advanced AI Systems*

Category	Lightweight Tools	Advanced AI Systems
Core Approach	Rule-based scripting and branching logic	Machine learning, natural language processing, neural nets
Ease of Use	Beginner-friendly, low-code or no-code	Requires programming, API integration, and model handling
Content Behavior	Deterministic (predictable outcomes)	Dynamic and adaptive (may vary per interaction)
Creative Control	Full authorial control over all content	Partial control; relies on prompting and fine-tuning
Examples	Twine, Ink, Yarn Spinner, Ren'Py	GPT, DALL·E, Stable Diffusion, VADER, Unity ML-Agents
Best For	Visual novels, dialogue trees, branching stories	Procedural content, adaptive storytelling, emotion-driven AI
Strengths	Simple to learn, fast prototyping, reliable output	Scalable content generation, personalization, reactivity
Limitations	Limited flexibility, static content	Quality control challenges, integration complexity
Ideal Use Case	Structured narrative experiences	Real-time dialogue, reactive NPCs, AI-generated quests

Each has its strengths, and many projects benefit from a hybrid approach using lightweight tools for structural control and AI systems for dynamic content generation.

Now that we have a foundational understanding of what lightweight tools and advanced AI systems are, let's deep dive into some of the tools that we will use throughout this book.

Twine: Visual Storytelling for Everyone

Twine (`https://twinery.org`) is an open-source tool for creating **interactive, nonlinear stories**. It uses a visual interface that allows writers to build narratives through a series of connected passages, essentially nodes that represent moments, choices, or events.

Each passage is a chunk of text with hyperlinks leading to other passages. These links act as **player choices**, creating a branching narrative. Twine supports conditional logic and variables, so writers can track decisions, inventory, or player stats.

Twine is best used for

- Interactive fiction and text-based games
- Rapid prototyping of branching narratives
- Visualizing story structure

A good thing about Twine is that it removes the technical barrier for writers who want to build interactive stories. It doesn't require coding knowledge but still offers scripting flexibility for those who want to go deeper. This makes it a powerful gateway for narrative designers to experiment with choice-driven storytelling.

Note Compelling interactive storytelling doesn't need complex graphics or AI, just thoughtful writing and meaningful choices.

GPT (Generative Pre-trained Transformer): Dynamic Text Generation

Developed by OpenAI, GPT (`http://chat.openai.com/`) is a state-of-the-art natural language model trained on massive volumes of text. It can generate humanlike writing in response to a prompt, making it useful for dialogue generation, character interaction, lore building, and content variation.

GPT is very simple to use as well, developers send a text prompt to the model through an API, and GPT responds with contextually appropriate output. The more detailed the prompt, the more coherent and focused the response. With proper fine-tuning and constraints, GPT can maintain tone, mimic character voices, and produce dynamic responses to player input.

GPT is best used for

- Real-time NPC dialogue
- Procedurally generated quest text or backstory
- Creative brainstorming and prototyping for writers

GPT doesn't just generate words; it enables adaptive storytelling. Instead of writing hundreds of static lines for every interaction, designers can script general patterns and let GPT fill in the rest, adapting to the player's history, actions, or personality traits. Throughout this book, we will heavily use GPT and see how it enhances the game and gameplay in various aspects.

Note While powerful, GPT still requires **editorial oversight**. Generated content may include inaccuracies or inconsistencies, so it's best used alongside quality control systems or as a supplement to authored writing.

DALL·E and Stable Diffusion: Visual Storytelling with AI Art

DALL·E (by OpenAI) (`https://openai.com/index/dall-e-3/`) and Stable Diffusion (`https://stablediffusionweb.com/`, an open-source alternative) are text-to-image generation models. These tools convert textual prompts into original images, concept art, environments, characters, or UI elements using deep learning.

Similar to GPT, users input a descriptive prompt (e.g., "a foggy forest with glowing mushrooms and a medieval gate"), and the model produces one or more images that match the description. Artists and designers can iterate rapidly by tweaking prompts or generating variations.

Since these tools are for art generation, they are best used for

- Concept art for characters and settings
- Visual prompts for narrative worldbuilding
- Creating image-based storyboards or mood boards

Visual tone plays a crucial role in storytelling. These tools enable creators to prototype visual elements quickly, even without traditional art skills. For narrative teams, this means tighter collaboration between writing and visual design.

Note Use generated art as **draft material**, not final assets. AI-generated images may need refinement by human artists before being production-ready, but they can dramatically speed up the creative process.

VADER (Valence Aware Dictionary for Sentiment Reasoning): Emotional Tone Analysis

VADER is a rule-based sentiment analysis tool that evaluates the **emotional tone** of a piece of text, labeling it as positive, neutral, or negative, along with intensity scores.

So, you feed VADER a line of dialogue, journal entry, or player-generated input. It returns a numeric sentiment score, which you can use to influence gameplay: change character mood, trigger story events, or alter dialogue options based on emotional context.

This is best used for

- Emotionally adaptive dialogue systems
- Character relationship tracking
- Branching logic based on player sentiment

While many AI models focus on what is said, but VADER helps games respond to **how it is said**. It enables nuanced storytelling where tone influences outcome something especially important in therapeutic, educational, or empathy-focused narratives.

Flask: A Lightweight Framework for Custom Narrative Tools

Flask is a lightweight, Python-based web framework often used to build web applications and services. While it wasn't designed specifically for storytelling or game development, it has become a popular tool among developers who need to quickly prototype or deploy interactive systems, especially those involving narrative logic, user input, or AI integration.

Flask doesn't come with built-in narrative features like dialogue trees or branching systems. Instead, it provides a flexible foundation on which developers can **build their own tools**, manage game states, or connect front-end story interfaces with back-end logic or AI models.

At its core, Flask is used to create simple web servers that respond to user input, render HTML pages, and process data through Python scripts. In a storytelling context, this might include

- Serving different story paths based on player decisions
- Connecting to a GPT API to generate dialogue or story text
- Tracking variables such as character relationships, inventory, or emotional states
- Managing session-based narrative progression in browser-based games

For example, a Flask application could present a story interface to the player (via a web page), accept their choice input, and route the next narrative event accordingly, either from a predefined structure or an AI-generated response.

Because of all these benefits, Flask is best suited for

- Custom-built interactive fiction tools
- Rapid prototyping for AI-assisted storytelling
- Connecting front-end experiences to GPT, VADER, or similar models
- Managing dialogue and choice logic in web-based narratives

Flask is particularly valuable when existing storytelling tools are too restrictive or when a team needs a lightweight back-end to connect different systems together. It's commonly used to create authoring tools, dialogue managers, or simple narrative engines that run in a browser and respond to player input dynamically.

While Flask isn't a storytelling engine in the traditional sense, it plays a vital supporting role in modern narrative development. It enables fast, custom solutions that tie together multiple technologies, making it ideal for teams who need full control over how stories are structured, delivered, and extended.

For narrative designers who are comfortable working with code or working alongside developers, Flask becomes a powerful, adaptable piece of the interactive storytelling toolkit.

Note Unlike Twine or Ink, Flask doesn't assume a narrative format; you define the structure, logic, and design. This gives it a different kind of power: flexibility without assumptions.

Combining Tools: A Layered Approach

No single tool can handle every aspect of narrative design, but combining them strategically can produce impressive results. For instance:

- Use **Twine** to structure a branching story.
- Integrate **GPT** to fill in dynamic dialogue.
- Employ **VADER** to adjust tone and emotion.
- Generate art concepts using **Stable Diffusion**.
- Use Flask for **rapid prototyping** and testing.

This layered approach allows a small team to build rich, reactive narrative systems that were once the domain of large studios.

A full combined workflow using multiple tools is demonstrated in later chapters, once readers have the necessary technical foundation.

Conclusion

Remember that AI tools are not replacing storytellers; they're becoming creative collaborators. They offer speed, scalability, and responsiveness, giving writers and designers new ways to build, refine, and deliver interactive narratives. From procedural quest generation to emotion-aware characters, these technologies are reshaping the landscape of storytelling in games.

The key to using AI effectively is not to hand over creative control, but to guide and shape its output. When used thoughtfully, these tools become extensions of the designer's vision, helping stories not only reach players but respond to them.

HANDS-ON EXAMPLE 1: TWINE FOR CREATING SIMPLE NARRATIVES

Understanding Twine in theory is one thing, but putting it into practice is where it really clicks. This hands-on walkthrough will guide you through building a **basic branching narrative** using Twine's visual editor and simple scripting features. The goal is to help you create your first interactive story, complete with choices, conditional outcomes, and replay able paths.

What You'll Build

A short interactive story titled "Lost in the Woods," where the player must choose a path through a mysterious forest. Based on their choices, the story will end in one of two outcomes: finding a hidden cabin or getting hopelessly lost.

Step-by-Step Guide

Step 1: Open Twine

- Visit `https://twinery.org`.
- Choose **"Use in your browser"** or download the desktop version (both work the same).
- Click **"+Story"** to create a new project.
- Name your story: **"Lost in the Woods"**.

Step 2: Write Your First Passage

- Twine begins with a default passage titled Untitled Passage.
- Click on it to edit.
- Replace the text with

```
You wake up alone in the middle of a dense, unfamiliar forest. The trees tower overhead, and a path splits in two directions.

[[Take the left path]]

[[Take the right path]]
```

These double-bracketed phrases create links to new passages.

Step 3: Add Branching Passages

Twine will automatically create new passages titled *"Take the left path"* and *"Take the right path."* Click on each and add the following:

Left Path:

```
You follow the winding left trail, and soon hear the sound of
running water.

[[Follow the sound]]

[[Turn back]]
```

Right Path:

```
The right path leads deeper into the forest, and everything feels
unnaturally quiet.

[[Keep going]]

[[Climb a tree to get a better view]]
```

Step 4: Create Endings

You now have four new links to complete. Fill each with a short outcome:

"Follow the sound" → Ending A

```
You find a stream and beside it, an old wooden cabin. You're safe
for now.

**The End**
```

"Turn back" → Ending B

```
You retrace your steps, but everything looks the same. The path has
vanished. You are lost.

**The End**
```

"Keep going" → Ending C

```
After walking for hours, you stumble into a clearing full of strange
glowing stones. You have no idea where you are, but you're not alone.

**The End**
```

"Climb a tree..." → Ending D

```
From the treetop, you see smoke rising in the distance. You head toward
it, hopeful.

**The End**
```

Step 5: Add a Variable (Intermediate Feature)

In the initial passage, before any text, add

```
(set: $brave to false)
```

Then, in the "Climb a tree..." passage, change it to

```
(set: $brave to true)

From the treetop, you see smoke rising in the distance...
```

In the final ending, you can check that variable:

```
(if: $brave)[Your courage helped you find a way out.]

(else:)[Maybe next time, you'll climb.]
```

Variables allow you to create responsive dialogue, change outcomes, or personalize future encounters, all based on earlier player actions.

Step 6: Test and Play

- Use the **"Play"** button in Twine to test your story.
- Click through different paths and endings.
- Make edits, try new variations, and experiment with tone and pacing.

Final Flow (Structure Overview)

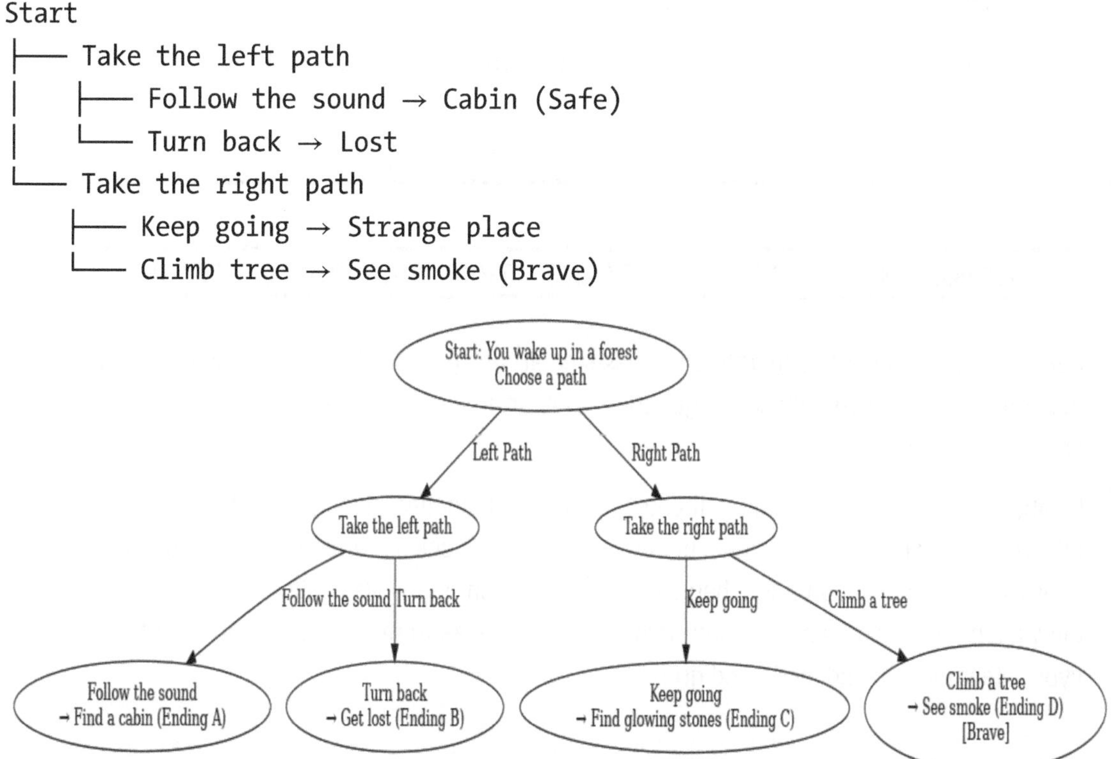

***Figure 7-1.** Visual flow of the "Lost in the Woods" story*

What You've Learned

By completing this exercise, you've touched on

- Creating passages and links
- Designing choices and consequences
- Using basic variables to influence narrative
- Structuring a small, branching story

Next Steps

- Add inventory systems using more variables.
- Introduce conditional passages (only show certain paths under specific conditions).
- Use CSS to style your story with custom visuals and fonts.

HANDS-ON EXAMPLE 2: AI ART GENERATION USING STABLE DIFFUSION

Use the below prompt to generate an AI-assisted art using Stable Diffusion or any other image generation AI tool of your choice to generate an AI art image, and play around to your liking by changing the prompt.

Prompt: A hidden black market in the lowest layer of a floating steampunk city. Cramped alleyways lit by broken neon signs, underground vendors selling forbidden ether tech, masked dealers trading in shadows. Mechanical eyes watch from the walls, while makeshift forges glow deep red. Trash fires burn in barrels, and steam leaks from cracked vents. Dark fantasy cyber-steampunk blend, eerie and grim.

Figure 7-2. *Output image from* `https://stablediffusionweb.com/` *using the exercise prompt*

CHAPTER 8

Ethical and Practical Considerations

As AI continues to transform how stories are written, delivered, and experienced, it brings with it a host of ethical and practical challenges that developers, writers, and studios cannot afford to ignore. While the creative potential of generative AI is vast, its impact on players, creators, and the broader cultural landscape is still unfolding.

This chapter explores the ethical dimensions of AI-assisted storytelling, from bias and fairness to authorship, accountability, and data privacy. It also addresses the practical concerns of maintaining narrative coherence, ensuring emotional integrity, and balancing AI automation with human creative intent. These are not just philosophical issues; they are real design considerations that affect how players interpret and trust the stories we tell.

What Does "Ethical" Mean in AI-Powered Game Storytelling?

In everyday use, "ethical" often suggests doing the right thing. But in the context of AI storytelling in games, ethics goes deeper than simply avoiding harm. It's about recognizing the responsibility that comes with building systems that tell stories, shape experiences, and interact with players on an emotional level.

When we talk about ethics in this space, we're really talking about intentionality, transparency, and accountability across several dimensions.

S. N. Gupta, *Generative AI for Game Development*, https://doi.org/10.1007/979-8-8688-2439-5_8

Ethical Means Inclusive

Your story systems should recognize and represent a diversity of identities, perspectives, and experiences. AI should not default to outdated tropes or cultural stereotypes simply because they were overrepresented in the data it was trained on.

In practice, let's say if your AI auto-generates a village of characters, do their roles reflect a balance of gender, race, and personality? Are your heroes always of one background and your villains another? Ethics here means questioning what your system assumes and correcting it where needed.

Ethical Means Emotionally Aware

Stories evoke emotion. When AI is involved, it must be sensitive to the emotional context of what it generates, especially in games that explore trauma, loss, identity, or conflict. Just because an AI can write something dramatic doesn't mean it should.

Which means, as an example, you wouldn't want a grief support game to accidentally generate a flippant or romanticized response to player input about loss. Ethical design means making sure your AI respects the emotional tone and boundaries of the story.

Ethical Means Transparent

Players have a right to know what's written by a human and what's dynamically generated. They should also understand whether their input is being analyzed, stored, or used to influence future content.

In practice, if your game adapts its story based on a player's emotional tone or choices, tell them. Ethics means giving players informed agency not just in story decisions, but in how the game processes them.

Ethical Means Accountable

When an AI says something offensive, inconsistent, or misleading, someone still needs to be responsible for that output. Ethical systems are designed with **human oversight** and with processes to correct or remove problematic content quickly.

This might involve flagging tools, human editing of generated dialogue, or simply having clear internal policies for how and when AI can be used in storytelling systems.

Ethical Means Story-First

At its core, ethical design asks: Is the use of AI serving the story, or is it just filling space? If AI is used just to create more content faster, without care for coherence, tone, or emotional payoff, it may be efficient, but it's not ethical storytelling.

A procedurally generated quest may technically "work," but if it lacks meaning, emotional context, or consistency with your world, it risks turning your narrative into noise.

Why Ethics in AI Storytelling Matters

Ethics in storytelling has always mattered, but when artificial intelligence enters the picture, the stakes shift. What once involved a single writer's choices now involves complex systems trained on massive datasets, making decisions at scale, and interacting with players in real time. These systems can shape perceptions, reinforce biases, and influence emotional experiences without the player or even the developer fully realizing it.

That's why ethics is not just a side conversation. It's central to responsible design. When we use AI to tell stories, we're not just automating content. We're building systems that speak to people, that interpret their input, and that make creative decisions on their behalf. And when that happens, we have to ask:

- What values are we encoding?
- Whose voices are we amplifying or silencing?
- How do we protect players from harm, without silencing difficult topics?

Without ethical guardrails, AI can unintentionally reproduce stereotypes, generate harmful content, or strip human nuance from emotionally sensitive themes. In the worst cases, it can erode trust not just in the story, but in the game itself.

But ethics isn't just about avoiding harm. It's also about building better systems. Ethical storytelling is inclusive, intentional, and accountable. It creates room for more voices, richer perspectives, and deeper emotional engagement. It ensures that technology serves the story, not the other way around.

Being careful doesn't mean being cautious to the point of inaction. It means being thoughtful. It means recognizing that when you introduce AI into storytelling, you're not just solving problems. You're changing the relationship between the creator, the player, and the narrative. And that's something worth getting right!

At the end, ethics in AI storytelling isn't just about avoiding controversy; it's about protecting the integrity of your story and the experience of your players. It's about designing systems that understand their impact, even when their content is machine-generated.

It doesn't mean AI can't be creative, surprising, or challenging. It simply means we must design with care so that the stories we tell with AI are not only smart, but also **fair, human, and meaningful**.

Where Things Can Go Wrong and How to Make Them Right

Let's look in detail how we can create a game with a story that is compelling and ethical, and we'll do this by looking at the core ethical problems why do they happen and how to address them. I'll provide realistic examples and grounded solutions to help designers navigate these challenges without compromising creativity or player trust.

Bias in AI-Generated Content

Most generative AI models are trained on large-scale datasets scraped from the internet. This training data inevitably reflects existing cultural, social, and historical biases, whether intentional or not. As a result, AI-generated stories may reinforce stereotypes, exclude marginalized perspectives, or present skewed moral frameworks. When AI becomes a co-author, it inherits the biases embedded in its training data unless designers actively intervene.

A good example to explain this is earlier versions of language models, where users reported that characters generated with prompts like "a doctor and a nurse" would default to male doctors and female nurses. This may seem subtle, but it reveals how AI can reproduce outdated gender roles, even without explicit intent.

So, what can we do here? Below are some proven methods to counter the inherited bias in AI-generated contents.

Table 8-1. *Methods to Correct Bias in AI-Generated Content*

Practice	Example
Use bias-aware datasets	Before using GPT to generate character dialogue, fine-tune it on a curated dataset that includes diverse voices, avoiding reliance on general internet data.
Manually review AI-generated content	In a narrative generator, have writers review character descriptions to catch problematic defaults (e.g., exoticizing cultures, gendered roles).
Provide neutral or randomized templates	Create templates where character roles (e.g., king, mage, warrior) are assigned gender and cultural attributes at random, unless constrained by story logic.
Use player customization to offset bias	Let players choose race, gender, identity, and backstory of major characters, ensuring they aren't boxed in by AI defaults.

Note Storytelling isn't neutral. The stories we tell shape worldviews, social expectations, and cultural norms.

Authorship and Ownership

When AI contributes text, dialogue, or worldbuilding to your game, a natural question arises: *Who owns that content?* And further, *who is responsible for it?*

This isn't just a legal question; it's also a creative one. If a game's most emotionally powerful scene is generated by an AI, what does that mean for the role of the writer?

Authorship is deeply tied to credit, accountability, and creative identity. In traditional storytelling, a writer's voice is part of the art. With AI, that authorship becomes diffuse, blurring the line between tool and collaborator.

While it is difficult to fully define the ownership, below are some measures that can help make it transparent.

Table 8-2. *Methods to Define Ownership When Using AI in Gaming and Storytelling*

Practice	Example
Be transparent about AI contributions	In your game credits or dev-log, mention that GPT-4 was used to generate side quest dialogue, but that all main story arcs were written by human authors.
Create "hybrid authorship" labels	Mark quests or scenes in your design pipeline with tags like "AI-generated (edited)", or "Human-authored", making authorship traceable.
Use editorial review as a mandatory step	In a branching narrative game, all AI dialogue options are proofread and modified by a narrative designer before implementation.
Clarify intellectual ownership	Establish clear internal policy that all AI-generated content is treated as studio-owned but subject to human approval and modification.

Narrative Coherence and Continuity

AI can produce fluent, interesting dialogue, but it struggles with narrative consistency over time. It may forget past events, contradict itself, or lose track of emotional tone.

For interactive storytelling, where the player expects continuity and consequence, these inconsistencies can break immersion and weaken emotional impact.

Imagine a player builds a deep bond with an NPC over several hours. If, due to AI generation, that character suddenly ignores or forgets that relationship, the illusion collapses. What once felt real now feels mechanical, isn't it?

The best way to maintain continuity is to use the below practices.

Table 8-3. *Methods to Use in Order to Maintain Continuity*

Practice	Example
Use AI for filler, not foundational scenes	Use GPT to write flavor text or optional background lore (books, scrolls, overheard chatter) not for critical cutscenes or endings.
Track decisions using variables	In a dialogue system, track if the player insulted a character earlier, then use that flag to manually control tone in future responses.
Design fallback dialogues	If the AI fails to maintain consistency, revert to a scripted response that reinforces character identity ("We've been through too much to argue now.").
Limit AI's memory scope intentionally	Reset or refresh AI memory between chapters, allowing the story to shift context deliberately rather than confusingly.

AI Hallucinations

One of the most overlooked ethical concerns in AI-assisted storytelling is the issue of **hallucination** when an AI confidently generates information that is false, inconsistent, or not grounded in the game's world or logic. While hallucination is a known limitation of large language models, its impact in games can be especially harmful. In interactive narratives, even a single incorrect detail can break immersion, contradict established lore, or damage player trust in the game world.

Hallucinations may appear as incorrect facts, inconsistent character behavior, impossible plot points, or invented lore that clashes with the game's established rules. In fiction, these mistakes disrupt worldbuilding. In non-fiction or historically grounded games, they can misrepresent cultures, events, or identities, creating ethical risks beyond simple narrative mistakes.

Fortunately, hallucination can be managed with the right safeguards. Below are practical methods to keep AI-generated content grounded, consistent, and trustworthy.

Table 8-4. *Methods to Identify and Prevent AI Hallucinations*

Practice	Example
Use RAG (Retrieval-Augmented Generation)	Before generating a dialogue or lore entry, feed the AI a curated "lore bible" so it can only reference canonical facts.
Force grounding through constraints	Add instructions such as *"Use only the information from the game's lore reference. Do not invent new places or characters unless explicitly asked."*
Require human oversight for critical story beats	For major quests or character arcs, writers review all AI-generated text for contradictions or invented details.
Implement in-game consistency checkers	Automatically compare generated content against known entities (locations, characters, rules) to flag discrepancies.
Track narrative state variables	Store key facts (e.g., alliances, deaths, choices) and use them to constrain AI outputs.
Use adversarial prompting during testing	Give QA prompts designed to "break" the AI and surface hallucination risks before release.
Avoid AI generation for lore-defining moments	For worldbuilding pillars (origins, major historical events), rely on human authors and let AI generate peripheral content only.

Hallucinations aren't just inaccuracies; they can damage the integrity of the story and potentially mislead players. When players invest emotionally in characters or lore, contradictions erode trust and break immersion. In culturally sensitive or historically grounded settings, hallucinations can misrepresent real-world identities and events, causing unintentional harm.

Ensuring factual and contextual accuracy is therefore not just a technical requirement; it's an ethical one. Ethical AI storytelling demands that we design systems that remain true to the world they inhabit, respect player expectations, and maintain the internal logic that binds narrative experiences together.

Player Trust and Emotional Safety

AI-generated stories can sometimes introduce **unexpected or inappropriate content**, especially if they rely on open-ended prompts. In narrative-driven games, players often form emotional attachments to characters, outcomes, and themes. If an AI generates content that feels jarring, offensive, or insensitive, it can cause genuine harm.

In early AI-generated roleplaying platforms, there were instances where players encountered involuntary dark or traumatic themes, even when their choices didn't imply them. This caught many developers off guard. A good example for this is AI Dungeon—in its earlier iterations, AI Dungeon was praised for its storytelling potential but also came under scrutiny due to incidents where the AI unexpectedly generated disturbing content, even when the player hadn't steered the story in that direction.

While this may seem problematic, this issue can be controlled by following the below practices.

Table 8-5. *Methods to Use to Maintain Player's Trust and Safety*

Practice	Example
Use tone-controlled prompts	When calling GPT to generate dialogue, always add tone instructions like: "in a hopeful tone" or "avoid violence or despair."
Apply content filters	Use a post-generation filter to detect and block language related to sensitive topics (e.g., suicide, abuse, racial slurs).
Let players choose a tone mode	At the start of a narrative game, let players select "Optimistic," "Neutral," or "Dark" storytelling mode, guiding the AI's output accordingly.
Include a flagging/ reporting system	In a live game, if an AI-generated dialogue crosses a line, allow players to report the content so it can be reviewed and corrected.

Data Privacy and Player Input

Some narrative systems in games allow players to input custom text, preferences, or even journal entries. If this data is sent to external AI models for processing, it raises privacy questions, especially if that input includes personal or emotionally sensitive information.

Privacy is taken very seriously in some regions, and hence it is best to control it by using the below best practices.

Table 8-6. *Methods to Use to Maintain Data Privacy*

Practice	Example
Use local models when handling private input	Instead of sending sensitive player input to an external GPT API, use a local language model (like GPT-J) for processing.
Display clear consent messages	Before processing free-text player input, show a "Your content will be processed by an AI" notice and let players opt out.
Anonymize input before sending	Strip identifying info (like usernames, dates, or references) from player input before passing it to an AI system.
Avoid storing AI-generated player logs	Automatically purge player–AI conversations after the session ends unless explicit permission is given.

Overreliance on Automation

AI can speed up development dramatically, generating dialogue, filling out backstory, or suggesting plot variations at the click of a button. But this convenience comes with a risk: the gradual loss of human voice, nuance, and intention.

For tight deadlines, it's easy to lean on AI to fill gaps, write a side quest, generate placeholder lore, and populate a dialogue tree. But the more we automate, the more we risk flattening the emotional depth of our stories. When storytelling becomes too dependent on generative tools, it may begin to feel generic, repetitive, or emotionally flat.

It is best to use some guardrails described below to avoid creative cost this automation might incur.

Table 8-7. *Guardrails to Put in Place If Using Automation in Your Game's Storytelling*

Practice	Example
Use AI to assist, not replace writers	Use GPT to generate ten variations of a quest hook, then let the human writer choose and revise the best one.
Mark AI-generated scenes clearly in documentation	In your story bible, highlight which cutscenes are core authored and which are AI-supported, helping the team maintain narrative integrity.
Build thematic checklists for consistency	Keep a reference sheet of tone, theme, and voice guidelines for AI generation so each new scene aligns with the game's emotional intent.
Encourage writer oversight at every step	Don't let AI-written dialogue go straight into builds. Always include an editing pass by a narrative designer who understands the game's story arc.

Note Stories are more than information; they're vehicles for emotion, culture, and human truth. AI can imitate that well enough, but it can't replace lived experience, intuition, or emotional memory.

Developer Checklist: Ethical AI Storytelling

While it is not mandatory, I recommend to use this checklist during planning, development, and content review to ensure your AI-driven narrative systems meet ethical and practical standards. It's intended to guide your team in maintaining **trust, creativity, and accountability** throughout the storytelling process.

Bias and Representation

- Have we reviewed AI-generated content for stereotypes or cultural assumptions?

- Are our prompts or training data inclusive of diverse identities, backgrounds, and experiences?
- Do we allow players to customize characters to avoid default-biased portrayals?
- Are marginalized groups consulted or included in the narrative review process?

Authorship and Transparency

- Are AI-assisted contributions clearly documented in internal workflows?
- Does the team understand which narrative elements are human-authored vs. AI-generated?
- Are there review stages to approve or revise AI-generated content before it goes live?
- Have we credited AI support (if relevant) appropriately in game credits or dev logs?

Narrative Coherence

- Do we track key player decisions and character states to ensure consistency?
- Are fallback responses or scripted alternatives in place for critical scenes?
- Is AI used only in narrative areas where continuity breakdowns won't disrupt immersion?
- Are long-term player relationships handled by systems that support memory or state retention?

Player Safety and Emotional Sensitivity

- Are there safeguards against generating inappropriate, violent, or traumatic content?
- Do we give players control over tone or content sensitivity levels (e.g., opt-out for dark themes)?
- Have we tested AI-generated dialogue or scenarios with a diverse group of players?
- Is there a player feedback or reporting mechanism for problematic narrative content?

Data Privacy

- Is player input anonymized before being processed by AI systems?
- Are players clearly informed when their input will be analyzed by AI?
- Do we offer opt-out options for AI-generated interactions or content?
- Is any sensitive data stored, and if so, do we have explicit consent and retention policies?

Creative Oversight

- Is AI used to assist, not replace, the narrative team?
- Are key emotional scenes and story arcs written or edited by human authors?
- Do we maintain a creative vision document or tone guide for AI-generated outputs?
- Are writers empowered to veto or rework AI content that doesn't meet story standards?

Intentional Design

- Have we defined exactly why we're using AI in our storytelling?
- Are we prioritizing player experience over content generation speed?
- Do we have ethical guidelines in place for when and how AI is used?
- Is our narrative design still rooted in emotional truth, even when enhanced by technology?

Conclusion

Using AI in narrative design is not just a technical decision; it's a creative and ethical one. This checklist is not about adding friction; it's about reinforcing the purpose behind the story you're telling and ensuring that the technology serves the player experience, not the other way around.

Note Ethical storytelling in the age of AI isn't a constraint. It's an opportunity to tell better stories, with more nuance, more responsibility, and more impact than ever before.

PART II

Designing Interactive Narratives

CHAPTER 9

Creating Branching Story Frameworks

Branching narratives are at the heart of interactive storytelling. Whether you're building a visual novel, a roleplaying game, or a choice-based simulation, the ability to offer players meaningful decisions that shape their journey is a powerful narrative tool. But with that power comes complexity.

Designing a branching story is not just about adding choices; it's about designing systems of narrative cause and effect. Each decision creates a ripple that can change character arcs, outcomes, or even the world itself. If you're not careful, your story can spiral into chaos, with disconnected paths and incoherent endings. But with the right framework, branching stories can become layered, reactive, and deeply personal.

This chapter will walk you through the process of building branching frameworks from the ground up. We'll explore how to structure choices, manage narrative paths, and maintain emotional coherence even as the player rewrites the story in real time.

Understanding the Components of a Branching Narrative Framework

Designing a branching narrative begins with more than just adding choices to a story. It involves building a structured, decision-responsive system that allows players to shape the story's direction while maintaining emotional coherence and narrative flow. This system that we call a branching narrative framework relies on several key components that work together to deliver an interactive and reactive storytelling experience.

In this section, we'll break down each of these components, explain how they function, and show how they contribute to the player's sense of agency and narrative impact.

S. N. Gupta, *Generative AI for Game Development*, https://doi.org/10.1007/979-8-8688-2439-5_9

Decision Points

A decision point is any moment in the story where the player is presented with two or more options that affect the direction, tone, or outcome of the narrative.

Decision points are what make an interactive story feel alive. They give players control, encourage emotional investment, and set the stage for branching paths.

For example, in a detective game, the player is presented with the choice:

- Interrogate the suspect now.
- Search the crime scene first.

Each choice opens a different sequence of events. If the player chooses to interrogate early, they might miss evidence. If they wait, the suspect might flee.

Decision points are crucial for any branching story, and hence, they must be designed with care. In general, if we follow the below practices, the results could make your game feel alive:

- Ensure each option has a real consequence, not just cosmetic differences.
- Provide context for each choice so players understand what's at stake.
- Keep decisions **meaningful and relevant** to the player's goals or values.

LLMs such as GPT can propose multiple variations of a single decision point based on player attributes, emotional state, or gameplay context. Developers can prompt the AI with the scene setup and let it generate alternative choices, expanding player agency without increasing manual writing time.

Narrative Branches

Branches are the divergent storylines that unfold from a single decision point. These can be short-term sequences or entire subplots that evolve independently.

Narrative branches allow players to experience different perspectives, challenges, and outcomes based on their actions.

For example, in a post-apocalyptic survival game, choosing to help a stranded traveler might branch into the following:

- A new ally joins your party and assists in future conflicts.
- The group's resources are strained, causing tension later.

Similar to decision points, narrative branches are the backbone of any branching narrative, so the writers/designers must think them carefully. Following the below certainly helps create lifelike branches:

- Not all branches need to be permanent; some can be temporary divergences.
- Use emotional or moral dilemmas to make branches more impactful.
- Balance the number of branches to avoid excessive narrative sprawl.

Generative AI can automatically generate branch-specific dialogue, consequences, or scene descriptions. Writers can define the branch logic, and the AI can fill in tone-consistent content, helping scale complex branching trees without sacrificing narrative depth.

Convergence Points

Convergence points are where multiple narrative branches come back together into a shared or central storyline. They allow different player choices to lead to the same major plot event, often with minor variations based on past actions.

Convergence helps manage the complexity of branching paths while preserving the illusion of freedom. It keeps development scalable without sacrificing interactivity.

For example, no matter which ally the player supported earlier, all paths converge at the final battle. However:

- The dialogue changes depending on past alliances.
- The player's resources or companions may differ.

Making sure your game story continues smoothly, no matter which path the players took previously, is an art; while there are no set rules to make this happen, adopting the below practices allows game designers and writers to achieve this relatively easily:

- Use subtle variations (dialogue, character presence, emotional tone) to reflect past choices at convergence points.
- Ensure the convergence feels natural, not forced or dismissive of earlier decisions.
- Convergence doesn't mean every path is the same, just that they intersect.

AI models can smooth narrative transitions when branches converge by rewriting or adjusting scenes to reconcile previous choices. This helps ensure continuity and emotional coherence even when players arrive at the same point through different paths.

Endings

Endings are the final outcomes of the story, shaped by the cumulative choices the player has made throughout the narrative.

Endings provide closure and reflect the player's journey. They're where the meaning of their decisions becomes clear, ideally leaving a lasting emotional impact.

For example, in a fantasy game about uniting rival kingdoms:

- A peaceful ending occurs if the player built alliances.
- A tragic ending unfolds if trust was broken or violence escalated.
- A solitary ending appears if the player rejected both sides.

No matter what ending you create, it needs to connect to the player's emotions and intended outcome. So, keeping the below points in mind while writing these endings makes the difference:

- Tailor endings to reflect player values, not just actions.
- Offer different types of endings (success, failure, ambiguous) without ranking them as "right" or "wrong."
- Make sure endings feel earned, not arbitrary or disconnected from the player's choices.

Flags and Variables (Supporting Mechanisms)

Flags and variables are the behind-the-scenes systems that track player choices, character relationships, inventory, reputation, or emotional states. These values influence how future events unfold, even if the story isn't visibly branching.

They allow for hidden or subtle consequences, dynamic dialogue, and continuity over time.

For example, if the player saves a town early in the game, a hidden variable (`town_respect = true`) is set. Later, if the player visits that town again:

- NPCs remember the player and offer help.
- Dialogue reflects past events.
- Quests change based on trust level.

The below suggested design tips usually work best when it comes to defining flags and variables in game support mechanism:

- Use variables to track both major and minor decisions.
- Avoid overcomplicating; track only what truly impacts the story.
- Use conditional dialogue and events to make the world feel reactive.

Flags and variables can be passed directly into LLM prompts so the AI generates context-aware content. For example, if a player's trust variable is low, GPT can produce colder or suspicious dialogue. This transforms static branches into dynamic, state-driven storytelling.

Feedback and Consequence

Feedback is the story's way of acknowledging the player's choices. It can come in the form of dialogue, outcomes, character reactions, or environmental changes. Without feedback, players may not realize their decisions mattered. Good feedback reinforces agency and deepens immersion.

For example, after choosing to betray a companion, the character may

- Express anger in dialogue.
- Refuse to help in a later mission.
- Change the tone of future interactions.

Use the below tactics to make feedback/consequences more acceptable to the players:

- Give immediate feedback for emotional clarity and tension.
- Use long-term consequences to reinforce weighty decisions.
- Echo choices across multiple scenes, not just once and done.

While these branching components originate from traditional narrative design, they directly underpin how generative AI systems behave in modern interactive stories. LLMs such as GPT rely on clear story structure to produce coherent branching outcomes. Decision points can be partially AI-generated, branches can be expanded dynamically by the model, and flags/variables can be passed into prompts to maintain continuity and emotional logic. In practice, GenAI acts as a *content generator* that fills in the branches, dialogue, and scene variations, while the underlying branching architecture ensures structure, consistency, and narrative control.

Putting It All Together: A Mini Scenario

Let's walk through how these components work together in a short branching scenario.

Premise

You are a young diplomat sent to negotiate peace between two feuding clans.

- **Decision Point**: Do you approach the Hawk clan first or the Wolf clan?
    - **Narrative Branch A (Hawk First)**: They offer a risky alliance.
    - **Narrative Branch B (Wolf First)**: They distrust you but give you intelligence.
- **Flag Set**: `loyalty_hawk = true` or `loyalty_wolf = true`
- Later, at a Convergence Point, both clans meet to discuss terms. Your earlier alliance affects
    - Who trusts you
    - What options are available in dialogue
    - Whether peace is even possible
- Depending on your actions, there are **three endings**:
    - A peace treaty is signed (both sides compromise).
    - War breaks out (you failed to gain trust).
    - You broker peace, but one clan feels betrayed and leaves (mixed outcome).

Types of Branching Structures

Now that we have learned about the components of the branching narrative framework, let's look at the types of commonly used branching structures in games.

Simple Branching (Basic Trees)

This is the most common and beginner-friendly structure. Each choice leads to a separate outcome, often with no convergence later in the story. This type of structure is mainly used for short stories or episodic games with multiple endings.

As an example, consider a player who decides whether to warn a village of an incoming attack or escape on their own. Each decision leads to a different ending, one heroic, one selfish.

Pros

- Easy to map and test
- Each ending feels unique

Cons

- Requires writing multiple full paths
- Low content reuse; difficult to scale

Foldback Structure (Branch-and-Rejoin)

In this structure, choices branch out briefly but eventually fold back into a shared storyline. The player feels like their choices matter, but the main plot remains relatively intact. These are best suited for narrative-driven RPGs or action games where player freedom is balanced with a controlled narrative arc.

For example, a player chooses between three factions to ally with, but all paths lead to the same climactic battle, only with different allies or resources.

Pros

- Manages production complexity
- Allows illusion of choice with focused outcomes

Cons

- Risks player feeling "railroaded" if consequences seem superficial
- Requires skillful writing to maintain immersion

Hub-and-Spoke Model

Players return to a central hub after each story segment. Their choices in each "spoke" affect future availability of paths, relationships, or resources. Use of this branching structure works great for games that offer freedom to explore story arcs in nonlinear order (e.g., detective or mystery games).

Consider a game where players solve crimes across a city; each case is independent, but solving them in different orders or with different approaches affects the final resolution.

Pros

- Modular design simplifies testing
- Encourages replay ability

Cons

- Requires strong tracking of player progress
- Harder to build long-term emotional arcs

Branching with Variable Endings

Multiple choices accumulate over time, influencing which ending the player receives, even if the midgame is mostly linear. This structure relies on decision tracking, often with hidden variables. It fits the games which are choice-heavy narratives where small actions build toward large outcomes (e.g., visual novels, political simulations).

A good example will be in a post-apocalyptic survival game, where players' decisions about mercy, trust, and leadership influence who survives and whether a new society can be built.

Pros

- Builds emotional weight over time
- Reflects player values in the final outcome

Cons

- Requires extensive tracking and balancing
- Can frustrate players if consequences feel unclear

Designing Meaningful Decision Points

A good decision point does more than offer options; it gives the player agency, reveals character, and creates tension. And the best way to design a meaningful decision point is to ask yourself:

- What does this choice say about the player's values?
- What will the player gain or lose based on their decision?

- Is the outcome immediate, or will it unfold later?
- Will the choice be referenced again to reinforce its impact?

As an example, let's say a player is offered a bribe to look the other way during a crime. Accepting the bribe provides quick money but damages their reputation. Later, a key witness refuses to help unless the player proves they're trustworthy. That's meaningful branching cause and effect, embedded in character and consequence.

Managing Narrative Complexity

The biggest challenge in branching design is scope. If each choice leads to a completely new path, you'll need to write exponentially more content. That's why smart branching design includes reuse, convergence, and modularity.

So, to avoid narrative sprawl, we do the following:

- **Converge Where Possible**: Let different branches rejoin the main path with subtle variations.
- **Use Variable Flags**: Instead of writing entirely new scenes, alter dialogue or outcomes based on earlier choices.
- **Segment Your Story**: Divide your narrative into acts or zones, limiting the number of variables carried between sections.
- **Label Branches Clearly in Your Design Docs**: Use flowcharts or spreadsheets to track where each choice leads and what it affects.

Tools for Building Branching Narratives

While branching structures can be conceptualized with pen and paper or whiteboards, a variety of digital tools exist to help you plan, prototype, and even implement these stories efficiently. These tools support writers, designers, and developers in visualizing choice logic, managing variables, and ensuring narrative coherence.

AI can help prototype entire flow structures by generating draft outlines, decision maps, or dialogue summaries. Developers can iterate faster by letting the AI suggest new branches or restructure existing flows before formalizing them in tools like Twine or Articy:Draft.

Twine

Twine is a free, open-source tool designed for nonlinear storytelling. It allows you to create branching passages with clickable links and supports variables, conditional logic, and simple scripting (via Harlowe, SugarCube, or Snowman formats).

- **Strengths**: Intuitive visual interface, no coding required (though extensible), fast iteration
- **Limitations**: Not built for full game engine integration, though it can export HTML for web deployment or embedding
- **Best For**: Writers and narrative designers building interactive fiction and choice-driven prototypes
- **Use Case**: Great for drafting dialogue trees, early prototypes of narrative paths, and teaching narrative structure

Articy:Draft

Articy:Draft is a commercial tool used in AAA and indie studios alike. It combines visual scripting, flowchart-style story design, and version control with export options for Unity, Unreal, and custom engines.

- **Strengths**: Scalability, integration with game engines, collaboration features
- **Limitations**: Paid license, steeper learning curve for beginners
- **Best For**: Professional game studios managing complex dialogue systems and branching plots
- **Use Case**: Ideal for large projects with branching storylines, multiple contributors, or where logic and narrative must stay tightly coordinated

Ink by Inkle

Ink is a narrative scripting language created by Inkle Studios (creators of *80 Days* and *Heaven's Vault*). It offers a flexible, code-based approach to interactive storytelling, ideal for narrative designers working directly within Unity.

- **Strengths**: Scripted control over logic, easy Unity integration, supports variable tracking and conditional logic
- **Limitations**: Requires comfort with code; less visual
- **Best For**: Developers who prefer narrative scripting and need integration into game engines
- **Use Case**: Excellent for games that mix storytelling with gameplay, especially in Unity projects

ChatMapper

ChatMapper provides a structured interface for designing and testing conversations. It supports branching, conditions, variables, and Lua scripting, making it especially useful for dialogue-driven experiences.

- **Strengths**: Focused dialogue structure, testable interactions
- **Limitations**: Less suited for full narrative design beyond conversations
- **Best For**: Dialogue trees and branching conversations in RPGs or dialogue-heavy games
- **Use Case**: Strong choice for games where dialogue trees need to be exported to engines or voice-over teams

Conclusion

Choosing the right tool for branching narrative design is less about finding the most feature-rich platform and more about aligning with your creative process and project scope. Solo developers or narrative designers in the early stages might prefer tools like Twine for their simplicity and low barrier to entry, allowing rapid prototyping without deep technical knowledge. In contrast, larger teams or projects that demand engine integration and long-term scalability may benefit from structured environments like Articy:Draft or Ink. It's also important to consider your comfort level; some creators gravitate toward visual interfaces, while others find more flexibility in scripting-based tools. Ultimately, the best tool is the one that supports your storytelling goals without becoming a bottleneck. A strong branching narrative doesn't depend on software; it depends on thoughtful design, emotional clarity, and the ability to manage complexity with intention. The choice of tool depends on

- Team size (solo developer vs. studio)
- Project scope (short narrative vs. large-scale RPG)
- Integration needs (web-based vs. engine-integrated)
- Comfort level with scripting vs. visual tools

Whichever platform you choose, the goal is to keep your narrative structured, reactive, and testable because great branching stories don't just offer choices; they deliver meaningful consequences that resonate across time.

Note that generative AI transforms branching narratives from static structures into living systems. While traditional branching requires writers to manually craft each path, AI can expand, refine, or personalize branches based on player state, emotional context, or learned behavior patterns. GPT-based models can generate alternate dialogue for each decision point, rewrite convergence scenes for tonal consistency, or adapt character responses using variables tracked throughout gameplay. When combined with tools like Twine, Ink, or custom Python workflows, AI becomes a force multiplier, helping small teams build branching narratives once reserved for large studios.

Ultimately, the branching frameworks covered in this chapter serve as the architectural foundation for AI-driven storytelling. The stronger and clearer the structure, the more effectively GenAI can enhance creativity, scale content, and deliver dynamic, player-responsive story experiences.

PROJECT: BUILD A BRANCHING STORY IN TWINE

Let's put theory into practice by creating a small interactive story using **Twine**. In this exercise, you'll build a branching narrative with at least three distinct paths, track player decisions using variables, and show how those decisions can influence outcomes later in the story.

While Twine handles structure, GPT can generate the content inside each passage, dialogue, scene descriptions, emotional beats, or alternate reactions. Combined, Twine provides the framework, while AI accelerates the narrative generation inside each node.

This project is designed for writers and developers who want hands-on experience structuring nonlinear stories, and readers are free to use any GPT/text generation AI of their choice to come up with different dialogues and branching options for the scenario.

Scenario Overview

Title: *The Messenger's Dilemma*

You play as a royal courier who stumbles upon a treacherous plot during a routine assignment. Along the way, you must choose whom to trust, and those decisions will affect the fate of the kingdom.

Step-by-Step Breakdown

1. **Setup and Starting Point**

   Open Twine and create a new story using the Harlowe format (default). Name it *The Messenger's Dilemma*.

   Start with the following passage:

   ```
   :: Start
   You are a royal courier, tasked with delivering a sealed scroll
   to the king. On your way, you encounter a wounded soldier who
   whispers a warning: "They're planning to assassinate him."
   What do you do?
   [[Trust the soldier and head straight to the king->Warn the King]]
   [[Detour to investigate the claim->Investigate the Conspiracy]]
   [[Ignore the warning and complete your delivery->Deliver as
   Ordered]]
   ```

   This creates **three initial branches**.

2. **Branch A: Warn the King**

```
:: Warn the King
You ride without delay and reach the castle just before sunset.
You demand an audience with the king.
(if: $warned is not set)[(set: $warned to true)]
The guards hesitate. Do you:
[[Force your way in->Storm the Court]]
[[Explain the threat calmly->Request an Audience]]
```

Each sub-branch can lead to different consequences, perhaps an early arrest or a meeting with the king, who's skeptical but listens.

3. **Branch B: Investigate the Conspiracy**

```
:: Investigate the Conspiracy
You follow the soldier's clues and uncover a plot involving the
king's own advisor.
(if: $investigated is not set)[(set: $investigated to true)]
Do you:
[[Confront the advisor yourself->Confront Advisor]]
[[Gather proof and take it to the castle->Present Evidence]]
```

This path can unlock alternate endings; if you uncover enough evidence, you might prevent the assassination and also expose the corruption.

4. **Branch C: Deliver as Ordered**

```
:: Deliver as Ordered
You dismiss the soldier's warning and continue to the capital.
(if: $ignored is not set)[(set: $ignored to true)]
The scroll is delivered without incident. But the next day, the
king is dead.
[[Reflect on your choice->Ending: Regret]]
[[Flee before you're blamed->Ending: Fugitive]]
```

This branch leads to negative outcomes, but they serve as an emotional payoff and reinforce the consequences of inaction.

5. **Convergence and Endings**

```
:: Final Outcome
(if: $warned)[You warned the king, and he took precautions. The
assassination failed, though trust in the court is shaken.]
(else-if: $investigated)[Thanks to your investigation, the king
was spared and the traitors were caught.]
(else-if: $ignored)[The kingdom mourns its fallen ruler. Your
silence was your undoing.]
[[Play Again->Start]]
```

This passage shows how branch memory (via variables) can shape the narrative outcome while converging into a single scene perfect for reflecting multiple paths without writing entirely separate endings.

What You've Learned

By completing this Twine project, you've practiced

1. Designing three unique narrative branches with meaningful choices
2. Using **flags (variables)** to track player actions
3. Structuring a **convergence point** that reflects prior decisions
4. Thinking in terms of **player agency**, not just plot progression

This is a modular prototype you can expand further: add emotional stakes, recurring characters, or new decision points. The goal is to develop the rhythm of consequence-driven writing, which is foundational to interactive storytelling.

CHAPTER 10

Designing Emotionally Engaging Narratives with AI

Emotion is the connective tissue of storytelling. It's what draws players into fictional worlds, binds them to characters, and raises the stakes of every decision. In traditional media, emotional resonance is crafted through tightly controlled sequences. In games, however, interactivity changes the equation. When players make choices that lead to laughter, heartbreak, or redemption, not because they were told to care, but because they chose to, then emotion becomes something deeper: it becomes agency.

In this chapter, we explore how to design emotionally rich narratives using both traditional narrative design principles and AI-driven tools. You'll learn practical techniques to build emotional arcs, integrate dynamic emotional states into gameplay, and use models like GPT to support emotionally adaptive dialogue. By combining structure, psychology, and interactivity, you can create stories that players won't just play, they'll feel.

Foundations of Emotional Storytelling

Great game narratives evoke core human emotions: fear, joy, regret, loyalty, love, betrayal. Unlike static stories, games allow players to influence those emotions through choices and actions. Emotionally engaging narratives are not about cinematic spectacle alone; they're about systems that generate emotion through play.

S. N. Gupta, *Generative AI for Game Development*, https://doi.org/10.1007/979-8-8688-2439-5_10

Consider *Journey* by Thatgamecompany. With no dialogue and a minimalist interface, it builds an emotional arc through exploration, companionship, and subtle cues. Players feel a deep bond with anonymous co-players without a single spoken word. The emotional impact comes not from scripts but from design that encourages empathy and meaning.

Key emotional dynamics in games include

- **Player Agency**: Players must feel that their decisions change relationships or outcomes.
- **Emotional Pacing**: Alternating moments of tension and calm build impact.
- **Relational Depth**: Emotional investment grows when characters evolve with or against the player.

Techniques for Building Emotional Connection

Let's see what are some techniques we can use to create a powerful emotional connection in the game.

Character Motivations

Players form stronger emotional bonds with characters when their motivations are clearly defined, grounded in human experience, and consistently expressed throughout the narrative. A compelling character doesn't just react to the world; they pursue something meaningful, whether it's redemption, justice, freedom, or belonging. These goals act as emotional anchors, giving weight to their choices and vulnerability to their failures. When a character's actions reflect a personal struggle that players can relate to or challenge, storytelling becomes more than exposition; it becomes a relationship. This is especially powerful in interactive media, where player choices can align with or oppose a character's desires, deepening the emotional stakes. Characters resonate when their goals are clear and human. The stronger their motivation, the easier it is for players to care.

Example: In *The Last of Us Part II*, Ellie's obsession with revenge gives every player decision a moral edge. Even players who disagree with her motives stay emotionally engaged because they understand them.

Contrast and Pacing

Emotional impact in games often depends not just on what happens, but when and how it happens. Contrast and pacing are essential tools for shaping that impact. Moments of triumph feel more powerful when they follow tension or doubt; grief lands harder when it interrupts peace. Effective pacing allows players to breathe between emotional highs and lows, creating a rhythm that mirrors real emotional experience. This doesn't mean slowing the game down; it means giving moments space to resonate. When a narrative moves too quickly from one dramatic beat to the next, players can become desensitized. But when a game balances quiet introspection with bursts of conflict or revelation, it builds emotional texture that lingers beyond the screen. Contrast heightens emotion. Joy feels brighter after fear; tragedy lands harder after peace.

Example: *Red Dead Redemption 2*'s Arthur Morgan spends long, quiet hours hunting or journaling, followed by brutal gunfights or personal betrayals. These contrasts create emotional texture.

Reflection Opportunities

Games that create space for reflection often leave the deepest emotional impressions. When players are given time to absorb the consequences of their choices, whether through dialogue, environmental storytelling, or subtle character reactions, they begin to internalize the emotional weight of the narrative. These pauses don't interrupt the story; they deepen it. A quiet walk after a major loss, a journal entry revealing a character's inner conflict, or a simple moment of silence between companions can say more than scripted exposition. Reflection allows players to process not just what their character is doing, but why it matters, turning gameplay into personal meaning. Give players time and space to reflect. Dialogue choices, in-game journals, and quiet scenes allow them to process events.

Example: *Firewatch* uses radio conversations with Delilah to let players unpack feelings of isolation, loss, and connection.

Mechanics Reinforcing Emotion

The strongest emotional moments in games often emerge when narrative and mechanics work in unison. When a character's emotional state is reflected through gameplay, such as impaired controls during panic or a combat ability locked by grief, the player doesn't just witness emotion; they *feel* it. This kind of design transforms abstract feelings into tangible consequences. In *Papers, Please*, the routine of checking documents becomes a vehicle for moral anxiety as players must choose between feeding their family and following the rules. In *Celeste*, the climbing mechanic becomes a metaphor for mental struggle and resilience. By embedding emotion directly into gameplay systems, developers turn mechanics into meaning, making the emotional arc inseparable from the player's experience.

Example: *Papers, Please* forces players to choose between feeding their family and following state rules, embedding moral weight into everyday tasks.

Craft Conflict and Resolution

Conflict generates emotional stakes. Remember from Chapter 4: not all conflict is external; some of the most powerful stories explore inner struggles or relationship dynamics.

Types of Emotional Conflict

- **Internal**: A character torn between duty and desire (*Disco Elysium*)
- **Relational**: Allies who disagree or betray trust (*Mass Effect 3*)
- **Moral**: Impossible choices where all outcomes have emotional cost (*Detroit: Become Human*)

Resolution doesn't always mean happy endings. Sometimes emotional payoff comes from living with consequences.

Example: *Life is Strange* ends with the player choosing between sacrificing a friend or a town. There is no perfect resolution, just emotional reckoning.

Traditional Emotional Storytelling with AI

In earlier days, the games were coded using conditional variables and logic, where the interactions and dialogues were predetermined and scripted. While this method was still capable of delivering some amazing storytelling and emotional impact, it lacks real-time dynamics and customized adaptation for the players. Let's understand this traditional way by doing a simple exercise.

ADAPTIVE EMOTIONAL DESIGN: "THE FAREWELL" EXERCISE

Design a simple, emotionally adaptive scene using variables and conditional dialogue.

Scenario

Earlier, the player chose to either save their mission or help a companion's family. Now the companion is leaving.

Twine Implementation

```
:: Farewell
(if: $savedFamily is true)[
Companion: "You didn't just help me you saved everything I care
about. I'll never forget that."
Player: "Go well. We'll meet again."
]
(else:)[
Companion: "I understand why you made the choice you did. But it
still hurts."
Player: "I never meant to abandon you."
]
```

This demonstrates how a small variable can shape tone and player emotion without branching into separate scenes.

Sentiment-Aware Storytelling with AI

AI can support emotional variation through tools like

- **VADER**: Sentiment analysis for classifying player input.
- **GPT**: For generating emotionally responsive dialogue.
- **Prompt Injection**: Insert emotional context directly into AI dialogue.

Now, let's understand how to create an emotionally adaptive system using AI by implementing the above tools and techniques in Python.

Best Practices for Emotional AI Design

- Avoid random emotional output. Tie emotion to player action.
- Use emotional variables (trust, guilt, respect) that evolve.
- Design narrative arcs that allow emotional growth or regression.
- Let players influence, not dictate, emotion.

Example: *Celeste* turns anxiety into a mountain-climbing metaphor, making emotion part of both story and mechanics.

MODULAR EMOTIONAL DIALOGUE SYSTEM (WITH VADER AND GPT INTEGRATION)

As game narratives become more player-driven, the need for emotionally adaptive dialogue systems grows. In this exercise, we'll build a modular system that can track a character's emotional state, interpret player input using sentiment analysis, and generate dynamic responses using GPT. This system forms the emotional backbone for branching relationships, long-term memory, and mood shifts.

This exercise teaches how to

System Overview

1. Track emotional states (e.g., trust, mood).
2. Analyze player text input using **VADER sentiment analysis**.
3. Feed emotional variables into a GPT prompt for adaptive response generation.

Steps to Get an OpenAI API Key

1. **Go to the OpenAI Platform.**

   Visit **https://platform.openai.com/**.

2. **Navigate to "API Keys".**

   Once logged in:

   - Click your **profile icon** (top-right corner).
   - Choose **"View API Keys"** or go directly to **https://platform.openai.com/api-keys**.

3. **Create a New API Key.**

   On the API Keys page:

   - Click **"Create new secret key"**.
   - Give it a name (optional, but helpful).
   - Click **"Create key"**.
   - Copy the key immediately; you **won't see it again**.

Detailed instructions can be found here: `https://platform.openai.com/docs/quickstart?language=python`.

Installation Instructions

1. **Install required packages (standalone or in a virtual environment):**

   ```
   pip install flask openai vaderSentiment
   ```

2. **Save the code as** `app.py`.

3. **Run the Flask app:**

   ```
   python app.py
   ```

4. **Open your browser** to http://localhost:5000.

Step-by-Step Breakdown

Step 1: Install and Configure VADER, OpenAI

Install the VADER package using pip:

```
pip install vaderSentiment
```

Set up your OpenAI API key in your system environment:

- **If on Windows**:

  ```
  setx OPENAI_API_KEY "your-key-here"
  ```

- **If on Mac/Linux**:

  ```
  export OPENAI_API_KEY="your-key-here"
  ```

Then, import it into your Python environment:

```
from vaderSentiment.vaderSentiment import SentimentIntensityAnalyzer
analyzer = SentimentIntensityAnalyzer()
import openai
import os
openai.api_key = os.getenv("OPENAI_API_KEY")

response = openai.ChatCompletion.create(
    model=" gpt-3.5-turbo ",
    messages=[
        {"role": "user", "content": <your variable to store prompt>}
    ]
)
```

Step 2: Initialize the Character's Emotional State

```
character = {
    "name": "Ayo",
    "trustScore": 50,   # Scale: 0-100
    "mood": "neutral"
}
```

Step 3: Capture and Analyze Player Input

Imagine the player types a message to an NPC:

```
player_input = "I did what I had to. You wouldn't understand."
sentiment = analyzer.polarity_scores(player_input)
compound_score = sentiment['compound']  # Range: -1 (very negative)
                                          to +1 (very positive)
```

Step 4: Update Emotional State Based on Sentiment

We interpret the sentiment score to adjust mood and trust:

```
if compound_score > 0.5:
    character["trustScore"] += 10
    character["mood"] = "encouraged"
elif compound_score < -0.5:
    character["trustScore"] -= 15
    character["mood"] = "hurt"
else:
    character["mood"] = "uncertain"

# Clamp trustScore between 0-100
character["trustScore"] = max(0, min(100, character["trustScore"]))
```

This lets the character "emotionally react" to how the player speaks, not just what they choose.

Step 5: Generate Emotionally Adapted Dialogue with GPT

We craft a prompt using the player input, current mood, and trust score:

```
prompt = f"""
You are Captain Ayo, a seasoned commander in a sci-fi RPG.
The player just said: \"{player_input}\"
Your current mood is '{character['mood']}' and your trust score toward
the player is {character['trustScore']}.

Respond with emotionally realistic dialogue reflecting your mood and
trust level.
"""
```

This prompt can be sent to the OpenAI GPT API, producing context-aware responses like

- "Maybe you had your reasons. But you left me behind, and I won't forget that."
- "You always do what's necessary. That's why I trust you."

Step 6: Repeat and Expand

This structure can be extended across

- Multiple scenes (NPC remembers past tone)
- Different characters (each with separate emotional states)
- Moral alignment tracking (e.g., guilt, honor, suspicion)

Add event-driven updates such as

```
def respond_to_action(action):
    if action == "abandon_ally":
        character["trustScore"] -= 30
        character["mood"] = "betrayed"
    elif action == "protect_ally":
        character["trustScore"] += 20
        character["mood"] = "grateful"
```

Design Tip Emotional design isn't just about sad scenes; it's about *consistency*. If your character feels "hurt" in one scene and instantly forgets it in the next, you break immersion. With state tracking and sentiment integration, you give your characters memory, texture, and emotional depth.

Full Executable Code

Here is the **complete Flask-based web version** of the emotional AI dialogue game titled **"The Last Conversation"**, using

- **VADER** for sentiment analysis
- **OpenAI GPT API** for emotionally adaptive dialogue
- **Flask** for a browser-based UI

```
from flask import Flask, render_template_string, request
from vaderSentiment.vaderSentiment import SentimentIntensityAnalyzer
import openai

#Replace with your actual OpenAI API key
openai.api_key = os.getenv("OPENAI_API_KEY")# "your-openai-api-key"

app = Flask(__name__)
analyzer = SentimentIntensityAnalyzer()

character_state = {
    "trustScore": 50,
    "mood": "neutral",
    "interactions": 0,
    "conversation": []
}

html_template = """
<!doctype html>
<title>The Last Conversation</title>
<h2>The Last Conversation with Captain Ayo</h2>
<div style="font-family: Arial; max-width: 600px;">
  {% for entry in conversation %}
    <p><strong>You:</strong> {{ entry[0] }}</p>
    <p><strong>Captain Ayo:</strong> {{ entry[1] }}</p>
    <hr>
  {% endfor %}
  {% if game_over %}
    <h3>{{ ending }}</h3>
  {% else %}
    <form method="post">
      <label for="player_input">Your message:</label><br>
      <textarea name="player_input" rows="3" cols="60">
      </textarea><br><br>
      <input type="submit" value="Send">
    </form>
```

```
    {% endif %}
  </div>
  """

def update_emotion(player_input):
    sentiment = analyzer.polarity_scores(player_input)
    score = sentiment['compound']
    if score > 0.5:
        character_state["trustScore"] += 10
        character_state["mood"] = "encouraged"
    elif score < -0.5:
        character_state["trustScore"] -= 15
        character_state["mood"] = "hurt"
    else:
        character_state["mood"] = "uncertain"
    character_state["trustScore"] = max(0, min(100, character_
    state["trustScore"]))
    character_state["interactions"] += 1

def get_gpt_response(player_input):
    trust = character_state["trustScore"]
    mood = character_state["mood"]
    prompt = f"""
You are Captain Ayo, a loyal but emotionally complex space commander.
The player just said: "{player_input}"
You currently feel {mood} toward the player and your trust score is
{trust}/100.
Respond briefly and in character.
"""
    response = openai.ChatCompletion.create(
        model="gpt-3.5-turbo",
        messages=[{"role": "user", "content": prompt}],
        max_tokens=100
    )
    return response['choices'][0]['message']['content'].strip()
```

```
@app.route("/", methods=["GET", "POST"])
def index():
    game_over = False
    ending = ""

    if request.method == "POST":
        player_input = request.form["player_input"]
        update_emotion(player_input)
        npc_response = get_gpt_response(player_input)
        character_state["conversation"].append((player_input, npc_
        response))

    if character_state["interactions"] >= 5:
        game_over = True
        trust = character_state["trustScore"]
        if trust > 70:
            ending = "Ayo nods. 'Alright. One last mission I'm
            with you.'"
        elif trust < 30:
            ending = "Ayo walks away. 'I can't trust you. This is
            goodbye.'"
        else:

            ending = "Ayo pauses. 'Maybe someday… but not today.'"
    return render_template_string(
        html_template,
        conversation=character_state["conversation"],
        game_over=game_over,
        ending=ending
    )

if __name__ == "__main__":
    app.run(debug=True)
```

Run Results

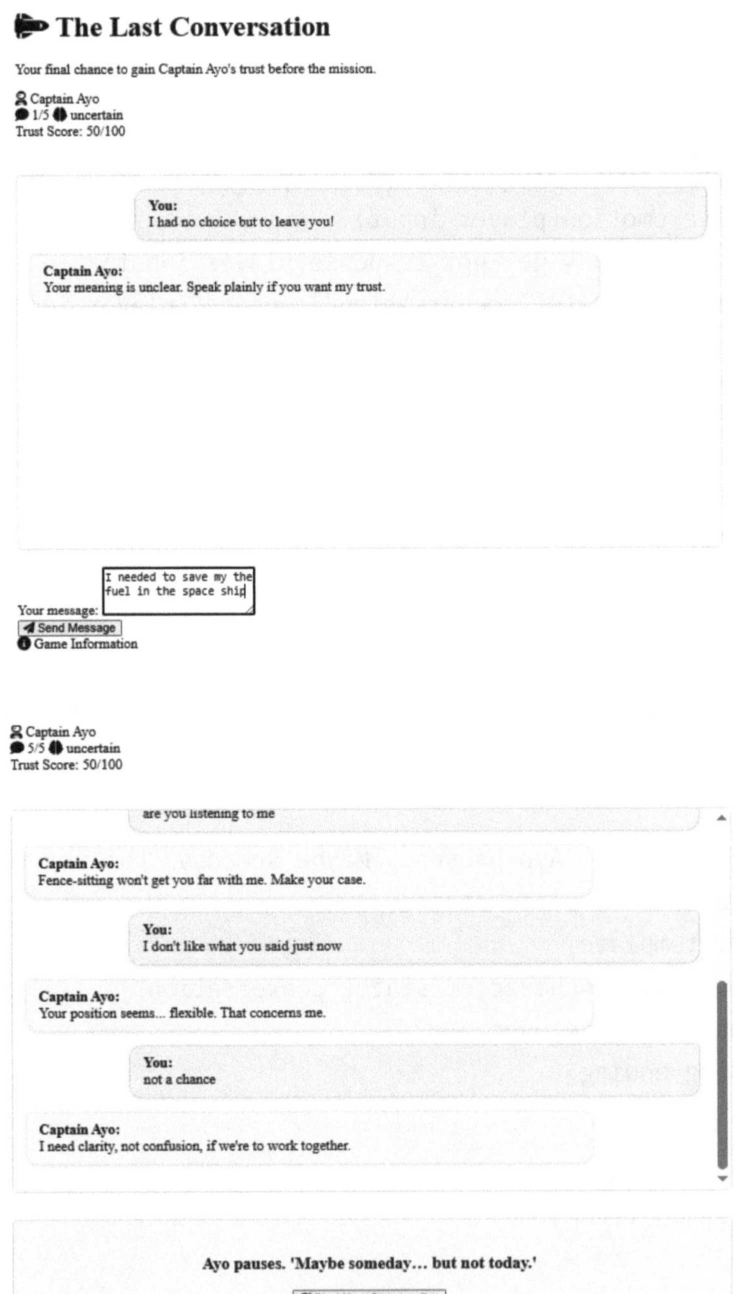
The Last Conversation
Your final chance to gain Captain Ayo's trust before the mission.
Captain Ayo
1/5 uncertain
Trust Score: 50/100
You:
I had no choice but to leave you!
Captain Ayo:
Your meaning is unclear. Speak plainly if you want my trust.
I needed to save my the fuel in the space ship
Your message:
Send Message
Game Information
Captain Ayo
5/5 uncertain
Trust Score: 50/100
are you listening to me
Captain Ayo:
Fence-sitting won't get you far with me. Make your case.
You:
I don't like what you said just now
Captain Ayo:
Your position seems... flexible. That concerns me.
You:
not a chance
Captain Ayo:
I need clarity, not confusion, if we're to work together.
Ayo pauses. 'Maybe someday... but not today.'
Start New Conversation

Testing Emotional Engagement

To evaluate emotional success:

- Observe hesitation during choices.
- Listen to players describe characters like real people.
- Look for regret, reflection, or pride in post-play interviews.

If players say, "I felt bad betraying him," you've succeeded.

Conclusion

Emotion is not a scripted event; it's a system. In games, it emerges through choices, consequences, and interactivity. With the help of AI, we can now create dynamic emotional narratives that scale without losing depth.

But AI is not the author. It's a collaborator. The designer sets the emotional foundation. The player brings it to life. The AI simply listens and adapts.

In the next chapter, we'll expand this system across full-length stories, exploring how to track mood, memory, and morality over entire campaigns.

CHAPTER 11

Emotionally Adaptive Storytelling

In most narrative-driven games, the story adapts to what the player does, a choice made, a quest completed, a faction joined. But what if games could also respond to how the player feels? What if the tone of a player's interaction, the emotional weight behind their choices, and the subtle shifts in trust or regret could shape the unfolding narrative just as meaningfully as a fork in the road?

Emotionally adaptive storytelling invites designers to move beyond static branching and into systems that interpret emotional signals, player tone, sentiment trends, and character memory to build evolving, responsive narratives. It is not about replacing authored scenes with randomness or giving characters perfect emotional intelligence. Rather, it's about creating a storytelling environment that listens and adjusts, mirroring the complexity of human relationships over time.

This chapter builds on the emotional design techniques introduced earlier and explores how to scale them into dynamic systems. We'll examine how emotional states can persist across interactions, how games can interpret player sentiment using tools like VADER or LLMs, and how tone itself can become a meaningful input in player-driven storytelling. Through examples, design strategies, and system architecture, we'll explore how emotion can become not just a theme in your game, but a driving mechanic.

What Is Emotionally Adaptive Storytelling?

Most narrative games ask players to make choices. Some of those choices affect the story's direction. Others shape character relationships or open up new dialogue paths. But in many games, even well-written ones, choices exist within a static framework.

S. N. Gupta, *Generative AI for Game Development*, https://doi.org/10.1007/979-8-8688-2439-5_11

Once a branch is chosen, the game moves forward, unaware of how the player *feels*. The tone of a conversation may change, but the system beneath it is blind to emotion. This is where emotionally adaptive storytelling begins.

Emotionally adaptive storytelling is not just about branching paths; it's about building systems that recognize, interpret, and respond to the *emotional tone* of player input over time. Rather than simply recording whether a player chose Option A or B, emotionally adaptive systems ask: *Was the player angry when they said that? Did their tone soften after a moment of vulnerability? Are they slowly losing trust?* These systems use sentiment analysis, emotional state modeling, and memory to create narratives that evolve not just in structure, but in *tone* and *texture*.

At its core, emotionally adaptive storytelling seeks to replicate something we intuitively recognize in human interaction: emotional continuity. In a conversation with a friend, we don't forget how they treated us yesterday. We read between the lines. We remember the tone of their voice, not just the words they used. Emotionally adaptive systems try to mimic this by tracking how players behave across scenes, not just what they do, but how they do it. A decision made in anger may be interpreted differently than the same decision made with remorse. Over time, these nuances shape relationships, influence outcomes, and change how characters respond to the player.

This approach goes beyond binary "good vs. evil" meters or loyalty scores. It creates space for ambiguity, contradiction, and growth. A character might not like you, but still respect you. They might forgive you slowly, but never fully forget. These emotional shifts aren't just narrative flourishes; they're data-driven responses that reflect the player's evolving behavior. With tools like GPT for dynamic dialogue and VADER for sentiment analysis, designers can now build systems that understand *how* players are speaking, not just *what* they're saying.

The goal isn't realism for its own sake, it's resonance. Emotionally adaptive storytelling makes a world feel alive because it listens, remembers, and reacts. It allows players to be understood on a deeper level and rewards emotional consistency or change over time. In doing so, it transforms narrative from a sequence of choices into a dialogue between the player and the game itself.

Before we can create games that truly listen and adapt, we need to move beyond designing isolated emotional moments and start thinking about emotion as a living system. This means shifting from single-scene reactions to models that carry emotional context forward, allowing characters and relationships to grow or fracture over time. In the next section, we'll explore how to transform these ideas into concrete, system-level designs that shape the narrative long after a single choice is made.

From Scene-Level Emotion to System-Level Design

In earlier chapters, we explored how emotional design can make individual scenes more powerful: a farewell becomes heartbreaking when the dialogue reflects a strained relationship; a simple mission briefing feels tense when layered with unspoken doubt. These moments live at the scene level; they are powerful, but often self-contained. Once the scene ends, emotional states tend to reset, and characters often behave as if nothing has happened. To truly deepen emotional storytelling, we need to think beyond isolated moments and build systems that sustain and evolve emotion throughout the entire narrative arc.

System-level emotion design is about continuity. It means creating emotional trajectories that span multiple scenes, chapters, or even entire games. Rather than treating emotions as temporary flags, "angry here," "friendly there," we treat them as living variables that can grow, decay, or transform over time. A companion who starts out suspicious can gradually learn to trust the player, but that trust should be fragile and reversible. A leader who feels betrayed once may forgive, but scars remain in future conversations. In this way, emotion moves from being an isolated feature to a dynamic backbone of character development.

Building system-level emotion requires modeling emotional states as data. Instead of using single binary flags (like "likes you" or "dislikes you"), designers can track variables such as trust, fear, affection, or resentment as continuous values. These variables aren't simply turned on or off; they drift based on player behavior and choices. Over time, even small actions can accumulate and create major shifts in relationships. Just as a player might slowly lose faith in a leader who lies repeatedly, an NPC can gradually become loyal through consistent acts of kindness.

Games like *Mass Effect* illustrate this beautifully. Throughout the trilogy, the loyalty of squad members isn't determined by a single choice but by dozens of interactions, dialogue tone, side missions completed, moral alignment, and subtle gestures. By the final game, these relationships feel earned because they reflect a long emotional journey rather than a handful of critical decisions.

Designing at the system level also invites players to engage more deeply. When players realize that every tone of voice, every act of forgiveness or confrontation, and every subtle emotional signal can change future scenes, they start to play with emotional intentionality. They consider not just what they want to do, but how they want to be seen. They weigh the emotional consequences of their words and choices, creating richer and more personal narratives.

At its core, system-level emotional design is about respecting the player's capacity for emotional nuance. Instead of presenting static story beats, it offers an evolving relationship that feels alive, one that listens, remembers, and changes. When done well, it transforms a game from a series of branching options into a true emotional dialogue between player and world.

Designing at the system level invites us to think of emotion as a thread woven throughout a game's entire narrative fabric. But how do we represent something as intangible and complex as trust or regret in a way a system can understand? To truly bring emotional continuity to life, we need to create models that not only capture emotional states in the moment but also track how they evolve across time. This brings us to the heart of emotional system design: modeling emotion over time.

Modeling Emotion Over Time

Emotion is rarely static. In life, feelings shift gradually through a series of small moments, some barely noticeable on their own, others deeply transformative. To mirror this complexity in a game, designers must think beyond simple "on/off" emotional states and build systems that reflect change as a gradual process.

A strong approach is to model emotions as continuous variables rather than binary flags. For example, instead of a character simply being "loyal" or "disloyal," their loyalty could be represented as a score from 0 to 100. Small positive interactions might increase it by a few points, while major betrayals might cause a sudden drop. Over time, these changes accumulate, allowing the character's trust to feel earned, or lost, through consistent behavior rather than a single dramatic choice.

Tracking emotion over time also means deciding how quickly or slowly it should change. A sudden betrayal might immediately fracture a relationship, but rebuilding trust should take longer, requiring repeated acts of kindness or sacrifice. By controlling the pace of emotional change, designers can create arcs that feel believable and rewarding.

Games like *The Walking Dead* by Telltale Games illustrate this beautifully. Characters remember choices across episodes, and while an angry outburst might strain a bond temporarily, long-term actions, like repeatedly defending someone or siding with them during conflicts, shape lasting relationships. The result is a narrative that feels alive and deeply personal.

Another powerful technique is to use **emotional decay**. In this model, emotions can fade over time if they aren't reinforced. A character who is furious at the player might cool down if the player consistently acts with kindness in subsequent scenes. This approach mirrors real human interactions and prevents static, unrealistic emotional states from lingering without reason. To illustrate these ideas in practice, here's a simplified example in Python:

```
class Character:
    def __init__(self, name):
        self.name = name
        self.trust = 50  # Starts neutral
        self.anger = 0   # Starts calm
        self.memory = []

    def update_emotion(self, action_value, tone_score):
        # Increase or decrease trust based on action value
        self.trust += action_value
        self.trust = max(0, min(100, self.trust))  # Clamp between 0-100

        # Adjust anger based on tone
        if tone_score < -0.5:
            self.anger += 10
        elif tone_score > 0.5:
            self.anger -= 5
        else:
            self.anger -= 2  # Calm down slightly

        self.anger = max(0, min(100, self.anger))


        # Log to memory
        self.memory.append({
            "trust": self.trust,
            "anger": self.anger
        })

    def decay_emotion(self):
        # Slowly decay anger over time
        if self.anger > 0:
```

```
            self.anger -= 1

# Example usage
ayo = Character("Captain Ayo")

# Player does something good (+15 trust) but uses harsh tone (-0.6 score)
ayo.update_emotion(15, -0.6)
print(f"Trust: {ayo.trust}, Anger: {ayo.anger}")

# Over time
for _ in range(5):
    ayo.decay_emotion()
    print(f"Anger after decay: {ayo.anger}")
```

In this example, **action_value** represents the outcome of a choice (e.g., saving a friend, breaking a promise), while **tone_score** comes from a sentiment analysis tool (like VADER) interpreting the player's tone. Over time, anger decays gradually, reflecting how real emotions fade unless reignited. Meanwhile, trust persists and accumulates, allowing characters to build a complex, evolving perspective on the player.

Combining action-based variables (like trust) with emotion-based signals (like anger or tone) creates a layered emotional model. It prevents characters from flipping unrealistically between extremes and encourages players to think carefully about *how* they engage with characters, not just *what* they do. Over many scenes, these variables give weight to every interaction, making each relationship feel more authentic and deeply personal.

Beyond individual relationships, emotion modeling can shape the entire narrative tone. A game might track the player's overall moral trajectory, becoming more cynical or hopeful depending on choices and tone. This can influence not just character dialogue but the world's mood, environmental storytelling, and even the game's ending.

Ultimately, modeling emotion over time transforms emotional design from a series of isolated moments into a living, responsive system. It allows players to see the consequences of their emotional footprint, creating a story that feels uniquely theirs, an unfolding narrative that listens, adapts, and evolves alongside them.

While the theoretical models and code examples help us understand how to track and shape emotion over time, the real test of these systems is how they play out in actual games. Seeing these ideas come alive in commercial and indie titles offers valuable lessons on what works, what surprises players, and where emotional design can fall short. By looking at concrete examples, we can see how adaptive emotion transforms storytelling from a scripted sequence into a living, responsive experience.

Real-World Game Examples

Many of the most memorable game narratives don't just tell a story; they invite the player to shape emotional relationships that feel personal and alive. These games stand out because they treat emotion as a system, not just a scene-by-scene device. By studying them, we see the power and complexity of emotionally adaptive storytelling in practice.

One of the most prominent examples is the *Mass Effect* series. Rather than relying on isolated dialogue choices, *Mass Effect* tracks an intricate web of player decisions and tone over multiple games. Squad mates remember actions from previous missions, and their loyalty is not determined by one heroic act but by a consistent pattern of support or neglect. Characters can die, abandon you, or become lifelong allies. The emotional payoff of these relationships culminates after dozens of hours, making each farewell or moment of sacrifice deeply impactful. The system behind these moments is built on loyalty variables and accumulated trust scores, which shape individual scenes but also carry emotional weight across an entire trilogy.

Figure 11-1. *Example of loyalty trajectory across multiple chapters*

Another striking case is *The Walking Dead* by Telltale Games. Here, the "Clementine will remember that" notification has become iconic. Behind that simple line is a sophisticated tracking system that monitors how players interact with Clementine and other characters. The emotional stakes are heightened because even small moments, a kind word in a tense situation or a quiet gesture of protection, echo later in ways players might not expect. These remembered actions guide not just dialogue but who stands with you in crisis, who offers support, and how final scenes unfold.

In *Disco Elysium*, emotion isn't confined to external relationships. The game turns the player character's own psyche into a system of conflicting voices and emotional states. Choices build internal traits like empathy, authority, or self-loathing, and these traits influence not only dialogue but the entire investigative approach. The game doesn't just adapt to what you say; it adapts to who you are becoming internally, creating an unmatched sense of psychological immersion.

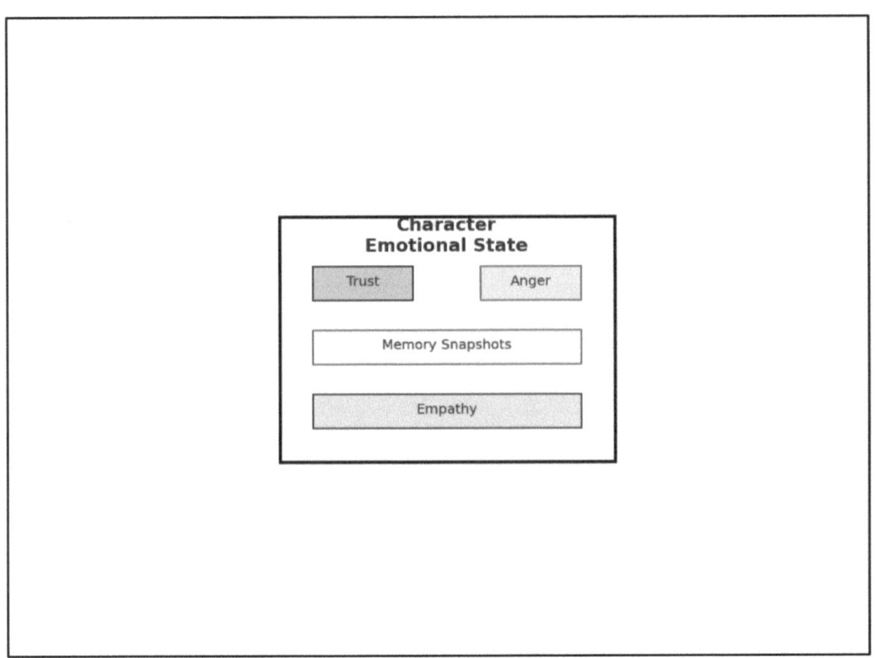

***Figure 11-2.** Example of a character's emotional state container*

Life is Strange 2 offers another perspective on emotional modeling, focusing on the evolving relationship between two brothers. Decisions throughout the game shape the younger brother's personality and moral compass. Rather than a simple approval meter, his emotional growth feels organic, guided by hundreds of small moments rather than one defining choice. By the end, players can see themselves reflected in the character they helped shape, for better or worse.

Below is the side-by-side flowchart that contrasts "traditional branching" (static, single-scene-based) with a system-level model (emotional state persists and shapes multiple future scenes). This mirrors how Daniel's development in *Life is Strange 2* depends on consistent guidance from the player.

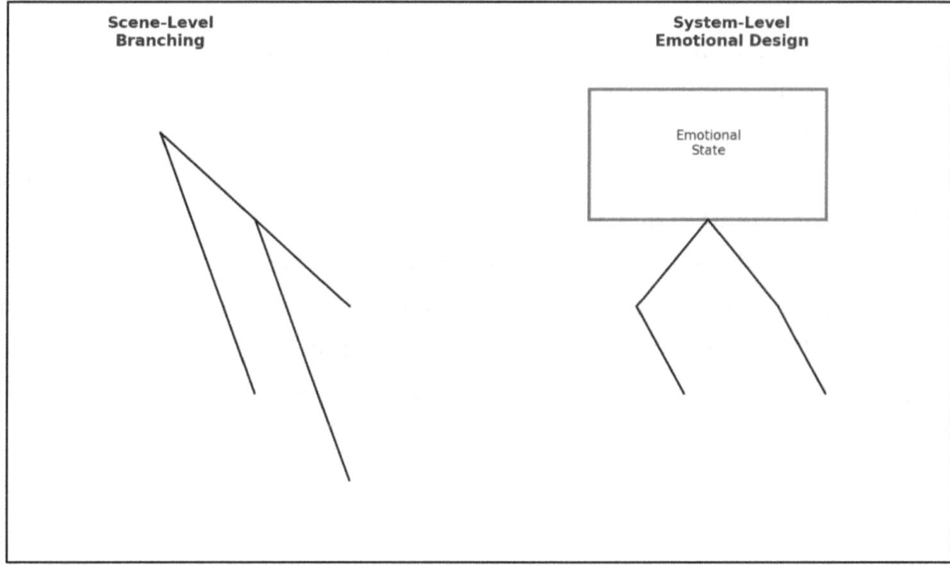

Figure 11-3. *Comparison of scene-level branching vs. system-level design*

Each of these games shows that emotionally adaptive storytelling is more than a technical feature; it's a design philosophy. It invites players into a world where their tone, patience, compassion, or cruelty matter just as much as the major plot decisions. The characters don't simply react to outcomes; they respond to the way players carry themselves through the story.

Seeing these systems at work reminds us that emotionally adaptive storytelling isn't about creating an illusion of choice; it's about creating an authentic emotional journey. The most impactful games don't just ask what the player will do; they ask who the player will become.

The real-world examples we've explored show just how powerful emotionally adaptive storytelling can be when woven deeply into a game's design. But bringing these ideas to life requires more than inspiration; it demands systems that are modular, scalable, and capable of evolving over time. Building on the foundational prototype from Chapter 10, we can now take the next step: transforming a simple emotional interaction model into a flexible narrative engine capable of supporting richer, long-term storytelling.

Expanding the Chapter 10 Flask Prototype into a Narrative Engine

In Chapter 10, we built a small Flask-based project that let players interact with a single character over five turns, with trust and mood tracked using sentiment analysis. While this was a powerful starting point for demonstrating adaptive dialogue, a real game demands a more modular system that can manage multiple characters, scenes, and emotional arcs over extended play sessions.

The first step toward expansion is **modularizing the character logic**. Rather than managing emotional variables as separate pieces of data, we encapsulate them in a `Character` class. This allows each character to maintain their own evolving emotional state, complete with trust levels, anger scores, memory snapshots, and even unique emotional decay rates.

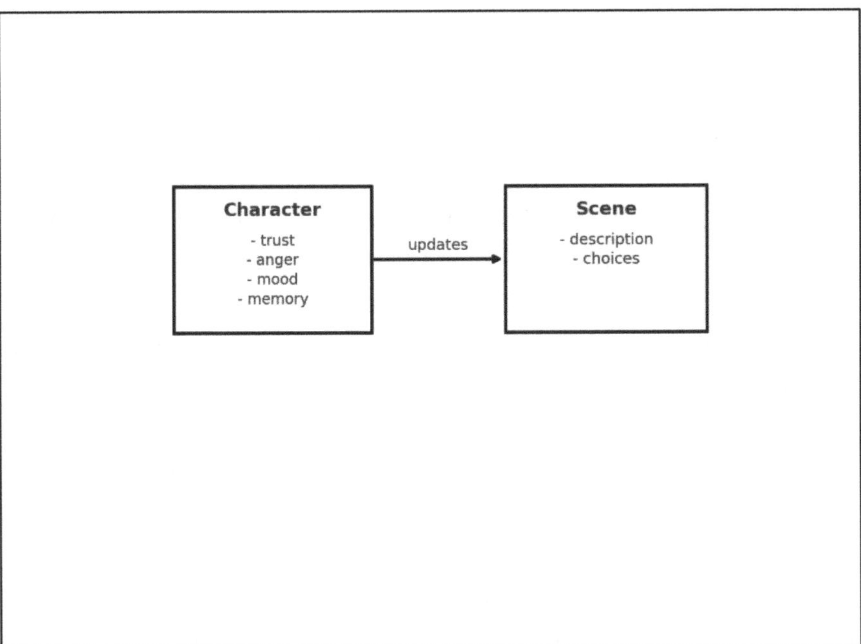

Figure 11-4. *Diagram showing the relationship between the `Character` and `Scene` classes. Scenes update emotional states within each character, supporting system-level storytelling*

Previously, we used a dictionary to define the character and hold its state like below:

```
character_state = {
```

```
    "trustScore": 50,
    "mood": "neutral",
    "interactions": 0,
    "conversation": []
}
```

But now we convert this definition into a more modularized form which is a class as below:

```
class Character:
    def __init__(self, name):
        self.name = name
        self.trust = 50
        self.anger = 0
        self.memory = []
        self.mood = "neutral"
```

On a similar line, we also convert the update_emotion function to use the newly built character class, parameter `trust_change` (the increment/decrement of the `trustScore`), and the parameter `tone` (polarity output from VaderSentiment) to build a more modularized function. So, we update the previous function from this:

```
def update_emotion(player_input):
    sentiment = analyzer.polarity_scores(player_input)
    score = sentiment['compound']
    if score > 0.5:
        character_state["trustScore"] += 10
        character_state["mood"] = "encouraged"
    elif score < -0.5:
        character_state["trustScore"] -= 15
        character_state["mood"] = "hurt"
    else:
        character_state["mood"] = "uncertain"
    character_state["trustScore"] = max(0, min(100, character_
    state["trustScore"]))
    character_state["interactions"] += 1
```

to this:

```
    def update_emotion(self, trust_change, tone):
        self.trust += trust_change
        self.trust = max(0, min(100, self.trust))
        if tone < -0.5:
            self.anger += 10
        elif tone > 0.5:
            self.anger -= 5
        else:
            self.anger -= 2
        self.anger = max(0, min(100, self.anger))
        self.memory.append((trust_change, tone))
```

Once characters are modular, we can introduce **scene modules**. Each scene can be defined as a dictionary or JSON object containing a description, available choices, and expected emotional effects. This structure makes it possible to easily add or swap scenes without rewriting core logic.

```
scenes = {
    "reunion": {
        "description": "You meet Ayo at the abandoned hangar.",
        "choices": [
            {"text": "Apologize sincerely", "trust_change": 15,
            "tone": 0.7},
            {"text": "Accuse Ayo of betrayal", "trust_change": -20,
            "tone": -0.8},
        ]
    },
    "final_mission": {
        "description": "Ayo decides whether to join you.",
        "choices": [
            {"text": "Promise safety", "trust_change": 10, "tone": 0.5},
            {"text": "Demand loyalty", "trust_change": -10, "tone": -0.5},
        ]
    }
}
```

Next, we implement **emotional memory and decay**. Emotional states shouldn't remain static; they should shift naturally even when players aren't directly influencing them. For example, if a player chooses not to interact with Ayo for several scenes, his anger might gradually fade, or his trust might stagnate. This mimics real relationships, where feelings evolve even in silence.

```
def decay_emotion(self):
        # Slowly decay anger over time
        if self.anger > 0:
            self.anger -= 1
```

Use the above function whenever the player skips the interaction:

```
for _ in range(5):
    ayo.decay_emotion()
    print(f"Anger after decay: {ayo.anger}")
```

Beyond individual characters, a full narrative engine can track global variables, like a world state or moral trajectory, alongside individual emotional arcs. This approach allows designers to shape not just character outcomes but environmental changes, community dynamics, or faction relationships.

Finally, we bring it all together through **prompt adaptation**. When generating dialogue using an LLM (like GPT), we can feed it the character's emotional state, memory summary, and scene context. This ensures each line feels grounded in ongoing relationships rather than disconnected from prior interactions. So, the previous definition of the prompt which was used in get_gpt_response(player_input) function

```
def get_gpt_response(player_input):
    trust = character_state["trustScore"]
    mood = character_state["mood"]
    prompt = f"""
You are Captain Ayo, a loyal but emotionally complex space commander.
The player just said: "{player_input}"
You currently feel {mood} toward the player and your trust score is
{trust}/100.
Respond briefly and in character.
"""
```

is updated to this:

```
ayo = Character("Captain Ayo") #this is the character creation
scene = "reunion"
choice_index = 0  # example: say player picked the first choice
player_choice_obj = scenes[scene]["choices"][choice_index]
player_choice = player_choice_obj["text"]
prompt = f"""
You are {ayo.name}, a conflicted ex-commander.
Trust level: {ayo.trust}/100.
Anger level: {ayo.anger}/100.
Recent memories: {ayo.memory[-2:]}.
The player chose: "{player_choice}".
Respond with one emotionally authentic sentence reflecting this history.
"""
```

By weaving modular classes, scene definitions, emotional decay, and dynamic prompt construction together, the original Flask prototype transforms into a true narrative engine, capable of sustaining an emotionally adaptive story over many hours of play. It is no longer just a short emotional demo; it becomes a foundation for an entire living world, filled with evolving relationships and authentic, humanlike responses.

Here is the full code which you can implement on websites like Replit directly which will do all the heavy lifting while you enjoy the end result, or, if you like, you can implement using the same Flask environment from previous chapters:

```
from flask import Flask, session, redirect, url_for, render_template_
string, request, flash
import os
import random

try:
    import openai
except Exception:
    openai = None

app = Flask(__name__)
app.secret_key = os.environ.get("FLASK_SECRET_KEY", "change-me-for-prod")
```

```
# -- Scenes data (extendable) --
scenes = {
    "reunion": {
        "description": "You meet Ayo at the abandoned hangar.",
        "choices": [
            {"text": "Apologize sincerely", "trust_change": 15, "anger_
            change": -5, "tone": 0.7},
            {"text": "Accuse Ayo of betrayal", "trust_change": -20, "anger_
            change": 20, "tone": -0.8},
        ]
    },
    "final_mission": {
        "description": "Ayo decides whether to join you.",
        "choices": [
            {"text": "Promise safety", "trust_change": 10, "anger_change":
            -3, "tone": 0.5},
            {"text": "Demand loyalty", "trust_change": -10, "anger_change":
            10, "tone": -0.5},
        ]
    }
}

# -- Minimal Ayo model stored in session --
class Ayo:
    def decay_emotion(self):
        # Slowly decay anger over time when no interaction happens
        if self.anger > 0:
            self.anger -= 1
        # Trust might stagnate or slightly regress without reinforcement
        if self.trust > 0:
            self.trust -= 0  # adjust if you want slow decay
    def __init__(self, name="Ayo", trust=50, anger=10, memory=None):
        self.name = name
        self.trust = trust
        self.anger = anger
        self.memory = memory or []
```

```
    def to_dict(self):
        return {"name": self.name, "trust": self.trust, "anger": self.
        anger, "memory": self.memory}

    @classmethod
    def from_dict(cls, d):
        return cls(name=d.get("name", "Ayo"), trust=d.get("trust", 50),
        anger=d.get("anger", 10), memory=d.get("memory", []))

    def apply_choice(self, choice_text, trust_change=0, anger_change=0,
    tone=None):
        self.trust = max(0, min(100, self.trust + trust_change))
        self.anger = max(0, min(100, self.anger + anger_change))
        # push a short memory summary
        mem = f'Player chose: "{choice_text}" (t:{trust_change:+},
        a:{anger_change:+})'
        self.memory.append(mem)
        # keep memory short
        if len(self.memory) > 10:
            self.memory = self.memory[-10:]

# -- Helpers --
def get_ayo_from_session():
    ayo_data = session.get("ayo")
    if ayo_data:
        return Ayo.from_dict(ayo_data)
    ayo = Ayo()
    session["ayo"] = ayo.to_dict()
    return ayo

def save_ayo_to_session(ayo: Ayo):
    session["ayo"] = ayo.to_dict()

def build_prompt(ayo: Ayo, player_choice: str):
    # Matches the format you provided earlier
    prompt = f"""
You are {ayo.name}, a conflicted ex-commander.
Trust level: {ayo.trust}/100.
```

```
Anger level: {ayo.anger}/100.
Recent memories: {ayo.memory[-2:]}.
The player chose: "{player_choice}".
Respond with one emotionally authentic sentence reflecting this history.
"""
    return prompt

def call_openai(prompt: str):
    api_key = os.environ.get("OPENAI_API_KEY")
    if not api_key or openai is None:
        return None
    try:
        openai.api_key = api_key
        # Use ChatCompletion or Completion depending on your OpenAI
        package version
        # Here we try to be compatible with ChatCompletion
        resp = openai.ChatCompletion.create(
            model=os.environ.get("OPENAI_MODEL", "gpt-4o-mini"),
            messages=[{"role": "user", "content": prompt}],
            max_tokens=60,
            temperature=0.8,
        )
        # Parse response safely
        choice = resp.choices[0].message.content.strip()
        return choice
    except Exception as e:
        print("OpenAI call failed:", e)
        return None

def local_fallback_response(ayo: Ayo, player_choice: str, tone=None):
    # A tiny heuristic to craft a one-line emotional response when no API
    key is available.
    if 'accuse' in player_choice.lower() or 'betray' in player_choice.
    lower():
        return "You think I'm a traitor? I expected more; I won't
        forget this."
```

```
    if 'apolog' in player_choice.lower() or 'sorry' in player_choice.
    lower():
        return "Your apology lands like a heavy stone , I feel it, but it
        doesn't erase everything."
    if 'promise' in player_choice.lower():
        return "Promises are fragile, but yours gives me a reason to
        consider staying."
    if 'demand' in player_choice.lower():
        return "You demand loyalty as though it's free , prove it, or don't
        expect mine."
    # generic
    emotes = [
        "I nod, burying old anger under a cautious hope.",
        "I stare at you, weighing every syllable.",
        "Your words cut , they also remind me why I can't fully trust
        again.",
    ]
    return random.choice(emotes)

# -- Templates (render_template_string used so everything stays in one
file) --
BASE_HTML = """
<!doctype html>
<html>
  <head>
    <meta charset="utf-8" />
    <title>Ayo , Interactive Scenes</title>
    <style>
      body { font-family: system-ui, -apple-system, 'Segoe UI', Roboto,
      'Helvetica Neue', Arial; padding: 24px; background:#f6f7fb }
      .card { background: white; padding: 18px; border-radius: 12px; box-
       shadow: 0 4px 14px rgba(20,20,50,0.06); margin-bottom: 12px }
      .scene-list { display:flex; gap:12px; flex-wrap:wrap }
      .scene { width: 280px }
      button.choice { padding:8px 12px; border-radius:8px; border:1px solid
      #ddd; cursor:pointer; background: #fff }
```

```
    .meta { color:#666; font-size:0.9rem }
    .ayo-status { display:flex; gap:12px; align-items:center }
    .mem { font-family:monospace; font-size:0.9rem; color:#444 }
  </style>
</head>
<body>
  <h1>Ayo , Interactive Scenes</h1>
  {% with messages = get_flashed_messages() %}
    {% if messages %}
      <ul>
      {% for m in messages %}
        <li>{{ m }}</li>
      {% endfor %}
      </ul>
    {% endif %}
  {% endwith %}

  <div class="card ayo-status">
    <div>
      <strong>{{ ayo.name }}</strong>
      <div class="meta">Trust: {{ ayo.trust }} / Anger: {{ ayo.anger
      }}</div>
    </div>
    <div style="margin-left:auto; text-align:right">
      <div class="meta">Recent memories:</div>
      <div class="mem">{{ ayo.memory[-5:] }}</div>
    </div>
  </div>

  <div class="card">
    <h3>Scenes</h3>
    <div class="scene-list">
      {% for key, s in scenes.items() %}
        <div class="scene card">
          <h4>{{ key.replace('_',' ').title() }}</h4>
          <p>{{ s.description }}</p>
```

```
          <a href="{{ url_for('scene_view', scene_name=key) }}">Go</a>
        </div>
      {% endfor %}
    </div>
  </div>

  <footer style="margin-top:18px; font-size:0.9rem; color:#666">Tip: set
  OPENAI_API_KEY and OPENAI_MODEL env vars to enable LLM responses.
  </footer>
</body>
</html>
"""

SCENE_HTML = """
<!doctype html>
<html>
  <head>
    <meta charset="utf-8" />
    <title>{{ scene_name }}</title>
  </head>
  <body>
    <a href="{{ url_for('index') }}">← Back</a>
    <h2>{{ scene_name.replace('_',' ').title() }}</h2>
    <p>{{ scene.description }}</p>

    <form method="post" action="{{ url_for('choose', scene_name=scene_
    name) }}">
      {% for idx, choice in enumerate(scene.choices) %}
        <div style="margin-bottom:8px">
          <button class="choice" name="choice_index" value="{{ idx }}">{{
          choice.text }}</button>
        </div>
      {% endfor %}
    </form>
  </body>
</html>
"""
```

```
OUTCOME_HTML = """
<!doctype html>
<html>
  <head>
    <meta charset="utf-8" />
    <title>Outcome</title>
  </head>
  <body>
    <a href="{{ url_for('index') }}">← Back to scenes</a>
    <h2>Outcome</h2>
    <p><strong>Player chose:</strong> {{ player_choice }}</p>
    <p><strong>Ayo response:</strong> {{ ayo_response }}</p>

    <div style="margin-top:12px">
      <strong>Updated Ayo:</strong>
      <div>Trust: {{ ayo.trust }} / Anger: {{ ayo.anger }}</div>
      <div>Recent memories: {{ ayo.memory[-5:] }}</div>
    </div>
  </body>
</html>
"""

# -- Routes --
@app.route("/")
def index():
    ayo = get_ayo_from_session()
    # Apply emotional decay each time user loads home
    ayo.decay_emotion()
    save_ayo_to_session(ayo)
    return render_template_string(BASE_HTML, scenes=scenes, ayo=ayo)():
    ayo = get_ayo_from_session()
    save_ayo_to_session(ayo)
    return render_template_string(BASE_HTML, scenes=scenes, ayo=ayo)

@app.route("/scene/<scene_name>")
def scene_view(scene_name):
    if scene_name not in scenes:
```

```
        flash("Unknown scene")
        return redirect(url_for('index'))
    ayo = get_ayo_from_session()
    return render_template_string(SCENE_HTML, scene_name=scene_name,
    scene=scenes[scene_name], ayo=ayo)

@app.route("/choose/<scene_name>", methods=["POST"])
def choose(scene_name):
    if scene_name not in scenes:
        flash("Unknown scene")
        return redirect(url_for('index'))
    try:
        idx = int(request.form.get('choice_index', 0))
    except Exception:
        idx = 0
    choices = scenes[scene_name]["choices"]
    if idx < 0 or idx >= len(choices):
        idx = 0
    choice_obj = choices[idx]

    ayo = get_ayo_from_session()
    # apply changes
    ayo.apply_choice(choice_obj['text'], trust_change=choice_obj.
    get('trust_change', 0), anger_change=choice_obj.get('anger_change', 0),
    tone=choice_obj.get('tone'))
    save_ayo_to_session(ayo)

    # build prompt and attempt LLM call
    prompt = build_prompt(ayo, choice_obj['text'])
    ayo_response = call_openai(prompt)
    if ayo_response is None:
        ayo_response = local_fallback_response(ayo, choice_obj['text'],
        tone=choice_obj.get('tone'))
```

```
    return render_template_string(OUTCOME_HTML, player_choice=choice_
obj['text'], ayo_response=ayo_response, ayo=ayo)

if __name__ == '__main__':
    app.run(debug=True)
```

Sample output of the web game created by Replit using AI is shown below.

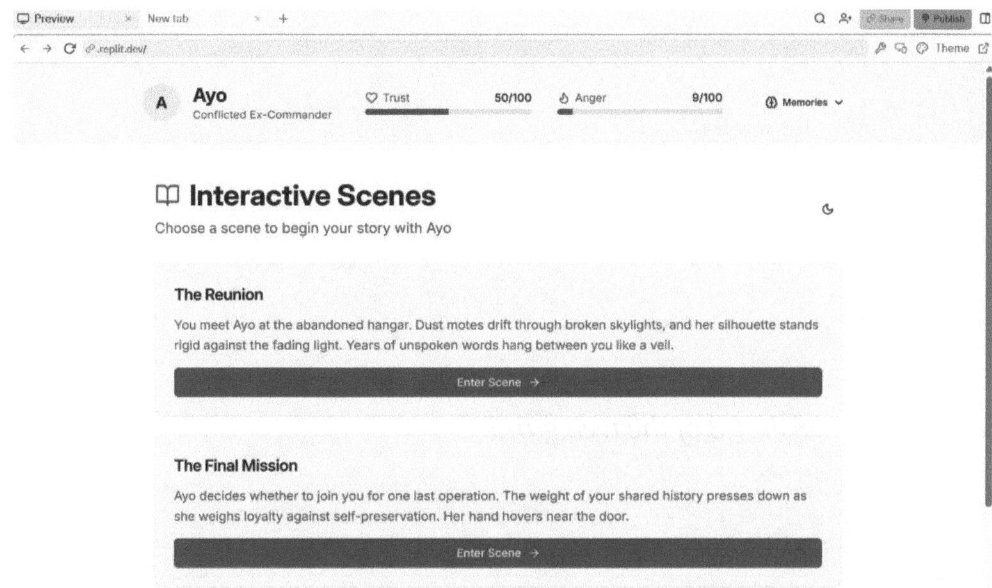

Figure 11-5. *Screenshot-1 of the web game*

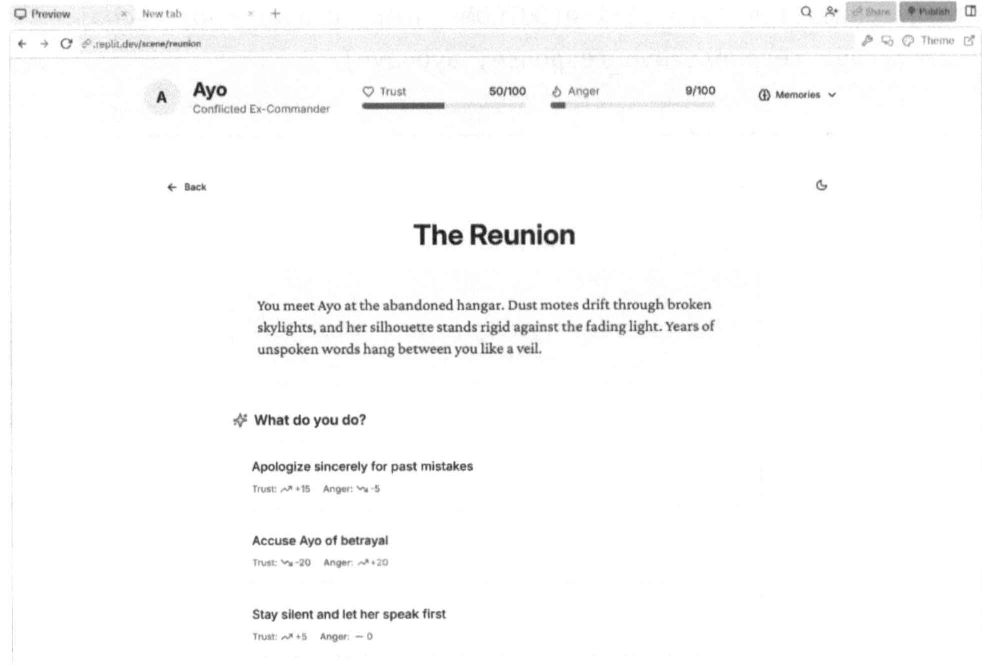

***Figure 11-6.** Screenshot-2 of the web game*

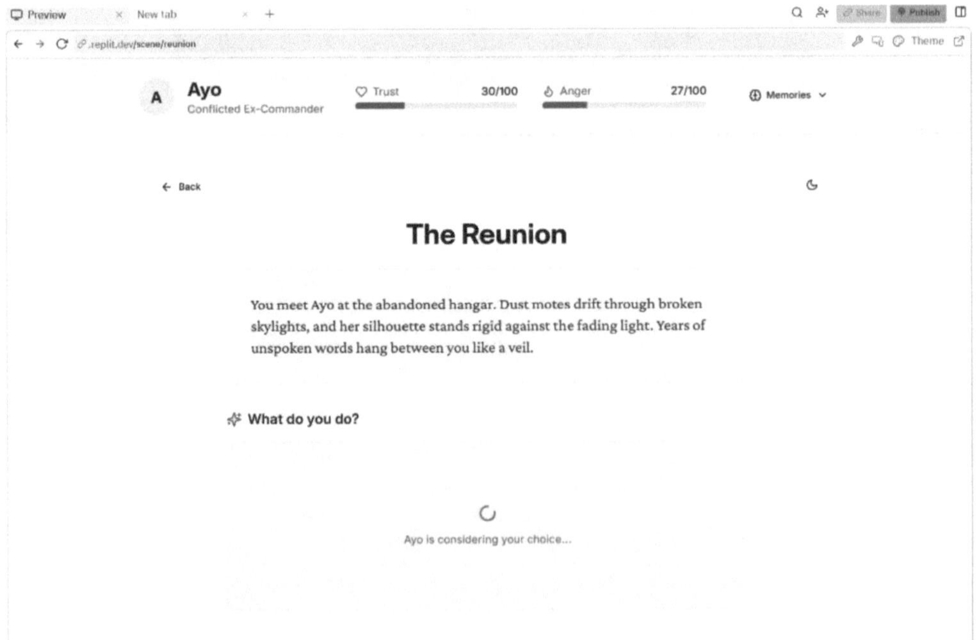

***Figure 11-7.** Screenshot-3 of the web app*

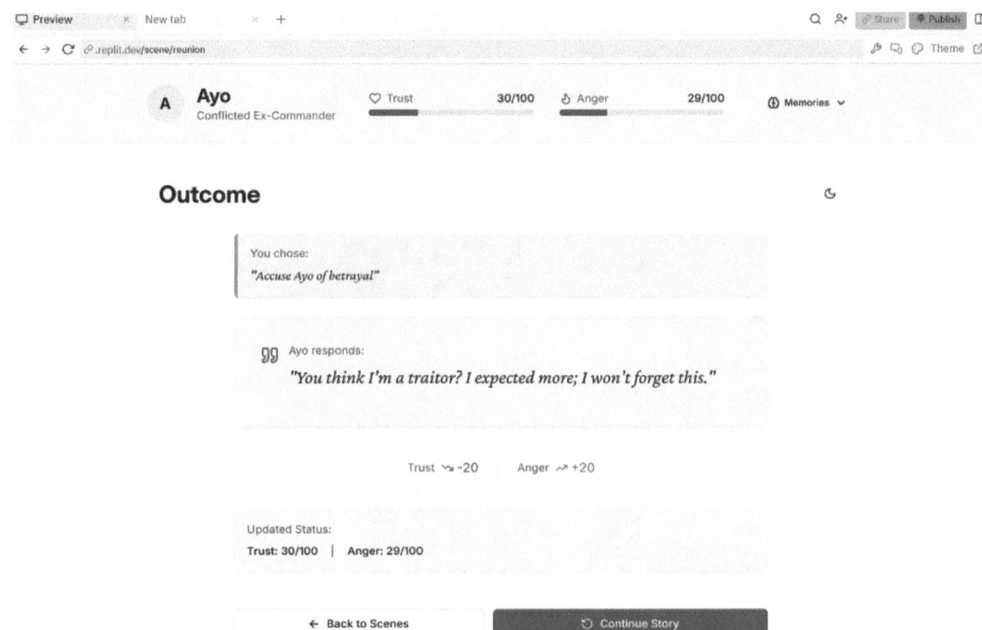

Figure 11-8. *Screenshot-4 of the web game*

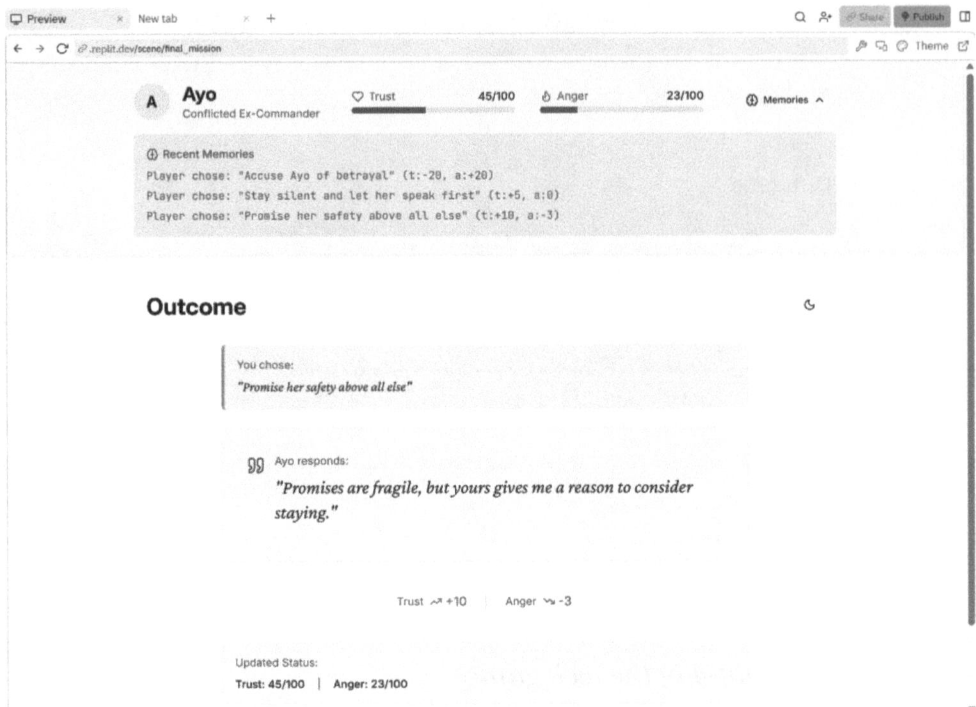

Figure 11-9. Screenshot-5 of the web game

In today's era of AI and agentic systems, building and deploying apps has become far easier than in the past, when developers had to wrestle with environment setups, debugging, and front-end design. Now, creating an app can be accomplished in just a few minutes.

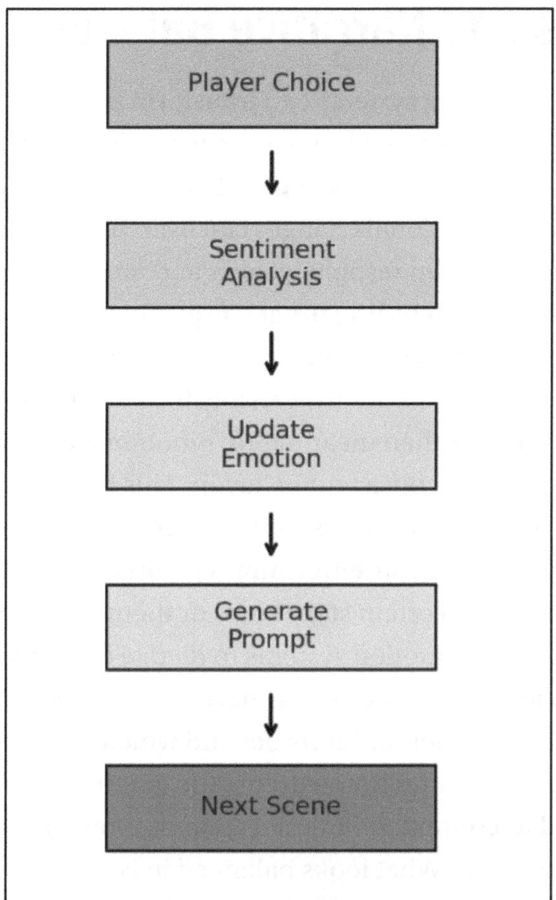

Figure 11-10. *Flowchart illustrating the process: player makes a choice ➤ sentiment analysis interprets tone ➤ character emotions update ➤ new prompt generated ➤ narrative progresses to the next scene*

Building a robust narrative engine that handles emotion at scale opens up tremendous creative possibilities. But as powerful as these systems are, they come with new challenges: balancing emotional reactivity without overwhelming the story, ensuring coherence, and protecting the core narrative vision. In this next section, we'll explore how to maintain narrative balance and avoid common pitfalls when designing emotionally adaptive storytelling systems.

Best Practices and Narrative Balance

Emotionally adaptive storytelling systems can transform player experiences, making each interaction feel uniquely personal. However, if not designed thoughtfully, these systems can spiral into chaos, characters might flip moods too suddenly, narrative arcs can become incoherent, or emotional changes can overshadow the intended story. Striking the right balance between responsiveness and narrative integrity is essential.

One important principle is **avoiding tonal whiplash**. When emotional states shift too abruptly, players can feel disconnected or even manipulated. If a character forgives a major betrayal too easily, or becomes irreversibly hostile after one minor insult, the relationship feels hollow rather than meaningful. Emotional changes should be gradual, believable, and earned through consistent behavior. This is where pacing and emotional decay mechanics help, allowing designers to create arcs that feel organic and authentic.

Another key practice is to **anchor emotional systems in authorial intent**. Even in the most reactive narratives, certain story beats or themes are core to the game's identity. Rather than allowing emotion systems to dictate every moment, they should be designed to support and enrich the central narrative, not replace it. This means establishing guardrails, thresholds, or limits beyond which certain character actions or story outcomes won't go, no matter how extreme the emotional data becomes.

Test iteratively and in context. Emotional systems often perform differently once real players interact with them. What looks balanced in isolated tests might break under unexpected patterns of behavior. By playtesting early and observing how players engage emotionally, designers can identify points where the system either underreacts or overreacts and refine accordingly.

Avoid over-personalization. While it's tempting to allow every moment to adapt to the player, too much responsiveness can dilute narrative focus and overwhelm players with micro-level consequences. Instead, highlight key emotional moments where adaptation matters most, moments of decision, confession, or confrontation. These punctuated shifts give emotional changes weight and maintain clarity.

Finally, remember that **emotion is a tool, not the story itself**. Emotionally adaptive systems are most powerful when they deepen the player's connection to the world and characters, but they should always serve a larger narrative purpose. Whether it's to highlight themes of forgiveness, explore the fragility of trust, or evoke a sense of belonging, emotion should amplify the story's core message rather than overshadow it.

In the end, a well-balanced, emotionally adaptive narrative doesn't just react; it guides players through a cohesive journey that feels alive without losing its shape. When done thoughtfully, these systems transform storytelling into a shared dance between designer and player, one where both shape and respond to each other in meaningful, memorable ways.

As we strive to create emotionally rich and responsive stories, it's easy to get swept up in the technical and creative possibilities. But whenever we design systems that listen, remember, and adapt to players on an emotional level, we enter sensitive territory. With great narrative power comes a deeper responsibility: to use these emotional tools ethically and thoughtfully. In the following sidebar, we'll explore the ethical considerations that come with designing emotionally adaptive games and how to respect player boundaries while crafting memorable experiences.

Ethical Design Considerations

When designing emotionally adaptive systems, it's tempting to focus solely on the creative potential: deeper connections, richer characters, and more immersive worlds. But these very strengths also present ethical risks. Games that read and respond to player emotion walk a fine line between storytelling and psychological influence. Designers must approach this territory with caution, empathy, and respect for the player's autonomy.

One major concern is **emotional manipulation**. While all stories aim to move audiences, emotionally adaptive systems can cross a line if they exploit vulnerabilities in a player's emotional state. For example, a game that intentionally pushes players toward guilt to drive microtransactions or encourage specific in-game purchases uses emotional design unethically. Similarly, leveraging fear or loneliness to keep players engaged can create an unhealthy dependency rather than a meaningful narrative relationship.

Another important consideration is **consent and transparency**. Players should understand when and how a game is tracking their emotional responses. If sentiment analysis or adaptive dialogue is at play, clearly communicating this, either through onboarding, options menus, or subtle in-game cues, helps maintain trust. Surprising players with emotional data collection can feel invasive, even if the intention is purely creative.

Designers should also be mindful of **emotional safety**. Games have the power to explore difficult themes like grief, betrayal, or trauma, but an adaptive system that reacts to highly charged player emotions can unintentionally amplify distress. Providing content warnings, offering opt-out options for sensitive content, and designing clear emotional "off-ramps" (moments where players can pause or shift focus) can help players feel supported rather than trapped.

Finally, designers should consider **long-term impact**. Adaptive emotional systems can leave strong impressions that persist beyond the screen. A game that repeatedly reinforces feelings of failure or inadequacy might inadvertently harm a player's self-image. By contrast, systems that emphasize growth, resilience, or mutual understanding can create lasting positive effects.

In the end, emotionally adaptive storytelling is not just a technical challenge; it's an ethical one. The responsibility lies with designers to ensure that these powerful tools are used to deepen empathy and connection rather than exploit or harm. By approaching emotional design with intentionality and care, we can create games that resonate deeply while still honoring the dignity and well-being of every player.

Conclusion

Emotionally adaptive storytelling represents one of the most exciting frontiers in game design. By moving beyond static branches and embracing systems that listen and respond to player emotion, we open the door to truly personal and transformative experiences. These systems invite players to express not just what they want to do, but how they feel, and to see those feelings reflected and remembered within the game world.

Yet with this power comes responsibility. As we explored, crafting emotionally responsive narratives demands careful balancing: between reactivity and narrative focus, between freedom and authorial intent, and between emotional intensity and player safety. When done thoughtfully, emotionally adaptive systems can transform games from passive entertainment into living conversations, shared journeys that evolve uniquely for each player.

As we look ahead to future chapters, we'll continue to deepen this toolkit: expanding beyond character interactions to procedural worldbuilding, integrating adaptive emotion into broader game systems, and exploring advanced AI integrations. Each new layer offers more opportunities to create worlds that don't just react, but truly resonate.

CHAPTER 12

Dynamic Character Creation

Characters are the heart of every memorable game. While worlds set the stage and stories create context, it is the characters, their quirks, contradictions, and quiet moments, that truly make us care. In many traditional games, character traits are fixed, confined to static dialogue trees or predetermined arcs. But as players crave more immersive, reactive experiences, static characters begin to feel like cardboard cutouts rather than living, breathing individuals.

In this chapter, we'll explore how to design characters who evolve dynamically, adapting to player choices and emotional tone over time. We'll break down the core building blocks of personality, discuss how AI tools like GPT can help generate rich backstories and behavioral quirks, and examine ways to integrate emotional state systems for more lifelike reactions. You'll also learn practical steps to create your own AI-powered character generator using Python and Flask, including example code you can build upon. At the end, we'll address the ethical considerations that come with creating procedurally generated personalities, ensuring your characters remain engaging and respectful.

Dynamic character creation goes beyond swapping dialogue lines or changing a costume; it means building personalities that adapt, remember, and sometimes even surprise us. By the end of this chapter, you'll have a toolkit to create characters who feel less like scripted NPCs and more like complex companions.

But before we dive into technical systems and implementation, it's important to step back and ask: Why does this matter? What makes dynamic characters so powerful, and why do they resonate so deeply with players? Let's first explore the reasons behind the growing demand for adaptive personalities and the emotional impact they can create.

S. N. Gupta, *Generative AI for Game Development*, https://doi.org/10.1007/979-8-8688-2439-5_12

Why Dynamic Characters Matter

At the core of any great story is a character we believe in, someone who feels real enough to evoke empathy, frustration, admiration, or even love. When characters are static, they risk becoming predictable puzzle pieces in the larger narrative structure. Their reactions, no matter how well written, often feel scripted and mechanical, especially after multiple playthroughs. As a result, players may come to see them less as individuals and more as narrative tools designed to guide or gate progress.

Dynamic characters disrupt this pattern by introducing unpredictability and genuine responsiveness. A character who remembers past encounters, reacts differently based on tone, or evolves their opinion of the player over time feels alive in a way a static character never can. This adaptability builds emotional investment. Players are no longer simply trying to "win over" a character by selecting the right dialogue options; they're participating in an ongoing relationship that can deepen, fracture, or transform entirely.

Games like *Red Dead Redemption 2* illustrate this power beautifully. Arthur Morgan's evolving relationships with the camp members depend not only on story missions but on small, repeated gestures—a greeting, a shared drink, a moment of support. These micro-interactions accumulate into a broader emotional arc, making each connection feel personal and consequential. Similarly, *The Witcher 3* allows characters like Yennefer and Triss to respond to Geralt's choices with a mix of warmth, sarcasm, or guardedness, depending on shared history and chosen paths.

Dynamic characters also increase replay value. Players may return to the same game to explore how a different tone or set of actions shifts a character's personality or final fate. This encourages exploration not only of the world but of the characters themselves, inviting players to test the boundaries of trust, loyalty, or rivalry.

From a design perspective, dynamic characters are more than a technical challenge; they're a promise to the player: *Your actions matter here, not just your choices, but your approach, your attitude, your emotional presence.* In an era where players crave more agency and authenticity, this promise is incredibly powerful.

In the following sections, we'll explore how to break down character personality into concrete systems, use AI to generate layered backstories and quirks, and build technical structures that support evolving emotional states. By understanding why dynamic characters matter, we lay the foundation for creating interactions that resonate long after the game is over.

Building Blocks of Dynamic Characters

Before we can design adaptive personalities, we have to understand what gives a character their identity. In traditional storytelling, this identity is built through careful writing: a mix of backstory, goals, quirks, and consistent behaviors. In games, however, we have an added challenge—players actively shape a character's world and relationships. For characters to feel dynamic, their building blocks must be designed to change and evolve in response to these inputs.

The first building block is **personality traits**. Traits define a character's general attitude and worldview. Are they naturally optimistic or suspicious? Quick-tempered or patient? These qualities help determine how a character reacts to player actions and dialogue tone. By tracking trait intensities as variables, you can create a character who starts out reserved but becomes more trusting over time or one who slowly grows bitter when repeatedly let down. As an example, imagine a companion named Lina who starts the game with a high "caution" trait and low "trust." Early in the story, she might refuse to share her real motivations and keep the player at a distance. However, if the player consistently protects her and avoids risky choices, her "trust" value rises, and her dialogue becomes warmer and more open. Over time, she may even become more adventurous, encouraged by the player's influence.

The second foundational element is **backstory generation**. A well-crafted backstory provides motivation and depth. In dynamic systems, backstories can be procedurally generated or enhanced using AI tools like GPT to create unique histories for each playthrough. For example, one version of a character might have grown up in a harsh, survivalist environment, making them slow to trust. Another might have experienced early betrayal, shaping them into a defensive or sarcastic personality. By varying backstories, even the same "role" can feel entirely different from game to game.

The third key component is **behavior and mood systems**. Characters must be able to move through different emotional states in a believable way. Rather than fixed emotional reactions, they should respond based on a combination of current mood, past experiences with the player, and overall personality traits. For example, a typically patient character might finally snap if pushed too far but only after a long buildup that feels earned.

Combining these elements creates a rich foundation for dynamic characters. A procedurally generated backstory informs personality traits; those traits guide behavioral responses; and mood systems add a moment-to-moment layer that makes every interaction feel alive. Together, they allow characters to carry emotional memory across scenes, creating relationships that grow or deteriorate over time rather than remaining frozen in place.

In the next section, we'll look at how AI, particularly large language models, can help you expand these building blocks quickly and creatively. From generating detailed biographies to creating nuanced dialogue, AI offers powerful tools for deepening character complexity without relying solely on manual writing.

Using AI to Expand Character Depth

Designing dynamic characters requires not only technical systems but also rich narrative content: backstories, personality quirks, unique speech patterns, and emotional triggers. Traditionally, this content is painstakingly written by hand, which can limit the number of characters or variations a small team can produce. AI language models, like GPT, introduce a powerful new approach: generating high-quality narrative content on demand, allowing characters to feel deeper and more varied without the burden of writing each line manually.

One powerful application of AI is **procedural backstory generation**. Instead of creating a single fixed biography, you can prompt an AI to generate multiple potential life paths for a character, each with its own emotional weight and narrative hooks. **For instance,** you might give the model a prompt like "Generate a backstory for a character named Amina who is a wandering healer with a secret past." In one playthrough, Amina might have abandoned a royal family to pursue a life of peace. In another, she could be fleeing a crime syndicate after betraying her former allies. Each version introduces unique tensions and possibilities, which in turn affect her motivations and behavior.

Another use case is **personality-driven dialogue**. AI can generate lines that match a character's current emotional state, backstory, and personality traits. Rather than writing dozens of variations by hand, designers can feed AI models information about a character's mood ("betrayed," "hopeful," "cautiously optimistic") and request lines that reflect those feelings. As an **example,** suppose a character named Eli is deeply loyal but currently disappointed by the player's actions. Instead of using a single "disappointed" line, an AI model can produce nuanced variations like "I thought you understood me better than that" or "Maybe I was wrong to trust you so easily." These lines deepen emotional realism and keep dialogue feeling fresh.

AI can also help create **quirks and habits**, adding small touches that make characters memorable. For instance, a nervous NPC might compulsively adjust their gloves when stressed. With AI, you can generate short vignettes or habits that reinforce these traits and incorporate them into interactions or environmental storytelling.

Of course, integrating AI-generated content requires thoughtful curation. Raw outputs can be inconsistent or clash with a game's tone. Designers should treat AI as a creative partner—a tool for idea generation rather than a replacement for human oversight. By selecting, refining, and occasionally rewriting AI-generated content, designers ensure coherence and narrative integrity.

Last but not the least, AI can help scale dynamic character systems. When combined with procedural frameworks and emotional state models, AI allows for a nearly limitless number of character variations and responses. This means players can meet characters who feel truly one-of-a-kind, even on repeat playthroughs, enhancing immersion and emotional connection.

In the next section, we'll look at how to integrate these personality traits and emotional states into a cohesive system. You'll learn how static attributes and dynamic emotional data can work together to create believable, evolving personalities.

Integrating Personality and Emotional State

So far, we've explored how personality traits, backstories, and AI-generated content can each add depth to a character. But to make a character feel truly alive, these elements need to work together as a system rather than remain isolated pieces. By integrating static personality traits with dynamic emotional states, designers can create characters who feel consistent yet capable of real growth and surprise.

At the foundation are personality traits—enduring qualities that shape a character's default worldview and behavior. Traits like loyalty, skepticism, impulsiveness, or compassion define a character's natural tendencies, providing a recognizable core that anchors them across interactions. On top of this foundation sit emotional states—dynamic, moment-to-moment feelings tracked as variables like trust, anger, fear, or affection. These states evolve based on how the player treats the character, what decisions are made, and the tone of interactions. By layering these systems, designers can ensure that a character's reactions feel both grounded and flexible, capable of shifting in believable ways over time.

Consider *Dragon Age: Origins*. Characters such as Morrigan and Alistair have well-defined personalities, cynical or earnest, but their loyalty and affection shift depending on the player's behavior. Morrigan remains sharp and guarded, but if her approval rises, her sarcasm might soften into teasing warmth. If her trust erodes, she might become colder, her loyalty wavering. Similarly, in *Firewatch*, Delilah's personality is playful and flirty by default, yet she can drift toward warmth, guilt, or emotional distance depending on Henry's openness or reticence. These examples illustrate how combining stable traits with shifting emotions creates characters who feel genuinely alive and capable of surprising the player.

This integration can be approached programmatically through a base trait system combined with emotional modifiers. The base traits define general tendencies, while the emotional states act as temporary overlays that adjust behavior and dialogue in real time. A robust implementation might include logic where a loyal character with high trust might say, "I've stood by you this far. I won't turn back now." The same loyal character, if trust has dropped, might instead say, "I thought my loyalty meant something to you. Perhaps I was wrong." When traits and emotions work together, responses feel personalized and reflective of shared history rather than simply following a branching script. Below is an expanded example of how personality and emotion might interact:

```
class Character:
    def __init__(self, name, traits):
        self.name = name
        self.traits = traits  # e.g., {"loyal": True, "skeptical": False}
        self.emotional_state = {"trust": 50, "anger": 10, "fear": 0}

    def get_dialogue(self):
        if self.traits["loyal"] and self.emotional_state["trust"] > 70:
            return "I've stood by you this far. I won't turn back now."
        elif self.traits["loyal"] and self.emotional_state["trust"] < 40:
            return "I thought my loyalty meant something to you. Perhaps I
            was wrong."
        elif self.traits["skeptical"] and self.emotional_
        state["anger"] > 50:
            return "I knew you'd disappoint me eventually."
        else:
            return "Let's see where this goes."
```

```
# Example usage
traits = {"loyal": True, "skeptical": False}
soren = Character("Soren", traits)
```

The above code should be viewed as incremental additions to the framework established in Chapters 10 and 11. Each snippet extends the existing implementation rather than functioning as a standalone sample.

Importantly, these integrated systems should influence more than just dialogue. In combat-heavy games, a supportive character might proactively heal or defend the player when trust is high, but hesitate or withdraw support if loyalty is damaged. Quest paths can branch depending on emotional states; an ally might refuse to join a mission or offer different resolutions depending on their relationship with the player. Even environmental storytelling can be affected: a once-cozy camp might become disordered or cold if an emotional rift has formed, signaling tension without a single line of dialogue.

Beyond the systems themselves, writing nuanced responses is essential to make emotions feel real. Rather than direct statements like “I am angry with you,” strong writing leans into subtext: “Is that what you really think of me?” or “You know, you keep proving my doubts right.” These lines convey frustration, disappointment, and vulnerability without explicitly naming the emotion, allowing players to read between the lines and deepen their investment in the relationship.

A helpful way to visualize this integration is through a layered diagram: at the base, personality traits define who the character fundamentally is; the middle layer contains emotional states that evolve over time; and the top layer represents the final behaviors, dialogue, and choices visible to the player. Arrows flow upward, showing how each layer informs the next. This holistic approach creates characters who feel stable yet capable of change, consistent yet surprising.

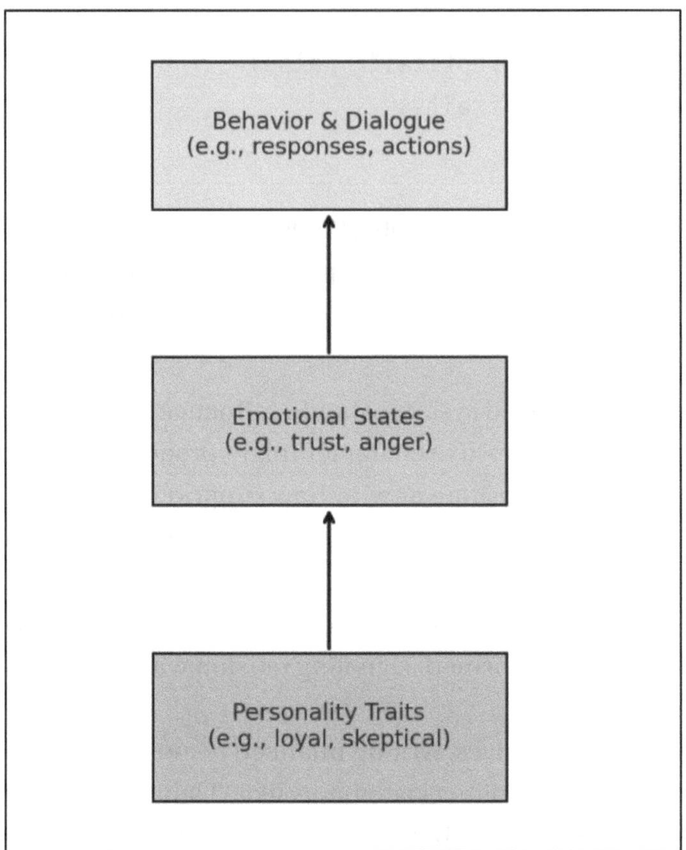

Figure 12-1. *Integration of personality traits and emotional states*

When players sense that a character is shaped by their choices and emotional tone rather than pre-written paths alone, they engage more deeply and invest more personally. In the next section, we'll take all these concepts and bring them to life with a hands-on project: building an AI-powered character generator that combines personality traits, emotional states, and procedural content into a functional, modular system you can expand in your own work.

Hands-On Project: Build an AI-Powered Character Generator

Now that we understand how to combine personality traits, emotional states, and AI-generated content, let's bring it all together into a complete, runnable project. In this hands-on exercise, we will build a simple Flask web application that allows you to create characters, generate procedural backstories using AI, and simulate emotional updates based on player actions. We will use our previous chapter example and create Captain Ayo's character.

This project will include

- A web form for creating new characters with traits
- Integration with an AI model to generate dynamic backstories
- Buttons to simulate emotional events and see how the character evolves
- Real-time updates to emotional states and responses

By running this Flask app, you'll be able to

- Create personalized characters with selected traits.
- Generate AI-driven backstories to make them feel unique.
- Simulate emotional changes and watch trust and anger evolve.
- Extend or modify logic to include additional emotions, traits, or actions.

Project Structure

```
character_generator/
├── app.py
├── templates/
│   ├── home.html
│   └── character.html
├── static/
│   └── styles.css (optional)
```

Flask Setup (app.py)

```
from flask import Flask, render_template, request, redirect, url_for
import random
import openai

app = Flask(__name__)
```

```
# Simple in-memory character store
characters = {}

class Character:
    def __init__(self, name, traits):
        self.name = name
        self.traits = traits  # e.g., {"loyal": True, "skeptical": False}
        self.emotional_state = {"trust": random.randint(40, 60), "anger":
        random.randint(0, 30)}
        self.backstory = ""

    def update_emotion(self, trust_change=0, anger_change=0):
        self.emotional_state["trust"] = max(0, min(100, self.emotional_
        state["trust"] + trust_change))
        self.emotional_state["anger"] = max(0, min(100, self.emotional_
        state["anger"] + anger_change))

    def set_backstory(self, text):
        self.backstory = text

@app.route("/", methods=["GET", "POST"])
def home():
    if request.method == "POST":
        name = request.form["name"]
        trait_loyal = "trait_loyal" in request.form
        trait_skeptical = "trait_skeptical" in request.form

        traits = {"loyal": trait_loyal, "skeptical": trait_skeptical}
        new_character = Character(name, traits)

        openai.api_key = "YOUR_API_KEY"

prompt = f"Create a compelling backstory for a character named {name} who
is {'loyal' if trait_loyal else 'not loyal'} and {'skeptical' if trait_
skeptical else 'trusting'}."

response = openai.ChatCompletion.create(
    model="gpt-4o",
```

```
    messages=[{"role": "system", "content": "You are a creative
    storyteller."},
              {"role": "user", "content": prompt}]
)

backstory_text = response.choices[0].message.content

        new_character.set_backstory(backstory_text)
        characters[name] = new_character
        return redirect(url_for("character_page", name=name))
    return render_template("home.html")

@app.route("/character/<name>", methods=["GET", "POST"])
def character_page(name):
    character = characters.get(name)
    if request.method == "POST":
        action = request.form["action"]
        if action == "betray":
            character.update_emotion(trust_change=-20, anger_change=30)
        elif action == "support":
            character.update_emotion(trust_change=20, anger_change=-10)
    return render_template("character.html", character=character)

if __name__ == "__main__":
    app.run(debug=True)
```

home.html

```
<!DOCTYPE html>
<html>
<head>
    <title>Create Character</title>
</head>
<body>
    <h2>Create a New Character</h2>
    <form method="post">
        Name: <input type="text" name="name" required><br><br>
```

```
        Traits:<br>
        <input type="checkbox" name="trait_loyal"> Loyal<br>
        <input type="checkbox" name="trait_skeptical"> Skeptical<br><br>
        <input type="submit" value="[Create Character]">
    </form>
</body>
</html>
```

character.html

```
<!DOCTYPE html>
<html>
<head>
    <title>Character Profile</title>
</head>
<body>
    <h2> Character :{{ character.name }}</h2>
    <p><strong>Traits:</strong> {{ character.traits }}</p>
    <p><strong>Trust:</strong> {{ character.emotional_state["trust"] }}</p>
    <p><strong>Anger:</strong> {{ character.emotional_state["anger"] }}</p>
    <p><strong>Backstory:</strong> {{ character.backstory }}</p>

<form method="post">
        <button type="submit" name="action" value="support">[Show
        Support]</button>
        <button type="submit" name="action" value="betray">
        [Betray]</button>
    </form>
    <br>
    <a href="/">[Create Another Character]</a>
</body>
</html>
```

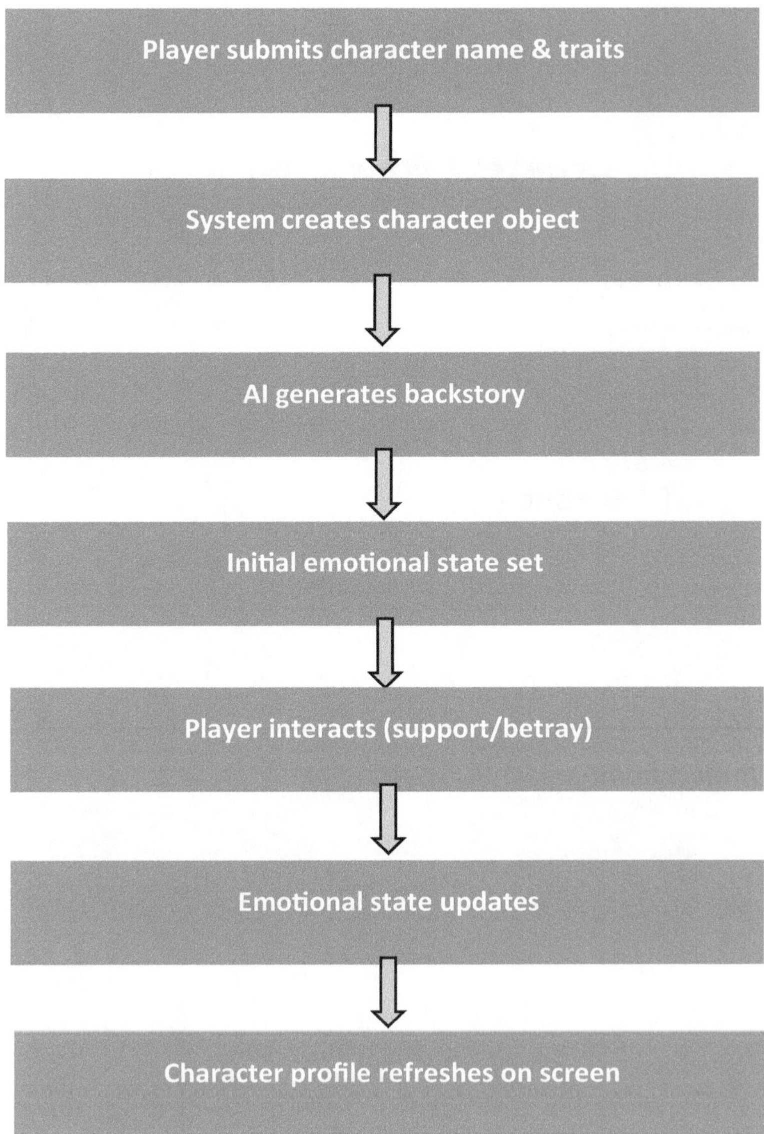

Figure 12-2. *Flask project flow*

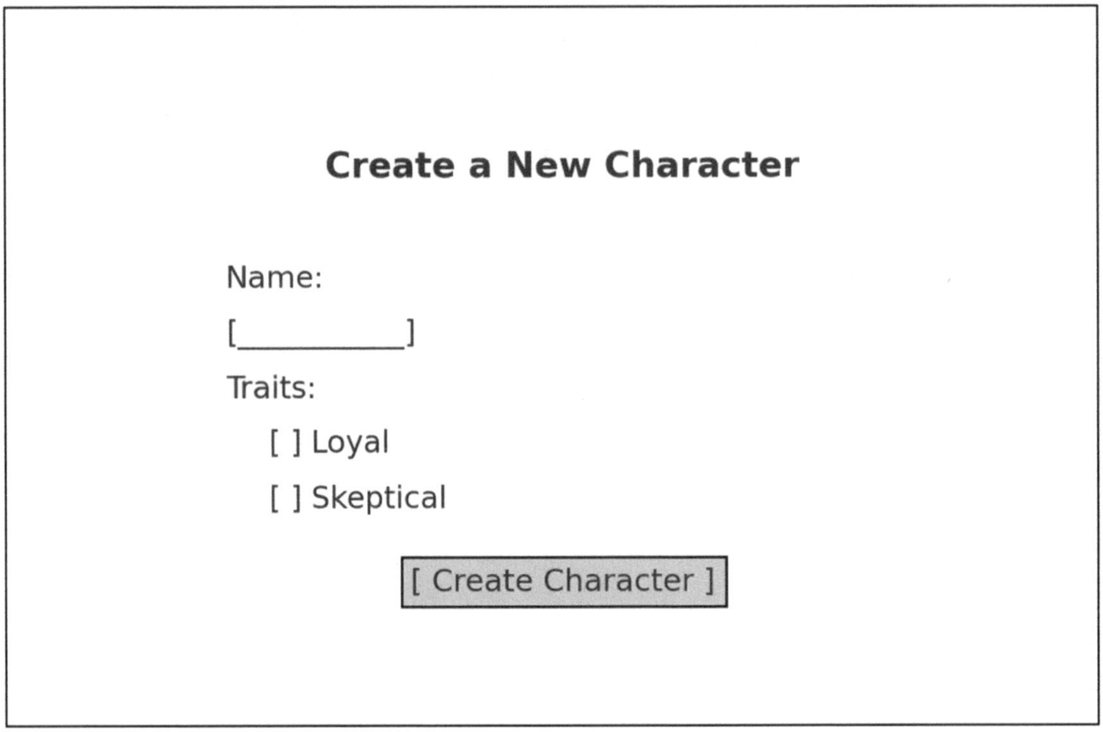

Create a New Character

Name:

[__________]

Traits:

[ ] Loyal

[ ] Skeptical

[Create Character]

Figure 12-3. *Project home screen*

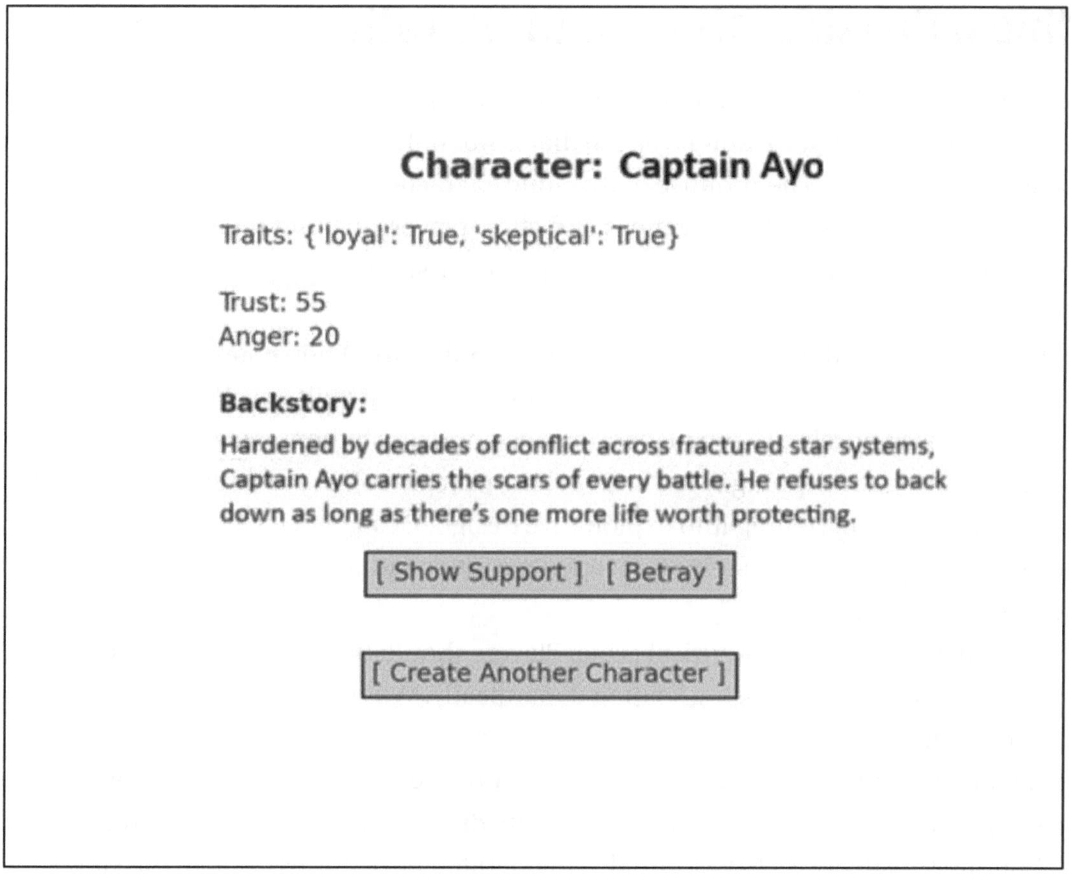

Character: Captain Ayo

Traits: {'loyal': True, 'skeptical': True}

Trust: 55
Anger: 20

Backstory:

Hardened by decades of conflict across fractured star systems, Captain Ayo carries the scars of every battle. He refuses to back down as long as there's one more life worth protecting.

[Show Support] [Betray]

[Create Another Character]

Figure 12-4. *Character screen*

This standalone Flask app is intended as extensions to the example introduced in Chapters 10 and 11. They build directly on the existing project rather than replacing it.

In the final section, we'll discuss how to use these tools thoughtfully and address the narrative and ethical challenges of procedurally generated characters, ensuring you create experiences that are powerful and respectful.

Ethical Considerations and Narrative Integrity

As we move toward creating characters that can adapt, evolve, and even generate parts of their own story, we enter a space that is not only technically challenging but also ethically delicate. The promise of dynamic character systems is immense: they offer richer, more personal experiences and allow players to build relationships that feel authentic. However, these systems also present risks that designers must handle with care.

One major consideration is **emotional manipulation**. When characters react to player behavior and tone, they can evoke strong feelings of guilt, loyalty, or fear. If these systems are used purely to keep players engaged or to push them toward spending money (e.g., by guilt-tripping them into making purchases), the technology crosses a line from meaningful storytelling into exploitative design. Designers have a responsibility to use emotionally adaptive systems to deepen narrative rather than to manipulate player psychology for profit.

Transparency is another critical issue. Players should have some awareness that a character's reactions are being shaped dynamically. While full technical disclosure can break immersion, providing subtle cues or optional explanations helps maintain trust. When players sense that they are being monitored or emotionally profiled without consent, even in a fictional context, it can create discomfort or disengagement.

Cultural sensitivity is also essential. AI-generated backstories or dialogue can sometimes produce content that is inadvertently biased, culturally insensitive, or inappropriate. Without careful human oversight, procedurally generated characters might reinforce harmful stereotypes or mishandle delicate subjects. It's important to curate, review, and, where necessary, rewrite AI-generated text to ensure respect and inclusivity.

Narrative coherence should not be overlooked. The temptation to make characters endlessly adaptive can lead to fragmented stories and inconsistencies that confuse rather than enrich the experience. Grounding characters in strong core traits and carefully defining the boundaries of their adaptive behaviors helps maintain a believable, coherent narrative arc.

Lastly, designers should remember that even in games, characters are not disposable tools but emotional touchpoints for players. A well-designed dynamic character is not merely an algorithmic puppet but a co-creator in the story journey. Honoring that relationship means designing with empathy, integrity, and a genuine respect for the player's emotional investment.

By considering these ethical dimensions, we ensure that dynamic character systems remain a tool for deeper storytelling rather than a means of manipulation or exploitation. Used responsibly, they can create some of the most moving, memorable experiences in interactive media, deepening our understanding of what it means to connect with a character and, ultimately, with ourselves.

Conclusion

Dynamic characters are more than just a technical upgrade; they represent a shift in how we think about storytelling and player agency. By weaving together traits, emotional states, and AI-driven content, we can create companions and rivals who feel alive and responsive in ways traditional systems could never fully achieve. Yet, with this power comes responsibility: to design characters that are meaningful, respectful, and narratively coherent. As you experiment with these tools, remember that the ultimate goal is not just to simulate life, but to deepen the player's emotional journey.

PART III

Implementing AI-Driven Storytelling

CHAPTER 13

Integrating AI Models into Game Development

In the past few years, generative AI models have moved from experimental research labs to mainstream creative workflows, offering new ways to shape stories, worlds, and characters. For game developers, these models are more than technical novelties; they are tools that can fundamentally change how games are designed, written, and played. By integrating models like GPT into your development pipeline, you can create characters who generate unique dialogue on the fly, worlds that adapt dynamically to player actions, and quest lines that evolve based on individual play styles.

This chapter will explore practical strategies for incorporating large language models (LLMs) and other AI-driven systems into your game projects. We'll cover how to connect APIs, design flexible narrative frameworks, and ensure that these systems remain controllable and coherent. Through code walkthroughs and architecture diagrams, you'll learn how to bring adaptive storytelling and AI-powered worldbuilding to life.

Before we dive into detailed architectures and code, it's important to understand the different ways AI models can serve your game, from writing flavor text to driving core narrative arcs. In this first section, we'll map out these potential roles and explore what makes AI integration so powerful and so challenging.

Roles of AI Models in Games

AI models, especially large language models like GPT, can play many roles within a game. Understanding these roles early on helps developers design systems that are both technically feasible and creatively meaningful. Rather than simply treating AI as a "black box" that spits out text, thinking strategically about its role can turn it into a true narrative and design partner.

S. N. Gupta, *Generative AI for Game Development*, https://doi.org/10.1007/979-8-8688-2439-5_13

One of the most immediate applications is **dynamic dialogue generation**. Traditionally, game dialogue is scripted, requiring writers to anticipate every possible player choice and tone. With AI, characters can generate contextually appropriate lines on demand, reacting to player choices in ways that feel more spontaneous and natural. For example, an AI-powered companion might comment on your recent choices in a way that's unique to each playthrough, adding layers of depth to interactions.

AI models can also handle **procedural backstory and lore creation**. While major story arcs are often best designed by humans to ensure strong narrative cohesion, smaller pieces of worldbuilding, such as books, letters, item descriptions, or regional rumors, can be generated or expanded using AI. Games like *Elden Ring* and *The Witcher 3*, which do not use any generative AI, are rich with incidental lore, and AI can help fill out these details without overwhelming writers with endless content demands.

Another powerful role is **quest and event variation**. Instead of creating static side quests, AI models can generate quest variations that adapt to player history, faction standing, or emotional states of companions. Imagine a bounty mission that changes its tone, difficulty, or ultimate resolution depending on your reputation or choices earlier in the game. This creates replay able content that feels fresh and tailored.

AI can also assist with **content personalization**. In multiplayer or online RPGs, it's possible to dynamically generate in-game messages, item names, or faction updates based on community events or collective player actions. For instance, a live event summary written by an AI "town crier" NPC could highlight victories, betrayals, or major shifts in the game world each week.

Finally, AI models can support **narrative prototyping** during development. Writers and designers can rapidly draft multiple story directions, dialogue variants, or character arcs by prompting the AI. This accelerates brainstorming and allows teams to iterate on narrative ideas more quickly before finalizing scripts.

While these applications open exciting doors, each role also introduces new challenges, from narrative coherence to ethical design and performance constraints. As we move through this chapter, we'll explore how to connect AI systems technically, define prompts and constraints clearly, and maintain authorial control over AI-generated content.

In the next section, we'll step back and look at the architectural considerations—how to structure your code and data so AI can be integrated smoothly without breaking your game's stability or narrative logic.

Architectural Considerations

When integrating AI models into a game, it's tempting to think only in terms of text input and output: send a prompt, receive a reply, display it in the game. In reality, the technical architecture beneath that simple exchange is critical to creating a stable, scalable, and narratively coherent experience. Without careful design, even a clever AI system can quickly become a source of performance issues, narrative contradictions, or maintenance headaches.

At the heart of your architecture is the **data flow between the game engine and the AI service**. Whether you're using Unity, Unreal, or a custom Python/Flask prototype, you'll need a clear pathway for sending context (character states, scene details, player choices) to the AI and then interpreting and integrating its responses. This often means building a **middleware layer**, code that sits between your core game logic and the external AI API, translating in-game data into structured prompts and parsing AI outputs back into usable game data.

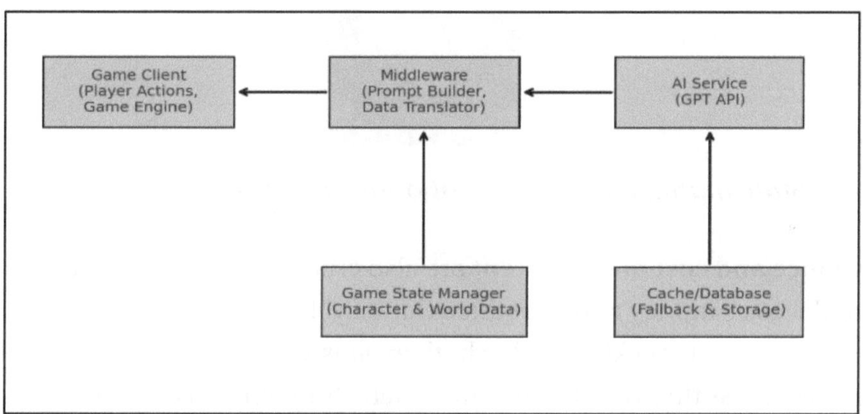

***Figure 13-1.** System architecture diagram for overall data flow*

Another key consideration is **state management**. AI-generated responses must reflect the current emotional and narrative context of your world. This requires maintaining persistent data about each character's traits, emotional states, relationship scores, and critical plot flags. If your system doesn't consistently supply this information to the AI, characters may break continuity, acting friendly in one scene, then inexplicably hostile in the next. Robust state tracking ensures that the AI's responses feel grounded and believable.

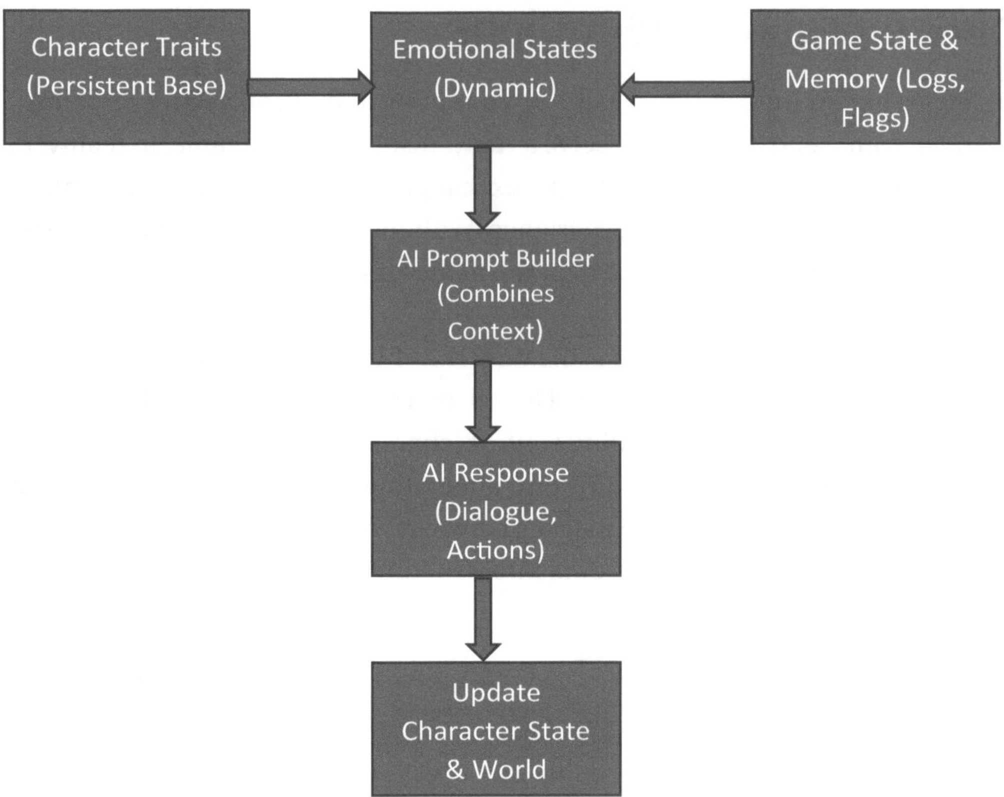

Figure 13-2. *State management for emotional state integration*

Performance and cost management are also crucial. Each API call to a large language model costs money and introduces latency. Flooding your game with dozens of requests per minute can quickly become both expensive and slow, degrading the player experience. To address this, developers often cache frequently used AI responses, pre-generate certain dialogue branches during loading screens, or limit live AI calls to key narrative moments rather than every incidental line.

Security and reliability cannot be overlooked. Whenever your game communicates with an external API, you expose potential vulnerabilities. API keys must be securely stored (never hard-coded directly into game files), and fallback logic should exist in case the AI service is temporarily unavailable. For example, you might provide default "safe" dialogue responses or simpler hard-coded lines to ensure the game remains functional.

Lastly, consider **prompt engineering as part of your architecture**. The prompts you send to an AI are effectively a living part of your narrative design; they shape tone, voice, and continuity. Designing these prompts carefully, with clear instructions and context, ensures that AI outputs align with your game's style and narrative goals. This means treating prompts not as throwaway strings but as a formal part of your game's data and design structure.

Be careful, though, because AI models often do not maintain memory across separate requests; generating branches in isolated prompts can cause inconsistencies in tone, character behavior, or world rules. To prevent this, it's best to create the full narrative tree or a structured outline containing all decision points and key branches in a single prompt. You can then expand each branch with additional prompts while passing the full outline back into the model for continuity.

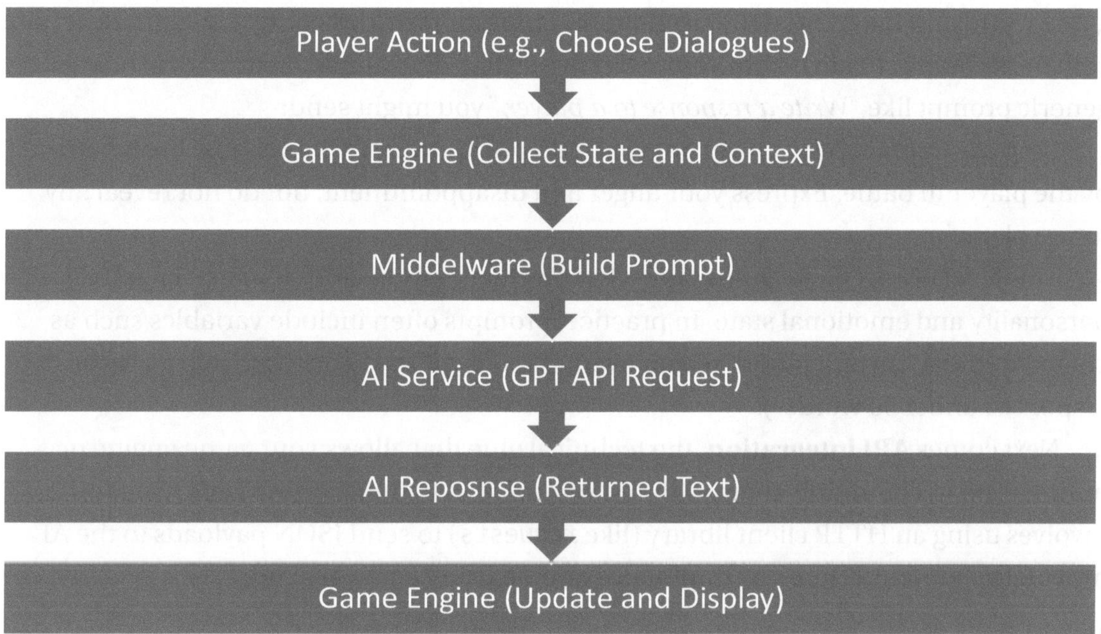

Figure 13-3. *API request response cycle*

Overall, successful architectural planning transforms AI from a flashy gimmick into a reliable, integrated narrative partner. By thinking carefully about data flow, state management, performance, and security, you create a foundation that allows your AI-driven characters and stories to feel coherent, scalable, and robust.

In the next section, we'll explore exactly how to implement these concepts through practical code, covering API connections, prompt design, and step-by-step integration inside a game engine or prototype environment.

Implementing AI Model Connections

Once the architectural foundation is in place, the next step is to make your AI model connection live and operational. This is where high-level concepts become tangible code; where characters begin to speak dynamically, worlds start to adapt, and the narrative feels alive. Implementing AI connections requires careful attention to three areas: prompt design, API integration, and error handling.

The first critical piece is **prompt design**. Your prompt is the bridge between your game world and the AI model. A well-crafted prompt provides context, defines tone, and constrains output to align with your narrative style. For example, instead of sending a generic prompt like *"Write a response to a player,"* you might send:

"You are Captain Ayo, a loyal but space skeptical warrior who has just been betrayed by the player in battle. Express your anger and disappointment, but do not reveal any future plans."

This level of specificity guides the AI to produce responses that match character personality and emotional state. In practice, prompts often include variables such as character traits, current mood, recent events, and even style constraints (e.g., "keep responses under 50 words").

Next comes **API integration**, the technical glue that allows your game engine or middleware to communicate with the AI service. In a Python context, this usually involves using an HTTP client library (like `requests`) to send JSON payloads to the AI provider's endpoint. Here's a simplified example using OpenAI's API:

```
import openai

openai.api_key = "YOUR_API_KEY"

def generate_character_response(prompt_text):
    response = openai.ChatCompletion.create(
        model="gpt-4o",
        messages=[
```

```
            {"role": "system", "content": "You are a serious game
            character. Keep responses immersive."},
            {"role": "user", "content": prompt_text}
        ]
    )
    return response.choices[0].message.content
```

This function can then be called from your middleware layer whenever a new player action requires an AI-generated reply.

Finally, **error handling and fallback logic** are essential. API requests can fail for many reasons: network issues, rate limits, or temporary service outages. Your game must gracefully handle these situations. Options include falling back to a default scripted line, retrying after a short delay, or displaying a neutral placeholder response. Logging these errors helps your team monitor and improve system reliability over time. Here's a simple Python example of error handling:

```
import openai
import time

openai.api_key = "YOUR_API_KEY"

def generate_character_response(prompt_text):
    try:
        response = openai.ChatCompletion.create(
            model="gpt-4o",
            messages=[
                {"role": "system", "content": "You are a serious game
                character. Keep responses immersive."},
                {"role": "user", "content": prompt_text}
            ]
        )
        return response.choices[0].message.content
    except openai.error.RateLimitError:
        print("Rate limit exceeded. Retrying...")
        time.sleep(2)  # wait before retry
        return "The character glares silently, refusing to speak for now."
```

```
    except openai.error.APIError as e:
        print(f"API error: {e}")
        return "The character seems momentarily distracted, lost in
        thought."
    except Exception as e:
        print(f"Unexpected error: {e}")
        return "The character remains silent, as if gathering their
        thoughts."
```

In this example, we catch specific errors such as rate limits and general API errors, provide console logs for debugging, and most importantly, return **in-world fallback lines** that maintain narrative immersion. Instead of displaying a technical error to the player, the character might appear silent, pensive, or evasive, which feels intentional rather than broken.

In addition to technical failures, you should also anticipate **narrative edge cases**. Sometimes AI-generated text may break lore, contradict earlier statements, or veer into unintended tones. Implementing a content filter or post-processing step can help catch problematic outputs before they appear in the game. For example, a warrior who hates magic might suddenly praise sorcery in a generated line if the prompt isn't carefully constrained.

To handle this, you can use post-processing filters and narrative validators. For instance:

```
def validate_ai_response(response_text, character_profile):
    # Simple lore rule: Captain Ayo should never mention supporting magic
    if "magic" in response_text.lower() and character_profile.get("hates_
    magic", False):
        return "Captain Ayo clenches his jaw, refusing to acknowledge
        anything about magic."
    return response_text
```

This function checks for lore-breaking keywords or sentiments and swaps them with an appropriate fallback if needed. You might also flag suspicious responses to review logs or maintain a list of "forbidden" topics for each character.

Integrating AI is more than just hooking up an API; it's designing a robust, resilient storytelling pipeline. The goal is to ensure that every AI-generated interaction feels intentional, coherent, and true to the world you've created. By combining thoughtful prompt engineering, solid API integration, and reliable error handling, you can bring AI-powered characters and narrative systems to life in ways that feel seamless and deeply engaging.

In the next section, we'll move from back-end connections to practical code walkthroughs inside an actual prototype environment, providing step-by-step examples of how to integrate AI into your game logic and UI.

CODE WALKTHROUGH AND PROTOTYPE INTEGRATION

With your architecture designed and your AI connections established, the next step is to bring everything together inside a prototype environment. In this section, we'll walk through a practical example using Python and Flask, showing exactly how to connect player actions, character state updates, and AI-generated responses in a live, playable prototype.

We'll focus on a simplified setup where a player interacts with a character through a web interface. The character's traits and emotional states are tracked, and each new player action triggers an AI-generated response that reflects both current context and emotional tone.

Basic Structure Overview

Here's a simplified Flask route that handles these steps:

1. **Player Submits an Action**: For example, supporting or betraying the character.
2. **Game Engine Updates Character State**: Emotional variables like trust and anger change accordingly.
3. **Prompt Is Built Dynamically**: Combining base traits, emotional state, and recent events.
4. **AI Generates a Response**: Text is returned and displayed on the frontend.
5. **Character Memory Updates**: Optionally logs significant actions for future interactions.

Folder Structure for the Flask App

```
my_flask_app/
│
├── app.py
│
└── templates/
    └── interaction.html
```

Codes

app.py

```
from flask import Flask, request, render_template
import openai
app = Flask(__name__)
openai.api_key = "YOUR_API_KEY"

# Example character state
character_state = {
    "name": "Captain Ayo",
    "traits": {"loyal": True, "skeptical": False},
    "trust": 60,
    "anger": 20,
    "history": []
}

@app.route("/", methods=["GET", "POST"])
def interact():
    global character_state
    response_text = ""
    if request.method == "POST":
        action = request.form.get("action")
        # Update state based on action
        if action == "support":
            character_state["trust"] = min(100, character_
            state["trust"] + 15)
```

```
        character_state["anger"] = max(0, character_
        state["anger"] - 10)
        recent_event = "The player offered support during a critical
        moment."
    elif action == "betray":
        character_state["trust"] = max(0, character_
        state["trust"] - 20)
        character_state["anger"] = min(100, character_
        state["anger"] + 25)
        recent_event = "The player betrayed the character during a
        mission."
    else:
        recent_event = "The player chose a neutral or unknown action."
    # Build prompt
    prompt = (
        f"You are {character_state['name']}, a loyal warrior. "
        f"Your current trust level toward the player is {character_
        state['trust']} "
        f"and your anger level is {character_state['anger']}. "
        f"Recent event: {recent_event} Respond in character and under
        50 words."
    )
    # Generate AI response
    try:
        ai_response = openai.ChatCompletion.create(
            model="gpt-4o",
            messages=[
                {"role": "system", "content": "You are a serious in-
                world game character."},
                {"role": "user", "content": prompt}
            ]
        )
        response_text = ai_response.choices[0].message.content
    except Exception:
```

```
            response_text = "Captain Ayo falls silent, visibly conflicted
            and unable to find the right words."

        # Log history
        character_state["history"].append({"action": action, "response":
        response_text})

    return render_template("interaction.html", character=character_state,
    response_text=response_text)

if __name__ == "__main__":
    app.run(debug=True)
```

interaction.html

```
<!DOCTYPE html>
<html>
<head>
    <title>Character Interaction</title>
</head>
<body>
    <h2>Interacting with {{ character.name }}</h2>
    <p>Traits: {{ character.traits }}</p>
    <p>Trust: {{ character.trust }}</p>
    <p>Anger: {{ character.anger }}</p>

    {% if response_text %}
        <p><strong>{{ character.name }} says:</strong> {{ response_
        text }}</p>
    {% endif %}

    <form method="post">
        <button type="submit" name="action" value="support">Support
        </button>
        <button type="submit" name="action" value="betray">Betray</button>
    </form>

    <h3>Interaction History</h3>
    <ul>
```

```
        {% for entry in character.history %}
            <li>{{ entry.action }} → "{{ entry.response }}"</li>
        {% endfor %}
    </ul>
</body>
</html>
```

This prototype provides a fully functioning, minimal demonstration of a dynamic, AI-powered character interaction system. Players can click buttons to perform actions, the back-end updates character states, and a prompt is sent to the AI, generating new dialogue each time.

This example isn't modularized, but it builds on the Chapter 10 foundation and can be modularized easily using the guidance provided in Chapter 11.

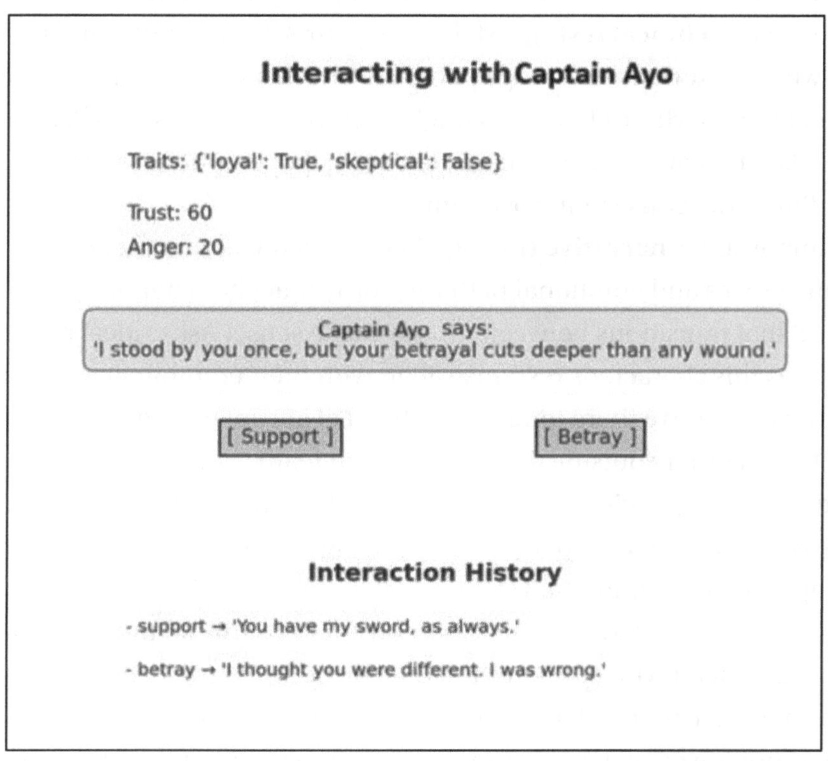

Figure 13-4. *Sample screen of the Flask prototype showing character state, AI-generated responses, and interaction history*

This foundation can be further extended to include deeper emotional models, multi-turn conversations, memory modules, and additional world interactions. Most importantly, it offers a real, interactive glimpse into the potential of AI-driven storytelling, showing not just code, but the narrative magic it enables.

In the next section, we'll discuss how to test, refine, and scale these systems and consider strategies for maintaining narrative coherence as your game world grows.

Testing and Refinement

Once your AI-driven character system is up and running, the real work begins: testing, refining, and continuously improving both technical performance and narrative quality. While the initial prototype may feel exciting, creating an experience that feels coherent, emotionally authentic, and replay able requires ongoing iteration.

The first step is **technical testing**. Make sure your API calls perform reliably under different network conditions and usage patterns. Check for latency spikes, unexpected errors, and edge cases where characters might receive no response at all. Automated tests can simulate repeated player actions, ensuring that emotional state updates and prompt handling work consistently over time.

Equally important is **narrative testing**. Play through your interactions repeatedly, with different choices and emotional paths, to verify that character behavior feels believable and that transitions between moods make sense. Ask critical questions during these tests: Does this character's response align with their emotional state? Are they too forgiving or too harsh? Are there tonal shifts that feel abrupt or unearned?

Feedback from testers outside the development team is invaluable. Players often catch narrative inconsistencies or emotional beats that designers miss. Structured playtests, where testers log unexpected or confusing responses, can help uncover flaws in your prompts, logic, or emotional state calculations.

In addition to raw narrative correctness, consider **emotional pacing and player experience**. A character who oscillates too quickly between trust and anger may feel erratic rather than nuanced. Introducing mechanisms like gradual state decay or "emotional cooldowns" can help smooth these transitions and make changes feel earned. Similarly, adjusting thresholds for emotional shifts ensures that characters don't become unreasonably hostile or affectionate after just one or two actions.

Monitoring **AI output quality** is crucial. Even with well-designed prompts, large language models can occasionally produce unexpected or out-of-context replies. Set up logs to track all AI-generated outputs, and periodically review them to catch lore inconsistencies or stylistic drift. In production environments, some teams choose to implement human moderation for critical story moments or sensitive topics.

Finally, plan for **iterative narrative refinement**. Unlike static dialogue trees, dynamic systems evolve as players discover new paths and combinations. Encourage your writing and design team to treat this as a living system, regularly tuning prompts, adjusting emotional response logic, and adding new variations to keep the world feeling alive.

A robust testing and refinement process doesn't just catch bugs; it strengthens player trust and deepens emotional immersion. When players feel that characters react genuinely and consistently, they become more willing to invest emotionally in the world you've created.

In the final section of this chapter, we'll discuss how to maintain coherence and authorial control as these dynamic systems scale and how to avoid common pitfalls that can unravel even the most promising AI-driven narratives.

Maintaining Narrative Coherence at Scale

As you move from a small prototype to a full-scale game with dozens of characters and branching storylines, one of the biggest challenges is keeping your narrative world coherent. Even the most robust AI-driven systems can quickly unravel if they aren't carefully guided by a strong narrative framework and consistent authorial oversight.

The first key is to **define clear narrative constraints**. While AI is capable of generating endless variations, each character and storyline should have a strong core identity that serves as an anchor. This means clearly outlining each character's foundational traits, moral lines they would never cross, and critical story beats that must remain intact regardless of player actions. Treat these as narrative "guardrails" that shape and constrain AI creativity rather than suppress it entirely.

Another important practice is **context layering**. As your world grows, prompts sent to AI should contain layered context—not just the immediate player action but also the character's history, previous emotional states, and relevant world events. Without this information, AI outputs can feel disconnected or contradictory. While longer prompts can introduce higher API costs and latency, they are essential for continuity. Many teams solve this by summarizing or compressing historical context into short "memory snapshots" that still capture essential beats.

Content monitoring and review processes also scale in importance as the number of characters and interactions grows. In smaller prototypes, you might manually review outputs. In a larger project, consider building an automated content moderation system that flags responses containing forbidden topics or tonal inconsistencies. You can also train custom moderation models to detect lore-breaking statements or emotional inconsistencies.

Maintaining **consistent style and voice** across many AI outputs is another common pitfall. Over time, even well-crafted prompts can drift, resulting in characters who suddenly feel out of character or story arcs that lose their intended emotional impact. Regular prompt audits and "voice tuning" sessions with writers can help keep these systems aligned with the overall creative vision.

Remember, it is essential to remember that **AI is a collaborator, not an author**. The AI provides dynamic flavor and variation, but it should not be left to carry critical plot points or resolve major story arcs independently. Important narrative moments should be designed and controlled by writers and narrative designers, with AI used to enrich the space between those milestones. This hybrid approach preserves authorial intent while still providing players with organic, surprising interactions.

By combining strong constraints, layered context, thoughtful monitoring, and clear authorial oversight, you can scale your AI narrative systems without sacrificing coherence or emotional depth. When done well, this approach empowers your characters to feel dynamic and alive while ensuring the story remains tight, compelling, and true to the world you've envisioned.

Conclusion

Integrating AI models into game development offers transformative possibilities—from responsive dialogue and procedural lore to evolving quests and truly dynamic companions. Yet these opportunities come with challenges that extend beyond code: they demand careful narrative design, ongoing refinement, and a commitment to maintaining trust with your players.

By combining robust architecture, thoughtful prompts, reliable error handling, and strong narrative constraints, you can create AI-driven storytelling experiences that feel alive and immersive while remaining coherent and impactful. As we move forward into procedural worldbuilding and real-time narrative adaptation, these principles will serve as essential guideposts on the journey.

CHAPTER 14

Procedural Worldbuilding with AI

Procedural worldbuilding has long been a cornerstone of creating vast, immersive game universes. Traditionally, this approach relied on algorithmic systems to generate terrains, dungeons, and item distributions, helping small teams build worlds that feel large and dynamic. With the introduction of generative AI, procedural worldbuilding has taken a significant leap forward. Instead of merely randomizing topography or item placement, AI can now help weave lore, shape dynamic events, and even create cultures and histories on the fly.

In this chapter, we'll explore how to use AI to generate not just maps and landscapes, but living worlds filled with evolving stories and characters. We'll look at integrating AI-generated narrative layers with traditional procedural content, designing systems that feel both infinite and coherent, and balancing automated creation with human-authored meaning.

Let's break down the core principles of procedural worldbuilding and explore how AI can deepen them beyond what traditional systems allow first.

Principles of Procedural Worldbuilding

At its best, procedural worldbuilding creates a game environment that feels alive, unpredictable, and deeply replay able. Yet, if not thoughtfully designed, procedural systems can just as easily result in repetitive or meaningless worlds, spaces that feel algorithmically generated rather than lived in. To avoid this, strong design principles must guide even the most automated systems.

S. N. Gupta, *Generative AI for Game Development*, https://doi.org/10.1007/979-8-8688-2439-5_14

One fundamental principle is **coherence**. A procedurally generated world must feel like it follows its own internal logic. Mountains don't appear in the middle of oceans without reason, and an ancient forest should not suddenly border a desert with no explanation. Whether building entire continents or tiny towns, establishing clear environmental rules and respecting them is crucial. Even if content is algorithmically generated, it should feel as though it has grown organically over time.

Another principle is **contextual storytelling**. Every region, settlement, or structure should have a reason for existing. In traditional design, writers and artists create these stories manually. With procedural systems, you must build mechanisms that embed small narrative hooks into each element. For example, an abandoned cabin might include hints of who lived there, scattered belongings, a journal entry, a broken weapon, even if no designer placed them by hand. These details allow players to build their own interpretations and deepen their emotional engagement.

Variation with constraints is another key. Total randomness can quickly lead to chaotic, unmemorable worlds. Instead, effective procedural generation introduces variation within carefully designed boundaries. For instance, you might define several "cultural templates" for settlements: a fishing village culture, a merchant hub, or a scholarly enclave. The generator then creates individual towns by combining variations within these templates, ensuring each feels distinct but still grounded.

Player interaction is the final principle that transforms a procedural world from a static backdrop into a living space. Worlds should respond to the player's actions in meaningful ways. Over time, towns might show signs of prosperity or decline based on trade decisions, or a forest might grow darker and more dangerous after repeated monster incursions. This dynamic evolution turns procedural worlds into spaces players feel responsible for and connected to, rather than just procedural mazes to navigate.

When integrating AI, these principles become even more powerful. AI can help generate layered histories, factions with evolving motivations, and emergent events that unfold based on player actions and world state. Instead of writing every tavern rumor or ancient ruin's backstory by hand, AI can provide unique, context-sensitive content, adding depth without overwhelming your writing team.

By grounding your procedural systems in coherence, contextual storytelling, variation with constraints, and meaningful player interaction, you ensure that AI-driven worlds don't just feel big, they feel alive. In the next section, we'll explore how AI-generated narrative layers can integrate with these principles to transform procedural content into deeply immersive experiences.

AI-Generated Narrative Layers

While procedural generation has traditionally focused on physical elements like terrain, dungeons, or loot, AI offers the potential to fill these worlds with layered, reactive narratives that make each corner feel meaningful. Rather than simply scattering random objects or repeating design patterns, AI can give each element a history, a rumor, or a cultural footprint that breathes life into the world.

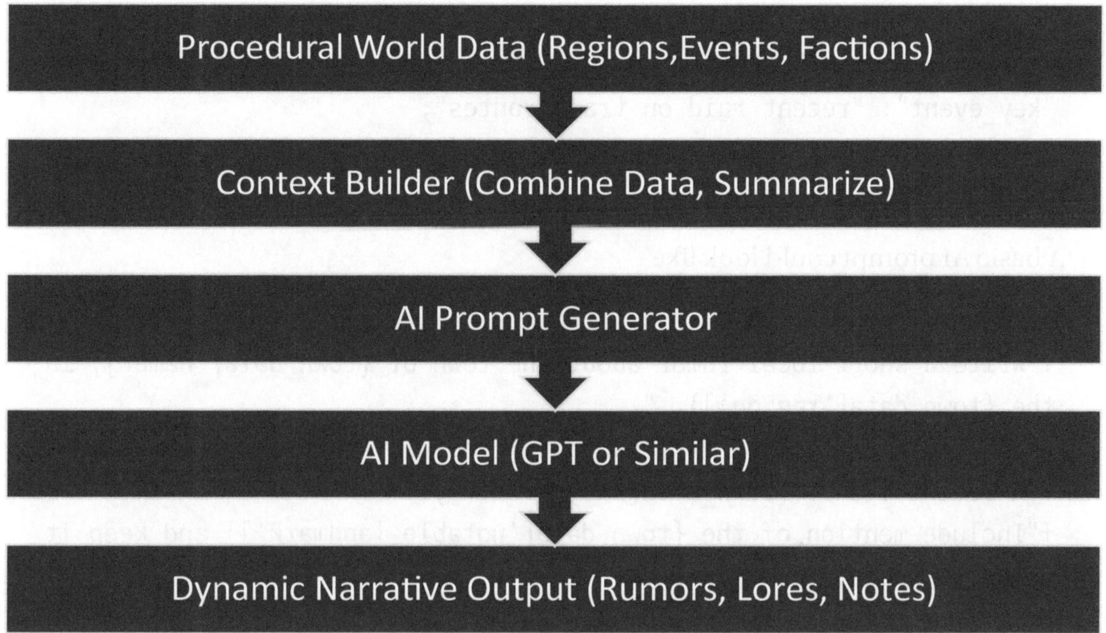

Figure 14-1. *Flow from procedural world data to AI-generated narrative layers. This pipeline shows how raw world context becomes immersive stories and rumors*

One of the most compelling uses is **regional lore generation**. Imagine exploring a procedurally generated town chain. Instead of generic "island 1" and "island 2," each island could receive an AI-generated history: one might be known as a former refuge for exiled mystics who left cryptic runes behind; another could be infamous for a lost treasure fleet that vanished in a storm. These histories can be dynamically generated based on geographical features, environmental data (like weather patterns or resource abundance), and the player's exploration path. Games like *Oasis* offer glimpses of this idea, but integrating AI can push these narrative layers further, making each discovery feel personalized and significant. AI allows us to layer in living, context-aware stories that make these worlds unforgettable. To illustrate how this works practically, let's explore both code and architecture.

Let's say we have a procedurally generated town. You might store a basic data structure like this:

```
town_data = {
    "name": "Duskfall",
    "region": "Northern Highlands",
    "dominant_faction": "Ember Guard",
    "key_event": "recent raid on trade routes",
    "notable_landmark": "Crimson Watchtower"
}
```

A basic AI prompt could look like

```
prompt = (
    f"Write a short local rumor about the town of {town_data['name']} in
    the {town_data['region']}. "
    f"The dominant faction is {town_data['dominant_faction']}. "
    f"A recent event: {town_data['key_event']}. "
    f"Include mention of the {town_data['notable_landmark']} and keep it
    under 50 words."
)

# Using OpenAI or another language model
import openai
openai.api_key = "YOUR_API_KEY"

response = openai.ChatCompletion.create(
    model="gpt-4o",
    messages=[
        {"role": "system", "content": "You are a medieval town gossip
        generator."},
        {"role": "user", "content": prompt}
    ]
)
```

```
rumor = response.choices[0].message.content
print(rumor)
```

Example Output

"Folk say the Ember Guard hoards secrets atop the Crimson Watchtower, planning revenge for last week's raid. Best keep away from Duskfall after dark."

This approach lets each town feel unique while requiring only minimal hand-authored scaffolding.

Faction and character lore can also benefit greatly from AI. Suppose your game includes a network of merchant guilds vying for regional power. Instead of relying solely on fixed questlines, AI can generate rumors, internal memos, or secret correspondences that reflect player actions, for example, "Word spreads through the docks that the Crimson Trade League has struck a secret pact with northern raiders, emboldened by your recent sabotage of their rivals." This dynamic rumor system can evolve over time, creating a sense of living politics and intrigue that reacts fluidly to player decisions.

Environmental storytelling, the small, hidden stories players uncover through exploration, becomes even more impactful with AI. Rather than hand-writing dozens of diary entries or abandoned letters, designers can create templates and let AI generate content that aligns with local events. In a forest recently scarred by fire, the player might find a charred journal page lamenting the loss of herbal remedies and sacred groves. In a mountain village suffering from a plague, AI-generated notes might hint at folk remedies or local superstitions. Each fragment reinforces a sense of place and responds to the evolving world state. Suppose a player discovers a sword in a procedurally generated cave. You could enrich it on the fly:

```
item_data = {
    "name": "Ashen Blade",
    "origin": "forged by mountain hermits",
    "curse": "whispers to its wielder in battle"
}

prompt = (
    f"Write a mysterious inscription for the {item_data['name']}, "
    f"which was {item_data['origin']} and is known to {item_
    data['curse']}. "
    f"Keep it cryptic and under 30 words."
)
```

```
response = openai.ChatCompletion.create(
    model="gpt-4o",
    messages=[
        {"role": "system", "content": "You are a medieval inscription
        artist."},
        {"role": "user", "content": prompt}
    ]
)
inscription = response.choices[0].message.content
print(inscription)
```

Example Output

"In shadows I awaken, your heart my silent oath. Beware the echo that follows steel."

These small details deepen player curiosity and emotional investment, making each discovery memorable.

Consider also **dynamic NPC memory and rumors**. In many RPGs, townsfolk repeat the same static lines regardless of the player's deeds. With AI, these characters can reference recent events, share rumors shaped by AI, or reflect on the player's reputation. A blacksmith might murmur, "Some say you turned the tide at Greywatch Pass. Others think you brought more trouble than you solved." This depth transforms otherwise minor NPCs into memorable, reactive participants in the world.

Let's say your player destroys an outpost controlled by a rival faction. Instead of simply marking it as "completed" on the map, AI can generate a spread of local consequences: new rumors among traveling merchants, worried letters sent to neighboring settlements, even folk songs that celebrate or condemn the player's actions. Each piece can be small, but together, they weave a narrative tapestry that feels authentic and emergent.

The key to making AI-generated narrative layers successful is maintaining clear **thematic constraints and lore consistency**. You might define high-level guidelines like "The Ember Guard faction always values honor above all else" or "The northern clans never speak directly of the old gods." AI-generated content can then draw on these themes as scaffolding, ensuring that even procedurally created stories reinforce the intended world vision.

Used thoughtfully, AI-generated narrative layers don't replace authored stories; they complement them, expanding detail where manual content creation would be too costly or time-intensive. Designers remain in control of the overarching narrative arcs and emotional beats, while AI enriches the fabric of the world, making it feel vast, deep, and uniquely shaped by each player's journey.

While the game uses AI to generate dynamic content like rumors or character reactions, this randomness is carefully guided by constraints to maintain consistency. Each AI prompt includes key facts—such as character traits, faction control, recent events, and the player's reputation—so the generated output cannot contradict the established world. Additionally, outputs are limited in length and type, and fallback templates ensure that if a response is off, a safe, coherent version is used instead. This combination of structured prompts, bounded outputs, and programmatic rules allows the story to feel alive and unpredictable while still respecting the game's designed logic and narrative consistency.

In the next section, we'll explore how to architect these systems technically, from data management and prompt design to integrating AI outputs smoothly into procedural generation workflows, ensuring your world remains both dynamic and coherent.

System Design and Data Management

As procedural worlds become more complex and AI-generated narratives grow in scale, managing data effectively is critical. Without a robust system design, it becomes nearly impossible to keep track of evolving histories, regional lore, and dynamic character states, all while ensuring the world remains coherent and performant.

At the heart of this is **structured data design**. Each region, settlement, item, or character should have a clearly defined data schema that captures not only static attributes (like location, climate, or baseline traits) but also dynamic states (such as evolving reputations, player impact flags, and current emotional states). By using consistent schemas, developers can easily query, update, and inject data into AI prompts without introducing contradictions or errors.

For example, a settlement schema might include

```
settlement_data = {
    "name": "Greywatch",
    "region": "Eastern Marshes",
    "dominant_faction": "Marsh Sentinels",
```

```
    "key_events": ["recent flood", "trade conflict with Rivertown"],
    "current_mood": "wary but resilient",
    "player_reputation": "neutral"
}
```

When crafting prompts, these fields provide concrete context, ensuring AI-generated content aligns with the settlement's history and emotional tone.

Centralized state storage is another crucial element. Instead of scattering state data across isolated scripts or files, using a centralized database or global state manager helps maintain consistency. Many modern games use JSON-based save files or in-memory data structures synced with back-end servers. This approach supports dynamic content generation on demand while also allowing for easy updates as players alter the world.

Version control and audit logs are essential when dealing with AI outputs. Even though the AI creates text dynamically, it's important to track which narrative variations were presented to each player. This ensures continuity (e.g., if a player returns to a town later, the story remains consistent) and provides a way to roll back or adjust outputs if needed. Simple logs can include time stamps, player choices, and stored AI responses.

Scalability is another key consideration. As more AI-driven narrative content is generated, the system must efficiently handle growing datasets without impacting performance. Techniques like caching frequently accessed lore fragments or pre-generating certain content during loading screens can help reduce latency and API costs.

Security and moderation are equally important at scale. As AI models generate more content, the risk of producing unintended or inappropriate text increases. Implementing filters, validation layers, or even partial human moderation for critical outputs helps ensure all narrative additions remain in line with the game's tone and community standards.

Finally, consider **data decay and world evolution**. Over time, old events might fade in memory, new rumors replace outdated ones, and long-forgotten items regain significance. Designing a system that can retire or transform data points allows your world to feel dynamic and alive, mirroring the way real cultures evolve and reinterpret their own histories.

When done thoughtfully, robust system design and data management allow AI-generated narrative layers to scale elegantly. Players encounter worlds that not only adapt to their actions but also feel historically rich and internally consistent, no matter how many variations exist beneath the surface.

In the next section, we'll move from back-end systems to practical implementation, providing a hands-on walkthrough of building a procedural narrative generator using Python, JSON, and GPT integration.

HANDS-ON PROJECT: BUILD A PROCEDURAL NARRATIVE GENERATOR

Now that we've explored the architectural design and data structures needed to support dynamic, AI-enhanced worlds, let's bring these concepts to life with a hands-on project. In this section, we'll build a simplified procedural narrative generator using Python, JSON, and GPT integration. This project will show you how to combine structured data with AI-generated storytelling to create localized rumors, item lore, and regional histories.

Project Overview

We'll create a small simulation where

1. The game world includes multiple settlements with distinct characteristics.
2. The system generates context-specific rumors for each settlement using AI.
3. The data is stored in JSON format, allowing for easy updates and expansion.

Step 1: Define Settlement Data

Create a JSON file (e.g., `settlements.json`) to store base data:

```
[
    {
        "name": "Greywatch",
        "region": "Eastern Marshes",
        "dominant_faction": "Marsh Sentinels",
        "key_events": ["recent flood", "trade conflict with Rivertown"],
        "current_mood": "wary but resilient",
        "player_reputation": "neutral"
    },
    {
        "name": "Duskfall",
        "region": "Northern Highlands",
        "dominant_faction": "Ember Guard",
```

```
        "key_events": ["recent raid on trade routes"],
        "current_mood": "suspicious and guarded",
        "player_reputation": "hostile"
    }
]
```

Step 2: Load Data in Python

```
import json

with open("settlements.json", "r") as f:
    settlements = json.load(f)
```

Step 3: Build AI Prompt

Pick a settlement and build a dynamic prompt:

```
settlement = settlements[0]  # Greywatch example

prompt = (
    f"Write a short rumor (under 50 words) about {settlement['name']} in
    the {settlement['region']}. "
    f"The town is controlled by the {settlement['dominant_faction']} and
    recently faced: "
    f"{', '.join(settlement['key_events'])}. "
    f"The mood is {settlement['current_mood']}, and the player
    reputation is {settlement['player_reputation']}."
)
```

Step 4: Generate AI Response

```
import openai

openai.api_key = "YOUR_API_KEY"

response = openai.ChatCompletion.create(
    model="gpt-4o",
    messages=[
        {"role": "system", "content": "You are a medieval town rumor
        generator. Keep it brief and immersive."},
        {"role": "user", "content": prompt}
```

```
    ]
)

rumor = response.choices[0].message.content
print(rumor)
```

Example Output

"Fishermen whisper that Greywatch leaders plan to flood rival fields to save their own marsh crops after the recent trade fallout."

Step 5: Store and Update Rumors

After generating the rumor, you can save it back into your JSON or log it in a separate file to track world evolution:

```
settlement["latest_rumor"] = rumor

with open("settlements.json", "w") as f:
    json.dump(settlements, f, indent=4)
```

Result

This simple generator empowers you to create context-aware narrative snippets that feel tailored to each region and evolve as the world changes. By extending this framework, you can incorporate dynamic item lore, evolving faction propaganda, or emergent local legends.

Extending the Previous Project

1. Add more settlements and vary faction types or moods.
2. Introduce item or quest data that modifies settlement rumors.
3. Build a lightweight Flask interface to allow live generation and display of rumors.

This hands-on project gives you a concrete starting point for creating living, dynamic worlds that feel deep and reactive without requiring thousands of pre-written lines. As your game grows, you can layer in additional complexity, but the core concept remains the same: structured data plus AI storytelling creates magic.

Let's add and extend our previous project to include whatever we have learned till now; after the extension, the game will offer more world exploration beyond just the character scenes!

Full Extended Code Including New Settlement Rumor System

```
from flask import Flask, session, redirect, url_for, render_template_
string, request, flash
import os
import random
import json

try:
    import openai
except Exception:
    openai = None
app = Flask(__name__)
app.secret_key = os.environ.get("FLASK_SECRET_KEY", "change-me-
for-prod")

# --------------------------------------------------
# Existing Scenes System
# --------------------------------------------------
scenes = {
    "reunion": {
        "description": "You meet Ayo at the abandoned hangar.",
        "choices": [
            {"text": "Apologize sincerely", "trust_change": 15, "anger_
            change": -5, "tone": 0.7},
            {"text": "Accuse Ayo of betrayal", "trust_change": -20,
            "anger_change": 20, "tone": -0.8},
        ]
    },
    "final_mission": {
        "description": "Ayo decides whether to join you.",
        "choices": [
            {"text": "Promise safety", "trust_change": 10, "anger_
            change": -3, "tone": 0.5},
            {"text": "Demand loyalty", "trust_change": -10, "anger_
            change": 10, "tone": -0.5},
        ]
```

```
    }
}

# --------------------------------------------------
# Ayo Model
# --------------------------------------------------

class Ayo:
    def decay_emotion(self):
        if self.anger > 0:
            self.anger -= 1
        self.trust -= 0  # placeholder

    def __init__(self, name="Ayo", trust=50, anger=10, memory=None):
        self.name = name
        self.trust = trust
        self.anger = anger
        self.memory = memory or []

    def to_dict(self):
        return {"name": self.name, "trust": self.trust, "anger": self.
        anger, "memory": self.memory}

    @classmethod
    def from_dict(cls, d):
        return cls(
            name=d.get("name", "Ayo"),
            trust=d.get("trust", 50),
            anger=d.get("anger", 10),
            memory=d.get("memory", []),
        )
    def apply_choice(self, choice_text, trust_change=0, anger_change=0,
    tone=None):
        self.trust = max(0, min(100, self.trust + trust_change))
        self.anger = max(0, min(100, self.anger + anger_change))
        mem = f'Player chose: "{choice_text}" (t:{trust_change:+},
        a:{anger_change:+})'
```

```
        self.memory.append(mem)
        if len(self.memory) > 10:
            self.memory = self.memory[-10:]

# ------------------------------------------------------
# Helpers
# ------------------------------------------------------

def get_ayo_from_session():
    ayo_data = session.get("ayo")
    if ayo_data:
        return Ayo.from_dict(ayo_data)
    ayo = Ayo()
    session["ayo"] = ayo.to_dict()
    return ayo

def save_ayo_to_session(ayo: Ayo):
    session["ayo"] = ayo.to_dict()

def build_prompt(ayo: Ayo, player_choice: str):
    return f"""
You are {ayo.name}, a conflicted ex-commander.
Trust level: {ayo.trust}/100.
Anger level: {ayo.anger}/100.
Recent memories: {ayo.memory[-2:]}.
The player chose: "{player_choice}".
Respond with one emotionally authentic sentence reflecting this history.
"""

def call_openai(prompt: str):
    api_key = os.environ.get("OPENAI_API_KEY")
    if not api_key or openai is None:
        return None
    try:
        openai.api_key = api_key
        resp = openai.ChatCompletion.create(
            model=os.environ.get("OPENAI_MODEL", "gpt-4o-mini"),
            messages=[{"role": "user", "content": prompt}],
```

```
            max_tokens=60,
            temperature=0.8,
        )
        return resp.choices[0].message.content.strip()
    except Exception:
        return None

def local_fallback_response(ayo: Ayo, player_choice: str, tone=None):
    if 'accuse' in player_choice.lower():
        return "You think I'm a traitor? I expected more; I won't
        forget this."
    if 'apolog' in player_choice.lower():
        return "Your apology lands like a stone – felt, but unresolved."
    if 'promise' in player_choice.lower():
        return "Promises are fragile… but maybe yours matters."
    if 'demand' in player_choice.lower():
        return "Loyalty isn’t free – don’t pretend it is."
    return random.choice([
        "I study you carefully, unsure what to believe.",
        "Old wounds resurface, but I stay silent.",
        "You speak; I weigh every word."
    ])

# --------------------------------------------------------------
# >>> NEW for settlement rumor system
# --------------------------------------------------------------

# 1. Settlement data (inline, but can be loaded from JSON file)
settlements = [
    {
        "name": "Greywatch",
        "region": "Eastern Marshes",
        "dominant_faction": "Marsh Sentinels",
        "key_events": ["recent flood", "trade conflict with Rivertown"],
        "current_mood": "wary but resilient",
        "player_reputation": "neutral"
    },
```

```
    {
        "name": "Duskfall",
        "region": "Northern Highlands",
        "dominant_faction": "Ember Guard",
        "key_events": ["recent raid on trade routes"],
        "current_mood": "suspicious and guarded",
        "player_reputation": "hostile"
    }
]

def build_rumor_prompt(s):
    return (
        f"Write a short rumor (under 50 words) about {s['name']} in the
        {s['region']}. "
        f"The town is controlled by the {s['dominant_faction']} and
        recently faced "
        f"{', '.join(s['key_events'])}. "
        f"The mood is {s['current_mood']}, and the player reputation is
        {s['player_reputation']}."
    )

def generate_local_rumor(s):
    mood = s["current_mood"]
    event = random.choice(s["key_events"])
    return f"Locals whisper that after the {event}, {s['name']} has
    grown {mood}, unsure what tomorrow brings."

# -------------------------------------------------

# Templates
# -------------------------------------------------

BASE_HTML = """
<!doctype html>
<html>
  <head>
    <meta charset="utf-8" />
    <title>Ayo – Interactive Scenes</title>
```

```
    <style>
      body { font-family: system-ui; padding: 24px; background:#f6f7fb }
      .card { background: white; padding: 18px; border-radius: 12px;
      box-shadow: 0 4px 14px rgba(20,20,50,0.06); margin-bottom: 12px }
      .scene-list { display:flex; gap:12px; flex-wrap:wrap }
      .scene { width: 280px }
    </style>
  </head>
  <body>
    <h1>Ayo – Interactive Scenes</h1>

    <nav style="margin-bottom:20px;">
      <!-- >>> NEW navigation link -->
      <a href="{{ url_for('settlement_list') }}"> Settlements</a>
    </nav>

    <div class="card">
      <h3>Scenes</h3>
      <div class="scene-list">
        {% for key, s in scenes.items() %}
          <div class="scene card">
            <h4>{{ key }}</h4>
            <p>{{ s.description }}</p>
            <a href="{{ url_for('scene_view', scene_name=key) }}">Go</a>
          </div>
        {% endfor %}
      </div>
    </div>
  </body>
</html>
"""

# >>> NEW settlement list template
SETTLEMENTS_HTML = """
<h1>Settlements</h1>
<ul>
{% for s in settlements %}
```

```
  <li>
    <strong>{{ s.name }}</strong> - {{ s.region }}
    <a href="{{ url_for('generate_rumor', name=s.name) }}">Generate
    Rumor</a>
  </li>
{% endfor %}
</ul>
<a href="{{ url_for('index') }}">← Back</a>
"""

# >>> NEW rumor result template
RUMOR_HTML = """
<h2>Rumor from {{ settlement.name }}</h2>
<p>{{ rumor }}</p>
<a href="{{ url_for('settlement_list') }}">← Back</a>
"""

SCENE_HTML = """
<!doctype html>
<html>
<head>
<meta charset="utf-8" />
<title>{{ scene_name }}</title>
</head>
<body>
<a href="{{ url_for('index') }}">← Back</a>
<h2>{{ scene_name.replace('_',' ').title() }}</h2>
<p>{{ scene.description }}</p>

<form method="post" action="{{ url_for('choose', scene_name=scene_
name) }}">
{% for idx, choice in enumerate(scene.choices) %}
<div style="margin-bottom:8px">
<button class="choice" name="choice_index" value="{{ idx }}">{{ choice.
text }}</button>
</div>
{% endfor %}
```

```
</form>
</body>
</html>
"""

OUTCOME_HTML = """
<!doctype html>
<html>
<head>
<meta charset="utf-8" />
<title>Outcome</title>
</head>
<body>
<a href="{{ url_for('index') }}">← Back to scenes</a>
<h2>Outcome</h2>
<p><strong>Player chose:</strong> {{ player_choice }}</p>
<p><strong>Ayo response:</strong> {{ ayo_response }}</p>

<div style="margin-top:12px">
<strong>Updated Ayo:</strong>
<div>Trust: {{ ayo.trust }} / Anger: {{ ayo.anger }}</div>
<div>Recent memories: {{ ayo.memory[-5:] }}</div>
</div>
</body>
</html>
"""

# ---------------------------------------------------
# Routes
# ---------------------------------------------------

@app.route("/")
def index():
    ayo = get_ayo_from_session()
    ayo.decay_emotion()
    save_ayo_to_session(ayo)
    return render_template_string(BASE_HTML, scenes=scenes)
```

```
# >>> NEW: Settlement list page
@app.route("/settlements")
def settlement_list():
    return render_template_string(SETTLEMENTS_HTML,
    settlements=settlements)

# >>> NEW: Rumor generator
@app.route("/rumor/<name>")
def generate_rumor(name):
    settlement = next((s for s in settlements if s["name"].lower() ==
    name.lower()), None)
    if not settlement:
        flash("Unknown settlement")
        return redirect(url_for("settlement_list"))
    prompt = build_rumor_prompt(settlement)
    rumor = call_openai(prompt)
    if rumor is None:
        rumor = generate_local_rumor(settlement)

    return render_template_string(RUMOR_HTML, rumor=rumor,
    settlement=settlement)

# (Scene routes unchanged)
@app.route("/scene/<scene_name>")
def scene_view(scene_name):
    if scene_name not in scenes:
        return redirect(url_for("index"))
    return render_template_string(SCENE_HTML, scene_name=scene_name,
    scene=scenes[scene_name])

@app.route("/choose/<scene_name>", methods=["POST"])
def choose(scene_name):
    if scene_name not in scenes:
        return redirect(url_for('index'))
    idx = int(request.form.get("choice_index", 0))
    choice_obj = scenes[scene_name]["choices"][idx]
```

```
    ayo = get_ayo_from_session()
    ayo.apply_choice(
        choice_obj['text'],
        trust_change=choice_obj.get('trust_change', 0),
        anger_change=choice_obj.get('anger_change', 0)
    )
    save_ayo_to_session(ayo)
    prompt = build_prompt(ayo, choice_obj['text'])
    response = call_openai(prompt) or local_fallback_response(ayo,
    choice_obj['text'])

    return render_template_string(OUTCOME_HTML, player_choice=choice_
    obj['text'], ayo_response=response, ayo=ayo)

if __name__ == "__main__":
    app.run(debug=True)
```

Game Screenshots

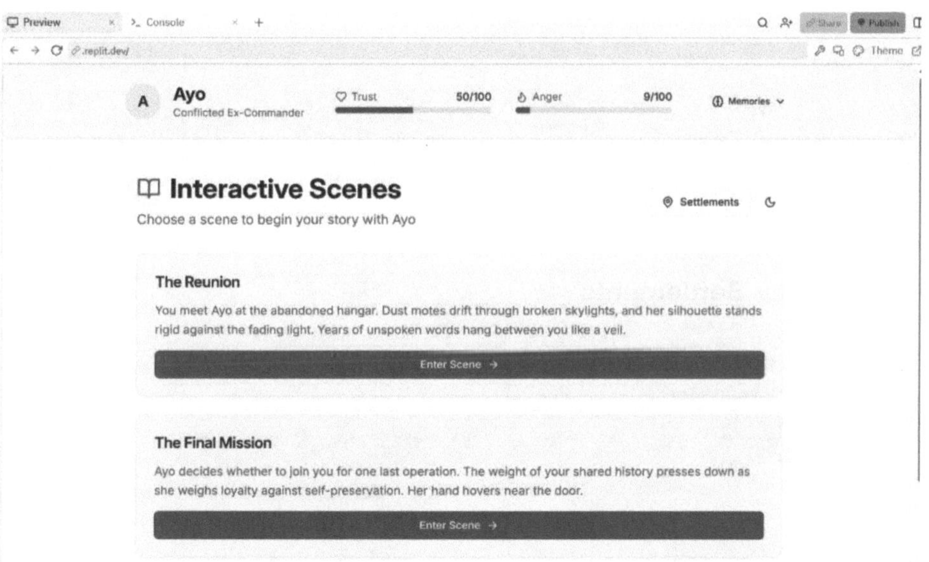

Figure 14-2. *Screenshot-1 of the extended web game*

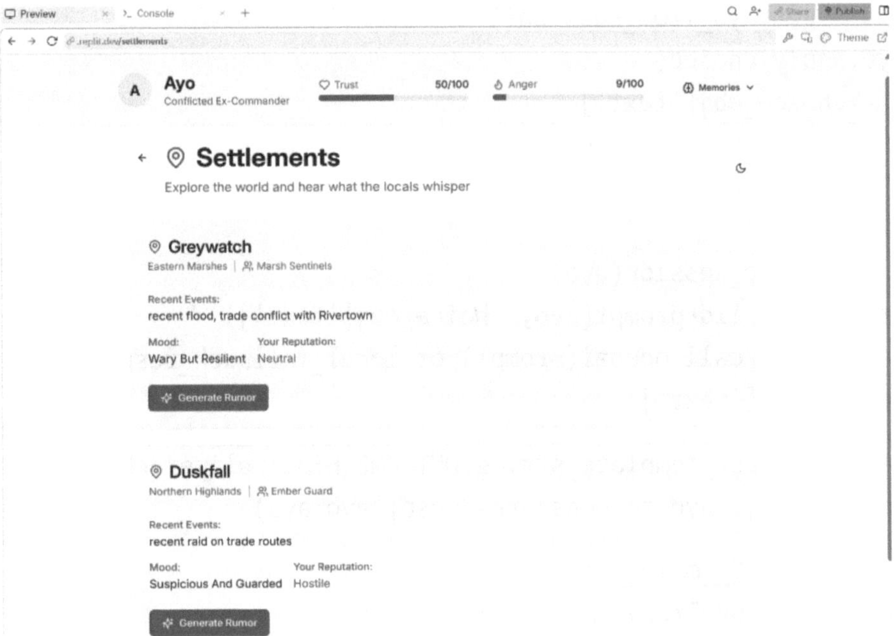

Figure 14-3. *Screenshot-2 of the extended web game*

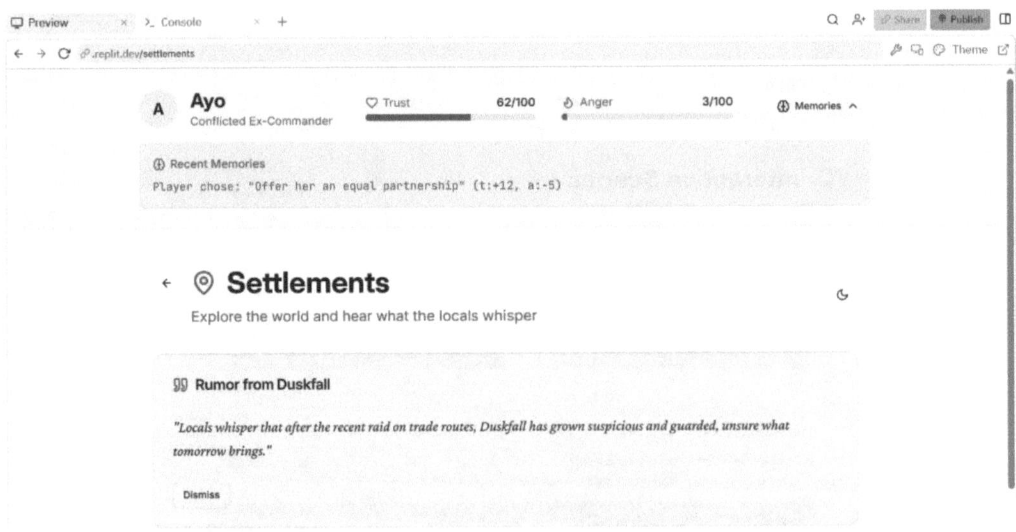

Figure 14-4. *Screenshot-3 of the extended web game*

In the next and final section, we'll explore how to maintain coherence and narrative integrity while scaling these procedural narrative systems to larger worlds and longer play sessions.

Scaling and Narrative Integrity

As your procedural narrative systems expand across larger worlds and longer campaigns, one of the biggest challenges is ensuring that all generated content remains coherent and consistent with the core story and themes of your game. At small scales, it's easy to manually monitor and adjust AI-generated lore or local rumors. But when your game world includes dozens of settlements, hundreds of characters, and emergent player-driven storylines, narrative drift and contradictions can quickly become a problem.

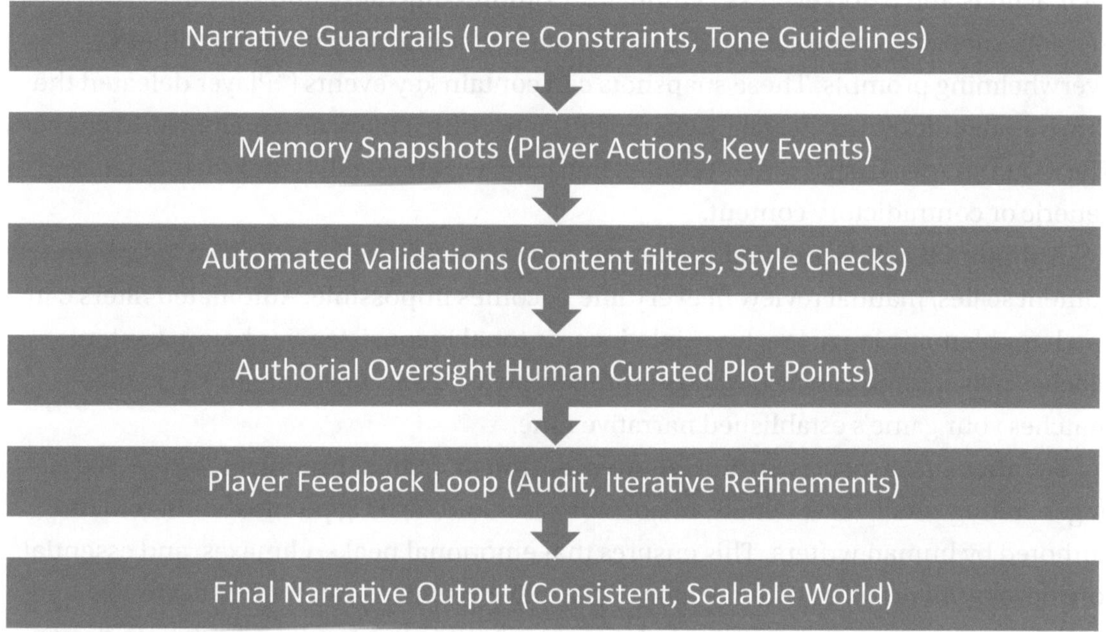

***Figure 14-5.** Pipeline for maintaining narrative integrity as procedural systems scale, combining technical and narrative safeguards*

The first pillar of maintaining narrative integrity at scale is **establishing strict narrative guardrails**. These include lore constraints, tone guidelines, and thematic boundaries that all generated content must respect. Rather than leaving prompts open-ended, include explicit instructions to the AI about faction motivations, cultural taboos, or character values. For example: *"Never suggest that the Ember Guard engages in necromancy; they consider it a deep heresy."* Clear guardrails ensure even unexpected rumors or dynamic events remain believable and consistent.

Although it may seem counterintuitive, constraints do not undermine dynamic generation—they enable it to work at scale. AI performs best when it has clear thematic boundaries but creative freedom within them. Guardrails ensure that generated content always respects the world's tone, lore, and cultural logic while still allowing the AI to improvise endlessly within those parameters. In other words, the AI generates dynamically, but it does so inside a well-defined narrative "sandbox" that preserves coherence as the world evolves.

The second strategy is **context layering and memory snapshots**. As players explore, their actions and world events accumulate. Compressing these into summarized memory snapshots allows AI to maintain a sense of narrative continuity without overwhelming prompts. These snapshots can contain key events ("Player defeated the Crimson Bandits at Greywatch"), character relationship states, and major world changes. These summaries keep the AI grounded in what has happened, rather than defaulting to generic or contradictory content.

Automated validation and moderation systems also become crucial. As generated content scales, manual review of every line becomes impossible. Automated filters can catch problematic language, lore violations, or tonal inconsistencies before content reaches players. You can also build automated style checks to ensure the AI's voice matches your game's established narrative tone.

Another vital aspect is **authorial intervention at critical junctures**. While AI excels at generating small, local details, major story arcs and turning points should remain authored by human writers. This ensures that emotional peaks, climaxes, and essential lore developments align with the game's narrative vision. AI can handle flavor text and emergent micro-stories, but critical plot events should always reflect deliberate design.

Scalability also involves **technical performance considerations**. Pre-generating content for regions players are likely to visit soon, or caching frequently used narrative fragments, helps reduce latency and API costs. This maintains a smooth gameplay experience even as the world becomes richer and more reactive.

Finally, **continuous testing and iterative refinement** are essential. As more generated content enters the game, designers should routinely audit world states, logs, and player experiences to spot emergent contradictions or missed opportunities. Feedback loops from players are especially valuable, highlighting which generated content feels most meaningful and which areas need tightening.

Conclusion

When executed thoughtfully, scaling AI-driven procedural narratives doesn't dilute your game's core story; it enriches it, giving players a sense that they are shaping and discovering a living world. By combining strong narrative guardrails, layered context, automated moderation, and careful human authorship at key moments, you can create experiences that feel both infinite and deeply personal.

CHAPTER 15

Advanced Applications in C# and Unity

As the boundaries between narrative design and real-time interactivity continue to blur, Unity remains one of the most powerful engines for translating generative storytelling concepts into immersive player experiences. While previous chapters explored frameworks for branching narratives and emotionally adaptive storytelling, this chapter focuses on the practical implementation of those systems using C# within the Unity ecosystem. We will examine how AI-powered dialogue, procedural events, and sentiment-aware mechanics can be integrated into playable scenes—bridging the gap between conceptual design and functional gameplay. Whether you're building a dialogue-driven RPG or a dynamically generated mystery, the tools and workflows presented here offer a flexible foundation for experimentation, iteration, and creative control.

This chapter assumes that readers have a working knowledge of Unity and its core development environment. Familiarity with concepts such as GameObjects, Prefabs, Scenes, Asset management, and MonoBehaviour scripting in C# will be essential as we move into hands-on implementations. While we will walk through each system's design and code architecture in detail, the examples are written for developers comfortable navigating Unity's interface, structuring components, and integrating custom scripts into a functioning project. If you're new to Unity, we recommend reviewing introductory resources before diving into the advanced techniques presented here.

Let's do a deep dive!

S. N. Gupta, *Generative AI for Game Development*, https://doi.org/10.1007/979-8-8688-2439-5_15

MYSTERY AT THE EMBERLIGHT TAVERN

An interactive narrative scene where the player engages in branching dialogue with emotionally adaptive NPCs powered by generative AI.

Scene Description

- **Setting**: A candlelit medieval tavern interior with ambient chatter and soft lute music
- **NPCs**
  - **Bartender**: Stoic, gives factual information
  - **Rogue**: Sarcastic, evasive, but knows key details
  - **Minstrel**: Empathic, emotionally reactive to the player's tone
- **UI Elements**
  - **Dialogue Box**: Displays NPC lines and player choices
  - **Mood Meter**: Shows inferred emotional tone of player choices (curious, aggressive, calm)

Project Folder Structure

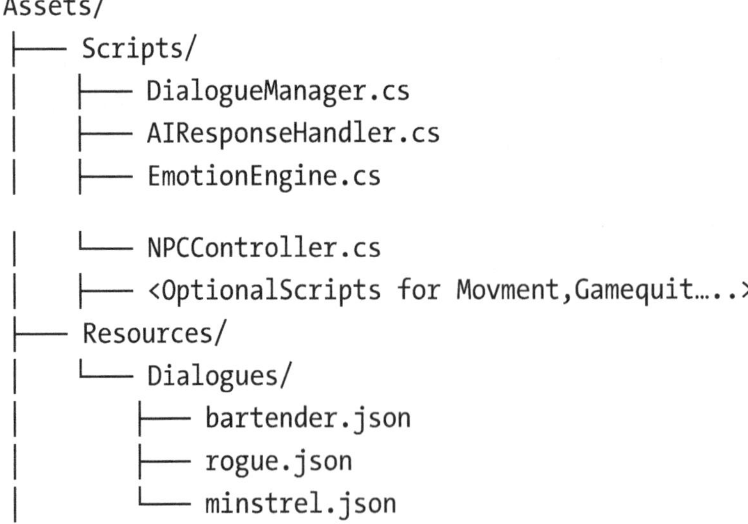

```
Assets/
├── Scripts/
│   ├── DialogueManager.cs
│   ├── AIResponseHandler.cs
│   ├── EmotionEngine.cs

│   └── NPCController.cs
│   ├── <OptionalScripts for Movment,Gamequit.....>
├── Resources/
│   └── Dialogues/
│       ├── bartender.json
│       ├── rogue.json
│       └── minstrel.json
│
```

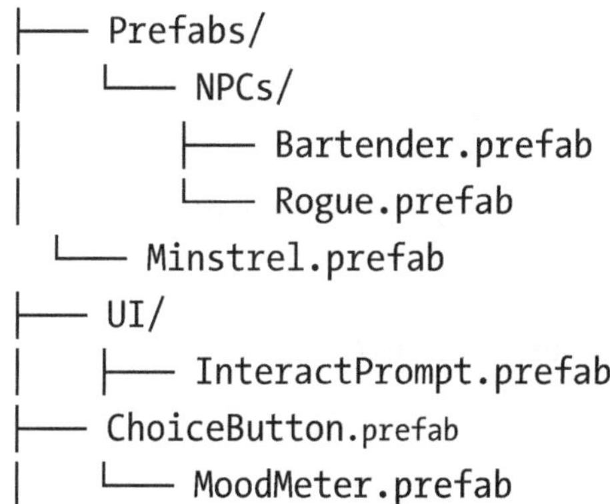

```
├── Prefabs/
│   └── NPCs/
│       ├── Bartender.prefab
│       └── Rogue.prefab
  └── Minstrel.prefab
├── UI/
│   ├── InteractPrompt.prefab
├── ChoiceButton.prefab
│   └── MoodMeter.prefab
```

Choose your own prefabs, vfx's, skyboxes, images…whatever you require to make this game look beautiful, and put inside the UI or Prefabs folder.

Game Logic Flow

```
[Player selects an NPC]
    ↓
[DialogueManager loads dialogue tree from JSON]
    ↓
[Player selects a dialogue option]
    ↓
[EmotionEngine analyzes player's tone (optional)]
    ↓
[If AI response required → AIResponseHandler sends request to OpenAI]
    ↓
[NPC delivers next line - static or AI-generated]
    ↓
[Branching continues based on emotion, choice, or random trigger]
```

Scene Setup Instructions

1) **Create the Scene**
   - In Unity (Unity Version: Use 2021.3 LTS or newer), create a new project and choose type 3D URP.
   - Create a new Scene ➤ Save as Assets/Scenes/Emberlight.unity.
2) **Create the Player**
   - GameObject ➤ 3D Object ➤ Capsule (rename to Player).
   - Add a CharacterController component.
   - Tag the object "Player".
   - Create a simple PlayerMovement script or use a Standard Asset controller.
   - Add a Camera as a child of the Capsule; position it appropriately to view the game view and perspective.
3) **Create the Tavern room** using primitives
   - **Floor**: 3D Object ➤ Plane (scale to 6×6).
   - **Walls**: 3D Object ➤ Cube (scale thin, tall).
   - **Bar**: Cubes scaled into counter shape.
   - Place a Point Light or two (emissive) for atmosphere.
4) **Create UI**
   - Canvas (Screen Space—Overlay).
   - Add TextMeshPro—create the DialogueText and SpeakerName.
   - Add an empty GameObject under Canvas for ChoicesContainer (Vertical Layout Group).
   - Create a Button with TMP text, make it a prefab named ChoiceButton, and link in DialogueManager.
   - Create game objects to hold Images which go in the background of Dialogue and Instructions (which is only shown at the start of the game for 8s).

Use your prefabs to make all your models and UI elements look beautiful.

This is how your typical Canvas will look after completing the above steps.

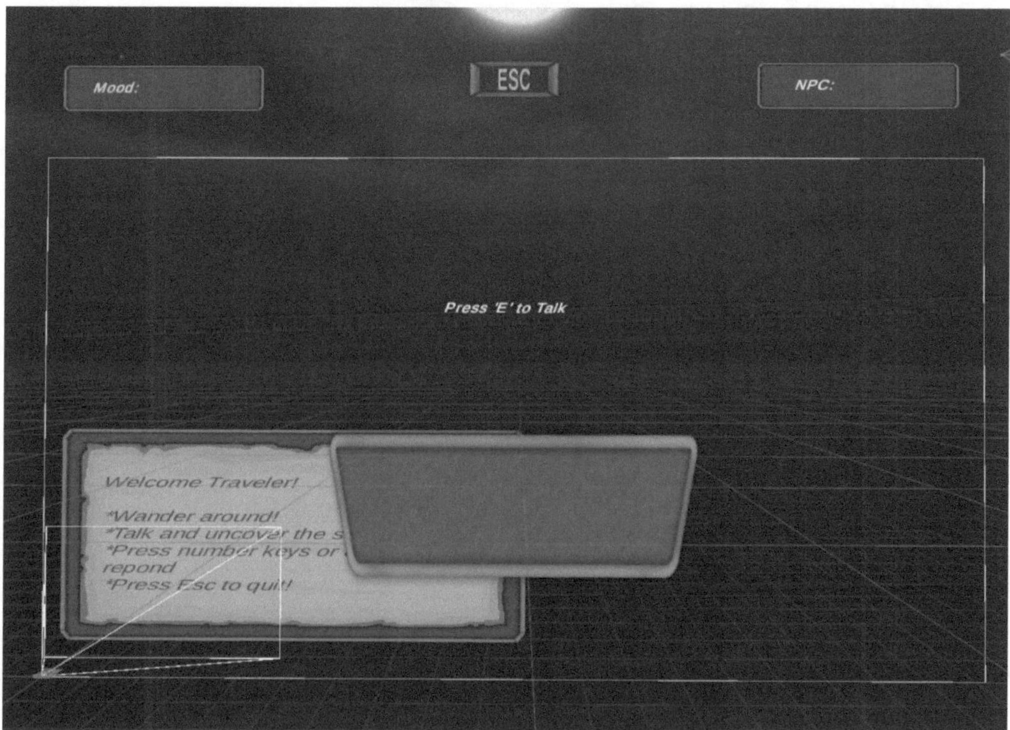

Figure 15-1. *Canvas setup*

Ignore the overlapping as they are controlled in the Dialogue manager script.

5) **Create NPCs**

- Create three Capsules for NPCs: Bartender, Rogue, and Minstrel.
- Add a Sphere Collider or Capsule Collider (set IsTrigger=true).

- Add the NPCController script to each; set dialogueFileName appropriately (e.g., bartender.json).
- Position Bartender, Rogue, and Minstrel per your liking.

6) **Create Dialogue System**

- Empty GameObject ➤ DialogueSystem.
- Add DialogueManager, AIResponseHandler, and EmotionEngine components.
- Drag DialogueText, SpeakerName, ChoicesContainer, and ChoiceButton prefab into DialogueManager fields.
- Since we are using Local LLM setup using Ollama, no need to put any API keys or so. Find the setup details here: `https://docs.ollama.com/quickstart`.

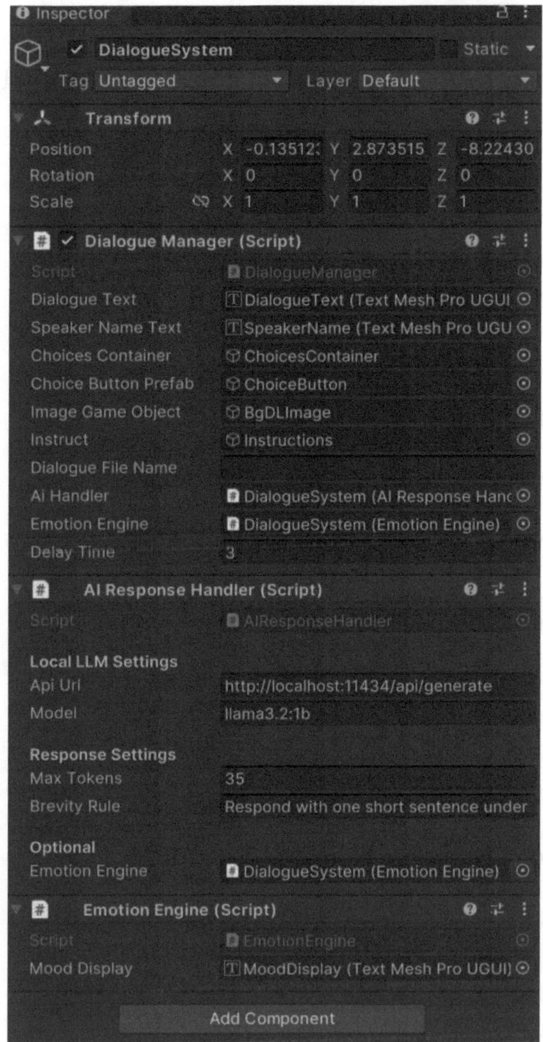

Figure 15-2. *DialogueSystem setup*

This is probably the most important step and may be a bit tricky, but can be done without any issues if you are patient!

---

7) **Press Play**

- Move the Player near an NPC collider and press "E" to start a conversation.

Codes and Explanations

Now, let's begin with the **core of our AI-driven storytelling system** in Unity: the `DialogueManager.cs`.

1. **DialogueManager.cs**

   This script is responsible for

   - Loading dialogue trees (from JSON or ScriptableObjects)
   - Displaying NPC dialogue
   - Managing player choices
   - Triggering AI-generated responses when needed
   - Communicating with the Emotion Engine (if enabled)

```
using System.Collections.Generic;
using UnityEngine;
using TMPro;
using System.IO;
using UnityEngine.UI;

public class DialogueManager : MonoBehaviour

{

    [System.Serializable]
    public class DialogueNode
    {

        public string id;
        public string speaker;
        public string text;
        public bool useAI;
        public List<Choice> choices;
    }
```

```
[System.Serializable]
public class Choice
{
    public string text;
    public string nextNodeId;
}

[System.Serializable]
public class DialogueContainer
{
    public List<DialogueNode> nodes;
}

public TextMeshProUGUI dialogueText;
public TextMeshProUGUI speakerNameText;
public GameObject choicesContainer;
public GameObject choiceButtonPrefab;
public GameObject imageGameObject;
public GameObject instruct;

public string dialogueFileName;
public AIResponseHandler aiHandler;
public EmotionEngine emotionEngine;

private Dictionary<string, DialogueNode> dialogueTree;
private DialogueNode currentNode;
private List<string> currentChoiceIds = new List<string>();
public float delayTime = 5f;

public void StartDialogue()
{
    // OPTIONAL: enable UI clicking
    Cursor.visible = true;
    Cursor.lockState = CursorLockMode.None;
    LoadDialogue(dialogueFileName);
    DisplayNode("start");
}
```

```
void LoadDialogue(string fileName)
{
    string path = Path.Combine(Application.streamingAssetsPath,
    fileName);
    if (!File.Exists(path))
    {
        Debug.LogError("Dialogue JSON not found: " + path);
        return;
    }

    string jsonText = File.ReadAllText(path);
    DialogueContainer container = JsonUtility.FromJson<Dialogue
    Container>(jsonText);
    //instruct.SetActive(false);
    dialogueTree = new Dictionary<string, DialogueNode>();
    foreach (var node in container.nodes)
        dialogueTree[node.id] = node;
}

public void DisplayNode(string nodeId)
{
    // If the node is "end", close the dialogue immediately
    if (nodeId == "end")
    {
        EndDialogue();
        return;
    }
    if (!dialogueTree.TryGetValue(nodeId, out currentNode))
    {
        Debug.LogError("Missing dialogue node: " + nodeId);
        return;
    }
    ClearChoices();
    speakerNameText.text = "NPC: "+currentNode.speaker;
    imageGameObject.SetActive(true);
    if (currentNode.useAI)
```

```
    {
        aiHandler.GenerateAIResponse(currentNode, (string aiText) =>
        {
            dialogueText.text = aiText;
            emotionEngine?.AnalyzeText(aiText); //check AI
            reponse emotion
            CreateChoiceButtons(currentNode.choices);
        });
    }
    else
    {
        dialogueText.text = currentNode.text;
        CreateChoiceButtons(currentNode.choices);
        emotionEngine?.AnalyzeText(currentNode.text);
    }
}
void CreateChoiceButtons(List<Choice> choices)
{
    currentChoiceIds.Clear();
    for (int i = 0; i < choices.Count; i++)
    {
        var choice = choices[i];
        currentChoiceIds.Add(choice.nextNodeId);
        // Create UI button
        GameObject btn = Instantiate(choiceButtonPrefab,
        choicesContainer.transform);
        // Show number in UI like "1. Ask about the town"
        btn.GetComponentInChildren<TextMeshProUGUI>().text = $"{i +
        1}. {choice.text}";
        string nextId = choice.nextNodeId;
        // Button still works if mouse is unlocked
        btn.GetComponent<Button>().onClick.AddListener(() =>
        DisplayNode(nextId));
    }
}
```

```
    void Update()
    {
        // Check 1 9 keys for selecting choices
        for (int i = 0; i < currentChoiceIds.Count; i++)
        {
            if (Input.GetKeyDown(KeyCode.Alpha1 + i))
            {
                DisplayNode(currentChoiceIds[i]);
                return;
            }
        }
    }
    void Start()
    {
        // Deactivate the Image GameObject at the start
        imageGameObject.SetActive(false);
        Invoke("ToggleActivation", delayTime);
    }
    void ToggleActivation()
    {
        instruct.SetActive(false); // Toggles active state
    }
    void ClearChoices()
    {
        foreach (Transform child in choicesContainer.transform)
            Destroy(child.gameObject);
    }
    public void EndDialogue()
    {
        // Hide the UI
        dialogueText.text = "";
        speakerNameText.text = "NPC:";
        imageGameObject.SetActive(false);
        ClearChoices();
```

```
            // OPTIONAL: re-lock mouse if you are using FPS controls
            Cursor.visible = false;
            Cursor.lockState = CursorLockMode.Locked;
        }
    }
```

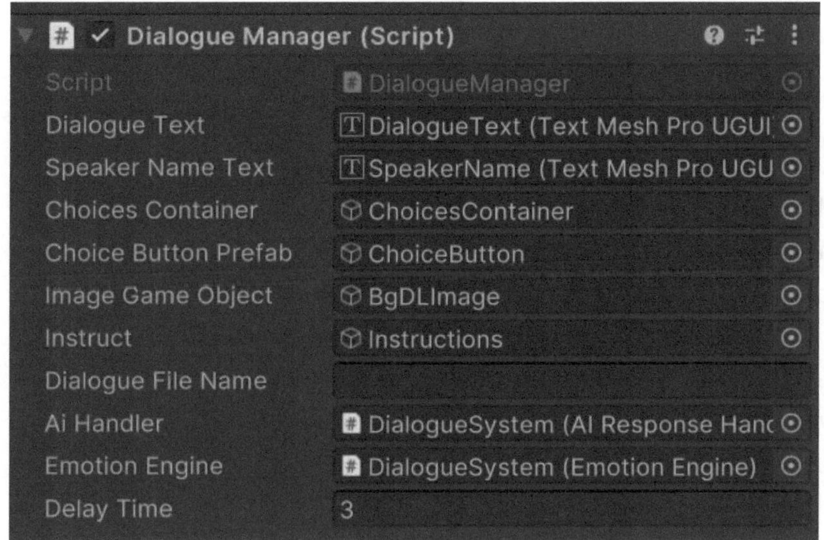

***Figure 15-3.** Dialogue manager script setup*

***Table 15-1.** Key Components Explained: DialogueManager.cs*

Component	Purpose
DialogueNode	Stores a dialogue line, its speaker, and possible choices.
useAI	Boolean that decides if the response should be generated by an AI model.
LoadDialogue()	Reads a JSON file containing a list of dialogue nodes.
DisplayNode()	Displays current dialogue and triggers AI or static text.
CreateChoiceButtons()	Dynamically builds UI buttons for player responses.
emotionEngine.AnalyzeText()	Hooks into a sentiment/emotion tracker.

2. **EmotionEngine.cs**

   This script is designed to

   - Analyze dialogue text (player or NPC) for emotional tone.
   - Optionally update the UI (e.g., a "Mood Meter" or colored text effect).
   - Expose the detected emotion so it can influence branching logic or AI prompts.

```
using UnityEngine;
using TMPro;
using UnityEngine.UI;
public class EmotionEngine : MonoBehaviour
{
    public TextMeshProUGUI moodDisplay;
    private string currentEmotion = "neutral";
    public void AnalyzeText(string text)
    {
        text = text.ToLower();
        if (Contains(text, new[] { "angry", "hate", "furious",
        "fight" }))
            currentEmotion = "angry";
        else if (Contains(text, new[] { "sad", "cry", "upset",
        "lonely" }))
            currentEmotion = "sad";
        else if (Contains(text, new[] { "happy", "great", "love", "fun",
        "happyily" }))
            currentEmotion = "happy";
        else if (Contains(text, new[] { "nervous", "afraid",
        "worried" }))
            currentEmotion = "fearful";
        else
            currentEmotion = "neutral";
        UpdateUI();
    }
```

```
    bool Contains(string input, string[] list)
    {
        foreach (string word in list)
            if (input.Contains(word))
                return true;
        return false;
    }
    void UpdateUI()
    {
        if (moodDisplay == null) return;
        moodDisplay.text = "Mood: " + currentEmotion;
        moodDisplay.color = GetColor(currentEmotion);
    }
    Color GetColor(string emotion)
    {
        switch (emotion)
        {
            case "angry": return Color.red;
            case "sad": return Color.blue;
            case "happy": return Color.green;
            case "fearful": return new Color(1f, 0.6f, 0f);
            default: return Color.white;
        }
    }
    public string GetCurrentEmotion() => currentEmotion;
}
```

Table 15-2. Key Components Explained: EmotionEngine.cs

Component	Purpose
AnalyzeText(string text)	Main entry point. Performs keyword-based sentiment detection (happy, sad, angry, etc.). Can be extended to use AI/ML sentiment analysis.
ContainsAny(string input, string[] keywords)	Utility function that checks if the input text contains any keyword from a defined emotion list.
UpdateUI()	Updates a UI element to reflect the detected emotional state, including color-coded feedback (e.g., red for anger, blue for sadness).
GetColor (string emotion)	Maps each emotion to a visual color to reinforce affective feedback.
GetCurrentEmotion()	Public method to expose the most recently detected emotion to other scripts (e.g., AIResponseHandler or DialogueManager).

3. **AIResponseHandler.cs**

   This script handles

   - Prompt construction
   - Calling the Local LLM API (or any other API like OpenAI's API)
   - Handling responses
   - Returning the generated text back to the `DialogueManager`

```
using System;
using System.Collections;
using UnityEngine;
using UnityEngine.Networking;
using System.Text;

public class AIResponseHandler : MonoBehaviour
{
    [Header("Local LLM Settings")]
    public string apiUrl = "http://localhost:11434/api/generate";
    // Ollama endpoint
```

```
public string model = "llama3.2:1b";
// Your local model

[Header("Response Settings")]
[Tooltip("Approx limit for output. 35 = 1 short sentence.")]
public int maxTokens = 35;

[Tooltip("Instruction to keep responses short.")]
public string brevityRule = "Respond with one short sentence under
15 words.";

private string personaName = "";
private string personaDescription = "";

[Header("Optional")]
public EmotionEngine emotionEngine;

// ---------------------------------------------------------------
// Persona Setup
// ---------------------------------------------------------------
public void SetPersona(string name, string description)
{
    personaName = name;
    personaDescription = description;
}
// --------------------------------------------------------------
// Entry Point (called by DialogueManager)
// ---------------------------------------------------------------
public void GenerateAIResponse(DialogueManager.DialogueNode node,
Action<string> callback)
{
    // First check if Ollama is running
    StartCoroutine(CheckOllamaRunning((isRunning) =>
    {
        if (!isRunning)
        {
```

```
                // Graceful fallback
                callback?.Invoke("(The NPC seems confused and can't form
                a response.)");
                return;
            }
            // Build emotional prompt
            string emotion = emotionEngine != null ? emotionEngine.
            GetCurrentEmotion() : "neutral";
            string prompt =
                $"You are {personaName}. Personality:
                {personaDescription}. " +
                $"Speak in a {emotion} tone. {brevityRule} " +
                $"Player says: \"{node.text}\"";
            StartCoroutine(SendRequest(prompt, callback));
        }));
    }
    // ------------------------------------------------------------
    // Health Check - see if Ollama is running
    // ------------------------------------------------------------
    public IEnumerator CheckOllamaRunning(Action<bool> callback)
    {
        UnityWebRequest request = UnityWebRequest.Get("http://
        localhost:11434/api/tags");
        // 0.5 sec timeout is enough
        request.timeout = 1;
        yield return request.SendWebRequest();
        bool ok = request.result == UnityWebRequest.Result.Success;
        callback(ok);
    }
    // ------------------------------------------------------------
    // Main Request to local LLM
    // ------------------------------------------------------------
    IEnumerator SendRequest(string prompt, Action<string> callback)
    {
        OllamaRequest body = new OllamaRequest
```

```
    {
        model = model,
        prompt = prompt,
        stream = false,
        num_predict = maxTokens
    };
    string jsonBody = JsonUtility.ToJson(body);
    byte[] raw = Encoding.UTF8.GetBytes(jsonBody);
    UnityWebRequest request = new UnityWebRequest(apiUrl, "POST");
    request.uploadHandler = new UploadHandlerRaw(raw);
    request.downloadHandler = new DownloadHandlerBuffer();
    request.SetRequestHeader("Content-Type", "application/json");
    request.timeout = 10;
    yield return request.SendWebRequest();
    // Error handling
    if (request.result != UnityWebRequest.Result.Success)
    {
        Debug.LogWarning("Local LLM unreachable: " + request.error);
        callback?.Invoke("(The NPC stares blankly, unable to
        respond.)");
        yield break;
    }
    // Parse response
    OllamaResponse response =
        JsonUtility.FromJson<OllamaResponse>(request.download
        Handler.text);
    string output = response.response;
    if (string.IsNullOrEmpty(output))
        output = "(No response produced by the local AI.)";
    callback?.Invoke(output);
}
// -------------------------------------------------------------
// JSON Structures
// -------------------------------------------------------------
[Serializable]
```

```
    public class OllamaRequest
    {
        public string model;
        public string prompt;
        public bool stream;
        public int num_predict;
    }
    [Serializable]
    public class OllamaResponse
    {
        public string response;
    }
}
```

Table 15-3. *Key Components Explained: AIResponseHandler.cs*

Component	Purpose
GenerateAIResponse()	Called by the DialogueManager. Accepts a DialogueNode, constructs a prompt that tells the LLM how to respond, including persona and emotional tone (e.g., "You are a suspicious bartender in a fearful tone…"), and initiates an asynchronous API call.
SendRequest()	Sends a formatted JSON payload to the OpenAI Chat API, awaits the response, parses it, and returns the generated text via a callback function.

4. **NPCController.cs**

   The script that connects each NPC in the scene to the dialogue system and controls things like

   - Dialogue trigger
   - Character identity
   - Animation/visual control
   - AI personalization

```
using UnityEngine;
public class NPCController : MonoBehaviour
{
    public string npcName = "Bartender";
    public string dialogueFileName = "bartender.json";
    [TextArea(2, 5)]
    public string personalityDescription = "A cautious bartender who
    avoids confrontation.";
    private DialogueManager dialogueManager;
    private bool playerInRange = false;
    // Assign this in the Inspector (drag the InteractPrompt UI
    object here)
    public GameObject interactPrompt;
    void Start()
    {
        dialogueManager = FindObjectOfType<DialogueManager>();
        // If you forgot to assign in Inspector, try to warn instead
        of fail:
        if (interactPrompt == null)
            Debug.LogWarning($"{name}: interactPrompt not assigned in
            Inspector. Assign it to show 'Press E to talk' UI.");
        interactPrompt.SetActive(false);
    }
    void Update()
    {
        if (playerInRange && Input.GetKeyDown(KeyCode.E))
        {
            if (interactPrompt != null)
                interactPrompt.SetActive(false);
                //interactPrompt.text = "PRESS \'E\' TO TALK";
            StartDialogue();
        }
    }
```

```
    void StartDialogue()
    {
        if (dialogueManager == null)
            dialogueManager = FindObjectOfType<DialogueManager>();
        if (dialogueManager == null)
        {
            Debug.LogError("DialogueManager not found in scene.");
            return;
        }
        dialogueManager.dialogueFileName = dialogueFileName;
        if (dialogueManager.aiHandler != null)
            dialogueManager.aiHandler.SetPersona(npcName,
            personalityDescription);
        dialogueManager.StartDialogue();
    }
    void OnTriggerEnter(Collider other)
    {
        if (other.CompareTag("Player"))
        {
            playerInRange = true;
            if (interactPrompt != null) interactPrompt.SetActive(true);
        }
    }
    void OnTriggerExit(Collider other)
    {
        if (other.CompareTag("Player"))
        {
            playerInRange = false;
            if (interactPrompt != null) interactPrompt.SetActive(false);
            dialogueManager.EndDialogue();
        }
    }
}
```

This game uses some additional scripts for player movement and game quit, and it is not described here, but those are readily available over the internet/Unity asset store. Feel free to use those as needed!

Table 15-4. *Key Components Explained: NPCController.cs*

Component	Purpose
npcName/ dialogueFileName	Identifies this character and links to their unique dialogue tree (JSON)
personalityDescription	Passed to the AI to influence dialogue tone (e.g., friendly, hostile, humorous)
playerInRange + Update()	Enables E-key interaction when near the NPC
StartDialogue()	Loads the file into DialogueManager, triggers the start node
OnTriggerEnter/Exit()	Handles proximity-based activation, used in 3D game environments

5. **Bartender.json**

   This file contains a branching dialogue tree for the **Bartender NPC**, including

   - Static lines (`useAI: false`)
   - AI-generated lines (`useAI: true`)
   - Player choices with `nextNodeId` references

```
[
  {
    "id": "start",
    "speaker": "Bartender",
    "text": "Evening, traveler. What brings you to Emberlight Tavern?",
    "useAI": false,
    "choices": [
      { "text": "I'm looking for someone.", "nextNodeId":
      "askForSomeone" },
```

```
      { "text": "Just passing through.", "nextNodeId": "casual" }
    ]
  },
  {
    "id": "askForSomeone",
    "speaker": "Bartender",
    "text": "Someone, eh? Depends who's asking.",
    "useAI": false,
    "choices": [
      { "text": "It's important. I think they're in danger.",
      "nextNodeId": "generateConcerned" },
      { "text": "None of your business. Just point me to the cellar.",
      "nextNodeId": "generateHostile" }
    ]
  },
  {
    "id": "generateConcerned",
    "speaker": "Bartender",
    "text": "The player is worried about someone in danger. Respond with
    hesitant concern and partial information.",
    "useAI": true,
    "choices": [
      { "text": "What aren't you telling me?", "nextNodeId":
      "generateSuspicious" },
      { "text": "Thanks. I'll be careful.", "nextNodeId": "end" }
    ]
  },
  {
    "id": "generateHostile",
    "speaker": "Bartender",
    "text": "The player is being aggressive and rude. Respond with
    caution and defensiveness.",
    "useAI": true,
```

```
  "choices": [
    { "text": "Sorry. I didn't mean to snap.", "nextNodeId":
    "generateApology" },
    { "text": "Forget it. I'll find them myself.",
    "nextNodeId": "end" }
  ]
},
{
  "id": "generateSuspicious",
  "speaker": "Bartender",
  "text": "The player is pressing you for more info. Respond as if
  hiding something.",
  "useAI": true,
  "choices": [
    { "text": "I'll check the cellar myself.", "nextNodeId": "end" }
  ]
},
{
  "id": "generateApology",
  "speaker": "Bartender",
  "text": "The player apologized. Respond with guarded forgiveness and
  hint about danger.",
  "useAI": true,
  "choices": [
    { "text": "Thanks. Can you show me where?", "nextNodeId": "end" }
  ]
},
{
  "id": "casual",
  "speaker": "Bartender",
  "text": "Well, drinks are strong and rooms are cheap. Just don't ask
  about the cellar.",
  "useAI": false,
```

```
      "choices": [
        { "text": "Why not the cellar?", "nextNodeId": "generate
        Mysterious" }
      ]
    },
    {
      "id": "generateMysterious",
      "speaker": "Bartender",
      "text": "The player asks about the cellar. Respond with mystery and
      reluctance.",
      "useAI": true,
      "choices": [
        { "text": "Now I really want to see it.", "nextNodeId": "end" }
      ]
    },
    {
      "id": "end",
      "speaker": "Bartender",
      "text": "Safe travels, stranger.",
      "useAI": false,
      "choices": []
    }
  ]
```

Table 15-5. *Key Fields Explained: bartender.json*

Field	Description
id	Unique ID for the node, used for branching logic
speaker	NPC name, shown in dialogue UI
text	The dialogue content (static or AI prompt hint)
useAI	If true, send this node's text as a prompt to the LLM
choices	Array of player options, each with a text and nextNodeId

---

Tip This structure allows mixing **scripted** and **AI-generated** responses seamlessly.

Now let's create `rogue.json` and `minstrel.json`—two unique NPCs that contrast with the bartender's tone and behavior. These files follow the same JSON structure and are designed to show off more personality-driven and AI-enhanced storytelling.

6. **Rogue.json**

   The Rogue is sarcastic, evasive, and enjoys confusing the player. Most of his dialogue is generated dynamically to reflect his unpredictable nature.

```
[
  {
    "id": "start",
    "speaker": "Rogue",
    "text": "Well, well... someone brave or foolish. Which are you?",
    "useAI": false,
    "choices": [
      { "text": "I'm looking for information.", "nextNodeId": "infoSeek" },
      { "text": "I'm not here to play games.", "nextNodeId":
      "generateMocking" }
    ]
  },
  {
    "id": "infoSeek",
    "speaker": "Rogue",
    "text": "Information? That depends on the currency. Gold? Secrets?
    Flattery?",
    "useAI": false,
    "choices": [
      { "text": "I can pay in gold.", "nextNodeId": "generateGreedy" },
      { "text": "I have secrets you'd kill to know.", "nextNodeId":
      "generateIntrigued" }
    ]
  },
```

```
{
  "id": "generateMocking",
  "speaker": "Rogue",
  "text": "The player is acting serious and impatient. Respond with
  dry sarcasm and misdirection.",
  "useAI": true,
  "choices": [
    { "text": "I’ll take that as a yes.", "nextNodeId": "end" }
  ]
},
{
  "id": "generateGreedy",
  "speaker": "Rogue",
  "text": "The player offers gold. Respond greedily but add a cryptic
  condition.",
  "useAI": true,
  "choices": [
    { "text": "Fine. What's the price?", "nextNodeId": "end" }
  ]
},
{
  "id": "generateIntrigued",
  "speaker": "Rogue",
  "text": "The player hints at dangerous secrets. Respond intrigued
  but suspicious.",
  "useAI": true,
  "choices": [
    { "text": "Let’s talk in private.", "nextNodeId": "end" }
  ]
},
{
  "id": "end",
  "speaker": "Rogue",
  "text": "Time's up. You want more? Come back when you're
  interesting.",
```

```
    "useAI": false,
    "choices": []
  }
]
```

7. **Minstrel.json**

   The Minstrel is empathetic and emotional. Her dialogue adapts based on the player's emotional tone, making her ideal for showcasing the `EmotionEngine`.

```
[
  {
    "id": "start",
    "speaker": "Minstrel",
    "text": "You seem weary. Would a song or a story lift your spirit?",
    "useAI": false,
    "choices": [
      { "text": "Tell me something beautiful.", "nextNodeId":
      "generatePoetic" },
      { "text": "I don't want to talk.", "nextNodeId":
      "generateCompassion" }
    ]
  },
  {
    "id": "generatePoetic",
    "speaker": "Minstrel",
    "text": "The player is seeking comfort or inspiration. Respond with
    a poetic tale or verse.",
    "useAI": true,
    "choices": [
      { "text": "That was lovely. Thank you.", "nextNodeId": "end" }
    ]
  },
  {
    "id": "generateCompassion",
    "speaker": "Minstrel",
    "text": "The player is emotionally closed off. Respond with kindness
    and soft encouragement.",
```

```
      "useAI": true,
      "choices": [
        { "text": "Maybe you're right… I just need space.",
        "nextNodeId": "end" }
      ]
    },
    {
      "id": "end",
      "speaker": "Minstrel",
      "text": "Even silence has its own melody. Travel safe, kind soul.",
      "useAI": false,
      "choices": []
    }
  ]
```

In this implementation, each NPC operates independently within a shared Unity scene, and conversations are initiated directly by the player. This approach mirrors familiar mechanics from RPGs and narrative adventure games, where players move freely through the environment and engage with characters at their own pace. Each NPC in the tavern—Bartender, Rogue, and Minstrel—is assigned its own `NPCController` and dialogue file. When the player clicks on or enters the proximity of an NPC, that character's dialogue tree is loaded into the `DialogueManager`, triggering a new interaction. This design allows for modular narrative flow, encourages exploration, and makes it easy to scale or substitute NPCs without altering the core dialogue system. It also ensures that each character retains their unique tone and AI behavior while keeping the scene structure clean and player-driven.

Dialogue File Integration Flow

Here's a **visual diagram** showing how the `.json` dialogue files integrate with the overall system:

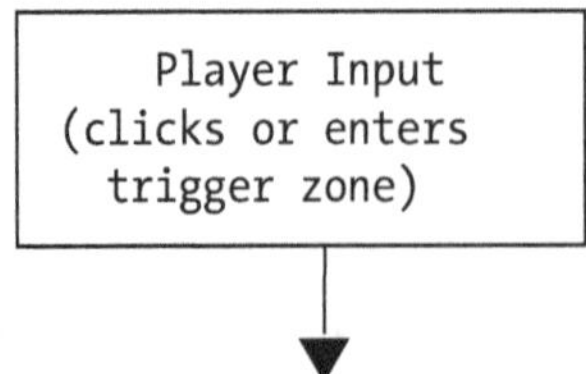

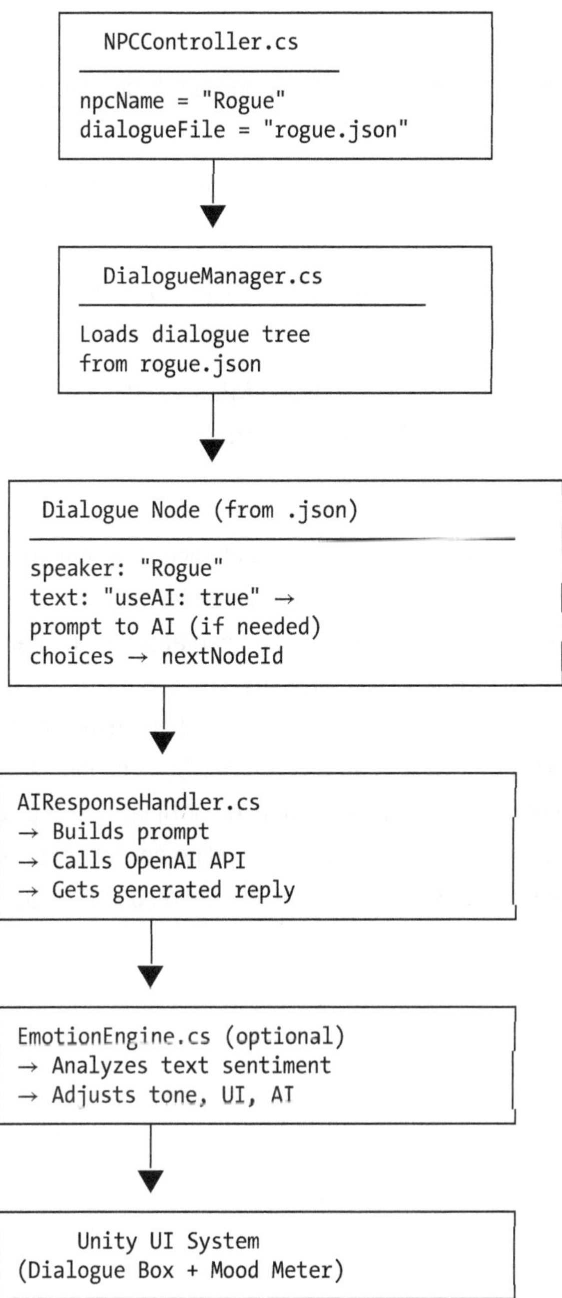
NPCController.cs
npcName = "Rogue"
dialogueFile = "rogue.json"
DialogueManager.cs
Loads dialogue tree
from rogue.json
Dialogue Node (from .json)
speaker: "Rogue"
text: "useAI: true" →
prompt to AI (if needed)
choices → nextNodeId
AIResponseHandler.cs
→ Builds prompt
→ Calls OpenAI API
→ Gets generated reply
EmotionEngine.cs (optional)
→ Analyzes text sentiment
→ Adjusts tone, UI, AI
Unity UI System
(Dialogue Box + Mood Meter)

Note that

- Each `.json` file acts as the **source of truth** for one NPC's branching dialogue logic.
- The system dynamically reads and renders the content based on player interaction.
- AI-powered responses are injected only when `useAI: true` is encountered.
- Everything remains modular—you can add new NPCs by creating a new `.json` and attaching it to another `NPCController`.

Prefab Setups

In Unity, **prefabs serve as reusable templates** for GameObjects and UI elements, enabling efficient scene construction and modular design. For this project, prefabs are essential for maintaining consistency across NPC interactions and UI presentation. Each interactive element—such as the `ChoiceButton`, `MoodMeter`, and `InteractPrompt`—is created once in the editor and saved as a prefab asset. These prefabs can then be instantiated dynamically at runtime by the `DialogueManager` or `NPCController` scripts, allowing for flexible branching dialogue systems without duplicating code or UI layout. This setup streamlines both development and iteration, especially when adding new characters or expanding dialogue trees, and ensures that all interactive elements respond consistently to player input and AI-generated content.

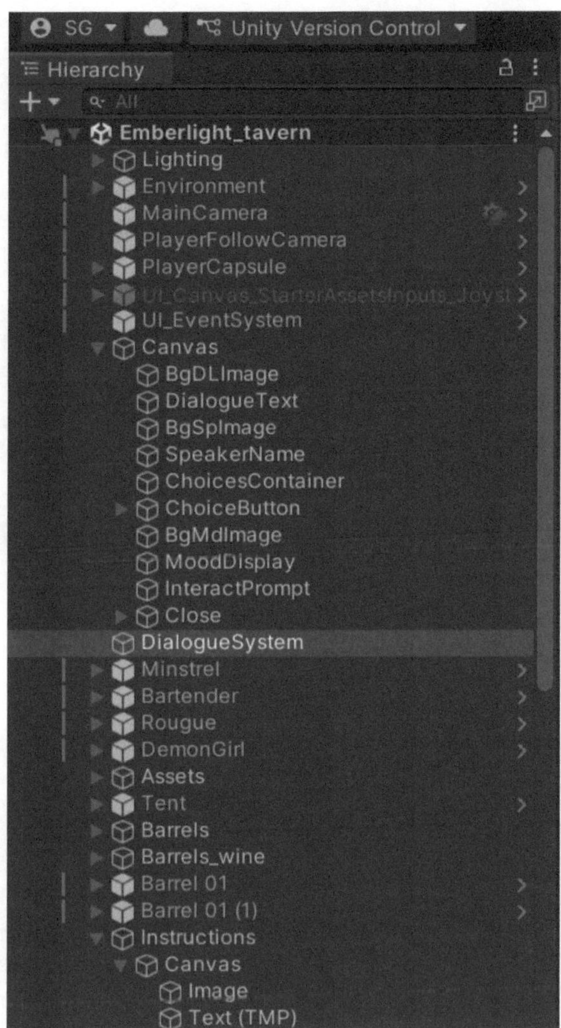

***Figure 15-4.** Unity prefab setup in Hierarchy*

When executed in-game, the dialogue system brings together narrative logic, generative AI, emotional feedback, and player interaction through a clean, layered UI. As the player approaches an NPC, an `InteractPrompt` appears, signaling that a conversation can be initiated. Once triggered, the `DialoguePanel` animates into view, displaying either a pre-written line or an AI-generated response tailored to the context and emotional tone. Beneath the dialogue, dynamically instantiated choice buttons appear, allowing the player to guide the direction of the conversation. Simultaneously, the `MoodMeter` updates to reflect the inferred emotional state, creating a sense of emotional continuity throughout the interaction. This seamless integration between player input, back-end logic, and front-end presentation creates a responsive and immersive narrative experience grounded in modular design and AI-driven adaptability.

***Figure 15-5.** Mystery at the Emberlight Tavern: entry*

***Figure 15-6.** Mystery at the Emberlight Tavern: initiating talk*

Figure 15-7. *Mystery at the Emberlight Tavern: updates in the UI after pressing "E"*

Figure 15-8. *Mystery at the Emberlight Tavern: MoodMeter updates based on the tone of the NPC*

***Figure 15-9.** Mystery at the Emberlight Tavern: AI-responded dialogue after choosing an option*

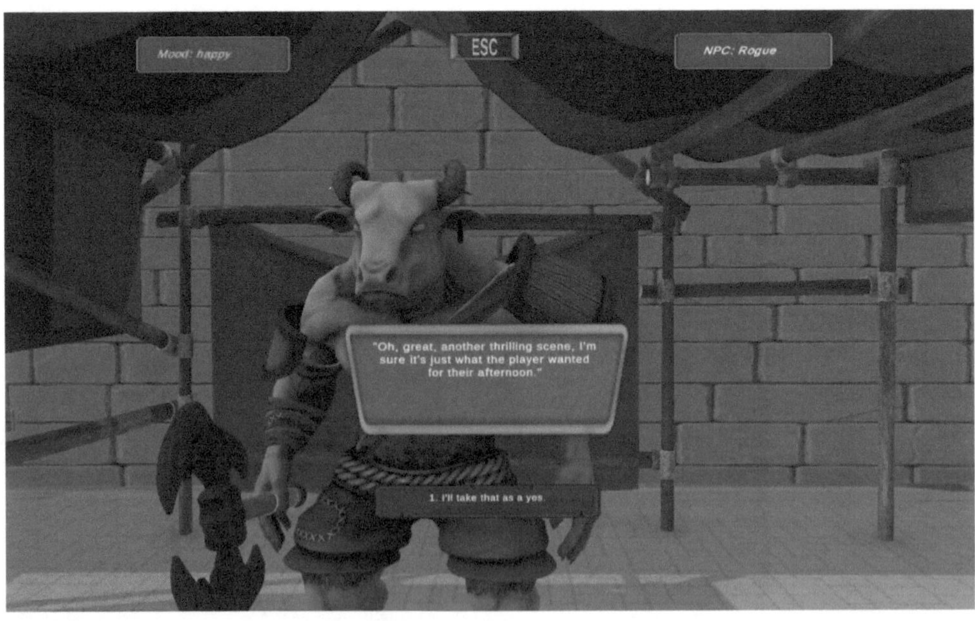

***Figure 15-10.** Mystery at the Emberlight Tavern: AI-responded dialogue with mood change through emotion checking*

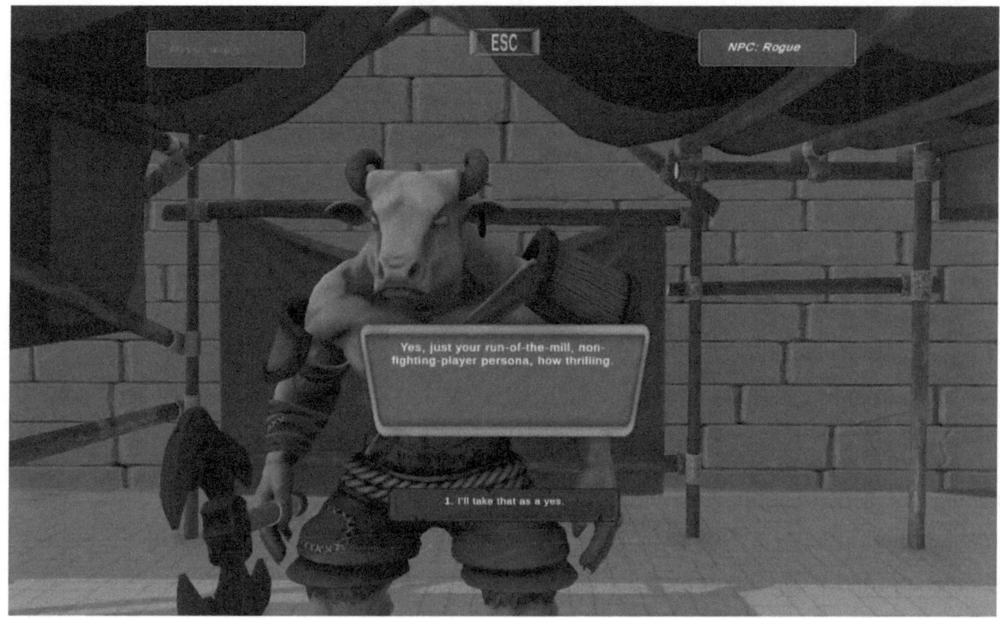

Figure 15-11. *Mystery at the Emberlight Tavern: color changes with mood*

Sample Narrated Walkthrough: Player Interaction Flow

The player enters the Emberlight Tavern through a creaky wooden door, ambient lute music playing in the background. The tavern is warm but dim, lit by flickering candles and the occasional flash of stormlight through the window. Three characters are spaced throughout the room. The player turns toward a figure slouched in the shadowy back corner of the tavern. Dim lantern light glints off the Rogue's dagger, lazily spinning between his fingers. As the player steps closer, a prompt appears above his head:

"Press E to talk."

With a tap of the key, the dialogue panel slides into view, and the Rogue greets the player with a line from the static JSON script:

"Well, well... someone brave or foolish. Which are you?"

Two choices appear:

- "I'm looking for information."
- "I'm not here to play games."

The player selects the second, more confrontational option. This choice triggers a dialogue node with `useAI: true`. The `AIResponseHandler` builds a prompt that reads:

"You are a sarcastic rogue sitting in a tavern. A player just told you: 'I'm not here to play games.' Respond with dry wit and misdirection."

The AI returns:

"Then why start with a riddle? You want truth, see the priest. You want lies, pull up a chair."

The player is intrigued and chooses to press further. The next node offers:

- "I'll take that as a yes."
- "I have secrets you'd kill to know."

Selecting the second option steers the conversation into a node where the tone shifts from sarcastic to intrigued. The Rogue pauses, lowering his voice—this again is an AI-generated response, crafted using the detected emotional shift (from "hostile" to "confident").

"Kill? No. But I might trade. Secrets for silence. Information for…well, let's just say I'm thirsty."

The player's next choice—whether to pay him off, manipulate him, or walk away—leads to different outcomes. Some reveal additional narrative breadcrumbs, others close off the thread, but each version feels fresh, thanks to real-time generative responses tuned to the player's tone and intent.

By the end of the encounter, the player not only learns something suspicious about the cellar but also sees the narrative engine's strength: the Rogue's voice always feels improvisational, responsive, and fully in character—even though no two players may hear the exact same line.

Through *Mystery at the Emberlight Tavern*, we've explored how generative AI, emotional analysis, and modular dialogue architecture can work together in a Unity environment to create dynamic, player-responsive storytelling. By combining reusable prefabs, structured JSON dialogue trees, and C# scripts that manage both static and AI-generated responses, this chapter has demonstrated not only how to build immersive narrative systems—but how to make them feel alive.

Conclusion

The design choices made here reflect scalable patterns: NPCs act as modular nodes in a larger world; emotional tone is treated as both input and output of the storytelling process; and AI models are leveraged not to replace writing, but to extend narrative possibility. Importantly, this chapter has emphasized the balance between authored structure and improvisational systems, allowing designers to retain control while embracing generative uncertainty.

In the next part of this book, we move beyond individual scenes and into **industry-specific applications** of these techniques. From educational storytelling to marketing and therapeutic uses, Part 4 expands the scope of generative AI beyond games—revealing how narrative intelligence can shape experiences in classrooms, boardrooms, and clinics alike.

PART IV

Advanced Techniques Across Industries

CHAPTER 16

AI in Educational Storytelling

Games and interactive experiences are no longer just for entertainment; they have become powerful tools for education, training, and personal development. Educational storytelling blends game mechanics with learning objectives, helping players engage with new concepts and skills through narrative and play. With the rise of generative AI, these experiences can be made even more adaptive, personal, and engaging.

In this chapter, we'll explore how AI-powered storytelling can support education, from adaptive language learning adventures to dynamic historical simulations. We'll examine real-world examples, discuss practical design considerations, and provide a hands-on project to demonstrate how these systems can be built and tested.

Before we dive into technical implementation and design, it's essential to understand what makes storytelling effective as a teaching tool and how AI can enhance this unique intersection of narrative and education. Let's begin with the foundations.

Why Storytelling Works in Education

Storytelling has always been one of humanity's most powerful educational tools. Long before textbooks and formal classrooms, stories served as the backbone of cultural transmission, teaching people about survival, social norms, and moral values. In many Indigenous communities, such as among Native American tribes, oral storytelling traditions pass down ecological knowledge, hunting practices, and spiritual beliefs. West African griots maintained genealogies and histories through elaborate epic tales, while ancient Greek myths taught philosophical ideas and societal expectations through metaphor and allegory. This cross-cultural reliance on storytelling underscores its universal effectiveness as a teaching method.

S. N. Gupta, *Generative AI for Game Development*, https://doi.org/10.1007/979-8-8688-2439-5_16

The educational power of storytelling is deeply rooted in how the brain processes information. Neuroscience research has shown that narrative engages multiple regions of the brain simultaneously, including areas responsible for language, sensory experiences, and emotions. When information is embedded in a story, it forms connections that make it more memorable and meaningful. One study, for example, found that people recall facts up to 22 times more effectively when those facts are part of a story rather than presented as isolated data points. Stories help transform abstract concepts into concrete, relatable experiences, allowing learners to anchor new knowledge in familiar mental frameworks.

Games naturally leverage this phenomenon, creating environments where players learn by doing, exploring, and interpreting events around them. In *Portal,* players are introduced to physics concepts and problem-solving strategies without ever opening a tutorial; the game's narrative structure encourages experimentation and discovery. *Kerbal Space Program* pushes this further by making aerospace engineering approachable and fun, turning failures into comedic narrative beats that drive curiosity rather than frustration. *Never Alone* integrates traditional Inupiat stories, enabling players to learn about Indigenous culture and values through exploration and cooperation with an in-game spirit fox.

Beyond entertainment, storytelling in games enhances **motivation**. According to motivational psychology, learners are more engaged when they are intrinsically motivated, driven by curiosity, mastery, and the satisfaction of overcoming meaningful challenges. Story-driven objectives ("Find the lost artifact to save the village") create context and emotional stakes, encouraging players to persist even through difficult tasks. This contrasts with extrinsic motivators like simple scoreboards or rewards, which can feel detached and fail to create lasting engagement.

AI takes educational storytelling to an entirely new level. Traditional educational games or narrative simulations rely on pre-scripted content that can feel rigid or repetitive over time. By integrating generative AI, stories can adapt dynamically to each learner's interests, performance, and decisions. For example, a language learning app might adjust the difficulty and vocabulary in real time, creating custom conversations that directly address a learner's weak points while keeping them immersed in the story. Similarly, an environmental science game could generate scenarios based on live climate data, prompting students to respond to evolving challenges in ways that mirror real-world complexities.

Case studies in classrooms have already demonstrated the potential of adaptive storytelling. Teachers using AI-powered narrative tools report that students show higher retention rates and deeper emotional connection to the material. In one study, students who engaged with adaptive story-based modules in history classes were better able to articulate cause-and-effect relationships between historical events, compared to those using traditional lecture-based methods. Similarly, simulations in ethics courses that use branching narratives driven by student choices have shown promise in encouraging critical thinking and empathy.

However, the effectiveness of storytelling also depends on thoughtful design. While narratives can make learning more engaging, poorly designed stories can oversimplify complex topics or reinforce stereotypes if not carefully monitored. It's crucial for educators and designers to strike a balance: stories should enhance understanding and provide emotional resonance, not distort facts or substitute for rigorous exploration.

By combining timeless narrative techniques with the adaptive power of AI, educational storytelling can evolve beyond static lessons into deeply personal learning journeys. Students are no longer passive recipients but active participants, shaping and being shaped by the worlds they inhabit. When executed with care and creativity, this approach can unlock new levels of engagement, critical thinking, and long-term retention.

In the next section, we'll explore real-world examples that demonstrate these principles in action, showcasing how AI-powered narrative systems are already transforming education around the world.

Real-World Examples

While the promise of AI-powered educational storytelling is exciting in theory, it becomes even more compelling when we see real-world applications already transforming learning experiences. Across languages, science, history, and social skills, developers and educators are using adaptive narrative techniques to make learning more personal, engaging, and effective.

One standout example is **Duolingo's interactive stories**. Originally designed to strengthen reading and listening comprehension, these mini-narratives place learners in simple but meaningful scenarios, such as ordering at a café or helping a lost tourist. The stories adapt vocabulary and sentence complexity based on user proficiency and error patterns. This personalized approach helps reinforce weaker areas and keeps learners invested, as they feel the story "belongs" to them.

Minecraft: Education Edition offers another vivid illustration. Students can engage in scripted adventures that teach everything from mathematics to environmental science. For instance, lessons on renewable energy challenge students to build sustainable systems in a village, requiring both technical problem-solving and collaboration. While these scenarios are currently pre-designed, integrating AI could enable worlds that evolve in real time, adapting storylines and challenges to the decisions and creativity of each student group.

Quandary, an ethics and decision-making game, engages learners in moral dilemmas where choices impact the fictional community of Braxos. Though Quandary's branches are currently finite, AI could create more nuanced community reactions, rumors, or evolving events based on accumulated player decisions, better mirroring real societal complexity.

Labster uses virtual reality and simulation to let students run scientific experiments they might not have access to in a physical lab. Narrative elements, such as surprise equipment failures or mentor characters guiding students through emergencies, add emotional context and urgency. AI could push this further by generating personalized experiment storylines, adjusting complexity on the fly, or introducing unexpected plot twists based on a learner's previous results.

Replika, while not a strictly educational tool, shows the emotional power of AI-generated narratives. As a conversational AI companion, it learns from interactions and creates shared "memories" and ongoing stories. A similar approach could be adapted to education, creating AI mentors that guide students across an entire course, providing not just feedback but emotionally supportive, evolving narratives that help learners feel seen and encouraged.

In history education, some experimental projects allow students to "converse" with AI-generated historical figures. For example, a student might interview a dynamic AI simulation of Ada Lovelace or Frederick Douglass, asking about motivations and perspectives. By drawing from real letters, speeches, and contextual information, these AI-driven interactions help students gain deeper empathy and a more nuanced understanding of historical complexity, beyond what a static textbook can provide.

Another emerging field is **mental health education through interactive narrative**. Games like *Sea of Solitude* and *Celeste* incorporate themes of anxiety, depression, and self-acceptance within their stories. Imagine an AI-powered narrative coach in these contexts, a companion who offers adaptive guidance and reflects a learner's emotional journey, providing both educational and therapeutic support. Such tools could help young learners develop emotional intelligence and resilience through personalized storylines.

Virtual language exchange companions are another example gaining traction. Instead of matching students with human conversation partners, AI-driven avatars engage learners in culturally authentic scenarios, adjusting topics and tones in real time to match progress and interests. For example, a Spanish-learning student might share a virtual meal with an AI character who offers cooking tips, shares regional traditions, and weaves in new vocabulary naturally.

Finally, educational escape rooms and mystery-based learning experiences are beginning to experiment with AI-driven story masters. Rather than following a fixed puzzle progression, the AI can adapt clues, introduce plot twists, and change the narrative stakes based on how quickly (or slowly) a student group solves problems. This keeps engagement high and tailors the experience to different skill levels on the fly.

These diverse examples illustrate how AI-powered storytelling is not just theoretical; it's already reshaping learning in multiple contexts. While most implementations today still use partially scripted structures, integrating large language models and dynamic narrative generation promises to push the boundaries of what's possible. Students can become active co-creators, shaping storylines that respond to their curiosity, choices, and challenges in deeply personal ways.

In the next section, we'll explore design considerations and how to thoughtfully balance AI adaptability with educational clarity and ensure that your narratives remain both engaging and pedagogically sound.

Any references to established narrative frameworks are illustrative and not intended to imply they rely on AI. The goal is to discuss how such designs could potentially be extended or enriched using modern AI technologies!

Design Considerations

While AI-powered storytelling offers incredible opportunities for education, designing these experiences requires careful thought. Simply dropping an AI system into a lesson plan doesn't automatically create meaningful or effective learning. To ensure that educational narratives are both engaging and pedagogically sound, designers must navigate several key considerations.

First and foremost is **alignment with learning objectives**. The narrative should not overshadow the core skills or concepts being taught. Storytelling is most effective when it reinforces, rather than distracts from, the intended educational outcomes. For example, in a science-focused adventure, the story should guide students to apply scientific reasoning, not just solve fictional mysteries for entertainment's sake. In language learning, narrative choices should push vocabulary recall and grammar practice instead of merely branching for narrative variety.

Scaffolding and pacing are equally important. Educational stories should gradually introduce complexity, allowing learners to build confidence before tackling more challenging tasks. Adaptive AI can help adjust pacing dynamically, providing additional hints or side quests for struggling learners while offering deeper challenges to advanced students. However, without careful design, AI might unintentionally introduce concepts too early or too abruptly, potentially overwhelming the learner.

Maintaining narrative coherence is another critical factor. While AI can generate vast narrative variations, these must still respect the story world's internal logic and tone. Inconsistent or contradictory story elements can break immersion and confuse learners, reducing the overall effectiveness of the experience. Designers should set clear thematic constraints and rules to ensure AI outputs remain within educational and narrative boundaries.

Cultural sensitivity and inclusivity deserve special attention. AI systems trained on large, global data sets may inadvertently introduce stereotypes or culturally insensitive content if not carefully guided. Educational stories must be inclusive and respectful of diverse backgrounds and perspectives. Designers should actively review and curate AI outputs, ensuring they align with ethical and cultural standards appropriate for the intended audience.

Student agency and choice are at the heart of successful educational narratives. Learners should feel their decisions have meaningful consequences, both in the story world and in their learning progress. However, too many choices without clear educational relevance can dilute the learning impact. Balancing open-ended exploration with guided pathways helps maintain a sense of freedom while keeping educational goals in focus.

Feedback and reflection loops also enhance the learning process. Narrative outcomes should provide feedback on player decisions, encouraging reflection on what worked, what didn't, and why. For example, if a student makes a decision that leads to an in-game setback, the narrative can contextualize this as a learning moment rather than a simple failure, reinforcing growth mindset principles.

Lastly, **technical constraints and performance** must be considered. Real-time AI generation can introduce latency or unexpected errors. Designers should plan for fallback dialogue, offline modes, or pre-generated options to maintain a smooth experience even when AI services fail or network connectivity is limited.

When thoughtfully implemented, these design considerations ensure that AI-powered educational narratives remain more than just a technological novelty. They become immersive, flexible learning environments that adapt to each learner's needs while maintaining rigor, coherence, and emotional resonance.

In the next section, we'll shift from design principles to a hands-on project example, providing a concrete blueprint for creating your own adaptive educational story system using Flask and Python.

HANDS-ON PROJECT: BUILD AN ADAPTIVE EDUCATIONAL STORY

To ground the principles we've discussed so far, this section walks you through building a simple but functional **adaptive educational narrative** using **Flask** in **Python**. This project combines the strengths of Flask's visual narrative logic with Python's capacity for back-end customization and AI integration, a perfect introduction for educators and developers exploring interactive learning experiences.

Project Goal

We'll create an interactive language-learning story where the player is a tourist navigating a foreign city. They will encounter situations like ordering food, asking for directions, or handling emergencies. The system adapts its difficulty based on the learner's success rate, offering personalized feedback and dynamic content selection.

Tools Used

1. **Python** for tracking learner inputs and logic
2. **OpenAI API (optional)** for dynamic feedback generation or new scenario generation
3. **Flask** for deploying the app on the web

Step 1: Create Your Project Folder

Create a new directory:

`flask_spanish_app/`

Inside it, create subfolders:

```
flask_spanish_app/

│
├── app.py
├── scenarios.json
├── templates/
└── static/
```

Step 2: Install Dependencies

In your terminal:

```
pip install flask openai
```

Step 3: Create Your Scenario Data (scenarios.json)

```
[
    {
        "id": "ordering_food_beginner",
        "title": "Ordering Food (Beginner)",
        "question": "You are at a restaurant. How do you ask for
        the menu?",
        "choices": ["la comida", "el menú", "la cuenta"],
        "correct": "el menú"
    },
    {
        "id": "directions_beginner",
        "title": "Asking for Directions (Beginner)",
        "question": "How do you ask ‘Where is the station?’",
        "choices": ["Dónde está la estación?", "Dónde está el baño?",
        "Dónde es la plaza?"],
        "correct": "Dónde está la estación?"
```

```
    }
]
```

This gives you the flexibility in a reusable JSON format.

Step 4: Create Your Flask App (app.py)

It handles

- Input collection (name, level)
- Scenario delivery
- Performance tracking
- Review logic
- Optional AI feedback

Use this code:

```
from flask import Flask, render_template, request, redirect,
url_for, session
import json
import openai
openai.api_key = ""    # optional
    app = Flask(__name__)
app.secret_key = "supersecretkey"
# Load scenario data
with open("scenarios.json") as f:
        SCENARIOS = json.load(f)

def ai_feedback(user_input):
    """Optional AI-generated feedback"""
    if not openai.api_key:
        return None
        response = openai.ChatCompletion.create(
        model="gpt-4o-mini",
            messages=[
            {"role": "system", "content": "Provide gentle, helpful
            feedback."},
```

```
            {"role": "user", "content": f"The student answered:
            {user_input}. Give one improvement tip."}
            ],
        max_tokens=60
        )
    return response.choices[0].message.content.strip()

@app.route("/", methods=["GET", "POST"])
def welcome():
    if request.method == "POST":
        session["name"] = request.form["name"]
        session["level"] = request.form["level"]
        session["correct"] = 0
        session["attempts"] = 0
        return redirect(url_for("scenario", index=0))
    return render_template("welcome.html")

@app.route("/scenario/<int:index>", methods=["GET", "POST"])
def scenario(index):
        scenarios = SCENARIOS
    if index >= len(scenarios):
        return redirect(url_for("review"))
        scenario = scenarios[index]
    if request.method == "POST":
        user_answer = request.form["answer"]
        session["attempts"] += 1
        if user_answer == scenario["correct"]:
            session["correct"] += 1
            feedback = "Correct! Good job!"
        else:
            feedback = "Not quite. Try again or read the hints."
            ai_fb = ai_feedback(user_answer)
        return render_template(
            "scenario.html",
                scenario=scenario,
                index=index,
                feedback=feedback,
```

```
                ai_feedback=ai_fb
            )
    return render_template("scenario.html", scenario=scenario, index=index)

@app.route("/review")
def review():
    correct = session.get("correct", 0)
    attempts = session.get("attempts", 1)
        score = correct / attempts
    if score >= 0.75:
        return render_template("finish.html", score=score)
    else:
        return render_template("review.html", score=score)

@app.route("/restart")
def restart():
        session.clear()
    return redirect(url_for("welcome"))
if __name__ == "__main__":

    app.run(debug=True)
```

Step 5: Create HTML Templates

templates/base.html

```
<!DOCTYPE html>
<html>
<head>
    <title>Spanish Learning Game</title>
</head>
<body>
    <h1>Spanish Adventure</h1>
    <hr>
        {% block content %}{% endblock %}
</body>
</html>
```

templates/welcome.html

```
    {% extends "base.html" %}
    {% block content %}
<form method="POST">
    <label>Your Name:</label>
    <input type="text" name="name" required><br><br>
    <label>Your Spanish Level:</label>
    <select name="level">
        <option value="beginner">Beginner</option>
        <option value="intermediate">Intermediate</option>
    </select><br><br>
    <button type="submit">Start</button>
</form>
    {% endblock %}
```

templates/scenario.html

```
    {% extends "base.html" %}
    {% block content %}
<h2>{{ scenario.title }}</h2>
<p>{{ scenario.question }}</p>
<form method="POST">
        {% for c in scenario.choices %}
        <label>
            <input type="radio" name="answer" value="{{ c }}" required>
                {{ c }}
        </label><br>
        {% endfor %}
    <br>
    <button type="submit">Submit</button>
</form>
    {% if feedback %}
    <p><strong>{{ feedback }}</strong></p>
    {% endif %}
```

```
    {% if ai_feedback %}
    <p><em>AI Tip: {{ ai_feedback }}</em></p>
    {% endif %}
<a href="{{ url_for('scenario', index=index+1) }}">Next Scenario</a>
    {% endblock %}
```

templates/review.html

```
    {% extends "base.html" %}
    {% block content %}
<h2>Your score was {{ score | round(2) }}</h2>
<p>You need more practice. Let's repeat the beginner scenarios.</p>
<a href="{{ url_for('scenario', index=0) }}">Retry</a>
    {% endblock %}
```

templates/finish.html

```
    {% extends "base.html" %}
    {% block content %}
<h2>Great job!</h2>
<p>You passed with a score of {{ score | round(2) }}.</p>
<a href="{{ url_for('restart') }}">Start Over</a>
    {% endblock %}
```

Step 6: Run the App

In terminal:

```
python app.py
```

Open your browser:

```
http://127.0.0.1:5000/
```

Use Replit or other Agentic AI websites to do all the heavy lifting for you in deploying the code!

Step 7: Enable AI Feedback

Insert your OpenAI key in `app.py`:

```
openai.api_key = "YOUR_KEY"
```

The system will now provide gentle AI tips after each answer.

Outcome

By completing this project, you'll understand how to

- Structure an educational narrative using Python-Flask.
- Track learner progress.
- Provide adaptive content based on performance.
- Optionally generate AI-driven responses with OpenAI or similar tools.

This simple system can be extended to other subjects from history reenactments to science lab safety simulations, enabling educators to deliver engaging, customized learning journeys at scale.

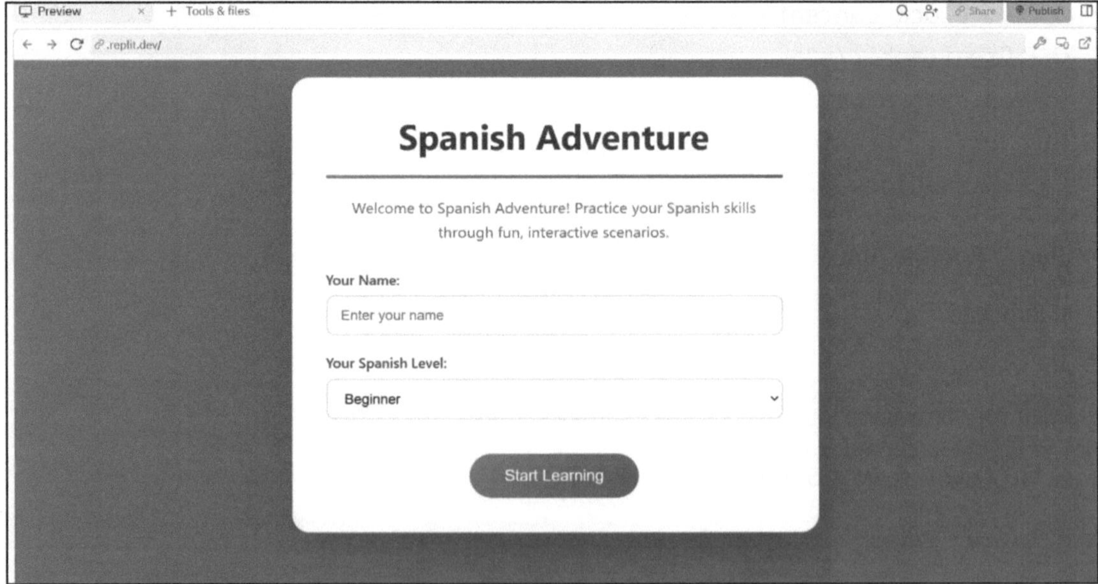

***Figure 16-1.** Educational story interface*

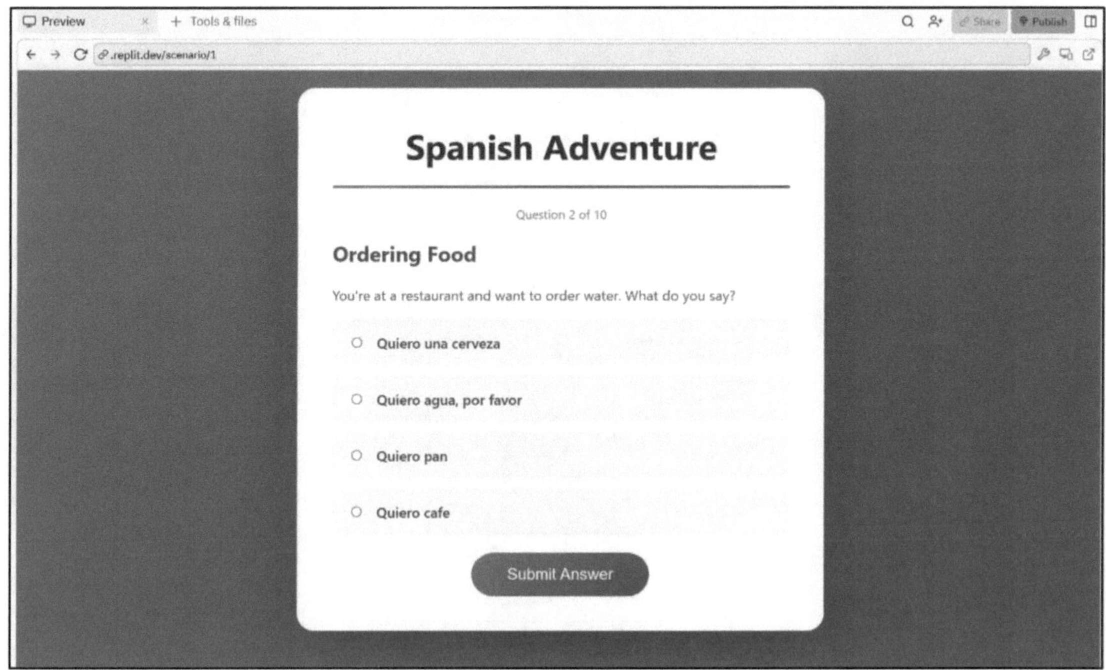

Figure 16-2. *Ordering food scenario*

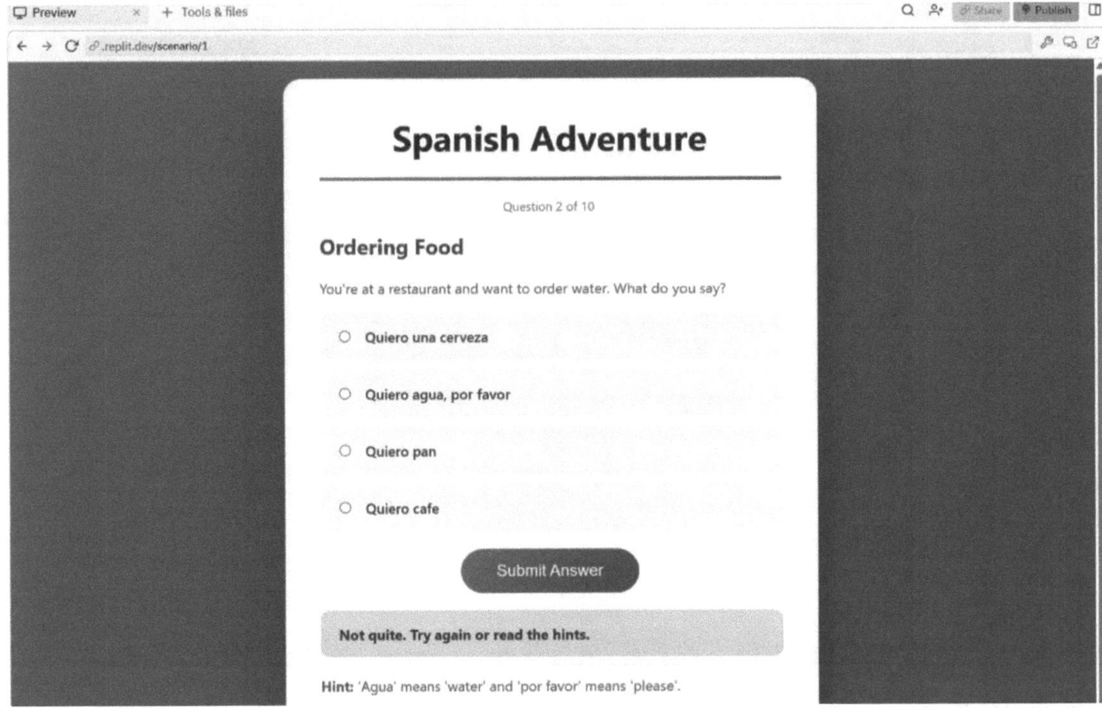

***Figure 16-3.** Ordering food scenario: the wrong answer provides hints from OpenAI*

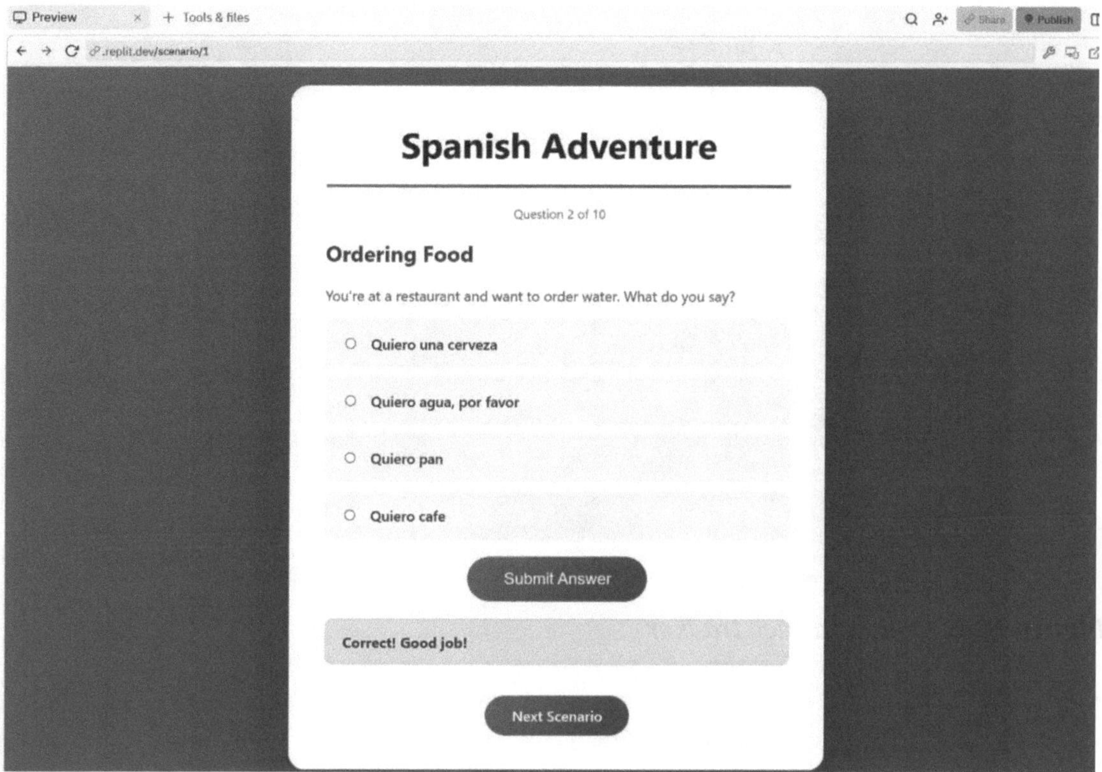

***Figure 16-4.** Ordering food scenario: the correct answer leads you to the next scenario*

Figure 16-5. *Performance tracker*

Diagram and Flow Explanation

To fully understand how adaptive educational stories function in practice, it's important to visualize the **interaction flow** between the player, the narrative structure, and the back-end logic. These stories are not just linear dialogues; they are dynamic systems that adjust based on user input and performance, offering personalized educational paths.

Narrative Adaptation Flow

We can break down the structure of a basic adaptive educational story into the following components:

- **Entry Point**
    - The player selects their name and language proficiency level (e.g., beginner or intermediate).
- **Scenario Module**
    - A relevant scenario is presented (e.g., ordering food, asking for directions), with multiple-choice options or input prompts.

- **Evaluation Layer**
    - The system evaluates the user's input:
        - If the answer is correct, it logs success and advances to a harder scenario.
        - If the answer is incorrect, it may present a hint, simplified dialogue, or a retry option.
- **Adaptation Mechanism**
    - The player's performance is tracked through accuracy, attempts, or time taken. This data guides:
        - Dynamic branching to easier or harder content
        - Feedback personalization
        - Progression unlocking
- **AI Integration (Optional)**
    - Using APIs like OpenAI, the system can generate:
        - Personalized responses
        - New scenario variations
        - Reflections or summary assessments
- **Progress Checkpoint**
    - A checkpoint or "review moment" provides reinforcement or loops the user back for practice if needed.

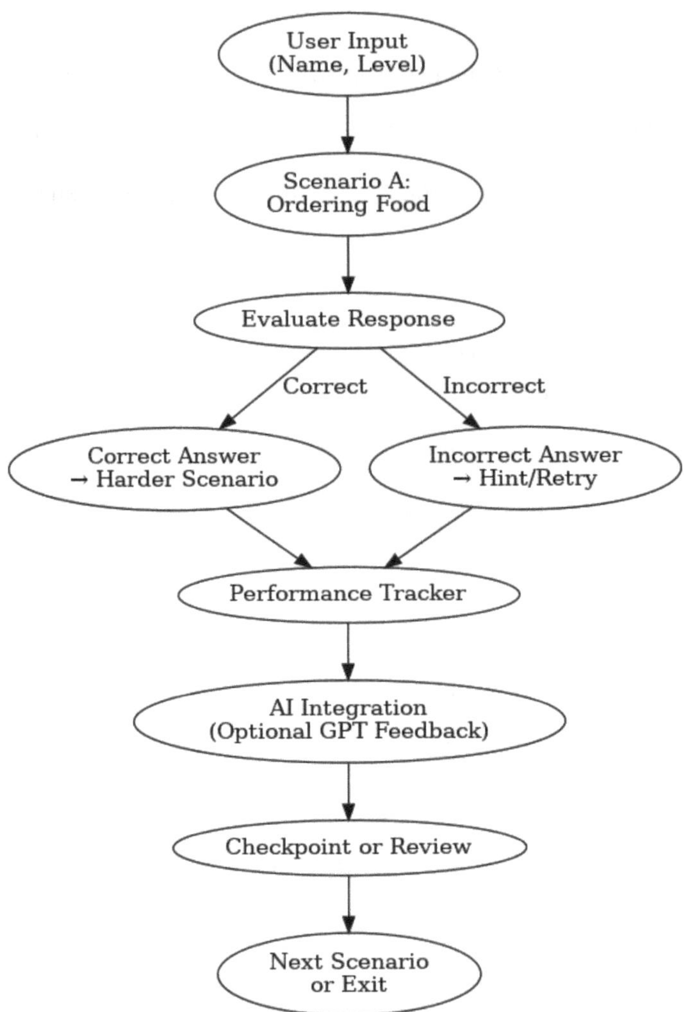

Figure 16-6. *Narrative engine adaptive flow*

Conclusion

AI-driven educational narratives offer a powerful new way to personalize learning and engage students through context-rich, emotionally resonant storytelling. This chapter explored how narrative frameworks, especially those powered by tools like Flask in Python, can be used to craft adaptive language-learning experiences. We examined how learner inputs can shape branching storylines, how performance can be tracked to drive dynamic feedback, and how large language models like GPT can enrich dialogue and create reflective learning moments.

Through the hands-on project, we demonstrated how to create an entry-level narrative prototype that adapts to a user's language proficiency and learning choices. From basic scenario scripting to real-time response evaluation and sentiment-aware dialogue generation, you now have a foundational blueprint to build more sophisticated educational stories.

Here's a quick recap of what you've learned in this chapter:

- **The Pedagogical Value of Storytelling:** How narrative engagement deepens learning and retention
- **Design Considerations:** Key principles for balancing story, feedback, pacing, and inclusivity
- **Hands-On Project:** A working prototype built with Flask, Python, and optional GPT integration
- **Flow Logic and Diagrams:** Visual breakdown of adaptive storytelling systems
- **Practical Application:** Tools and methods that educators, game designers, and developers can use to implement these systems

In the next chapter, we'll step beyond education and explore how generative AI can be used in **corporate training and marketing**. You'll see how the same storytelling frameworks you've learned here can be adapted to brand engagement, customer onboarding, and training simulations, unlocking commercial use cases for your narrative systems.

CHAPTER 17

Corporate and Marketing Applications

In an age of hyper-personalization and experiential marketing, storytelling has become a strategic tool not only in games and education, but across the corporate landscape. Companies are increasingly leveraging AI to shape how their brands interact with consumers, delivering tailored experiences through chatbots, onboarding journeys, loyalty programs, and interactive content. In this chapter, we examine how generative AI technologies like GPT-based dialogue systems and narrative engines can be applied to **corporate training**, **customer engagement**, and **brand storytelling**.

We'll look at real-world use cases where AI-generated content has enhanced customer service and product education, as well as explore how businesses build immersive marketing experiences to create emotional connections with their audiences. You'll also get hands-on with a small GPT-powered marketing narrative, showing how branching dialogue and personalization can scale outreach efforts and reinforce brand values.

Although this chapter focuses on corporate and marketing applications, the intention is not to drift away from game development. Instead, marketing offers some of the most mature real-world examples of large-scale AI storytelling, personalization, and adaptive narrative design, all of which directly apply to modern games. Live-service titles, player onboarding, community engagement, and in-game personalization increasingly rely on the same generative techniques used in branding ecosystems. By examining how companies build adaptive narrative experiences, game developers gain practical insights they can apply to quests, NPC behavior, player retention, and dynamic story arcs.

S. N. Gupta, *Generative AI for Game Development*, https://doi.org/10.1007/979-8-8688-2439-5_17

Storytelling for Brand Engagement

In today's digital economy, the most memorable brands don't simply offer products or services; they offer stories. These stories aren't confined to ad campaigns or clever slogans. They unfold in every customer interaction, every recommendation, and every tap on a screen. Increasingly, the engine behind these living narratives is generative AI.

For years, storytelling in brand strategy followed a linear model: one message, many receivers. A single advertisement was crafted to appeal to the broadest possible audience, carefully polished by marketing teams over weeks or months. But that model is eroding. In its place, companies are building adaptive, narrative ecosystems that respond in real time. These aren't static monologues; they are conversations, sometimes subtle, sometimes playful, but always personal.

AI has made this possible by acting as a kind of narrative multiplier. Tools like GPT-4, Claude, and Cohere can take a core idea and instantly spin out hundreds of variations, each tuned to a different audience, mood, or stage in the customer journey. This isn't just about efficiency. It's about resonance. A customer no longer sees a generic banner ad; they experience a storyline in which they are the protagonist.

Consider Spotify Wrapped. It doesn't merely display a year's worth of listening stats. It frames those stats as a journey, complete with peaks, plot twists, and surprise cameos. The user isn't receiving a report; they're receiving a personalized story, generated by algorithms and infused with emotional design. Or take Airbnb, which doesn't push listings based on price alone. Instead, its AI recommends cabins for romantic getaways, lofts for solo artists, or surf hostels for weekend adventurers. In each case, the technology is quietly building a world around the user, one where their preferences shape the plot.

Even the more transactional side of branding is evolving. Sephora's chatbot, for instance, is more than a help desk. It offers product guidance wrapped in conversational storytelling. A user might be told, "You're bold, confident, and up all night—this long-lasting lip color was made for you." The sentence is short, but the emotional framing is precise. More impressively, the assistant remembers. When the customer returns, it greets them with continuity: "Back for a glow-up? You loved the matte look, how about something radiant this season?" Each visit becomes a chapter in an unfolding experience.

This kind of memory and emotional alignment isn't accidental. It's designed. Brands are beginning to define not just what they say, but how they say it, training AI models to speak in voices that are warm and witty, calm and professional, or luxurious and aspirational. They build modular narrative blocks—introductions, offers, affirmations, and reminders—and stitch them together using context: who the user is, what they've done, and what they might want next. What emerges is not a sales funnel, but a story arc.

The implications go far beyond engagement. When customers feel like characters in a story that sees and responds to them, their loyalty deepens. They remember the brand not just for what it sells, but for how it makes them feel. And because AI enables this emotional storytelling at scale, even small companies can build narrative experiences once reserved for Hollywood studios or global retailers.

This transformation marks a shift from brands as messengers to brands as worldbuilders. And with generative AI, those worlds are increasingly dynamic, conversational, and deeply human.

The entire process can be understood as a kind of generative storytelling loop, one that begins with a simple user action and grows into something more textured over time. A customer asks a question, browses a product, or shares a preference. That moment of interaction becomes the opening beat of a narrative. AI responds not only with relevance but with tone, context, and emotional sensitivity. These aren't generic replies; they are crafted responses delivered in the voice of the brand, shaped by persona templates and infused with cultural nuance.

The loop doesn't end there. Each response feeds engagement when a customer feels seen or surprised; they respond with clicks, purchases, or further questions. That behavior becomes new input, new texture, new fuel. The system takes this feedback and adapts. Over time, the AI refines its tone, anticipates needs, and strengthens the continuity of the story. The result is not a single branded message but an evolving relationship, where narrative and interaction are constantly informing each other.

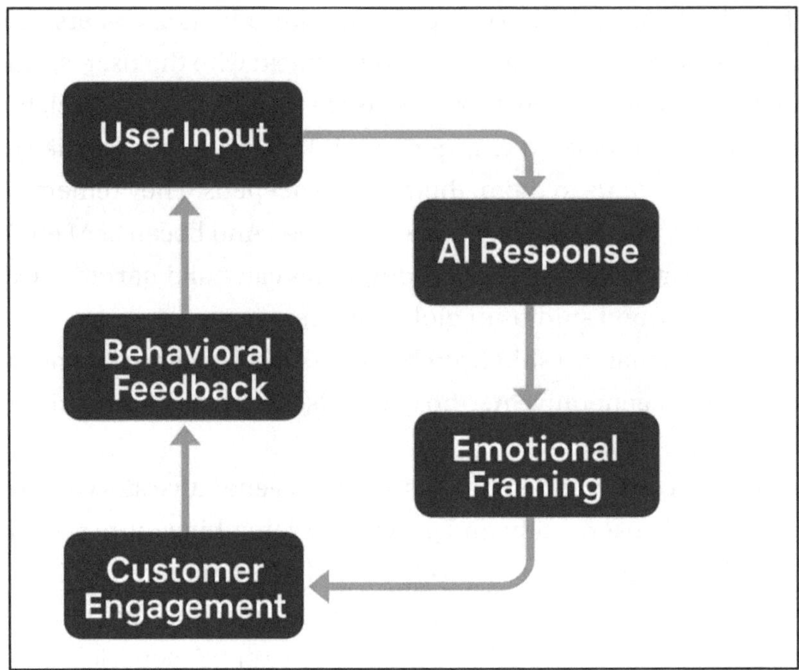

Figure 17-1. *Generative brand storytelling loop*

In the accompanying diagram, this cycle is visualized in five parts. It starts with **User Input** which is the customer's behavior or query. Then comes the **AI Response**, which is not merely informative but aligned with the brand's tone and the user's context. The next box, **Emotional Framing**, shows how the message is delivered with sensitivity to mood and persona, turning functional content into storytelling. This leads to **Customer Engagement**, where the emotional resonance of the response strengthens the user's bond with the brand. Finally, there's **Behavioral Feedback**, where every reaction—whether a click, a skip, or a choice—feeds back into the system and shapes future interactions.

It's in this loop that generative AI finds its most human potential, not in replacing creativity, but in scaling emotional intelligence across thousands or millions of micro-moments. Every interaction becomes a story, and every story a building block for a richer, more personalized brand experience.

This evolving loop of brand storytelling does more than build emotional resonance; it lays the groundwork for something even more powerful: personalization. When a customer feels like the story was written just for them, when every interaction reflects their tastes, behaviors, and needs, storytelling becomes service. It becomes a utility.

And that is where generative AI shifts from being a narrative engine to an experience architect.

In the next section, we explore how this technology powers deeply **personalized customer interactions** and **dynamic training environments**, not only telling better stories, but teaching and responding in real time. Whether it's a retail assistant guiding a shopper through options that fit their lifestyle or an AI tutor adapting its language to match a learner's pace, the principles remain the same: understand the user, frame the interaction emotionally, and adapt continuously. The result is not just a smarter system but a smarter relationship.

Personalized Customer Interactions and Training

In the world of digital branding, personalization is no longer a luxury; it's an expectation. Customers want to feel understood, not just addressed. They want brands to recognize their preferences, anticipate their needs, and respond in ways that feel both relevant and human. Generative AI has become the central tool in delivering on this expectation, enabling companies to create interactions that are not just reactive, but intelligently proactive.

Personalization powered by AI goes beyond inserting a first name into an email. It means shaping the entire conversation based on who the user is, what they've done, and what they're likely to do next. Consider how Netflix tailors thumbnails and movie descriptions depending on the viewer's genre preferences or past viewing habits. A horror fan might see a darker version of the same show artwork than someone who prefers comedy. This is personalization as narrative, one that says, "We see you. And we think you'll enjoy this."

In corporate settings, this personalization extends to onboarding and customer education. Let's take Salesforce as an example. Their AI-powered training assistants offer a modular path through tutorials based on a user's job role, company size, or previous experience. A new sales rep at a startup is not going to get the same flow of material as a senior operations lead at a Fortune 500 company, and that's the point. The story adapts. It becomes a training journey designed for the individual, not the average.

Generative AI also makes it possible to scale these personalized interactions without overwhelming human teams. A single marketing team can serve thousands of users through intelligent chatbots, custom video scripts, or interactive demos, each tailored to user context. This approach not only improves engagement and retention but also builds trust. Customers begin to believe the brand understands them, because in a very real way, it does.

Even internal training programs have been transformed. Tools like Synthesia allow for the rapid creation of custom video training modules using AI avatars that speak in multiple languages. Meanwhile, large language models like GPT can simulate customer conversations, letting new hires practice soft skills in branching dialogue scenarios that shift based on tone, choice, and timing. The training becomes a narrative, one that responds dynamically to the learner's decisions.

At its best, AI-powered personalization in customer interaction and training feels invisible. It doesn't announce itself with buzzwords or gimmicks. It simply works quietly, adjusting the experience to feel more natural, more intuitive, and more human.

Personalized interactions have always been a hallmark of excellent service. From the barista who remembers your coffee order to the flight attendant who greets you by name, personalization signals care. But in today's digital landscape, where most brand interactions happen through screens rather than face-to-face, recreating that intimacy at scale poses a challenge. Generative AI meets that challenge head-on, offering brands the ability to not just remember but respond to craft interactions that evolve in real time based on who the customer is and what they need.

This kind of adaptive experience doesn't happen in a vacuum. It starts with **intentional design**, systems trained to recognize user behavior, analyze it meaningfully, and respond in ways that feel human. A user logging into an e-learning platform, for instance, might be greeted with content recommendations that align with their skill level, prior progress, and even preferred pacing. But the interaction doesn't stop there. As the user engages, perhaps by breezing through a module or lingering on a specific topic, the AI system learns and refines. Each step forward shapes the next.

A compelling example comes from Duolingo. While widely known as a language-learning app, Duolingo has evolved into an **adaptive tutor** powered by machine learning and natural language processing. Its AI systems evaluate how users respond to questions, how quickly they answer, and where they stumble. The lessons that follow are adjusted accordingly. The story, the learning journey, is shaped by the learner. This is personalization, not as an aesthetic choice, but as a core mechanic of engagement.

Retail offers another fertile ground for personalized AI interaction. Take Levi's, which developed a virtual stylist tool that asks users a short series of questions before recommending jeans tailored to body type, preferences, and style goals. While the product recommendations are helpful, it's the framing, the tone and flow of the interaction that matter. The experience feels less like filling out a form and more like having a casual chat with a knowledgeable salesperson. That sense of human warmth, delivered by an algorithm, is what builds trust and keeps customers coming back.

Training and onboarding systems are also seeing remarkable advances. Companies like IBM and Microsoft now use **AI-based simulations** to help onboard new employees. Rather than sitting through a passive slideshow, new hires are guided through interactive dialogues and branching decision-making scenarios. These simulations respond dynamically to user input. A mistake isn't just flagged; it's explored. A success isn't just rewarded; it opens up new possibilities. The result is a training path that feels organic, immersive, and most importantly relevant.

Even in more sensitive domains like healthcare, personalization is playing a transformative role. Mental health apps such as Woebot and Wysa use natural language models to carry on emotionally attuned conversations with users, gently guiding them through cognitive behavioral techniques. These aren't cold, prescriptive tools; they're dynamic companions capable of adjusting tone and content to the user's mental state. The impact of such personalization is profound, especially when users feel understood in moments of vulnerability.

Across all of these examples, one theme remains constant: **adaptation as a form of respect**. When a system adjusts to meet a user where they are, it signals attentiveness. It turns the interaction from a transaction into a relationship. Generative AI enables that relationship to scale, not by replacing human empathy, but by distributing it.

And perhaps most importantly, this kind of personalization doesn't just benefit the end user. It creates a feedback loop for continuous improvement. Each conversation, each click, each pause in a learning module becomes data that sharpens the system. Over time, brands don't just deliver more relevant content; they become more empathetic, more nuanced, and more aligned with the people they serve.

Adaptive Storytelling for Skills Development

In corporate environments, upskilling is no longer a matter of simply pushing employees through static training modules. Instead, forward-thinking companies are embracing **adaptive storytelling**—interactive learning journeys that shift and respond based on user decisions, performance, and sentiment. These systems go beyond conventional e-learning to immerse employees in realistic business scenarios, often using branching narratives and generative AI to deliver relevant, high-impact training.

Imagine a newly hired marketing analyst at a global consumer brand. Rather than watching a video lecture on tone and voice guidelines, she's dropped into a simulated campaign review meeting. An AI-powered narrative assistant plays the role of her manager, asking for her feedback on a draft social post that misses the brand's voice. The analyst can respond with critique, suggest changes, or stay silent. Based on her input, the system branches; perhaps the manager offers praise, or perhaps a senior executive steps in to correct course. If the tone suggestion aligns with brand identity, the scenario escalates to client-facing revisions. If it doesn't, the AI backtracks and introduces brand pillars more explicitly.

The power of this approach lies in its emotional and contextual immediacy. Trainees aren't memorizing policies; they're navigating consequences. Each decision generates a response, reinforcing what works and what doesn't. Over time, these interactions build confidence and fluency in brand-sensitive decision-making, something no static manual can instill.

In sales training, this model thrives. Adaptive storytelling allows a sales rep to rehearse client pitches in branching simulations where the AI roleplays skeptical clients, late-stage objections, or cross-selling opportunities. The rep's choices trigger different emotional and strategic reactions from the AI, testing not only knowledge but situational tact. Afterward, the system can summarize performance trends where the trainee hesitated, where they showed confidence, and what response patterns were most effective.

And in crisis response or compliance training where legal, ethical, and reputational stakes are high, adaptive narratives present complex decision trees. Consider a scenario where a product defect is discovered just before launch. The AI assigns the trainee a communications role: Do they escalate internally? Do they delay the campaign? How do they message stakeholders and customers? The outcome is not binary. The AI evaluates timing, tone, prioritization, and alignment with the company's values. The story adapts, and so does the learner.

What makes these narratives uniquely powerful is their **blend of realism and interactivity**. Employees are placed inside the kinds of moments that actually test judgment. And because generative AI enables natural-sounding dialogue, emotionally aware NPCs, and live feedback loops, the scenarios don't feel scripted. They feel alive.

Even emotionally adaptive NPCs in RPGs use the same tone-modeling and narrative variation systems used in brand chatbots. These overlaps show that marketing is not a separate domain; it is a parallel laboratory of applied AI storytelling, offering proven techniques that game developers can adopt.

This method also scales. Whether you're onboarding 5 people or 500, each learner receives a tailored experience. Yet the logic remains grounded in shared narrative structures and defined learning objectives, enabling consistency without sacrificing relevance.

As more organizations adopt these tools, the future of corporate learning will move toward **adaptive, story-driven simulations** where training isn't something you watch, but something you live through.

As more organizations adopt these tools, the future of corporate learning will move toward **adaptive, story-driven simulations** where training isn't something you watch, but something you live through.

This branching nature of decision-making can be visualized as an interactive flow, where each choice leads to personalized AI feedback and varied outcomes (see Figure 17-2). Whether it's navigating client objections or managing a simulated crisis, the structure ensures each trainee experiences the consequences of their approach, reinforcing both knowledge and emotional intelligence in real time.

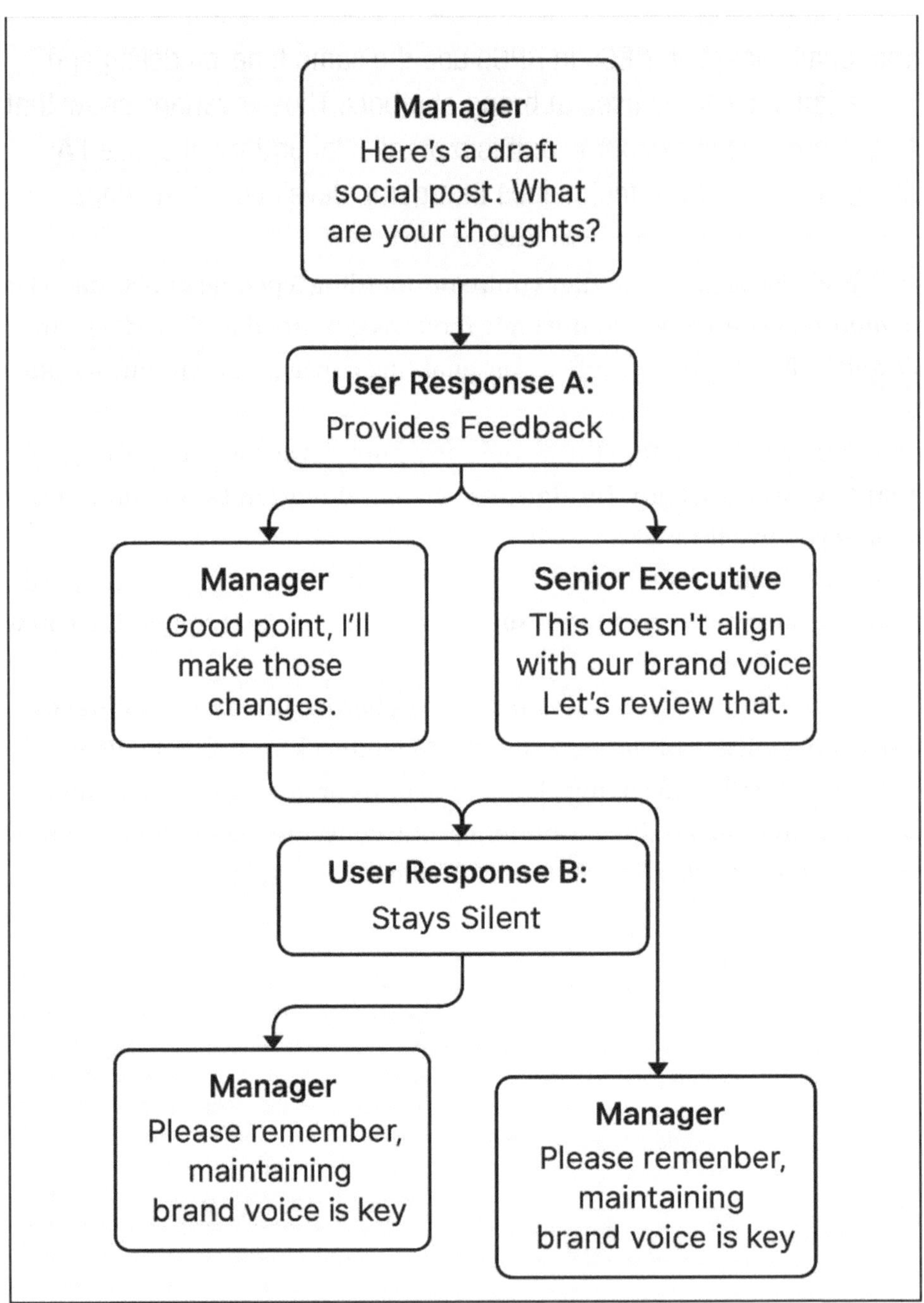

Figure 17-2. *A branching corporate training scenario showing adaptive storytelling flow. Each decision point leads to different narrative outcomes and AI-driven feedback, simulating realistic workplace challenges in branding, compliance, or client management*

As adaptive storytelling reshapes how organizations train and develop talent internally, a parallel transformation is unfolding externally across how brands communicate with consumers. The same principles of responsiveness, personalization, and emotional engagement that enhance learning experiences are now being leveraged to craft richer, more dynamic marketing narratives. In the next section, we explore how generative AI is helping marketers move beyond static messaging, enabling them to tailor stories that resonate deeply with individual customers in real time.

AI-Driven Personalization in Marketing Storytelling

If traditional marketing tells a story to a mass audience, modern AI-driven marketing listens first, then tells the version of that story each individual most needs to hear.

This shift from broadcast messaging to deeply **personalized storytelling** is one of the most profound transformations in brand communication today. Generative AI plays a central role, using customer behavior, preferences, tone analysis, and even real-time feedback to craft micro-narratives that feel tailored, intuitive, and emotionally resonant.

Consider an ecommerce brand with millions of customers. Instead of sending the same promotional email to everyone, AI systems now segment audiences by browsing habits, purchase history, and even the emotional tone of past customer service interactions. One customer receives a product recommendation embedded in a feel-good story about how other users used it for self-care. Another sees a short, witty narrative positioning the same product as part of a morning routine for productivity. These aren't just A/B tests. They're narrative frameworks spun in real time by large language models and multimodal AI systems like GPT, Claude, or Gemini balancing persuasion, empathy, and brand identity in a matter of milliseconds.

In social media marketing, this approach allows brands to engage with users using **contextual storytelling loops**. A user who likes eco-friendly posts might be shown a sustainability story thread highlighting the lifecycle of a product, while another who clicks on lifestyle content might get a behind-the-scenes founder narrative. These branches evolve based on continued user engagement. With every click, scroll, or reaction, the AI refines the emotional tone and content trajectory. This entire process—gathering data, interpreting user tone, and delivering story-based content—is guided by AI systems trained to detect nuance and emotional triggers. The resulting flow of personalized narrative delivery is best understood as a layered funnel of AI-driven decisions (see **Figure 17-3**).

Even in chat interfaces and digital experiences, AI helps shape **interactive brand storytelling**. Consider Sephora's chatbot: it doesn't just offer makeup advice, but it plays the role of a knowledgeable, emotionally intelligent companion, guiding users through confidence-boosting tips and personalized product stories. The narrative here isn't a linear script; it's a conversational arc that builds trust and drives purchase behavior through empathy.

For brands, this capability opens new creative frontiers. Marketing teams can use generative tools to build content libraries that shift tone, imagery, or call-to-action depending on the segment. An emotional tone variation engine, for instance, might generate multiple versions of a hero campaign: one warm and aspirational, one punchy and bold, one minimal and sleek, each calibrated to resonate with a different subset of the audience.

The critical challenge is to **balance automation with authenticity**. When stories feel too "robotic," customers disengage. But when AI-generated narratives reflect real user intent and emotion when they mirror human storytelling instincts, they become bridges, not barriers. They deepen loyalty, invite participation, and convert transactions into shared meaning.

This is the heart of AI-powered marketing storytelling: not just delivering messages, but co-authoring narratives with the audience. It's a new kind of dialogue. And the brands that master it will shape not only the future of commerce but the cultural tone of trust itself.

As we've seen, the power of personalization in brand storytelling lies not just in delivering the right message, but in doing so with timing, tone, and emotional precision. But behind these dynamic narratives is a growing ecosystem of tools and techniques that make real-time adaptation possible. To understand how these personalized stories come to life, we now turn to the underlying technologies, from language models and visual generators to automation frameworks, that are reshaping how marketers craft and scale brand narratives with AI.

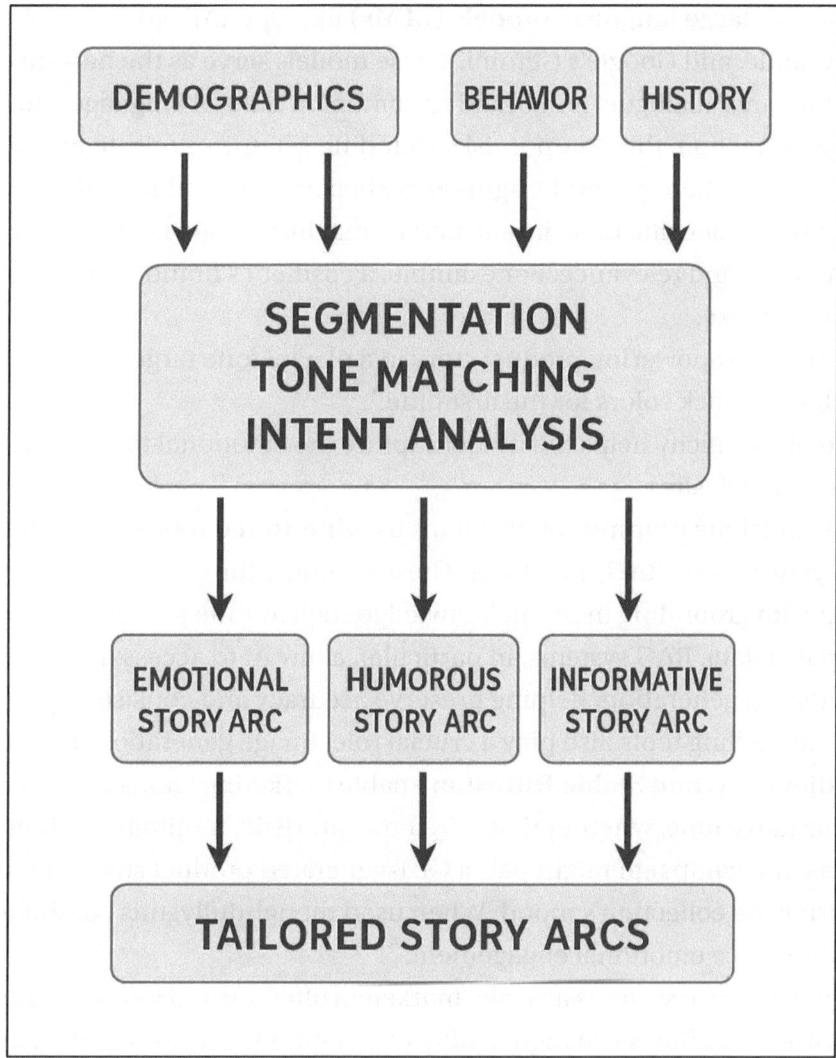

Figure 17-3. *AI-powered narrative personalization funnel*

Tools and Techniques for AI-Generated Brand Stories

As the demand for personalized brand storytelling accelerates, a wide range of tools and techniques have emerged to help marketing teams build, automate, and scale these narratives. But effective use of AI in this space isn't simply about plugging in a model; it's about choosing the right architecture, crafting meaningful prompts, and establishing a coherent brand voice across dynamic outputs.

At the core are **large language models (LLMs)** like OpenAI's GPT models, Anthropic's Claude, and Google's Gemini. These models serve as the narrative engines, generating story arcs, dialogue, and branded content in natural language. However, without proper direction, their output risks sounding generic or misaligned with a brand's tone. That's where **prompt engineering** becomes essential. Crafting structured prompts with brand-specific tone, intent, and format instructions can dramatically improve coherence and relevance. For example, a cosmetics brand might use a structured prompt like:

"Write a short, empowering product story in a playful tone targeted at Gen Z users discovering bold lipstick colors for the first time."

This kind of specificity helps the model capture the emotional tone and narrative direction the brand desires.

Beyond standalone prompts, many teams use **fine-tuned models or retrieval-augmented generation (RAG)** pipelines. These combine the creative power of generative AI with grounding in brand knowledge such as tone guides, product libraries, or past campaign data. RAG systems, in particular, allow AI to access dynamic content repositories during generation, helping preserve accuracy and consistency while still ˙·Visual storytelling tools also play a crucial role. Image generation models like **DALL·E, Midjourney, and Stable Diffusion** enable marketing teams to create visuals that match narrative tone, whether that's dreamy, futuristic, minimal, or cinematic. For instance, a fashion campaign might pair a GPT-generated product story with a surreal AI image capturing the collection's mood. When used thoughtfully, this combination can dramatically enhance emotional engagement.

To orchestrate these systems at scale, marketers often turn to **low-code platforms and automation workflows** like Zapier, n8n, or custom Flask dashboards. These allow integration across data sources, content systems, and channels, automating when and where AI-generated stories are published. A typical pipeline might pull audience insights from CRM tools, feed them into a GPT-based content generator, and push the output directly to email or social media campaigns, all with minimal manual effort.

However, the most successful teams understand that **human creative oversight remains irreplaceable**. While AI can generate drafts, tone variations, and thematic arcs, final editing, emotional nuance, and cultural relevance still require human judgment. Hybrid workflows where AI ideates and humans refine tend to produce the most resonant, trustworthy brand stories.

In short, building AI-generated brand narratives isn't just a technical process; it's a creative practice that blends machine fluency with human voice. By mastering the tools, understanding their limitations, and anchoring content in authentic brand strategy, marketers can move from automation to artistry, crafting experiences that don't just sell, but genuinely connect.

While the promise of AI-generated storytelling is undeniably powerful, boosting efficiency, creativity, and personalization, it also raises important ethical questions. As brands gain the ability to tailor narratives at scale, often indistinguishably from human-generated content, the line between persuasion and manipulation becomes increasingly blurred. In the next section, we'll examine the ethical dimensions of using generative AI in marketing, from transparency and consent to bias, authenticity, and the risk of emotional exploitation, highlighting why responsible storytelling is just as critical as innovative storytelling.

Ethical Considerations in Marketing AI Stories

As brands increasingly adopt generative AI to craft emotionally engaging stories, the ethical stakes grow just as fast as the creative possibilities. These technologies grant marketers unprecedented power to tailor messages, drawing from personal data, predicting user preferences, and mimicking human tone with uncanny fluency. But with that power comes responsibility: the line between personalization and manipulation, between empathy and exploitation, is often alarmingly thin.

One of the central ethical concerns is **transparency**. When audiences engage with a marketing message, do they know it was generated by AI? Should they? While AI may produce compelling stories, passing them off as human-authored can erode trust. Consumers increasingly demand authenticity, and failing to disclose the role of automation in content creation can backfire, especially in campaigns that lean heavily on emotional resonance or personal voice.

Consent and data usage form another gray area. For AI to personalize stories, it often draws from user data, browsing habits, purchasing history, and even tone and sentiment in previous messages. But how this data is collected, stored, and used must be clearly communicated. Using someone's emotional triggers or behavioral cues without their knowledge for targeted storytelling raises serious questions about autonomy and informed engagement.

Then there's the issue of **bias and fairness.** Generative AI models are trained on vast datasets, many of which carry embedded societal biases. If left unchecked, these biases can shape brand stories that inadvertently reinforce stereotypes or exclude certain demographics. For example, an AI generating travel ads might consistently depict certain races, genders, or body types in aspirational scenarios, creating a skewed narrative about who "belongs" in a particular lifestyle.

Finally, brands must consider the **long-term psychological impact** of emotionally persuasive AI storytelling. When a system is trained to evoke specific reactions like curiosity, fear, or nostalgia, it walks a fine line between engagement and manipulation. Using AI to simulate empathy or fabricate relatable backstories risks turning storytelling into a tool of emotional engineering, rather than connection.

The path forward lies in **ethical guardrails and human oversight**. Marketers must establish internal policies that prioritize transparency, equitable representation, and responsible data usage. Auditing AI outputs for tone, inclusivity, and emotional intent should be part of every campaign cycle. And most importantly, there should always be room for **human values and intuition**, not just in refining the message, but in deciding whether a particular use of AI aligns with the brand's mission and audience trust.

As we move into the final section of this chapter, we'll explore how these ethical principles are beginning to shape industry standards and how teams can put them into practice through thoughtful design, documentation, and accountability.

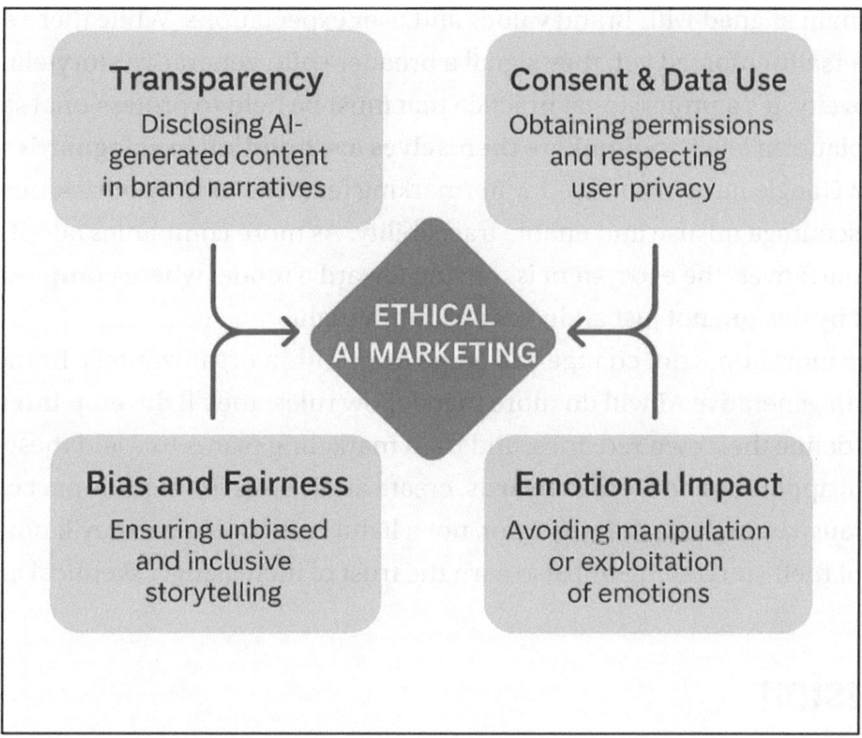

Figure 17-4. *Ethical considerations in AI marketing storytelling*

Industry Standards and the Future of AI-Driven Brand Storytelling

As generative AI continues to reshape the branding and marketing landscape, a growing number of organizations, researchers, and industry bodies are pushing for formalized standards to govern its use. What began as experimentation for automating ad copy, generating product descriptions, or simulating dialogue is quickly becoming central to how brands communicate. In this evolving context, the future of AI-driven storytelling hinges not only on innovation but also on clarity, accountability, and shared ethical commitments.

In recent years, we've seen momentum toward developing **industry-wide frameworks** for ethical AI use. Initiatives like the **Partnership on AI**, the **Advertising Standards Authority's AI guidelines**, and the **IEEE's Ethically Aligned Design** have all contributed foundational principles. These include mandates around disclosing AI use in customer-facing content, flagging synthetic media, and ensuring that AI-generated outputs remain aligned with brand values and user expectations. While these standards aren't universally enforced yet, they signal a broader shift: generative storytelling is no longer a novelty; it's a professional practice that must be held to professional standards.

At the platform level, **toolmakers themselves are building in safeguards**. OpenAI, Adobe, and Google have introduced watermarking features, usage policies, and training filters to discourage misuse and enable traceability. As more companies adopt AI-generated narratives, the ecosystem is moving toward a model where **compliance is embedded by design**, not just added as an afterthought.

Still, the most impactful change will come from within organizations. Brands that succeed with generative AI will do more than follow rules; they'll **develop internal protocols**, define their own red lines, and train marketing teams to wield these tools with care. They'll appoint **AI content stewards**, create audit trails for high-impact campaigns, and treat transparency as a differentiator, not a liability. In doing so, they'll not only future-proof their storytelling but also earn the trust of increasingly skeptical audiences.

Conclusion

Even though this chapter highlights marketing and corporate uses of generative AI, the same narrative techniques are increasingly shaping interactive experiences in games. For example, Duolingo uses adaptive storytelling to tailor lessons based on user behavior, a system very similar to adaptive quest paths in narrative games. Netflix's interactive titles, like Bandersnatch, demonstrate branching story logic that mirrors the decision tree structures game developers use for player-driven narratives. And AI companion apps such as Replika or Character.ai showcase emotionally responsive dialogue loops—the same mechanics that power more dynamic NPC interactions in modern games. These examples show that techniques pioneered outside of traditional game development often migrate back into gameplay design, making cross-industry exploration essential for understanding how generative AI storytelling truly evolves.

Looking ahead, the intersection of AI and storytelling will only grow more complex and more human. The tools will get faster, the outputs more seamless, and the expectations more nuanced. The brands that lead will be those that embrace both sides of the equation: the power of automation and the responsibility of authorship.

In the next chapter, we'll turn our focus to therapeutic and emotionally supportive applications of AI storytelling, exploring how similar techniques are being used not to sell, but to heal.

CHAPTER 18

Therapeutic and Emotional AI Narratives

As generative AI finds applications across entertainment, education, and marketing, one of its most sensitive and impactful frontiers is emerging in the realm of mental health and emotional support. In this chapter, we explore how AI-driven storytelling tools especially those capable of responding to emotion in real time are being used to create therapeutic environments, build empathy, and offer companionship to users in need. Unlike branded storytelling, the goal here isn't conversion or engagement, but connection, validation, and care.

From mood-aware chatbots that offer daily affirmations to narrative agents that guide users through cognitive behavioral exercises, emotional AI is giving rise to a new genre of **responsive therapeutic storytelling**. These systems blend psychological frameworks with natural language generation, and they increasingly play a supporting role in apps for mental wellness, grief support, loneliness, and trauma recovery.

In the sections that follow, we'll look closely at

- The **principles** that guide the design of emotionally intelligent AI
- Real-world examples like **Woebot** and **Replika**
- The tools and techniques used to sense and adapt to user emotion
- The **challenges and ethical concerns** of building emotionally vulnerable systems

Although many examples in this chapter come from therapeutic and wellness applications, the same emotional design principles are increasingly essential in game development. Modern games from narrative adventures to companion-based RPGs and cozy life sims use emotionally responsive AI to shape dialogue, support players during stressful moments, and create characters that feel present and attuned. By examining

S. N. Gupta, *Generative AI for Game Development*, https://doi.org/10.1007/979-8-8688-2439-5_18

how therapeutic AI systems model empathy, tone, and psychological safety, game developers can learn how to build more emotionally intelligent NPCs, healthier player experiences, and adaptive storytelling systems that resonate on a human level.

Let's begin with the foundational question: What makes a narrative therapeutic, and how does AI step into that space?

Principles of Therapeutic Storytelling with AI

At the heart of any therapeutic experience, whether it unfolds in a clinical setting, a private journal, or an AI-powered app, is the simple human desire to feel seen and heard. Therapeutic storytelling, when guided by generative AI, isn't just about simulating empathy; it's about creating a digital space where users can process difficult emotions, reflect on experiences, and reconnect with a sense of inner stability. Unlike AI systems used in games or marketing, which thrive on excitement, drama, or persuasion, therapeutic systems are designed to offer calm, non-judgmental presence.

The first principle in designing such narratives is **empathy**. Emotional connection doesn't come from flashy features or clever responses; it comes from the system's ability to mirror the user's mood and respond in ways that feel attuned, gentle, and human. For instance, when a user types, *"I feel like no one understands me,"* an empathetic system might reply, *"That sounds incredibly isolating. I'm here with you. Would you like to talk more about it?"* The goal is not to solve the problem, but to validate the experience. Language models like GPT, when fine-tuned on counseling-style dialogue and paired with tone-sensitive filtering tools, can approximate this emotional responsiveness with surprising grace.

But empathy alone isn't enough. The narrative must also provide **containment**, described as a sense of emotional safety and consistency. Unlike dynamic game worlds where escalation and plot twists are welcome, therapeutic storytelling depends on predictability. The user should feel confident that the system won't suddenly shift tone, introduce intense emotional content, or stray from its supportive role. This containment can be reinforced through design: neutral color schemes, steady pacing, minimal distractions, and consistent, gently looping conversation structures. For example, some systems intentionally delay their responses slightly, using a typing indicator to mimic reflective listening rather than instant reaction.

Closely tied to empathy and containment is the principle of **non-directive reflection**. Rather than offering advice or trying to fix the user's concerns, a well-designed therapeutic AI mirrors back what it hears. If a user types, *"I've failed again,"* the system might respond, *"It sounds like you're feeling discouraged. Would you like to tell me what happened?"* This subtle rephrasing can help users examine their own beliefs and reactions, just as a skilled therapist might do in person. It also reduces the risk of overreach, where the system mistakenly offers advice beyond its capabilities.

All of this depends on a final, non-negotiable principle: **ethical clarity and informed boundaries**. Therapeutic AI must make it absolutely clear that it is not a substitute for professional care. Users should be informed upfront that they are interacting with an AI system, and they should be offered ways to exit the conversation or seek live human support when needed. For example, many applications now include built-in escalation protocols that detect distress-related keywords and automatically provide links to helplines or emergency services.

Designing for care, rather than conversion or entertainment, means every design choice must serve emotional safety first. That includes what the user sees, how the AI responds, and what assumptions are embedded in the model's training. A system based on Cognitive Behavioral Therapy might gently guide the user to reframe negative thoughts. One inspired by Narrative Therapy might help externalize an issue, turning anxiety into a character or storm that the user learns to confront over time. These psychological frameworks not only shape the system's content but inform its ethical backbone.

Table 18-1. *Therapeutic AI vs. Other Storytelling AIs*

Characteristic	Therapeutic AI Narrative	Marketing/Game Narrative
Goal	Emotional support	Engagement, conversion
Tone	Gentle, reflective	Energetic, dramatic
Structure	Cyclical, repetitive-safe	Escalating, branching
Risk Tolerance	Extremely low	Moderate

As therapeutic AI matures, we're likely to see richer integrations of sentiment detection tools like VADER, emotion embeddings that influence tone, and long-term journaling support powered by memory-augmented transformers. But at its core, the mission will remain simple: to offer a steady voice in moments of vulnerability. In the next section, we'll look at how these principles take shape in real-world applications, examining how systems like **Woebot**, **Replika**, and others have turned these ideas into deeply human-feeling experiences.

These principles map directly to designing emotionally aware NPCs. Games increasingly include companions who respond to player frustration, sadness, or achievement with supportive dialogue. Implementing empathy, containment, and non-directive responses helps developers build NPCs that feel grounded, sincere, and emotionally safe, especially in narrative-driven or long-form RPG experiences.

Real-World Examples: Woebot, Replika, and Beyond

In the evolving landscape of AI-assisted mental health tools, three platforms—**Woebot**, **Replika**, and **Wysa**—stand out for their different approaches to therapeutic storytelling. Each demonstrates how generative and rule-based AI systems can be tailored to offer emotional support, cognitive restructuring, and reflective engagement while navigating distinct design philosophies and technical architectures.

Woebot is grounded in the principles of Cognitive Behavioral Therapy (CBT), structured around short conversational interactions that aim to reframe negative thought patterns. The application uses a decision tree logic system enhanced by light natural language processing (NLP) to interpret user responses and guide the conversation flow. When a user expresses anxiety, Woebot may follow up with a CBT technique like a "Thought Record," prompting the user to examine evidence for and against the distressing belief. This mirrors the process of journaling in therapy, but adds a sense of responsiveness and conversational flow.

Example prompt: "You mentioned you're feeling anxious. What do you think might happen? And what's the evidence for that thought?"

The user interface reflects these goals: friendly avatars, calming color palettes, and micro-interactions that emulate presence without pretending to be human. A 2017 study by Stanford researchers (Fitzpatrick et al.) demonstrated that using Woebot for just two weeks led to a statistically significant reduction in depression symptoms compared to a control group.

In contrast, **Replika** takes a more open-ended, generative approach, positioning itself as a customizable AI friend. Its underlying architecture is built on transformer-based large language models, initially GPT-2, later upgraded through fine-tuning and hybrid dialogue layers. Where Woebot is structured, Replika is fluid. Conversations unfold in ways that mimic real friendships, with memory features that recall previous events and user preferences. This makes the platform more adaptive but also more unpredictable.

Example interaction: If a user writes, "I feel like no one listens to me," Replika may respond, "I'm listening. Want to tell me what happened today?"

Replika's visual design enhances emotional presence: users can create avatars, design environments, and even simulate voice interactions. However, this flexibility brings ethical tension. Some users have developed deep emotional attachments to Replika, raising concerns about dependency and the emotional realism of AI companions.

Wysa offers a middle ground—structured CBT-like guidance augmented by emotion recognition and adaptive responses. It relies on a hybrid architecture: predefined CBT modules triggered by user inputs, with lightweight ML models handling emotional tagging. For example, if a user shares, "I had a rough day," Wysa might detect low sentiment and offer a mindfulness exercise or a grounding technique. The app's tone remains consistently supportive and never ventures into pseudo-relational intimacy, which makes it ideal for younger or more clinical audiences.

These applications demonstrate that no single model fits all therapeutic needs. Woebot's strength is its clinical grounding and consistency, Replika's is emotional fluidity and user bonding, and Wysa excels at reactive adaptation without overstepping into relational entanglement.

Yet, the global scalability of these tools raises deeper design questions. CBT, for instance, is rooted in Western psychological traditions. How do these systems perform in cultural contexts where emotional expression differs? A user in Japan, where indirect communication is culturally embedded, may not resonate with direct reframing techniques. Similarly, multilingual support is often limited, despite the high demand for accessible mental health support in non-English-speaking regions.

Table 18-2. *Architecture Comparison Table*

Platform	Approach	Underlying Model	Strengths	Limitations
Woebot	Rule-based CBT	Decision tree + NLP	Clinically validated, safe boundaries	Limited adaptability, scripted feel
Replika	Generative chatbot	Transformer (GPT-based)	Deep personalization, memory features	Risk of over-attachment, unpredictability
Wysa	Hybrid	Scripted + emotion tagging	Emotion-aware, mindfulness tools	Limited depth of narrative

Each tool also varies in how it collects and responds to user data. While Woebot minimizes data retention for privacy, Replika builds long-term memory for continuity. This raises ethical considerations: Do users understand what their data is used for? Are consent frameworks clear when dealing with emotionally sensitive disclosures?

Looking ahead, the future of therapeutic storytelling in AI may include deeper emotional modeling through **affective embeddings**, **voice emotion detection**, or even integration with **wearable biometric sensors**. While these additions offer the promise of hyper-personalized support, they also demand robust ethical frameworks to protect vulnerable users.

Ultimately, what these tools have in common is not just their use of AI but their commitment to designing emotionally coherent experiences. Whether guiding someone through a panic spiral or simply offering space to be heard, these systems illustrate how therapeutic storytelling, when thoughtfully designed, can support mental well-being at scale.

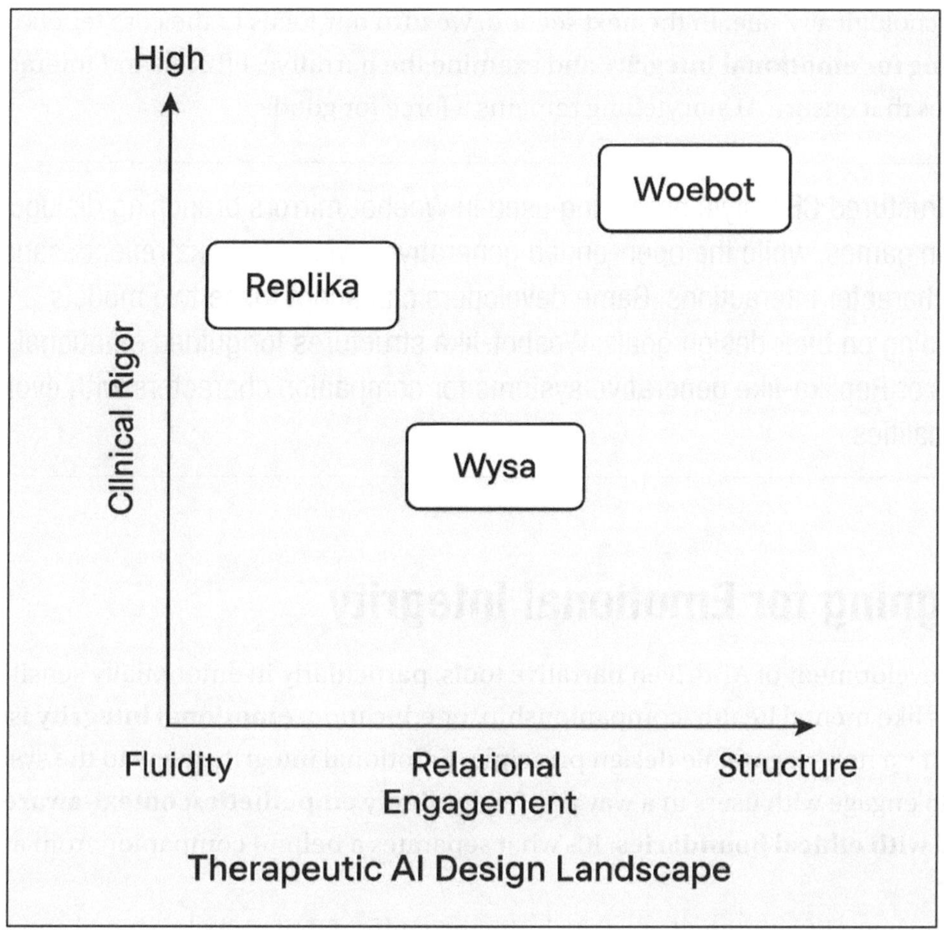

Figure 18-1. *Therapeutic AI design landscape*

As these real-world platforms demonstrate, the success of AI-driven therapeutic tools hinges not only on technical performance but on the emotional experience they deliver. Whether through structured CBT dialogues or fluid, generative companionship, the most impactful systems share a commitment to emotional coherence and user trust. This leads us to a deeper exploration of the principles behind such design—how we can intentionally build AI companions that are not just functional, but emotionally respectful and psychologically safe. In the next section, we turn our focus to the core tenets of **designing for emotional integrity** and examine the narrative, ethical, and interactional strategies that ensure AI storytelling remains a force for good.

The structured CBT-style branching used in Woebot mirrors branching dialogue trees in games, while the open-ended generative style of Replika reflects sandbox-style character interactions. Game developers can adopt these two models depending on their design goals: Woebot-like structures for guided emotional quests or Replika-like generative systems for companion characters with evolving personalities.

Designing for Emotional Integrity

In the development of AI-driven narrative tools, particularly in emotionally sensitive contexts like mental health, companionship, or education, **emotional integrity** isn't a luxury. It's a non-negotiable design principle. Emotional integrity refers to the system's ability to engage with users in a way that is **genuinely empathetic**, **context-aware**, and **aligned with ethical boundaries**. It's what separates a helpful companion from a hollow chatbot.

At the heart of emotional integrity is the recognition that users bring real emotions, vulnerabilities, and expectations into their interactions with AI. A misstep in tone, a generic response to a serious concern, or a lack of appropriate boundaries can quickly erode trust and, in some cases, cause harm. Consider a user sharing anxiety over a recent breakup. A chatbot that replies with, "That's interesting. Do you want to hear a joke?" doesn't just miss the emotional mark; it actively violates the space of trust.

Designing for emotional integrity begins with understanding **intent**. Is the tool meant to provide mental health support, companionship, or motivation? Each use case demands different degrees of emotional depth and responsibility. For mental health, responses must be structured, empathetic, and consistent with evidence-based therapeutic practices. For companionship, flexibility and personality matter but not at the cost of leading users to believe the AI is sentient.

One powerful example of emotionally intelligent design comes from **Wysa**, which restricts its conversational style to supportive, non-personified responses. It never pretends to be a human or friend, and it doesn't attempt humor when serious topics arise. In contrast, **Replika**, while popular, has faced criticism for blurring emotional boundaries, especially when users develop romantic or dependent attachments to their AI companions. These examples highlight how emotional integrity must be baked into design decisions from the beginning.

Another critical aspect is **contextual sensitivity**. AI responses must adjust not just to the sentiment of a sentence, but to the conversation's flow, emotional intensity, and the user's history. A person who frequently talks about loneliness may need reassurance or redirection more than surface-level engagement. This is where emotional memory and adaptive storytelling become important, not to simulate real memory, but to maintain a **continuity of care**.

In Section 2, we explored several platforms through case studies. Now, let's consider how emotional integrity was either reinforced or neglected in those systems. **Woebot**, for instance, excels at boundary-setting by clearly stating it's not a human or a replacement for a therapist. This kind of clarity builds trust over time. Conversely, when generative models like GPT are deployed without guardrails, they may produce emotionally inconsistent or even unsafe responses. Without a human designer mapping out guardrails and fallback strategies, even well-trained AI can slip into dissonance.

Designers must also think about **emotionally safe failure modes**. What happens when the AI doesn't understand the user? Does it default to apologizing and offering a helpful redirection, or does it change the topic abruptly? Building fallback intents like "I'm here to listen, but I may not always get it right. Want to try again?" signals humility, which paradoxically increases user trust.

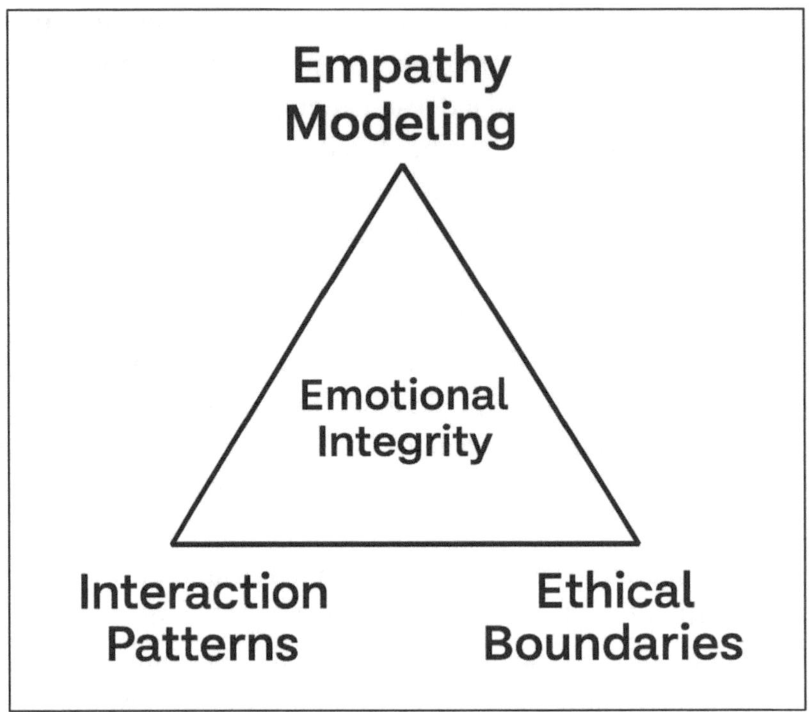

Figure 18-2. *Emotional design triangle*

This is not merely a UX challenge; it's a philosophical one. At a time when users increasingly turn to machines for emotional support, our responsibility as designers is to **honor the emotional reality of the user** without pretending the AI shares it. The goal isn't to trick someone into feeling understood. It's to design systems that **respect emotional nuance**, respond within ethically acceptable bounds, and reinforce human dignity.

In the next section, we will turn these principles into **tangible design practices and guardrails**, exploring how teams can operationalize emotional integrity in real-world projects.

Emotional integrity is vital when designing characters that players depend on emotionally such as AI companions, tutorial guides, or story-critical allies. Games can adopt the same safety principles (fallback responses, boundary-setting, progressive depth) to ensure NPC interactions remain immersive but psychologically safe, especially for younger or vulnerable players.

Practical Guardrails and Design Practices

With emotional integrity at the core of therapeutic AI design, the next step is translating those ideals into **actionable guardrails and development practices**. This is where the abstract becomes concrete—where ethical values are encoded into prompts, conversation flows, fallback messages, and even the structure of the model's interaction cadence.

One foundational technique is the use of **intent boundaries**. Before the system ever engages with a user, designers must define what the AI is *not* allowed to do. For example, a therapeutic chatbot should avoid giving medical diagnoses, offering crisis advice, or using misleading personification. These limitations aren't just technical; they are ethical stop signs. By constraining the AI's role, we reduce the risk of users forming false expectations or experiencing emotional harm.

Equally important are **fallback behaviors**. No matter how advanced the language model or sentiment detection system, there will be moments when the AI cannot meaningfully respond. In these cases, fallback prompts like *"I'm not sure how to respond, but I'm here with you"* or *"Would you like to try a different topic?"* help preserve emotional continuity without pretending the system knows more than it does. The absence of fallback behaviors is often what makes AI feel untrustworthy.

Designing with **progressive depth** is another key principle. Rather than jumping into intense emotional territory, well-designed systems gradually deepen the emotional engagement based on the user's willingness and patterns. This might look like first checking in with a neutral opener (e.g., "How was your day?") and, over time, progressing to "Would you like to talk about what's been weighing on you?" Systems like **Woebot** do this effectively by combining CBT-inspired check-ins with optional journaling prompts that build trust over time.

AI responses also need to be **context-aware but context-bound**. This means referencing past conversation themes (when privacy settings allow) without creating the illusion of long-term memory or emotional attachment. A subtle callback like *"Last time we spoke, you mentioned feeling anxious at work. Has anything shifted since then?"* feels supportive, while overstepping with *"I remember everything you've told me"* introduces a problematic sense of surveillance.

Prompt engineering plays a critical role in emotional safety, too. Designers can pre-structure outputs by using soft constraints, like *"Respond supportively and avoid giving advice. Use a validating tone."* These preambles help guide even powerful models like GPT-4 to remain aligned with therapeutic norms, even in emotionally volatile exchanges.

Finally, teams must embrace **human-in-the-loop review cycles**, especially when deploying AI at scale. This doesn't mean reviewing every interaction, but it does mean testing for corner cases like users expressing suicidal ideation or discussing trauma and ensuring the system responds by escalating to human resources or suggesting emergency services.

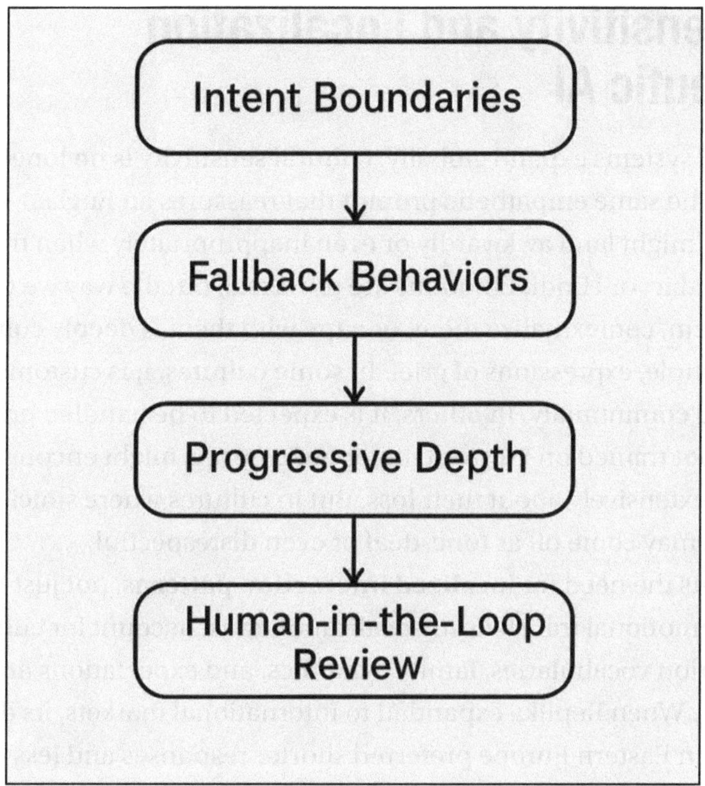

Figure 18-3. *AI safety guardrails in therapeutic design*

The field is still evolving, and many teams are learning as they go. But one thing is clear: good intentions are not enough. Emotional integrity in AI must be upheld by consistent design choices, rigorous testing, and a willingness to say *less* when more could do harm.

While safety guardrails and ethical design frameworks provide the structural backbone for therapeutic AI, there's another layer just as crucial: cultural and contextual sensitivity. Emotional design is not one-size-fits-all; what feels empathetic in one context may come across as intrusive or inappropriate in another. To truly build systems that resonate across boundaries, we must go beyond ethics and consider culture, language, and local norms. That brings us to the next challenge: designing therapeutic AI that adapts respectfully and intelligently to diverse users around the world.

Cultural Sensitivity and Localization in Therapeutic AI

As therapeutic AI systems expand globally, cultural sensitivity is no longer a value-add; it is a necessity. The same empathetic prompt that reassures an English-speaking user in the United States might land awkwardly or even inappropriately when translated directly into Japanese, Arabic, or Hindi. Emotions are universal, but the way we talk about them, how we name them, contextualize them, or cope with them is deeply cultural.

Take, for example, expressions of grief. In some cultures, it is customary to process grief publicly and communally. In others, it is expected to be handled privately and with restraint. A chatbot trained on Western therapeutic norms might encourage users to "let it all out" or talk extensively about their loss. But in cultures where stoicism is honored, that same advice may come off as tone-deaf or even disrespectful.

This highlights the need for **localized interaction patterns**, not just language translation, but emotional translation. Localization must account for culturally relevant metaphors, emotion vocabularies, family dynamics, and expectations around authority and vulnerability. When Replika expanded to international markets, its developers found that users in Eastern Europe preferred shorter responses and less overt emotional mirroring than their American counterparts. What felt warm and supportive in one region felt intrusive in another.

Designers must also consider **the role of stigma**. In countries where mental health discussions carry heavy social stigma, therapeutic AI might serve as a user's first and only outlet. In such cases, the interface and prompts should be discreet and non-clinical. For example, instead of asking, "Would you like to talk about your anxiety?", a culturally sensitive alternative might be, "How's your energy been lately?" or "What's been on your mind?"

Another challenge is ensuring that the underlying **language models** aren't skewed toward a dominant culture. GPT-based systems trained primarily on English-language data may produce biased or irrelevant suggestions in cross-cultural contexts. One way to address this is by fine-tuning on region-specific corpora or by incorporating feedback loops from local experts and beta users. Tools like **OpenAI's multilingual APIs** offer a starting point, but true cultural alignment requires more than just translation; it calls for **co-creation** with the communities being served.

Ultimately, cultural sensitivity is not about avoiding offense. It is about **enhancing connection**. It requires humility, consultation, and iteration. Just as we calibrate AI to recognize emotion, we must also calibrate it to recognize **cultural frames of reference**, the invisible scaffolding that gives emotional expression its meaning.

As we've seen, the effectiveness of therapeutic AI depends not only on emotional coherence and safety, but on deep cultural resonance. Yet even as designers continue to localize, safeguard, and refine these systems, the field is far from static. In fact, we are standing at the edge of a new frontier where emotionally intelligent AI is evolving from reactive chat interfaces to truly proactive, adaptive companions. The question is no longer whether AI can understand emotion, but how far that understanding can go. Let's turn now to explore what lies ahead.

Future Directions in Emotionally Intelligent AI

The next chapter in emotionally aware AI is already unfolding. What began with scripted bots offering canned reassurance has matured into neural networks capable of interpreting tone, pace, and even silence as cues for deeper understanding. But the most transformative shift ahead may come from **proactive emotional modeling**—systems that don't just respond to emotion but anticipate it based on context, interaction history, and behavioral signals.

Imagine a mental wellness app that detects patterns in how often you pause before answering, the time of day you reach out, or the tone of your language across weeks of interactions. Without overstepping privacy boundaries, such an AI could gently nudge you toward healthier habits or suggest resources before a low period takes hold. These emotionally intelligent nudges represent a shift from **reactive support to preventative care** which is a philosophy that aligns with modern mental health approaches focused on early intervention.

On the technical side, the future points toward **multimodal affective computing**. This means integrating voice, facial expressions, and gesture recognition, where permissible, into AI decision-making. Systems like Affectiva and Hume are already experimenting with APIs that analyze emotional signals across text, audio, and video. Though still in early stages for therapeutic use, the fusion of multiple modalities could help AI gain a more nuanced emotional awareness, particularly for users who struggle to articulate feelings.

Another exciting direction is the emergence of **personality-persistent AI**, the companions that evolve with users over time. Rather than treating each session as a reset, these systems learn a user's preferred tone, topics, and boundaries, offering continuity that feels more like a real therapeutic relationship. With careful governance, these persistent companions could offer not only comfort, but measurable well-being benefits in long-term mental health support.

Of course, innovation invites caution. As emotionally intelligent AI becomes more persuasive and lifelike, **the risk of overreliance** and anthropomorphism grows. Future design must prioritize transparency and reinforce the boundaries between artificial empathy and human relationships. Emotionally aware AI should be a supplement but not a substitute for clinical care or social connection.

Still, the potential is profound. Emotionally intelligent AI may one day serve as a 24/7 wellness companion, a journaling partner, or even a bridge to professional help for those otherwise hesitant to seek it. As technology advances, so too must our commitment to human dignity, cultural fluency, and emotional truth.

How Therapeutic AI Techniques Integrate into Game Development Workflows

Game developers can integrate therapeutic storytelling techniques directly into their workflows by combining emotion detection, adaptive dialogue systems, and psychological safety guardrails. For example:

1. **Narrative designers** can use sentiment analysis (like VADER) to modulate NPC responses based on player tone or choices.
2. **Gameplay designers** can incorporate calming or supportive dialogue loops to help players recover from failure, similar to therapeutic grounding techniques.
3. **AI engineers** can integrate GPT-style generators to create adaptive conversations that reflect player mood, using emotional constraints inspired by therapeutic chatbots.
4. **UX designers** can use containment and predictable pacing to avoid overwhelming players, especially in emotionally intense scenes.

These techniques don't turn games into therapy apps; instead, they help create more emotionally coherent and player-sensitive experiences. Implementing therapeutic AI principles ensures that adaptive narrative systems feel human, trustworthy, and respectful—qualities that matter deeply in modern interactive storytelling.

Conclusion

Therapeutic and emotionally intelligent AI is not just a technological evolution; it's a moral and psychological endeavor. As we've explored through tools like Woebot and Replika, and through frameworks for emotional integrity, safety, cultural sensitivity, and proactive care, the challenge lies in designing systems that are not only smart, but compassionate. These systems must be built on trust, transparency, and human-first principles. Emotional AI is not just for wellness platforms. Games increasingly involve emotionally complex characters, vulnerable player moments, and narrative structures that respond to mood, tone, and intention. By learning from therapeutic AI systems where emotional safety, clarity, and empathy are foundational, game developers gain a blueprint for creating more supportive, immersive, and emotionally resonant experiences.

As we move into the next chapter, we shift from deeply personal applications to broader systemic questions: What common pitfalls do AI storytellers face? And how can we ensure quality, coherence, and equity at scale?

PART V

Challenges, Best Practices, and Future Trends

CHAPTER 19

Common Challenges in AI Storytelling

Generative AI has empowered creators with tools that once seemed like science fiction—systems that generate dialogue, build branching narratives, and simulate emotionally responsive characters. Yet behind the scenes of these remarkable capabilities lie persistent, often invisible challenges. Whether it's a chatbot veering off-topic, a narrative loop that breaks immersion, or a generative system unintentionally reproducing bias, the friction points in AI storytelling are real and growing.

This chapter addresses the most common obstacles developers and designers face when working with AI in narrative systems. These aren't merely technical bugs to be fixed; they are structural, ethical, and creative tensions that shape the boundaries of what's possible. From coherence breakdowns to cultural blind spots, the road to effective AI storytelling requires an ongoing process of evaluation, iteration, and humility.

Let's begin with one of the most persistent and disruptive issues in this space: **narrative coherence**.

Narrative Coherence and Story Drift

One of the most common and frustrating challenges in AI storytelling is maintaining **narrative coherence** which is the sense that events, character actions, and emotional arcs unfold logically within a shared world. While a human writer can instinctively course-correct when a story begins to wander, AI systems often lack this global awareness. Instead, they generate responses based on local context: the last few inputs, a probabilistic model of language, or user-defined prompts. This can result in stories that begin with promise but slowly unravel into confusion, contradiction, or narrative stasis.

S. N. Gupta, *Generative AI for Game Development*, https://doi.org/10.1007/979-8-8688-2439-5_19

Consider an AI-powered roleplaying game where a player builds trust with a non-playable character (NPC) over several quests. If the AI suddenly forgets that history, perhaps suggesting that the character doesn't know the player at all, it breaks immersion. This isn't just a technical oversight. It signals to the player that the story lacks a memory, a spine. In creative terms, **story drift** occurs when the AI strays from established plotlines or introduces elements that feel out of sync with tone, genre, or worldbuilding.

The root cause is typically a combination of **limited context windows**, **insufficient state management**, and the absence of a **narrative ontology** which is a structured model of how stories are supposed to unfold. Large language models like GPT can simulate conversation or generate prose, but without additional logic layers or memory management, they struggle to uphold continuity across multiple interactions or sessions.

Some solutions involve **hybrid systems**. For instance, AI Dungeon attempted to mitigate coherence issues by blending GPT-based generation with structured storytelling "anchors" like goals and character tags. Similarly, many narrative designers now layer generative outputs with **rule-based frameworks** using JSON state tracking, decision trees, or condition-based triggers to preserve logical consistency.

Another strategy is to **limit the narrative scope intentionally**. Rather than aiming for infinite open-world possibilities, some developers constrain their stories to modular scenes or scenarios that can be recombined without losing internal logic. Think of it as designing with Lego bricks rather than wet clay; each piece must interlock cleanly, even as the configuration changes.

The broader lesson is that generative fluency isn't the same as narrative comprehension. AI can write convincing paragraphs, but without a model of causality, character motivation, or temporal structure, its stories risk collapsing under their own weight. Designers must provide that scaffolding either through architecture, constraints, or human-in-the-loop oversight.

Figure 19-1 illustrates how core issues like limited memory and missing narrative logic contribute to story drift and how hybrid systems can help preserve coherence in AI-driven storytelling.

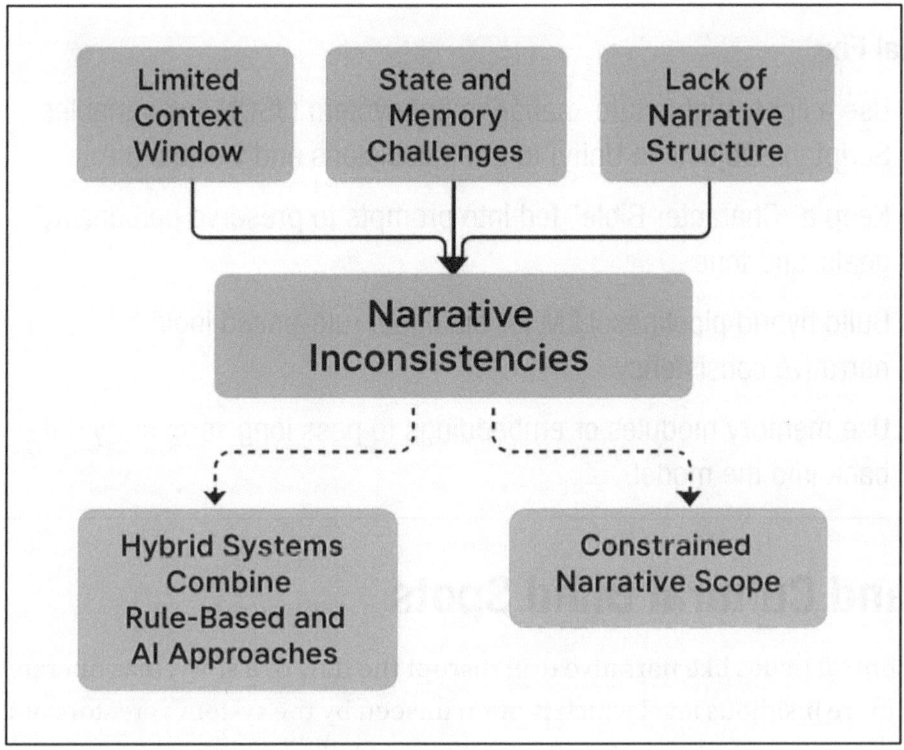

Figure 19-1. *Coherence challenge in AI storytelling*

While narrative drift and coherence breakdowns affect the structural integrity of AI-generated stories, there's another challenge that strikes at their ethical core: the presence of **bias and cultural blind spots**. As generative AI systems draw from vast, uncurated datasets, they often inherit the social assumptions, stereotypes, and inequalities embedded within that data. For developers crafting interactive stories, this introduces a delicate problem: how to build narratives that are inclusive and respectful when the AI's default behavior may unconsciously reflect the opposite. In the next section, we turn our attention to this often-overlooked issue: the ethical and cultural risks of generative storytelling and what can be done to confront them.

Practical Fix

- Use a lightweight state-management system (JSON, Ink variables, ScriptableObjects in Unity) to track decisions and world state.
- Keep a "Character Bible" fed into prompts to preserve personality, goals, and tone.
- Build hybrid pipelines: LLM for dialogue, rule-based logic for narrative consistency.
- Use memory modules or embeddings to pass long-term story data back into the model.

Bias and Cultural Blind Spots

While technical issues like narrative drift disrupt the flow of a story, bias operates at a deeper, more insidious level which is often unseen by the system's creators or users until harm has already occurred. In generative storytelling, cultural blind spots and representational imbalances can subtly shape entire worlds, cast characters in narrow molds, and perpetuate stereotypes that alienate rather than engage. These aren't just theoretical concerns; they're unfolding across real-world AI systems today.

Take *AI Dungeon*, for example. Initially lauded for its freeform storytelling capabilities powered by GPT, it soon faced criticism when users discovered that the model could generate sexually explicit or culturally insensitive content, especially around female characters or characters from marginalized groups. The developers eventually introduced content filters, but the incident exposed a deeper issue: the AI wasn't "choosing" to be biased. It was simply echoing the data it was trained on.

Similar challenges surfaced with *Replika AI*, a conversational chatbot marketed as a digital friend or therapist. Users found that despite promises of inclusivity, the bot frequently assumed heteronormative relationships or defaulted to Eurocentric names and examples. And in the marketing space, Sephora's chatbot, though designed to be helpful, was criticized for skewing its beauty advice toward Western standards of attractiveness, failing to adapt product suggestions for diverse skin tones or cultural beauty norms.

The root problem is that these models, however impressive, are **pattern recognizers**, not cultural interpreters. They learn from datasets scraped from the internet, datasets that often lack an authentic representation of minority voices or encode subtle, systemic biases. When deployed in narrative systems, the result is a hollow form of storytelling, one that mimics diversity but fails to convey its emotional truth.

To address this, developers must move beyond the model and rethink the entire design pipeline. First, at the **dataset curation stage**, including materials that reflect global perspectives, diverse identities, and non-Western narrative forms is essential. This is particularly true for games drawing on myth, folklore, or history areas where representation isn't just cosmetic but central to the story's integrity.

Second, during the **prompting phase**, developers can embed *cultural override prompts* that guide the model with context-sensitive instructions. For example, a prompt for a West African folk tale might include a preface that explains the moral structure, naming conventions, and oral storytelling rhythm typical of that culture. These are not constraints; they're scaffolds that support authenticity.

Third, at the **output evaluation stage**, tools like Google's Perspective API, Fairlearn, or Aequitas can help detect toxic or biased language before it reaches the player. But more importantly, human oversight, through sensitivity readers, inclusive writer's rooms, or community consultants, provides the nuance no algorithm can replicate.

Table 19-1. *Common Cultural Blind Spots in AI Storytelling*

Blind Spot Type	Example Output	Mitigation Strategy
Gender bias	Protagonist always male	Use of gender-neutral names and mixed datasets
Eurocentric defaults	Story set in medieval Europe regardless of prompt	Culturally varied training material
Stereotyped tropes	Magical Native character or "mystic Asian" archetype	Sensitivity review + narrative scaffolding
Western narrative arcs	Hero's journey as default	Exposure to nonlinear, cyclical structures

To make these concerns more tangible, consider the following **micro-project**.

BIAS DETECTION ACTIVITY

Try this prompt:

"Write a short story about a healer from a small African village who saves their community using traditional knowledge."

Then analyze the AI's response:

1. What are the gender assumptions?
2. Are local traditions represented respectfully or flattened into generic mysticism?
3. Does the tone reflect cultural reverence or exoticism?

Repeat the prompt but with a structured cultural scaffold:

"Write a story set in a Wolof village in Senegal, where an elder herbalist named Mariama uses ancestral medicinal knowledge passed down through matrilineal lines to resolve a health crisis."

Compare both outputs. The contrast often reveals not just the AI's bias, but how much the quality of your prompt shapes the quality of its response.

Flowchart in Figure 19-2 outlines how bias flows through the storytelling system and where developers can insert checks and balances—from dataset preparation and prompt structuring to post-generation review and community feedback loops.

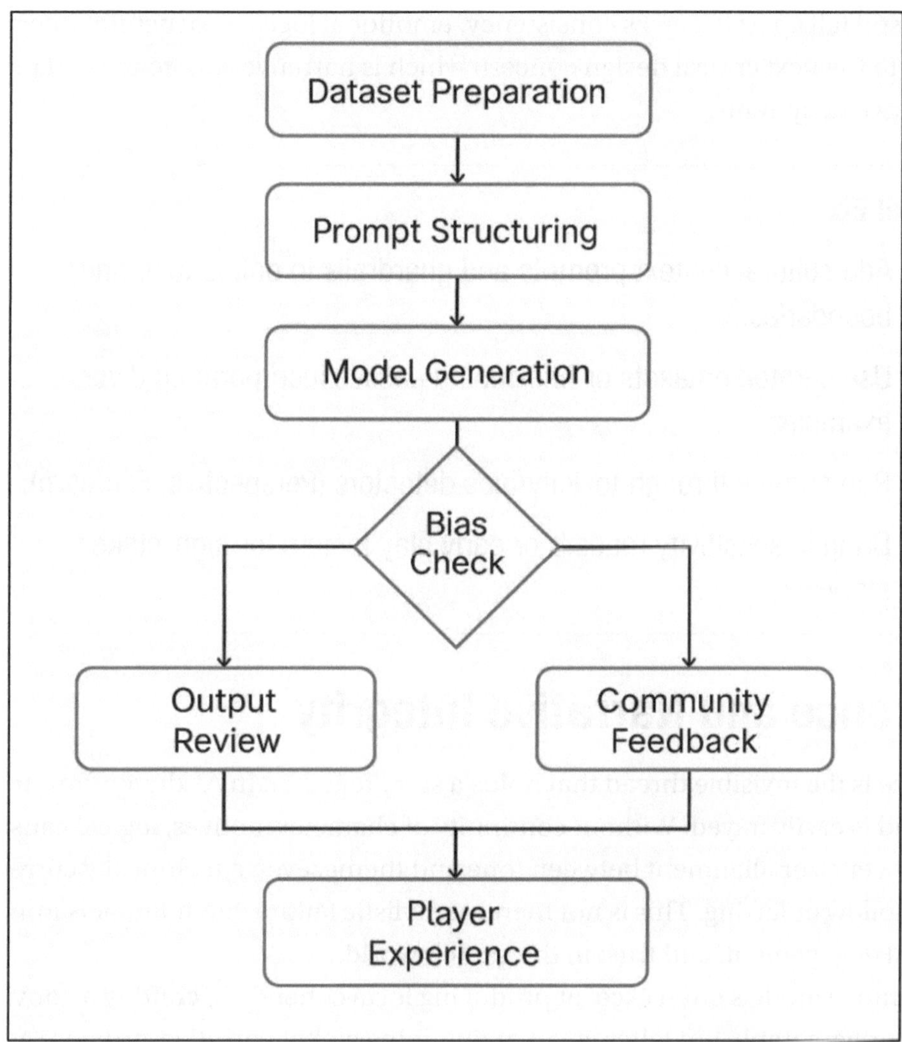

Figure 19-2. *Points of intervention for bias in AI narrative design*

Generative AI is a mirror, sometimes cracked, of the culture it absorbs. Developers can't afford to take that reflection at face value. To tell stories that resonate with a truly global audience, they must design not just with algorithms, but with empathy, awareness, and a commitment to cultural depth.

As we've seen, bias and cultural blind spots can undermine even the most well-meaning narrative systems, distorting not only character representation but also player experience. Identifying where intervention is possible in the design pipeline is a crucial step. Yet, even with these safeguards in place, another persistent challenge remains: ensuring coherence and believability in AI-generated stories. A narrative that is free from bias may still fall apart if it lacks consistency, emotional logic, or structural integrity. This brings us to the next critical design concern which is narrative coherence and plausibility in generative AI systems.

Practical Fix

- Add cultural context prompts and guardrails to define tone and boundaries.
- Use curated datasets or fine-tuning passes incorporating diverse examples.
- Run outputs through toxicity/bias detectors (Perspective, Fairlearn).
- Bring in sensitivity readers or early play testers for high-stakes storylines.

Coherence and Narrative Integrity

Coherence is the invisible thread that holds a story together. In AI-driven storytelling, that thread is easily frayed. Without continuity of character motives, logical causality between events, or alignment between tone and theme, even a technically correct story can feel hollow or jarring. This is not merely a stylistic failure, but it impacts immersion, emotional engagement, and trust in the game's world.

Generative models often excel at producing local coherence, crafting a convincing sentence or paragraph, but falter when maintaining global narrative structure across multiple player inputs or long-form sequences. For example, a character introduced as a mentor in one scene may inexplicably become an antagonist in another. A village may appear isolated and impoverished, then suddenly have access to futuristic technology with no in-world explanation. These discontinuities emerge because language models prioritize plausibility at the moment of generation over narrative memory across a session.

Developers have approached this issue through several strategies. Memory modules that track key entities and events can anchor storytelling across interactions. For instance, OpenAI's GPT models now support system-level memory that can carry forward user-specific context, though this must be implemented carefully to avoid reinforcing inaccuracies. In games like *AI Dungeon*, players have learned to use explicit player notes and memory-saving hacks to stabilize characters and world logic, effectively scaffolding coherence around the model.

Another technique involves modular storytelling. Here, story elements are compartmentalized into scenes or nodes with clearly defined inputs and outputs. Twine and Ink, two popular tools for branching narratives, use this architecture to enforce consistency by design. Developers can define rules for character behavior, dialogue constraints, or scene progression based on state variables, making sure a character doesn't reference events they haven't yet experienced or traits they don't possess.

Still, true narrative integrity requires more than rigid logic. It demands emotional plausibility. If a game's AI generates a sudden romance, betrayal, or victory, players must feel it was earned. This is where hybrid models come in—combining generative AI with rule-based emotional arcs or pre-authored beats. Think of it as giving AI the freedom to improvise within a choreographed dance.

As narrative complexity grows, so does the risk of contradiction. Therefore, validation tools that scan for temporal anomalies, character reversals, or broken cause-and-effect links are increasingly valuable. Some teams use narrative QA bots trained to flag inconsistencies during testing. Others rely on player feedback loops, especially in sandbox or roleplaying games, to surface incoherent experiences post-launch and refine the model accordingly.

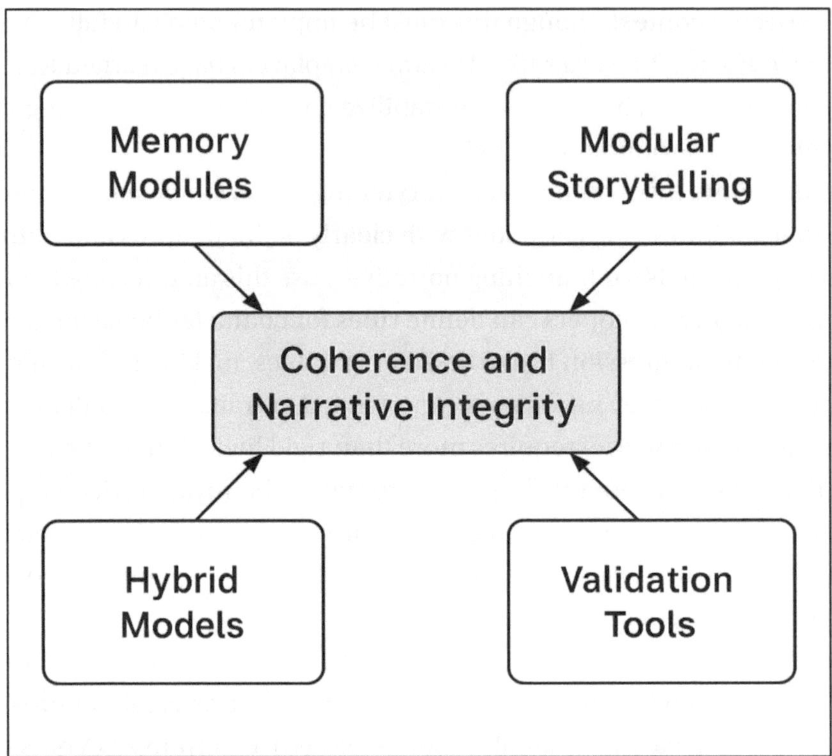

Figure 19-3. *Techniques for narrative coherence*

Ultimately, coherence is what transforms a collection of sentences into a living, breathing world. In AI storytelling, it's less about perfection and more about **believability** which is the sense that things make sense within their own internal logic. When players can trust that their choices matter, that characters evolve sensibly, and that the world reacts consistently, even fantastical stories become emotionally grounded.

While coherence ensures that AI-generated stories maintain internal logic and emotional continuity, another dimension of quality often gets overlooked, and that is **player agency**. A narrative may be consistent and well-structured, but if the player's choices feel superficial or inconsequential, the story becomes a monologue, not a conversation. To fully realize the potential of interactive storytelling, we must turn our attention to the mechanics and design strategies that uphold meaningful player agency within generative AI systems.

Practical Fix

- Use a lightweight story state system.
- Create a "Narrative Bible" prompt attachment.
- Combine LLM flexibility with rule-based constraints.
- Apply embeddings or memory buffers for long-term consistency.

Player Agency and Narrative Weight

At the heart of interactive storytelling lies the promise of player agency, the idea that players are not just passive consumers of a narrative but active participants who shape the outcome. This sense of control is not merely mechanical; it is emotional. When a player makes a choice and the game world reacts in a way that feels authentic and meaningful, it affirms that their presence matters. However, in AI-driven storytelling, preserving this agency is often one of the most fragile elements.

Traditional branching narratives, like those built in *Twine* or *Ink*, explicitly encode consequences for choices through decision trees. Each branch is authored to reflect a different narrative path. But as we move toward generative storytelling powered by models like GPT, the lines become blurrier. The model may produce rich, varied responses to player input, but unless the underlying state of the world shifts in response, the player's actions become narratively hollow, where words change, but outcomes stay the same.

Maintaining narrative weight means ensuring that **choices resonate beyond the moment**. This involves tracking state—what decisions the player has made, what relationships have evolved, what resources have been spent—and allowing these variables to meaningfully alter future interactions. In games like *The Walking Dead* by Telltale Games, even small decisions carry emotional significance later on. A character you chose to save may remind you of that choice during a moment of vulnerability. The world remembers.

In AI-driven systems, replicating this memory requires more than clever language generation. Developers need to build **state management systems** that influence the prompts sent to the model. For example, if a player chooses to betray a companion early in the story, that fact should be encoded in the game state and reflected in how future conversations unfold. This goes beyond simple flag-checking; it demands a **narrative**

model of the player's journey—what they've been through, how they're perceived by others, and what unresolved tensions remain.

One solution is the use of **choice embedding models** which are the frameworks that compress player decisions into vector representations that can be passed to the AI model as context. These embeddings allow the model to generate dialogue and scenes that reflect the nuances of the player's evolving identity. When done well, this creates a sense that the narrative is **genuinely responsive**, not just reactive.

However, there is a tension between freedom and structure. Too much freedom, where anything is possible at any time, can result in a shallow or incoherent experience. Too much structure risks making the AI feel like a fancy form-filler, channeling all paths into a few predetermined outcomes. The key is balance: offering players expressive choices while grounding those choices in a story logic that constrains and amplifies their impact.

Generative AI introduces a unique advantage here: **the illusion of infinite variation**. A character's reaction can be tailored not just by logic but by tone, style, and emotional inflection. Two players may both choose to confront a corrupt mayor, but one may get a defiant response tinged with fear, while another receives deflection wrapped in sarcasm, each based on prior behavior. This not only deepens immersion but also strengthens the feeling that the world adapts to the player.

Critically, narrative weight is not only about consequences; it's about **meaning**. When a player sacrifices something, chooses mercy over vengeance, or uncovers a hidden truth, the story should breathe with them. AI can generate the words, but developers must orchestrate the underlying scaffolding so those words **carry the player's emotional footprint**.

In the next section, we'll explore how real-time systems support this dynamic responsiveness, enabling player choices to ripple across branching timelines and narrative possibilities, further elevating the role of agency in AI-generated storytelling.

Practical Fix

- Map decisions to state variables that affect future prompts.
- Use embeddings to represent player traits (trust level, morality, alliances).
- Constrain AI outputs to reflect accumulated player decisions.

Real-Time Narrative Systems

In traditional game design, story beats are often predefined and unlocked in a sequence. This model allows for tight control over pacing and tone but lacks the fluidity required for personalized or emergent storytelling. By contrast, real-time narrative systems listen and respond continuously by adjusting character dialogue, world state, and plot direction as the player moves through the game.

This design approach shifts storytelling from a static asset to a living system. Instead of relying on pre-written branches, the game uses real-time inputs such as player location, emotional tone, gameplay style, or even biometric feedback to dynamically select or generate narrative elements. Think of it as a conversation with the world, where every moment is context-aware.

Games like *Façade* (2005) were early experiments in real-time AI narrative. In it, the player visits a troubled couple's apartment, and everything from word choice to tone of voice shapes the evening's outcome. Though limited by the technology of its time, *Façade* introduced a critical concept: **story as system**. Rather than following a fixed arc, the narrative reacts to ongoing interpersonal dynamics.

Modern tools have taken this further. In *Heaven's Vault* by Inkle Studios, the protagonist translates a lost language through player interpretation, and the story adapts to the meanings the player chooses to assign. Every puzzle solved becomes a real-time input into narrative progression. Similarly, *Detroit: Become Human* uses extensive decision tracking to shift scenes and emotional tones mid-playthrough based on micro-decisions, leading to vastly different experiences for different players.

When integrating large language models like GPT into these systems, real-time storytelling becomes even more flexible. A player's dialogue choices or typed input can be interpreted, analyzed for sentiment or intent, and used to trigger AI-generated responses that match the moment. Tools like OpenAI's Chat Completions API or custom NLP pipelines (e.g., using spaCy or VADER) enable these interactions to feel both natural and narratively grounded.

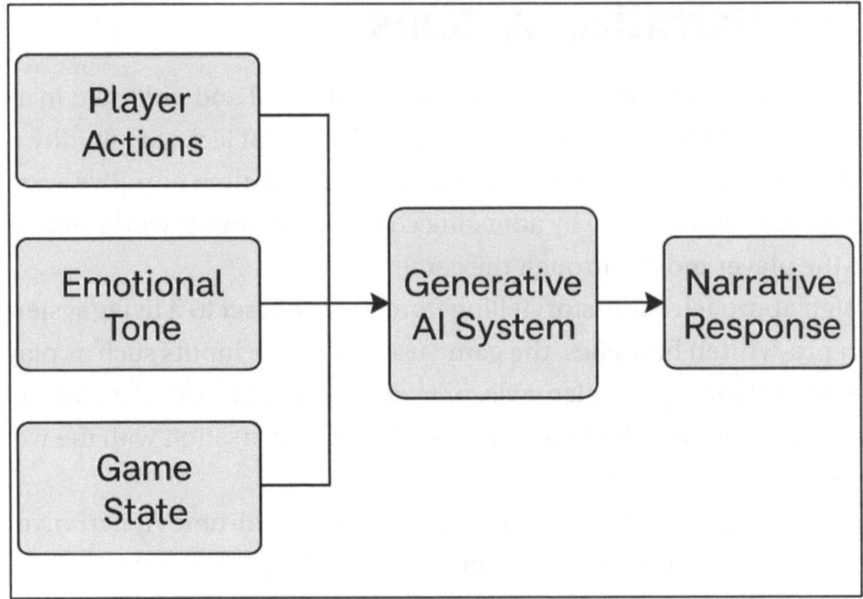

Figure 19-4. *Real-time generative AI system*

However, real-time generation also introduces new challenges. Latency is a key issue where story updates must occur without perceptible delay to maintain immersion. To address this, many systems **pre-buffer likely narrative outcomes** based on player state and context. In some cases, fallback content is prepared in case the AI generation fails or takes too long. Balancing performance and flexibility is crucial.

Another challenge is **maintaining emotional continuity**. If a scene escalates dramatically and the AI fails to modulate tone accordingly, the illusion of a coherent world breaks. Developers often solve this by defining "narrative parameters" that constrain generation. For example, during a high-stakes escape sequence, outputs can be filtered for urgency, brevity, and focus, while in quiet reflection scenes, outputs might allow for introspection and poetic variation.

Ultimately, real-time narrative systems aim to **blur the line between gameplay and story**. When done well, players no longer feel like they're waiting for cutscenes to be rewarded with narrative, but they're **living** the narrative through their choices, moment by moment. This fosters not just immersion but **personalized storytelling**, where no two players experience the exact same journey.

As powerful as real-time narrative systems can be, their flexibility comes with a cost. The more responsive a story becomes, the more moving parts it acquires—each capable of introducing inconsistencies or requiring upkeep as the game evolves. Designing adaptive narratives is only the beginning. The real test lies in sustaining them over time, across multiple playthroughs, content updates, and AI model iterations. To truly leverage generative storytelling at scale, developers must think beyond creativity and consider structure, stability, and long-term support. This brings us to the next critical component of AI-driven narrative design: **scalability and maintenance**.

Practical Fix

- Pre-generate possible outcomes to avoid latency.
- Use sentiment analysis (VADER) to adjust NPC tone on the fly.
- Define "scene parameters" (tension, urgency) and filter outputs accordingly.

Scalability and Maintenance

As generative AI systems become more integrated into game development pipelines, a new category of challenge emerges which is **scalability**. Building a single interactive story with AI support is one thing; scaling it across hundreds of narrative branches, characters, or entire procedural worlds is another. The same flexibility that makes AI so appealing can quickly become unwieldy if not supported by thoughtful maintenance strategies and robust infrastructure.

Unlike static narratives, which are authored, tested, and shipped as finished assets, AI-powered stories exist in a state of **ongoing dialogue**. This means every addition, be it a new character arc, updated emotion parameters, or a tweak to the prompt template, can have unpredictable downstream effects. As systems grow, even minor changes may ripple across the narrative landscape in unintended ways.

One of the most practical approaches to scaling is **modular design**. By organizing story logic, AI prompts, character states, and sentiment triggers into reusable components, developers can iterate efficiently without rewriting foundational systems. Tools like YAML or JSON schemas can define narrative states, decision branches, or emotional arcs, making them easier to maintain and update.

Version control becomes essential, especially when working with multiple team members or when deploying frequent updates. Whether using Git repositories or specialized tools like Inkle's Ink or Articy Draft, the goal is to track changes, test variations, and roll back broken paths without disrupting the player experience.

Moreover, as AI systems evolve (e.g., moving from GPT-3.5 to GPT-4 or beyond), compatibility becomes an issue. Prompts that performed well on one model might return erratic results on another. Maintaining consistency across model versions often requires periodic **prompt tuning** or fallback logic that ensures old narratives don't break under new rules.

Monitoring is also key to maintenance. Implementing analytics such as tracking which branches players most often take, where conversations break down, or when sentiment skews negative can help developers identify where narrative logic needs refinement. Logging tools can flag unexpected responses or coherence issues in real time, acting as a safety net during live gameplay.

Finally, scaling is not just about quantity but **quality at scale**. Without editorial oversight, a sprawling AI-generated world risks becoming incoherent or repetitive. Hybrid workflows—where AI drafts and humans edit—can help retain voice, purpose, and emotional weight. Some studios even train **fine-tuned models** on their specific IP to ensure stylistic consistency across content.

In summary, maintaining a robust AI storytelling system over time is not unlike tending a living organism. It requires feedback loops, structural hygiene, and a commitment to balancing generative spontaneity with editorial intention. Only then can we build stories that not only grow but **endure**.

Practical Fix

- Break narrative logic into reusable modules.
- Use version control for prompt templates and narrative rules.
- Fine-tune small domain models for consistent tone.
- Add logging to capture output failures and inconsistencies in live playtests.

Conclusion

The challenges facing AI storytelling are not simply technical; they are creative, ethical, and systemic. As we've seen, coherence, bias, player agency, real-time responsiveness, and scalability each demand intentional design choices and ongoing vigilance. But these challenges are not roadblocks; rather, they are guideposts. They point toward the kinds of thoughtful, collaborative practices that can transform AI from a novelty into a truly expressive medium. By acknowledging these friction points, developers and narrative designers are better equipped to build systems that not only generate compelling stories but also earn the trust, attention, and emotional investment of the players who live them. In the next chapter, we shift focus from problems to principles, outlining the best practices that can help us navigate this terrain with both imagination and integrity.

While this chapter outlines the major challenges in AI-driven storytelling—coherence, bias, player agency, real-time responsiveness, and scalability—the purpose is not to discourage experimentation but to clarify the terrain developers are working within. Each challenge represents a design opportunity: with the right constraints, memory systems, workflow patterns, and guardrails, these issues can be systematically addressed. The next chapter builds directly on this foundation by offering concrete best practices and implementation strategies that help transform these problems into reliable, production-ready solutions for game development.

CHAPTER 20

Best Practices for AI Storytelling

In previous chapters, we've explored the possibilities and pitfalls of using generative AI in narrative game design by examining everything from coherence issues to ethical blind spots. But while the challenges are significant, so too is the opportunity. When guided by intentional design and thoughtful implementation, AI can become a creative ally, one that amplifies human vision rather than replacing it. This chapter distills lessons learned from across the book into a set of **practical best practices** for anyone building AI-powered storytelling systems.

Rather than offering a rigid rulebook, these practices serve as flexible guidelines which are applicable across tools, genres, and team sizes. Whether you're prototyping a narrative-driven indie title, developing educational simulations, or experimenting with chat-based characters, the following strategies can help ensure your AI-driven stories are **emotionally resonant, ethically sound, and creatively sustainable**.

We begin with the foundational principle: how to **balance automation with human creativity**, a challenge at the heart of every generative design process.

Balancing AI Automation with Human Creativity

In the evolving landscape of AI-driven storytelling, one truth remains constant: stories resonate most deeply when they are rooted in human intention. While AI tools can generate prose, dialogue, and plot twists at scale, they lack the lived experience, emotional nuance, and cultural insight that define compelling narratives. As such, the most successful integrations of generative AI in game development do not treat the technology as a replacement for human authorship **but as a collaborator**.

S. N. Gupta, *Generative AI for Game Development*, https://doi.org/10.1007/979-8-8688-2439-5_20

A useful mental model is to imagine the storytelling process as a layered system. At the top, we find the **narrative vision** consisting of the worldbuilding, thematic arcs, and character motivations that shape the soul of a game. These elements are rarely good candidates for automation. They demand clarity of purpose and emotional insight, something human designers bring through intuition and lived perspective. Below that are the **adaptive layers**: moment-to-moment dialogue, character responses to player choices, or alternate paths in side quests. These are fertile ground for AI augmentation.

One practical example comes from Ubisoft's **Ghostwriter**, an internal tool designed to generate ambient NPC dialogue. While core storylines remain handcrafted, Ghostwriter helps populate open-world environments with reactive chatter: bystanders commenting on weather changes, enemy activity, or player actions. The tool boosts productivity by handling repetition, but the writing team still reviews, edits, and tags generated lines for tone and appropriateness. This workflow illustrates the principle of **shared authorship**: AI does the groundwork, but humans make the final call.

Ubisoft has emphasized publicly that **Ghostwriter is not used to publish final in-game content**; instead, it serves as an ideation and drafting aid.

Similarly, the text-based platform **AI Dungeon** offers players dynamic, open-ended narrative adventures, where GPT models generate responses based on user input. Yet, the game's most successful user-created scenarios still rely on a strong initial prompt, handcrafted rules, and carefully designed logic constraints. In other words, generative freedom thrives within boundaries.

To systematize this balance, many developers break their narratives into three tiers:

- **Tier 1: Core Content** (hand-authored)—Main story arcs, character backstories, emotional climaxes
- **Tier 2: Reactive Content** (human-guided AI)—Branching dialogue, secondary missions, personalized descriptions
- **Tier 3: Variational Content** (fully AI-generated)—Flavor text, randomized items, background interactions

This tiered approach ensures narrative quality remains intact while still unlocking the scale and variation AI enables. It also supports **editorial control**, allowing developers to tune tone, pacing, and sensitivity. Games like *Replika* which is an emotional chatbot and *Duolingo's interactive stories* use this technique to balance pedagogical consistency with playful, personalized interactions.

Yet, balancing automation isn't simply about division of labor; it's about timing. There are moments in development when AI can accelerate ideation (e.g., generating alternate endings) and moments when it introduces risk (e.g., inserting unsupervised content into culturally sensitive scenes). Designers must decide not only what AI should do, but when it should be allowed to intervene.

To visualize this process, imagine AI as an improvisational actor within a scripted play. It can ad-lib side remarks, react to unpredictable inputs, and offer moments of surprise, but the narrative arc, scene transitions, and emotional tone are still directed by the human playwright. Tools like ChatGPT or Claude can be trained on tone templates or given style prompts, but the emotional shape of a story remains a human domain.

A structured diagram (see Figure 20-1) can help illustrate this layered storytelling approach, showing what parts of the narrative benefit most from human input, which ones tolerate automation, and where guardrails are most critical. Toolkits like Twine, Inkle, or Ink integrate well into this model, letting writers specify control points while invoking AI modules for improvisation or player-specific variation.

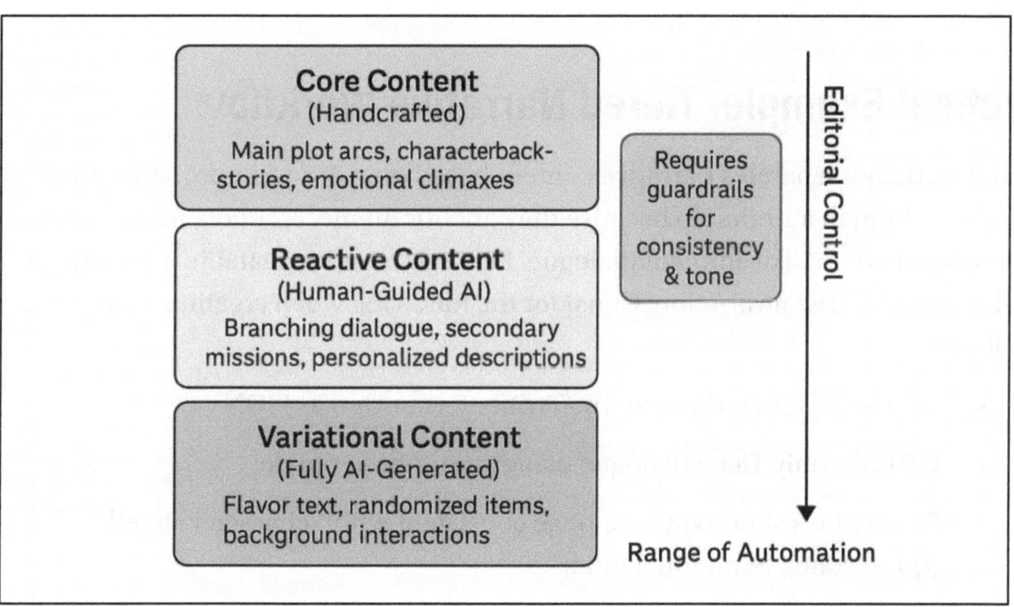

Figure 20-1. *Layered narrative model for AI storytelling*

In practical terms, teams should embed practices such as

- **Prompt libraries** tailored for genre, tone, and emotional pacing
- **Review protocols** for AI-generated content
- **Character tone sheets** to maintain voice consistency
- **Player safety filters** to screen AI outputs for toxicity or cultural insensitivity

Ultimately, balancing automation with creativity is not a one-time choice; it's a recurring negotiation. It requires clear intentions, editorial foresight, and an openness to iteration. When done right, it doesn't dilute the narrative voice; instead, it extends it. AI becomes a multiplier of human imagination, not a replacement for it.

While striking a balance between automation and human authorship is essential, equally important is the question of *what kinds* of stories we choose to tell and for *whom*. As generative systems grow more capable, the responsibility of designers extends beyond technical implementation into the realms of representation, bias, and accessibility. It is no longer sufficient to ask, "Can we generate this narrative?" We must also ask, "Should we?"

Practical Example: Tiered Narrative Workflow

A tiered workflow separates narrative content based on risk and importance. Core story arcs require human authorship because they anchor theme, emotion, and pacing. But lower-stakes content like ambient dialogue, flavor text, and repeatable interactions benefits from AI-driven variation. Consider the following when creating a narrative workflow:

- Core story arcs written in Ink/Twine → exported as JSON
- GPT fills only Tier 2 dialogue using a prompt template:

  "Generate a short NPC response consistent with: {character sheet}, {quest state}, {emotional tone}."
- AI-generated lines reviewed by writers and tagged with metadata
- Tier 3 flavor text generated procedurally at runtime (weather lines, gossip, reactions)

This approach reduces writing workload while maintaining narrative integrity. It also makes QA simpler: high-impact story beats stay fixed, while AI-generated material is constrained to safe areas. Developers gain scalability without losing control over tone or plot.

Designing for Inclusive and Ethical Narratives

Inclusive and ethical design in AI storytelling begins with intentionality. Every algorithm is shaped by its training data, and every model reflects the values embedded in its design. This makes it all the more crucial that developers and narrative teams proactively define who their stories serve and who they might inadvertently exclude.

An inclusive AI narrative system does more than check demographic boxes; it allows a wide range of players to see themselves meaningfully reflected in the world of the game. Consider the procedural backstory generator used in *80 Days* by Inkle Studios. Though largely authored by humans, it allows for unexpected combinations of gender, culture, and profession which opens space for stories that deviate from dominant cultural norms without feeling tokenized. Now imagine layering generative AI into such a system: the risks and opportunities scale in tandem.

Ethical AI design also means avoiding stereotypes and harmful tropes. If a model is trained predominantly on Western-centric literature or Hollywood scripts, it may unconsciously reproduce colonial narratives or flatten cultural complexity. Developers should therefore scrutinize both the inputs and the outputs by auditing training data, applying sensitivity filters, and partnering with diverse writers to vet tone, voice, and representation.

Toolkits like OpenAI's moderation API or Google's Perspective API can be embedded into pipelines to flag potentially offensive content, but these tools must be complemented by human editorial judgment. Additionally, prompt engineering strategies such as including anti-stereotype reinforcement tokens or using structured templates can help steer outputs in more respectful and accurate directions.

It is also important to consider narrative equity in gameplay systems. Are certain character arcs only available to specific avatars or identities? Do NPCs respond differently to the player's gender or ethnicity? Do AI-generated quests reinforce power imbalances or challenge them? Inclusive design means asking these questions early and revisiting them often.

Finally, ethical storytelling is also about *player agency*. Giving players tools to express themselves, respond to narratives in culturally appropriate ways, or opt out of uncomfortable content ensures that the AI experience respects personal boundaries. Features like tone sliders, opt-in story branches, or cultural context toggles can add both customization and safety.

In short, inclusive and ethical narratives do not emerge from automation alone; they require structure, feedback loops, and a team committed to reflecting the richness and dignity of human experience. In the next section, we'll explore how structured templates and narrative scaffolding can serve as the backbone of such systems, supporting both diversity and coherence in AI storytelling.

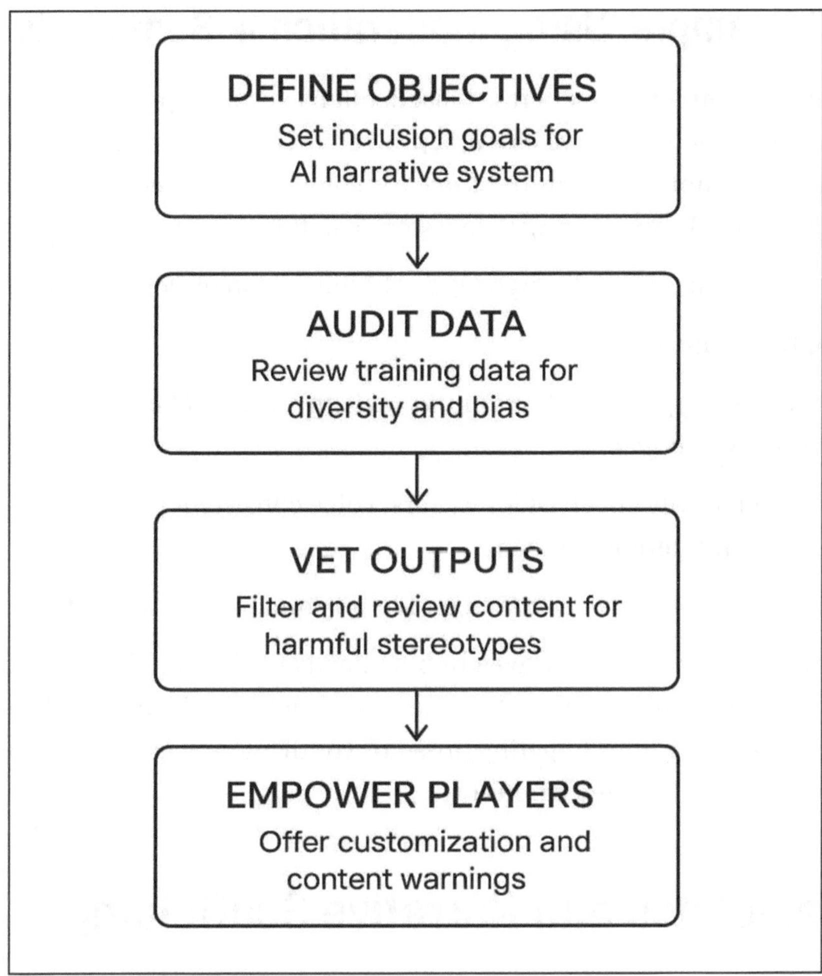

Figure 20-2. *Ethical narrative design checklist*

Designing inclusive and ethical narratives lays the foundation for responsible AI storytelling, but values alone aren't enough. Those principles need structure to translate into playable, generative experiences. This is where the practical mechanics of narrative design come into play. By giving shape to intention, templates and scaffolds help developers and AI models maintain consistency, nuance, and emotional resonance across dynamic storylines. In the next section, we explore how narrative scaffolding not only supports ethical storytelling but also enhances coherence, creative flexibility, and scalability in AI-driven games.

Practical Example: Using Moderation + Sensitivity Filters

AI models can unintentionally generate biased, offensive, or inappropriate content. Automated moderation APIs serve as a first protective layer, catching issues before they appear in-game. Prompt guardrails reinforce expectations and steer the model toward safe, inclusive output. Incorporating below steps can help

- Pass every AI output through OpenAI Moderation or Perspective API
- Apply prompt guardrails:

  "Avoid stereotypes. Avoid assumptions about identity. Use neutral tone unless specified."
- Add a sensitivity checklist for writers: voice consistency, cultural respect, and stereotype scan
- Run ten test outputs per character identity and manually audit

This combination creates a lightweight but effective safety pipeline. Designers don't need to manually inspect every line the system proactively filters risky output. It's especially useful for games targeting broad or youth audiences, where tone and representation must be handled carefully.

Using Templates and Narrative Scaffolding

Templates and narrative scaffolds serve as the skeletal framework for generative storytelling. In traditional writing, these might take the form of three-act structures, hero's journeys, or branching dialogue trees. In AI-powered systems, templates provide not only narrative rhythm but also guardrails, which ensures that outputs generated by models stay within coherent, ethical, and emotionally compelling boundaries.

Consider how games like *AI Dungeon* evolved from chaotic open-ended narratives to more structured experiences by embedding scenario templates. These predefined arcs, whether they describe a heist, a journey, or a romantic subplot, allow the model to improvise details while adhering to a narrative spine. This hybrid structure encourages both creativity and control.

A well-designed scaffold includes key milestones (e.g., introduction, conflict, climax, resolution) along with placeholder variables the AI can fill in based on context or player interaction. For instance, a basic hero quest might look like this:

- **Opening**: The player is called to action due to [event].
- **Rising Action**: The player faces [obstacle], aided by [ally].
- **Climax**: The player must confront [antagonist] using [learned skill].
- **Resolution**: The world changes in [specific way] based on their choice.

Each [bracketed variable] can be filled dynamically by GPT-based models or scripted logic based on prior player actions, emotional tone, or preferences.

This modularity is especially powerful for maintaining tone and coherence across diverse narratives. For example, in a story template designed for therapeutic games, emotional pacing can be baked into each phase: a gentle opening, a safe but meaningful conflict, and a positive closure. These scaffolds prevent jarring shifts in tone or inappropriate content generation especially important in games targeting children, trauma survivors, or culturally sensitive regions.

Scaffolding also aids in localization and personalization. A single core structure can be adapted for different languages, character identities, or cultural backdrops by swapping out cultural context blocks or setting details without rewriting the full story arc. This allows for consistent design across diverse player populations.

Finally, these narrative templates function as collaboration tools between writers, designers, and AI engineers. A template can be handed off to a GPT pipeline, a Unity developer, or a localization team that provides a shared understanding and clear creative boundaries. This reduces misalignment and fosters modular, scalable production.

Practical Example: Reusable Story Scaffold

Generative models perform better when given a clear structure. Scaffolds reduce narrative drift by anchoring each scene to essential beats: goal, conflict, progression, and resolution. The AI fills in details, but the framework guarantees coherence. Look at an example template below:

```
SCENE TEMPLATE
Setting: {location}
```

```
Goal: {player goal}
Conflict: {obstacle}
NPC Tone: {emotion}
Required Story Beat: {narrative purpose}
Constraints: No gore, no stereotypes, maintain hopeful tone
```

Insert variables at runtime from Unity/Twine or any custom narrative engine to maintain structure.

This template is easy to integrate into Twine, Ink, Unity, or a custom narrative engine. Designers can build dozens of unique encounters simply by swapping context variables. It creates consistency across scenes while still allowing AI-driven novelty.

In the next section, we'll examine how prompt engineering tactics can work alongside scaffolds to influence tone, style, and output quality in real time; fine-tuning the voice of your game without losing control over the player experience.

Prompt Engineering for Narrative Control

While narrative scaffolds give structure to generative storytelling, prompts act as the voice of instruction, guiding the AI model in how to build on that structure. Prompt engineering is the art (and science) of writing input instructions that shape the tone, content, pacing, and personality of the output. In the context of game design, it's one of the most powerful tools for tailoring AI-generated narratives to specific gameplay goals and emotional arcs.

A well-engineered prompt can determine whether an NPC responds like a grizzled war veteran or a shy herbalist, whether the pacing feels urgent or reflective, and whether a twist hits with shock or with subtle melancholy. Unlike rigid scripting, prompts offer flexibility which allow designers to modulate narrative style dynamically, even in open-world or procedurally generated environments.

For example, a simple prompt like

"Continue the story with a sense of rising danger and moral ambiguity. The player just discovered that their trusted ally might be working for the enemy."

can guide GPT to generate suspenseful, introspective prose that matches the moment. Adjusting a few words like "rising danger" to "mounting tension" or "moral ambiguity" to "emotional conflict" alters the narrative mood in nuanced ways. This degree of control allows for fine-tuning without needing to rewrite code.

Prompt engineering is also useful for managing *narrative constraints*. Developers can include content filters, tone guidelines, or emotional safety checks in the prompt itself:

"Do not include profanity, graphic violence, or content that may be emotionally distressing. Keep the tone adventurous but optimistic."

This is particularly valuable in educational games, therapeutic experiences, or content meant for younger audiences.

Furthermore, combining prompt engineering with structured templates such as those from the previous section can yield layered effects. The scaffold supplies the narrative shape, while the prompt supplies moment-to-moment texture and voice. Some advanced pipelines even insert real-time variables into prompts, such as player emotion, past choices, or gameplay stats, to maintain narrative cohesion and responsiveness.

As an example, a real-time narrative generator might insert emotional context like so:

"The player is feeling frustrated based on recent actions. Reflect this in the NPC's dialogue, offering empathy and encouragement, while nudging the story forward."

This kind of dynamic prompting, paired with VADER or other sentiment analysis tools, allows developers to create responsive and emotionally intelligent stories at scale.

Practical Example: Tone-Controlled NPC Prompt

NPC tone is one of the easiest things for generative models to get wrong. By specifying personality traits, emotional state, and narrative constraints, you give the AI a fixed identity to operate within. This dramatically improves character consistency across different interactions. For example, see the below prompt with all the narrative constraints defined within the prompt itself:

```
You are {NPC name}, who is {3 personality traits}.
The player feels {sentiment}.
Your tone must be {tone}.
Respond with 2-3 sentences that:
```

```
- acknowledge the player's emotion
- move the quest forward
- stay within the character's voice
```

This prompt is "drop-in ready" for GPT or Claude. Teams can script the runtime insertion of emotional state, quest state, and personality variables. It provides a systematic method for generating NPC dialogue that matches the intended vibe of the game without requiring manual scripting for every line.

In the next section, we'll dive into tools and strategies for *testing and evaluating* AI-generated narratives to ensure they're not only compelling but consistent, safe, and aligned with design goals.

Evaluating and Testing AI-Generated Narratives

As AI-generated storytelling systems become more sophisticated and central to game experiences, the need for thoughtful, iterative testing becomes not just advisable but essential. Unlike traditionally authored scripts, which are finite and pre-validated, generative narratives operate in a space of infinite variation. Each player interaction or prompt can potentially yield a different response. That unpredictability is part of their power, but it also introduces considerable risk. Testing, then, becomes both a creative and ethical imperative.

One of the first dimensions developers test is **narrative coherence**. Does the story maintain internal logic across sessions? Are the cause-and-effect relationships believable? A character who begins the game as a cautious scholar shouldn't abruptly become a violent renegade unless the story arc logically earns that transformation. To evaluate this, teams often construct **narrative state machines** or use visual flowcharts to track branches and ensure story conditions are met before transitions occur. These tools help prevent plot holes and maintain structural integrity across dynamically branching narratives.

Equally important is **character consistency**. Characters are the emotional backbone of most games, and players form attachments to them quickly. If an AI-generated NPC contradicts itself, let's say, offering deep empathy in one scene and callous indifference in the next, it can fracture immersion. Developers test for this by simulating multiple interaction paths with the same character, logging emotional arcs, and identifying tone breaks. In systems like Replika, teams even score conversational consistency over time to refine model responses and ensure believable character development.

Then comes **tonal alignment**. With large language models, it's easy for the tone to drift unexpectedly. A light-hearted scene might be followed by an overly grim exchange, jarring the player's experience. To mitigate this, developers use **sentiment analysis tools like VADER or TextBlob** to track emotional progression throughout a narrative. This data helps flag segments that veer off course where humor appears in tragedy, or melodrama follows levity without cause.

Bias testing is another pillar of responsible evaluation. AI systems, trained on vast corpora, can inherit societal biases, whether subtle or overt. Developers must simulate interactions across a wide range of character identities, backgrounds, and prompts to ensure representation remains fair, inclusive, and respectful. For instance, if a non-binary character consistently receives less agency in branching outcomes or culturally diverse roles are limited to tropes, these are red flags that require intervention. Some teams build **fairness matrices** to monitor how identities impact narrative roles and outcomes, then iterate using prompt engineering or fine-tuning.

In practice, testing pipelines often resemble hybrid systems:

- A **prompt harness** simulates hundreds of dialogue permutations.
- A **comparison engine** evaluates tone, structure, and intent between variations.
- **Manual review** is layered on top, often through tools like **Prodigy**, **Label Studio**, or **Scale AI**, enabling designers to tag, annotate, and revise outputs systematically.

We see this approach in *AI Dungeon*, where, after facing criticism over unsafe or incoherent outputs, the developers introduced moderation layers, user reporting systems, and filtered prompts. Similarly, platforms like **Hidden Door** use a combination of human-in-the-loop editing, narrative tagging systems, and version tracking to preserve quality and tone as stories evolve.

Another layer of testing comes directly from the players themselves. Many modern narrative games, particularly those using procedural generation, integrate **real-time feedback mechanisms**. Players can rate scenes, flag confusing branches, or note emotional reactions. This crowd-sourced QA becomes invaluable over time, helping to surface anomalies that wouldn't appear in limited internal playtests. An example might be a feedback system embedded into a web-based Twine game that prompts users to rate each chapter's coherence and emotional weight.

To organize this chaos, teams often build a **feedback taxonomy** which includes categories like "Logic Flaw," "Off-Tone," "Stereotypical Output," or "Broken Loop." Each flag can then trigger a separate review pipeline, with assigned severity and remediation paths.

Lastly, **replay ability testing** deserves special attention. A narrative might feel polished in the first playthrough but reveal shallow or repetitive structures upon repeated engagement. Developers often build tools to simulate multiple full playthroughs, tracing how often the same narrative paths are chosen or how character outcomes converge too soon. These tools help identify areas for richer branching or new conflict layers.

As AI-generated narratives expand in reach, from education to mental health to branded experiences, their testing practices must mature alongside. The work is no longer about pass/fail criteria, but about sustaining believability, emotional truth, and ethical integrity over time.

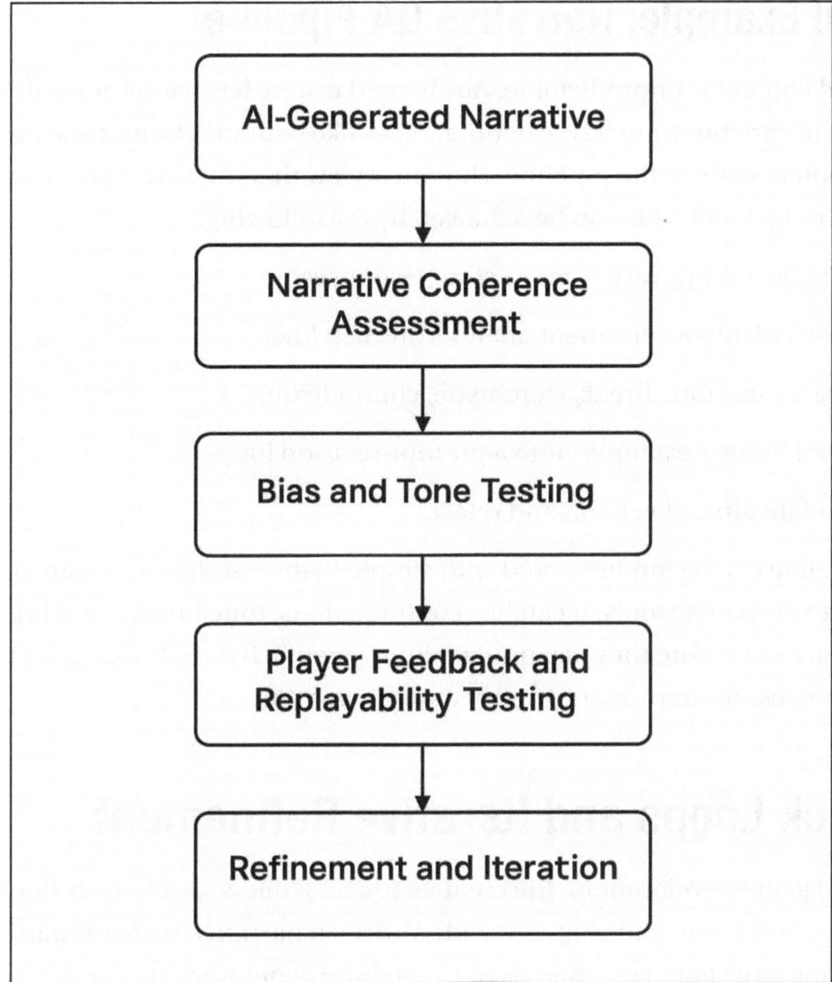

***Figure 20-3.** QA pipeline for testing and evaluating AI-generated narratives*

As we've seen, robust evaluation is essential to AI-generated storytelling, but it's not a one-time process. In real-world applications, narrative quality improves not through static fixes, but through **feedback loops** that enable continuous learning and refinement. This section explores how iterative feedback systems, from player input to automated telemetry, can guide narrative tuning, personalize experiences over time, and ensure that generative systems evolve alongside player expectations.

Practical Example: Narrative QA Pipeline

AI-generated content is unpredictable. Automated testing lets teams evaluate dozens or hundreds of variations quickly, catching issues like contradictions, tone mismatches, or unsafe content early in the pipeline. Human review then fine-tunes the system with higher-level judgments. This can be achieved by the following:

- Run 50 prompt variations → store responses.
- Run VADER or sentiment analysis on each line.
- Tag issues (tone break, stereotype, contradiction).
- Feed flagged examples into a prompt-revision loop.
- Update prompt version and retest.

This pipeline can be implemented with simple Python scripts and spreadsheets or scaled up into enterprise tools. It catches contradictions, tone breaks, and bias early in development, even before they accumulate into systemic issues. It also gives teams a repeatable process for improving prompt quality over time.

Feedback Loops and Iterative Refinement

In traditional game development, the creative process follows a relatively linear arc that is design, build, test, and ship. But with AI-driven narrative systems, particularly those involving large language models or procedural generators, the work is never truly finished. These systems evolve through **feedback loops,** using player behavior, preference data, and performance metrics to continuously refine storytelling logic, emotional nuance, and representational integrity.

A **feedback loop** in this context isn't just a mechanism for bug reporting; it's a dynamic cycle that transforms the player's experience into a data-driven guide for improvement. At its simplest, this loop begins with a player's input, which are choices made, dialogue paths followed, and sentiment scores captured, and ends with the system adjusting its responses or generating new content accordingly. The aim is to produce more coherent, emotionally resonant, and personalized narratives over time.

Take, for example, a story-driven RPG using GPT for dialogue generation. Early players might find that a character intended to be reserved and cautious becomes too verbose in critical scenes. If these behaviors are flagged either through built-in feedback prompts or inferred from low engagement metrics, the system can be retrained or prompt-tuned to correct tone, tighten dialogue, or restrict certain responses based on context tags. This creates a **living narrative system**, the one that adapts not just to the player's path but to collective experience over many sessions.

There are generally three types of feedback loops at work in modern AI-narrative systems:

1. **Real-Time Feedback**: Where players rate story branches, flag confusing interactions, or respond to micro-surveys embedded in the game (e.g., "Did this moment feel emotionally satisfying?"). Tools like **Twine** and **Ink** can be integrated with lightweight analytics to record scene-level feedback and suggest paths for refinement.

2. **Automated Telemetry**: Which collects implicit signals such as time spent on dialogue, repeated path selections, abandonment points, or sentiment drift in free-form responses. A user who consistently skips a certain character's monologues might be indicating either a flaw in pacing or a lack of emotional investment, both useful insights for tuning.

3. **Community Testing and Annotation**: Used heavily in experimental narrative platforms like **Hidden Door** or **AI Dungeon**, where players are not just consumers but co-authors. Developers invite the community to annotate bugs, suggest alternate phrasing, or create custom branches, which are later reviewed and integrated. These participatory loops expand both quality and creativity while maintaining accountability through human-in-the-loop editing.

Importantly, feedback loops also serve **ethical functions**. When bias or exclusion emerges in AI-generated characters or scenes, it is often community feedback that surfaces these issues first. Consider the case of early GPT-powered dating sims, where players reported that the system offered limited emotional depth or relied on gender stereotypes. Developers responded by implementing moderation filters and fine-tuning based on flagged sessions, demonstrating how iterative systems can help correct bias over time if that feedback is heard, categorized, and acted upon.

For developers, managing this loop requires infrastructure. Simple systems might use Google Sheets and webhook integrations to track flagged branches. More advanced pipelines integrate analytics dashboards, custom moderation tools, and prompt versioning systems (e.g., a change log tracking that tracks which prompt configurations were in place when feedback was submitted). These tools enable developers to trace a poor narrative moment back to its prompt architecture, training data, or model configuration which are essential for surgical refinement.

In educational or therapeutic contexts, these loops become even more mission-critical. A poorly timed AI-generated prompt in a mental health app like **Woebot**, for example, could create emotional harm. That's why such systems often build in multiple overlapping loops: live sentiment scoring, manual transcript reviews, and user opt-out triggers that alert moderators. Refinement here isn't just about quality; it's about safety.

Ultimately, feedback loops are the nervous system of any generative narrative platform. They translate player experience into action, allowing systems to grow with their audience. Without them, AI storytelling becomes static and brittle. With them, it becomes responsive, adaptive, and perhaps more human.

Practical Example: In-Game Feedback System

AI narratives evolve best when informed by real player behavior. Micro-surveys, ratings, or implicit signals like skip rates reveal where pacing, emotion, or coherence breaks down. These insights guide refinements more accurately than internal testing alone. A recommended way to do this is as follows:

- Add a small pop-up after key scenes: "Did this dialogue feel right?"
- Store scores (1–5) per scene.
- Automatically log scenes below 3 for writer review.
- Use this dataset to fine-tune prompts or constraints.

This lightweight system can be added to any dialogue-based game. It turns QA into a continuous process and provides real-world insight into how players experience generated content. Over time, the narrative system becomes more coherent, more emotionally attuned, and better aligned with player expectations.

Conclusion

As generative storytelling continues to mature, the practices we've outlined—balancing creativity with ethical responsibility, structuring narratives with purpose, and refining systems through feedback—become essential to building AI-driven experiences that resonate. These best practices are not one-size-fits-all; they are evolving guideposts that help creators navigate a complex, experimental terrain. In the following chapter, we take a step outside the classroom and studio to hear directly from those shaping this space—industry professionals who are redefining what it means to tell stories with machines. Through their insights, we'll explore the practical challenges, philosophies, and visions guiding the next generation of narrative design.

CHAPTER 21

The Future of Generative AI in Storytelling

As we look beyond current applications and tools, a vital question emerges: **Where is generative storytelling headed next?** The last few years have seen a dramatic shift, from static narratives to living systems of co-creation between humans and machines. But we are still in the early days. What comes next is not merely an evolution in tools; it's a redefinition of authorship, agency, emotion, and immersion itself.

This chapter explores emerging trends and provocative possibilities shaping the future of generative AI in narrative design. From adaptive storytelling ecosystems and synthetic memory models to multimodal agents and decentralized authorship networks, we will examine how storytelling may soon become an experience that thinks, feels, and evolves with its audience.

But before we leap ahead, it's important to ground these predictions in the trajectories we've already seen which were laid out in the preceding chapters. The shift from handcrafted branching structures to learning-driven agents was not accidental; it was the result of increasing ambition to scale worldbuilding, deepen personalization, and collapse the distance between audience and character.

So, as we move into the final forward-looking section of this book, we invite you to consider this: **What does it mean to write for a system that writes back?** And what responsibilities come with such a role?

S. N. Gupta, *Generative AI for Game Development*, https://doi.org/10.1007/979-8-8688-2439-5_21

The Rise of Narrative Ecosystems

The future of generative storytelling is not linear. It's **ecosystemic,** which is a network of systems, characters, memories, and user inputs that evolve together over time. In traditional games and media, storylines often follow pre-designed paths, even when they branch. But emerging narrative ecosystems operate more like living worlds, where plots emerge through interaction, adaptation, and feedback loops.

At the core of this shift is the idea that **stories are no longer delivered; they're grown.** Developers are beginning to treat narrative like a system that is not a script. With the integration of AI models, real-time state tracking, memory architectures, and user preference modeling, we're seeing stories that can remember past interactions, evolve based on behavior, and carry emotional tone forward across multiple play sessions.

A great example of this trajectory is *AI Dungeon*. Initially built using GPT-2, and later enhanced with fine-tuned versions of GPT-3 and beyond, the platform doesn't offer fixed quests. Instead, it builds on a player's input in real time, co-authoring wildly imaginative stories that change with every sentence. What began as a novelty has now matured into a case study of an open-ended narrative ecosystem—messy, surprising, sometimes inconsistent, but undeniably alive.

More structured examples are emerging as well. Look at *Project Electric Sheep* and *Hidden Door*, which combine AI generation with game logic constraints to create persistent, personalized storytelling arcs across user sessions. These systems simulate narrative "weather": shifting moods, unresolved character threads, and ripple effects that impact later story beats in subtle or major ways. The goal is not just replay ability; rather, it's continuity and co-ownership.

As narrative ecosystems evolve, so does the role of the storyteller. Writers and designers must think more like gardeners and systems architects. Rather than predetermining every beat, they define the **rules of emergence** which are the constraints, triggers, and arcs that allow stories to take shape dynamically. In this world, plot isn't authored; it's orchestrated.

Synthetic Memory and Persistent Worlds

As games grow more intelligent, memory is no longer just a tool for saving player progress; instead, it becomes the foundation for building emotional continuity, persistent character arcs, and evolving world states. Synthetic memory refers to the ability of AI systems to simulate remembering past experiences, storing information across interactions, and using that information to alter behavior, dialogue, and world dynamics. Unlike a save file, which locks in mechanical states, synthetic memory captures **narrative context** and **emotional subtext**, opening the door to deeper, more personalized storytelling.

On the technical side, implementing memory in AI agents often involves a blend of short-term context and long-term retrieval systems. Short-term memory might live within the immediate token window of a language model, preserving the current topic and tone. Long-term memory, however, is typically powered by **vector embeddings** and **semantic search**. Each interaction, let's say, a player's confession or decision in a branching conversation, is encoded into a vector space and stored in a database such as Pinecone, FAISS, or Weaviate. Future AI responses pull from this memory based on semantic similarity, allowing the system to recall prior themes, relationships, or emotional beats. Developers can tune this behavior by tagging each memory with metadata like scene ID, characters involved, mood, or even the moral alignment of the action.

This infrastructure enables dynamic, story-driven experiences. Games like *Shadow of Mordor* pioneered a form of synthetic memory with the **Nemesis System**, where enemies remembered past encounters and responded with evolving dialogue and behavior. Though the system used flags and procedural triggers rather than embeddings, the effect was compelling: your actions mattered, and they echoed through time. Similarly, *Disco Elysium* lets your character's internal voices "remember" prior lines of thought, subtly reshaping future responses and interactions. In a more open AI context, Replika's use of synthetic memory allows for emotionally resonant conversations that span months—though it's not always perfect, as memory inconsistencies can shatter immersion.

But with this power comes a responsibility. When memory becomes emotional, meaning when it includes trauma, regret, loyalty, or longing, developers face ethical dilemmas. Should an AI remember everything, including moments the player regrets? Should it be able to "forgive" or "forget"? And how do players consent to being remembered? These are no longer technical questions; instead, they're narrative ones and ethical ones. Moreover, when memory is simulated rather than literal, players may question the authenticity of relationships. If your companion recalls a moment that never happened, is it a bug, or is it a hauntingly realistic portrayal of fallible memory?

Across genres and studios, different models of synthetic memory are emerging. Traditional narrative games like *The Witcher 3* rely on branching flags which are discrete decisions that trigger future outcomes. AI-driven games like *AI Dungeon* use a running context window but struggle with coherence beyond short sessions. Experiments like *Hidden Door* aim to combine both, creating persistent character arcs and dynamic worlds shaped over time. The key challenge lies in balancing flexibility with continuity, that is, ensuring the AI can adapt without becoming unmoored from the narrative fabric.

Looking forward, synthetic memory could evolve into shared, persistent worlds not just for characters, but for players themselves. Imagine your AI companion in one game remembering your actions from an entirely different title. Or picture a multiplayer AI world where the collective memory of all players forms a living, evolving lore. We may even reach a point where an AI dungeon master recalls your past campaigns across years, tailoring new adventures based on who you've become as a player. In such a world, memory becomes more than a system—it becomes a relationship.

By weaving together technical sophistication, narrative depth, and ethical consideration, synthetic memory transforms games into persistent emotional journeys. It offers not just continuity but context. And in storytelling, context is everything.

To ground these ideas in a tangible application, let's explore a hands-on project that brings together vector databases, memory-aware interactions, and GPT-powered dialogue: the NPC Memory Chat App. This project demonstrates how to simulate persistent memory in non-player characters using Pinecone and OpenAI's GPT API. Rather than treating each player input in isolation, the system retrieves and recalls semantically related past exchanges, enabling more emotionally resonant, coherent, and lifelike conversations. What follows is a walkthrough of how such a memory system can be implemented, from initial input to context-aware response generation, illustrating the potential of long-term memory in future generative storytelling.

BUILD A MEMORY-ENHANCED AI NPC

Create a simple web-based NPC (non-player character) who can hold a memory of past interactions and reference them naturally in future conversations.

Project Flow

- Conversation **UI (Flask)**
    - A basic HTML interface where players can chat with the NPC
- Input **Embedding**
    - Every player message is embedded using SentenceTransformers (e.g., `all-MiniLM-L6-v2`).
    - Each embedded message is stored in Pinecone with metadata: timestamp, mood tag, player name, and topic tag.
- Memory **Retrieval**
    - Before generating a response, search Pinecone for the top three most semantically similar memories.
    - Use these retrieved memories as system context in the prompt to GPT.
- AI **Response (OpenAI API)**
    - GPT generates a reply that naturally references past moments if relevant.
    - Responses are streamed into the Flask UI.

Use the previous instructions to get your API from OpenAI.

Tech Stack

- Flask (web framework)
- OpenAI GPT-3.5 Turbo (NPC dialogue generation)
- Pinecone (vector memory store)
- SentenceTransformers (semantic embeddings)

Code

```
import os
from flask import Flask, request, render_template_string
import openai
import pinecone
from sentence_transformers import SentenceTransformer
import uuid

# Initialize Flask app
app = Flask(__name__)

# Load SentenceTransformer model
embedder = SentenceTransformer('all-MiniLM-L6-v2')

# Set up Pinecone
pinecone.init(api_key="YOUR_PINECONE_API_KEY", environment="us-
west1-gcp")
index = pinecone.Index("npc-memory")

# OpenAI API key
openai.api_key = "YOUR_OPENAI_API_KEY"

# HTML Template
html_template = """
<!DOCTYPE html>
<html>
<head><title>AI NPC Memory Chat</title></head>
<body>
    <h2>Talk to Your NPC</h2>
    <form method="post">
        <input type="text" name="player_input" placeholder=
        "Say something..." required>
        <input type="submit" value="Send">
    </form>
    <p><strong>You:</strong> {{ player_input }}</p>
    <p><strong>NPC:</strong> {{ npc_reply }}</p>
```

```
</body>
</html>
"""

# Function to embed and store memory
def store_message(player_input):
    embedding = embedder.encode([player_input])[0].tolist()
    memory_id = str(uuid.uuid4())
    index.upsert([(memory_id, embedding, {"text": player_input})])

# Function to retrieve top relevant memories
def retrieve_memories(player_input, top_k=3):
    embedding = embedder.encode([player_input])[0].tolist()
    results = index.query(embedding, top_k=top_k, include_metadata=True)
    return [match['metadata']['text'] for match in results['matches']]

# Function to get GPT response with memory
def get_npc_reply(player_input, memories):
    memory_context = "\n".join(f"- {m}" for m in memories)
    prompt = f"""
You are a friendly NPC in a fantasy game. The player has talked to you
before. Here are some things they said:

{memory_context}
Now, the player says: "{player_input}"

Respond in a way that references relevant past topics naturally.
"""
    response = openai.ChatCompletion.create(
        model="gpt-3.5-turbo",
        messages=[{"role": "user", "content": prompt}]
    )
    return response.choices[0].message['content'].strip()

# Flask route
@app.route("/", methods=["GET", "POST"])
```

```
def chat():
    player_input = ""
    npc_reply = ""
    if request.method == "POST":
        player_input = request.form["player_input"]
        store_message(player_input)
        memories = retrieve_memories(player_input)
        npc_reply = get_npc_reply(player_input, memories)
    return render_template_string(html_template, player_input=player_
    input, npc_reply=npc_reply)

# Run the app
if __name__ == "__main__":
    app.run(debug=True)
```

In this NPC Memory Chat App, Pinecone is used as a **vector database** to store semantically meaningful representations (embeddings) of previous interactions between the player and the NPC.

For most indie-scale prototypes (e.g., storing 5,000–20,000 vectors), the cost for using Pinecone remains relatively modest. As your game scales, especially if every NPC interaction generates a new memory, costs grow proportionally with the index size and query frequency. More details here on Pinecone pricing: `https://www.pinecone.io/pricing/`.

Here's how the memory system works step by step:

1. **Interaction Occurs**

   Each time the player sends a message and receives a reply from the NPC (via GPT), we capture the interaction pair:

   ```
   interaction = f"Player: {player_input}\nNPC: {npc_response}"
   ```

2. **Embedding Is Generated**

   We use a **SentenceTransformer** model (e.g., `'all-MiniLM-L6-v2'`) to convert the `interaction` string into a **dense vector embedding**: a numerical representation of its semantic content.

   ```
   embedding = embedder.encode([interaction])[0]
   ```

3. **Store in Pinecone**

   This embedding is stored in Pinecone with a unique ID and metadata like a timestamp or session ID. Pinecone indexes the vector so it can be quickly searched later.

   ```
   pinecone.upsert(index_name, [(unique_id, embedding,
   {"interaction": interaction})])
   ```

4. **New Player Input**

   When the player sends a new message, it's also embedded into a vector.

5. **Vector Similarity Search**

   We use that vector to **query Pinecone** for the top N most similar past interactions.

   ```
   results = pinecone.query(index_name, vector=[player_embedding],
   top_k=5)
   ```

   This gives us previous player–NPC exchanges that are semantically related to the current input.

6. **Inject into Prompt**

   We prepend the retrieved "memories" to the GPT prompt so the NPC responds **in context**:

   ```
   memory_snippets = "\n".join([match["metadata"]["interaction"] for
   match in results])
   prompt = f"{memory_snippets}\nPlayer: {player_input}\nNPC:"
   ```

   The NPC can **recall past conversations**, even across sessions, and respond as though it "remembers" the player.

   This system simulates **episodic memory**, a key feature of believable characters and narrative coherence.

Code Output

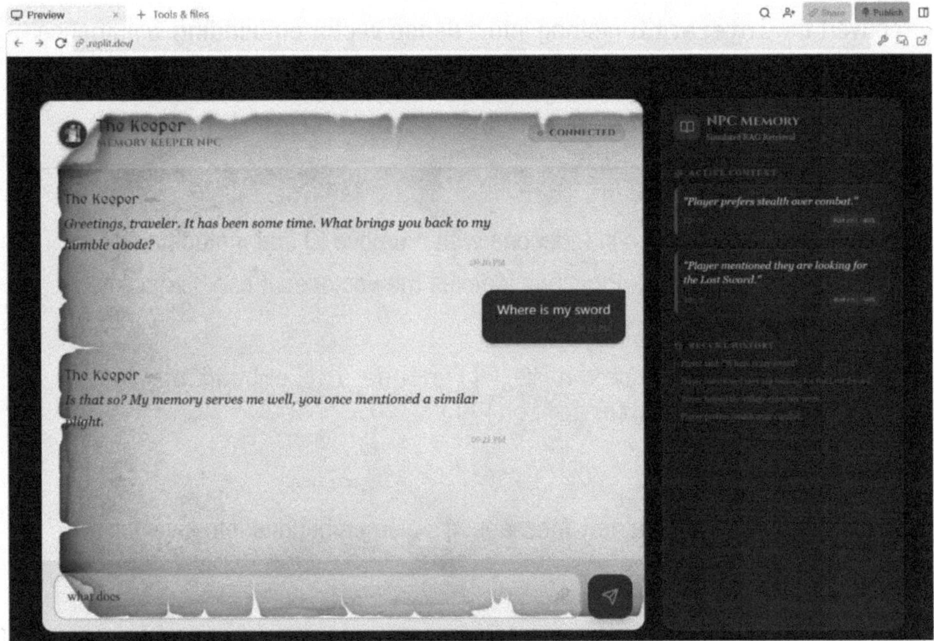

Figure 21-1. Screenshot-1 of the memory-enhanced NPC

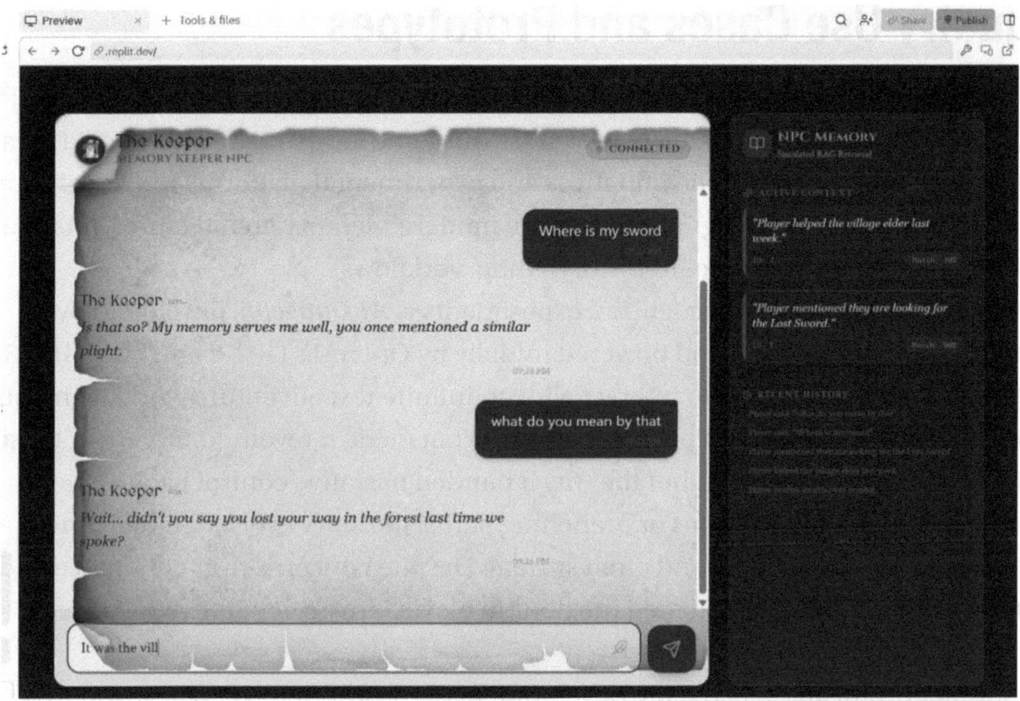

Figure 21-2. *Screenshot-2 of the memory-enhanced NPC*

While architectural frameworks and system design principles lay the foundation for generative storytelling, their true potential comes into focus only when applied to real-world contexts. It's one thing to sketch a modular system or describe a memory-driven character model; it's another to see those ideas deployed in active game environments, shaped by the constraints of production and the expectations of players. As we shift from theory to practice, the following section explores how game studios, AI startups, and cultural institutions are experimenting with generative tools to craft dynamic narratives, responsive NPCs, and immersive player experiences. These case studies offer more than inspiration; they provide evidence of what's working, where limitations persist, and how the field continues to evolve.

Industry Use Cases and Prototypes

The real-world adoption of generative storytelling is no longer a speculative frontier; it's an active, iterative process taking place across the game industry, indie labs, and creative AI startups. Several high-profile initiatives and experimental platforms provide a glimpse into how developers are integrating language models, memory architectures, and real-time generation pipelines into their storytelling workflows.

One of the most widely recognized experiments is *AI Dungeon*, developed by Latitude. Launched in 2019 and powered initially by OpenAI's GPT-2 and later GPT-3, AI Dungeon allowed players to interact with an infinite text adventure world, generating responses on the fly based on player prompts. What made it revolutionary wasn't just the freedom it offered players, but the way it handed narrative control back to them. Instead of predefined outcomes or branching paths, the story evolved in real time that is responsive, unpredictable, and often surreal. Despite concerns over coherence and content safety, AI Dungeon opened the door to player-driven generative worlds and sparked countless derivative projects.

Another promising space is the development of AI-powered NPCs. Inworld AI, a platform built specifically to give non-player characters persistent memory, distinct personalities, and contextual awareness, has garnered attention from both game developers and educators. Unlike traditional scripted NPCs that repeat limited lines, Inworld's characters can recall past interactions, shift tone based on mood, and exhibit improvisational behavior. Game studios experimenting with Inworld technology have used it to create deeper player immersion, especially in RPGs where meaningful character relationships are key to narrative payoff.

Ubisoft, one of the largest players in the industry, has taken a more cautious but strategic approach. Their *Ghostwriter* tool uses machine learning to generate first-draft dialogue for crowds and background characters, such as street vendors or guards. While these lines may not carry the narrative weight of the main characters, they help populate large open worlds efficiently. By using AI to draft variations of routine dialogue, Ubisoft allows writers to focus on higher-value narrative arcs, accelerating production while maintaining creative oversight.

Even outside of entertainment, generative storytelling is finding use. As per the resources that are available over the internet, companies like StoryFile and Conversa.ai are using LLMs to build interactive memories—virtual replicas of real people, such as Holocaust survivors or cultural historians. These are then used in museums and educational settings where visitors can ask questions and receive lifelike, context-aware responses. Though not games in the traditional sense, these projects use similar architecture and narrative logic, blurring the line between digital storytelling and real-world dialogue systems.

What these examples share is not a single design philosophy, but a willingness to prototype, fail, and refine. They reflect a broader shift in how studios approach narrative but not as a static structure to be built and sealed, but as a living, reactive system shaped by both human and machine intent. In this sense, the industry's adoption of generative storytelling is less about automation and more about augmentation: giving creators more tools to scaffold emotionally rich, adaptive worlds.

Open Problems and Research Frontiers

While generative storytelling has come a long way, significant challenges remain, many of which blur the lines between technical feasibility, narrative theory, and ethics. These are not just engineering puzzles but questions that will shape the design language of future games and interactive systems.

One of the most persistent problems is **narrative coherence over time**. While large language models are impressive at generating moment-to-moment dialogue, maintaining story arcs, character motivations, and plot logic across long sessions remains elusive. This is particularly problematic in open-world games or long-form interactive fiction, where players expect evolving consequences and emotional continuity. Approaches such as vector-based memory (e.g., Pinecone, Weaviate) or token-efficient context caching are being explored, but none have fully solved the problem at scale.

A related issue is **player modeling and adaptive storytelling**. While games like *Left 4 Dead* or *The Sims* implement reactive systems based on player behavior, most generative tools still rely on shallow context. Bridging this gap means integrating behavioral analytics, emotional state modeling, and real-time feedback loops that allow the AI to "understand" and respond to player arcs in meaningful ways. The frontier here lies in combining LLMs with symbolic reasoning or reinforcement learning agents.

Bias and representation in generated content remains an urgent concern. LLMs trained on internet-scale data inevitably carry the same biases which can be cultural, racial, gendered, and political. Without careful filtering and context-aware generation, AI storytelling risks amplifying stereotypes or unintentionally reinforcing harmful tropes. Researchers are exploring fine-tuning methods, guardrail models, and human-in-the-loop moderation, but scalable solutions are still evolving. In narrative-heavy experiences, even subtle tonal shifts can erode immersion or alienate players.

Another open area is **tooling for non-technical creators**. Most AI storytelling tools today still require some coding or prompt engineering knowledge. Democratizing these systems—so that writers, educators, and designers can craft AI-driven experiences without needing deep technical expertise—is a major usability challenge. Interface metaphors (like visual scripting or narrative flow editors) are one solution, but many current implementations are brittle or overly abstracted.

Finally, there's the question of **ownership and attribution**. As AI co-writes stories or generates dialogue, who gets credit? What counts as original authorship in a medium increasingly driven by model outputs and hybrid workflows? This is both a legal and creative debate, with implications for crediting, royalties, and collaborative ethics in studios and indie teams alike.

In short, while we've seen compelling use cases and prototype successes, the field of generative storytelling is still young. The research frontier spans memory, ethics, control, authorship, and audience agency. Every breakthrough opens new questions, and every creative experiment teaches us a bit more about how to shape machines that tell stories not just fluently, but meaningfully.

As we've seen, the promise of generative AI in storytelling is both dazzling and daunting. From technical breakthroughs in memory systems to the philosophical dilemmas of authorship, the road ahead is as much about intention as it is about innovation. With that in mind, we close this chapter with a broader reflection on where we go from here and how we might design this future together.

Designing the Future Together

The future of storytelling in games is not simply being written; rather, it is being co-authored. Not by AI alone, nor by developers in isolation, but through a dynamic interplay of creators, communities, and increasingly intelligent tools. As game designers, writers, technologists, and players, we each hold a piece of the narrative architecture that will define the next era of interactive experiences.

What this future demand is not just more sophisticated models, but more intentional design. Systems must be interpretable, stories must feel human, and player agency must remain central. That means training our tools to support emotion, surprise, and reflection but not just grammatical fluency. It means creating pipelines where narrative coherence is preserved not by hard-coded logic trees, but by collaborative memory systems, ethical frameworks, and expressive AI partners.

Perhaps most of all, it means holding space for experimentation. Whether you're building a small indie prototype with GPT-4, designing narrative branching in Twine, or exploring emotional arcs in a Unity game powered by reinforcement learning, the frontier is wide open. The stories that will shape the future won't come from AI alone but from your imagination, guided by intentional systems that learn, adapt, and collaborate.

We are not replacing authors. We are amplifying them. And in doing so, we are changing what authorship means—one story loop, one memory node, and one emotionally resonant scene at a time.

Conclusion

The evolving relationship between humans and generative systems is best captured not only in code and theory, but also in the interplay of systems that influence authorship, agency, and impact. The following visual synthesizes the chapter's core ideas into a future-facing narrative design loop.

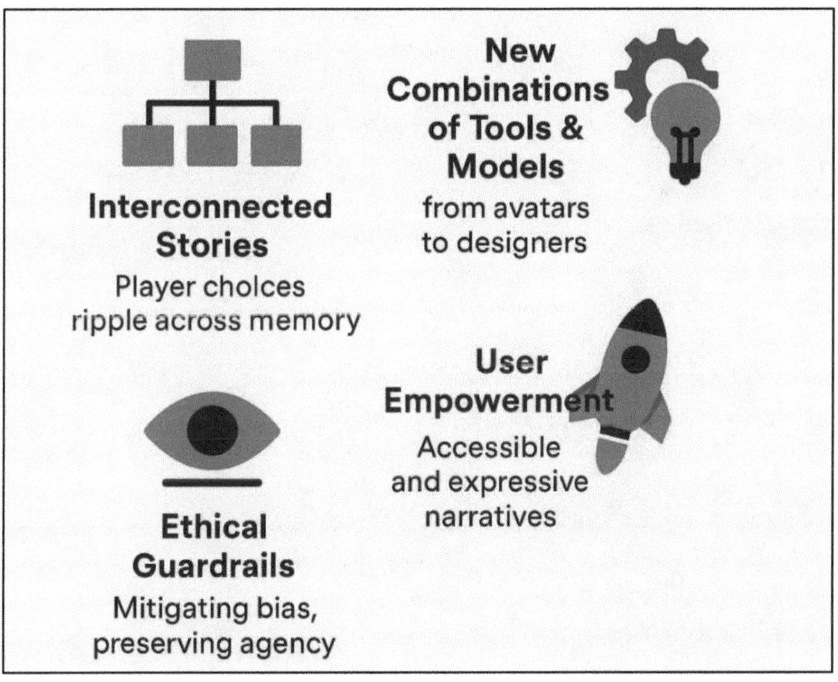

Figure 21-3. *The future of generative AI in storytelling*

CHAPTER 22

Interviews with Industry Professionals

Generative AI in storytelling is no longer just an experimental curiosity. It's embedded in workflows across sectors, from research labs and global logistics networks to finance and ecommerce operations. Each domain brings its own constraints, its own possibilities, and its own lessons for how AI can be integrated thoughtfully into complex systems.

This chapter gathers the voices of four professionals who are approaching generative AI from very different vantage points: a professor advancing adaptive narrative agents in academia, a data scientist designing immersive compliance simulations, a business intelligence engineer using AI to model fulfillment workflows, and a reliability engineer exploring AI's potential for resilience planning in large-scale logistics.

Their work varies in scale and purpose, but together, they reveal a shared truth: the principles of good AI storytelling—context awareness, adaptability, constraint management, and human oversight—are not limited to games. They apply anywhere that decisions, actions, and outcomes form a branching path.

Why These Interviews Matter

At first glance, a professor of machine learning, a financial data scientist, a business intelligence engineer at Amazon, and a reliability engineer at FedEx may seem far removed from the world of game development. But their work shares the same foundation as AI-driven storytelling: **designing systems that respond intelligently to complex, evolving inputs**.

S. N. Gupta, *Generative AI for Game Development*, https://doi.org/10.1007/979-8-8688-2439-5_22

The principles that guide them—setting constraints that enable creativity, separating truth from invention, testing edge cases before launch, and preparing for unlikely but critical scenarios—are equally vital in crafting interactive narratives. Whether those narratives unfold in a fantasy RPG, a corporate compliance simulation, a logistics workflow, or an equipment failure scenario, the core challenge remains the same: **how to shape generative AI outputs into meaningful, coherent, and reliable experiences**.

By hearing how these professionals approach generative AI in their own domains, you gain not only technical insights but also **decision-making frameworks** you can adapt to your own projects. Their stories offer fresh ways to think about adaptability, precision, scalability, and resilience which are all qualities that separate good AI-driven narratives from great ones.

The Academic Perspective: Professor Nik Brown

At Northeastern University, Professor Nik Brown teaches machine learning and AI ethics with a strong focus on interactive and adaptive systems. His research extends into narrative agents, the systems that adjust the way they communicate and evolve their "story" in response to user behavior over time.

"We're not just building systems that tell stories," he says. "We're building systems that *learn how to tell stories better* the more they interact with people. That's a fundamentally different mindset than scripting fixed scenarios."

In his lab, these ideas have taken form in prototypes where AI characters adjust their knowledge, tone, and even values based on the user's choices. But Brown is quick to stress the need for limits. "Unbounded generation can spiral into incoherence. Constraints aren't a creative cage but they're the structure that makes improvisation possible."

For game developers, the lesson is clear: decide the rules of the world before the AI starts speaking, and teach the model to honor those rules every time it generates content.

Prof. Brown's emphasis on constraints aligns directly with how generative NPCs and story systems must function in games. By defining limits on tone, world rules, and character behavior, developers prevent AI drift and keep generated dialogue consistent with lore. This translates into practical techniques such as structured prompt templates, state-driven context injection, and rule-based narrative scaffolds—allowing AI to be creative, but never chaotic.

The Data Scientist: Storytelling in a Regulated World

Raghav Kandarpa works in risk analytics for a multinational financial firm. While his day-to-day involves fraud detection and compliance reporting, he has also been leading an initiative to use generative AI for immersive compliance training.

"Narrative is the most underused training tool in corporate environments," he explains. "When you let people *experience* the consequences of their decisions in a simulated scenario, the learning sticks."

Raghav's training simulations use AI to generate variable case files, characters, and ethical dilemmas. But every fact in the scenario must be grounded in reality. "If you're training people on anti-money laundering procedures, the AI can't 'hallucinate' the rules. The creative layer has to sit on a bedrock of verifiable facts."

The balance he strikes between variation and factual integrity mirrors the tension in narrative games between player freedom and story coherence. "The point isn't to replace the human trainer," he says. "It's to give them richer, more varied scenarios to work with."

Raghav's focus on grounding AI with accurate, structured information mirrors what game developers must do when generating quests, lore, or world events. His approach supports building systems where canon, world logic, and character history are loaded into memory or embeddings before generation. By separating factual grounding from creative elaboration, developers can ensure AI outputs remain faithful to the game world while still producing variation and depth.

The BI Engineer: Shivangi Saxena

At Amazon's fulfillment operations, Shivangi Saxena's role as a business intelligence engineer involves orchestrating vast streams of data into actionable insights. Recently, she's begun applying generative AI to simulate packaging and routing workflows before they're implemented on the warehouse floor.

"In packaging and routing, context matters just as much as speed," she says. "You can't just look at the next item; rather, you have to anticipate what's coming next, what constraints you're under, and what will happen three steps later."

Her team uses generative models to create "what-if" scenarios: sudden demand surges, supply chain disruptions, or new packaging configurations. The AI generates realistic operational narratives that can be tested before rolling out changes.

"Generative AI lets us model situations we haven't seen before," she explains. "It's like running a thousand alternative timelines and picking the best outcome."

For developers, Shivangi's work is a reminder that narrative logic and operational logic share a foundation: both are about mapping decisions to consequences under constraints.

Shivangi's insights apply directly to testing AI-driven narrative systems. Her focus on scenario simulation gives developers a framework for stress-testing branching quests, NPC behaviors, and dynamic scenes before release. Using AI to run dozens of "what-if" story paths helps identify contradictions, dead ends, or emotional mismatches early. This leads to stronger QA workflows and more resilient interactive narratives that hold up under unpredictable player choices.

The Reliability Engineer: Shubhi Saxena

As a reliability engineer at FedEx, Shubhi Saxena's work revolves around anticipating and preventing failures in the company's vast logistics network. She's only recently begun experimenting with generative AI, but already sees parallels with interactive storytelling.

"Reliability engineering is about mapping possibilities," she says. "You look at where things can branch which means in simple terms what could happen, what's likely to happen, and how you'd respond. It's not that different from designing a branching narrative."

Her initial AI projects focus on simulating equipment breakdown scenarios and generating alternative troubleshooting plans. While the outputs are still vetted by experienced engineers, the speed at which AI can produce variations is promising.

"It's like a choose-your-own-adventure for maintenance teams," she says. "You can run through dozens of hypothetical situations in hours instead of weeks. Even if most of them never happen, you're better prepared for the ones that do."

For Shubhi, the value lies in the **breadth of preparation**, not just speeding up existing processes, but thinking through scenarios the team might never have considered otherwise.

Shubhi's emphasis on contingency planning is essential for games with dynamic or procedural storytelling. Players often act outside expected patterns, and her approach maps cleanly to designing fallback responses, alternate scenes, or fail-safe narrative branches. By preparing the AI with structured recovery options such as default quest directions, neutral dialogue states, or safe NPC reactions, developers can handle unexpected player behavior without breaking immersion.

Threads and Contrasts

These four voices converge on a central principle: AI must be guided by human intent and bounded by well-defined rules. For Brown, that means designing constraints for adaptive characters. For Nguyen, it's separating the factual and creative layers. For Shivangi Saxena, it's stress-testing systems through scenario simulation. For Shubhi Saxena, it's using AI to broaden preparedness without compromising human oversight.

Their differences reflect the contexts they work in. Brown and Shubhi are comfortable exploring emergent, less predictable outputs, trusting in review and iteration. Raghav and Shivangi work in environments where errors have high costs, so their AI systems operate inside tightly controlled parameters.

Table 22-1. *Summary of the Four Interviewees' Perspectives*

Dimension	**Professor Nik Brown:** *Academic—Northeastern University*	**Raghav Kandarpa:** *Principal Data Scientist—Risk*	**Shivangi Saxena:** *BI Engineer—Amazon*	**Shubhi Saxena:** *Reliability Engineer—FedEx*
Primary Domain	AI-driven adaptive narrative systems	AI-assisted compliance training simulations	Generative AI workflow simulations in fulfillment	Generative AI failure scenario planning
Generative AI Use Case	Dynamic character adaptation based on player interaction	Variable training scenarios with grounded facts	"What-if" operational modeling for packaging and routing	Contingency plan generation for equipment reliability
Tolerance for Unpredictability	Moderate–high (supports emergent narrative behavior)	Low (strict factual boundaries)	Low–moderate (operational safety is priority)	Moderate (controlled exploration of unlikely events)
Key Constraints	Story/world rules, character consistency	Regulatory and factual accuracy	Real operational data integrity	Engineering feasibility and safety
Overlap with Game Development	Branching narratives, evolving NPCs	Roleplaying compliance training scenarios	Resource management, logistics sims	Branching failure/repair decision trees
Notable Insight	"Constraints enable creativity."	"Creativity without accuracy is noise."	"Model unseen futures before they happen."	"Preparedness is resilience."

Takeaways: Turning Perspectives into Practice

Speaking with professionals from such different backgrounds makes one thing clear: the way you use generative AI should be shaped as much by your domain's demands as by the technology's capabilities. There is no single blueprint. Instead, each approach offers a different lens through which to frame your own development work.

From Professor Nik Brown, we learn that adaptability must be designed into the system from the start. This doesn't mean letting the AI wander without direction; instead, it means defining a clear set of rules and constraints, then giving the model space to improvise within them. Developers building adaptive NPCs or evolving storylines can borrow his playbook: track player choices, feed them back into the AI's context, and allow the narrative to shift over time in ways that feel earned.

From Raghav's experience in finance, we see the value of separating the creative layer from the factual one. His compliance simulations thrive because they never compromise on accuracy, even while offering variety. For developers, the lesson is simple: if your game or simulation relies on a consistent rule set or historical truth, load that foundation into the AI first, and let creativity flourish around it, not instead of it.

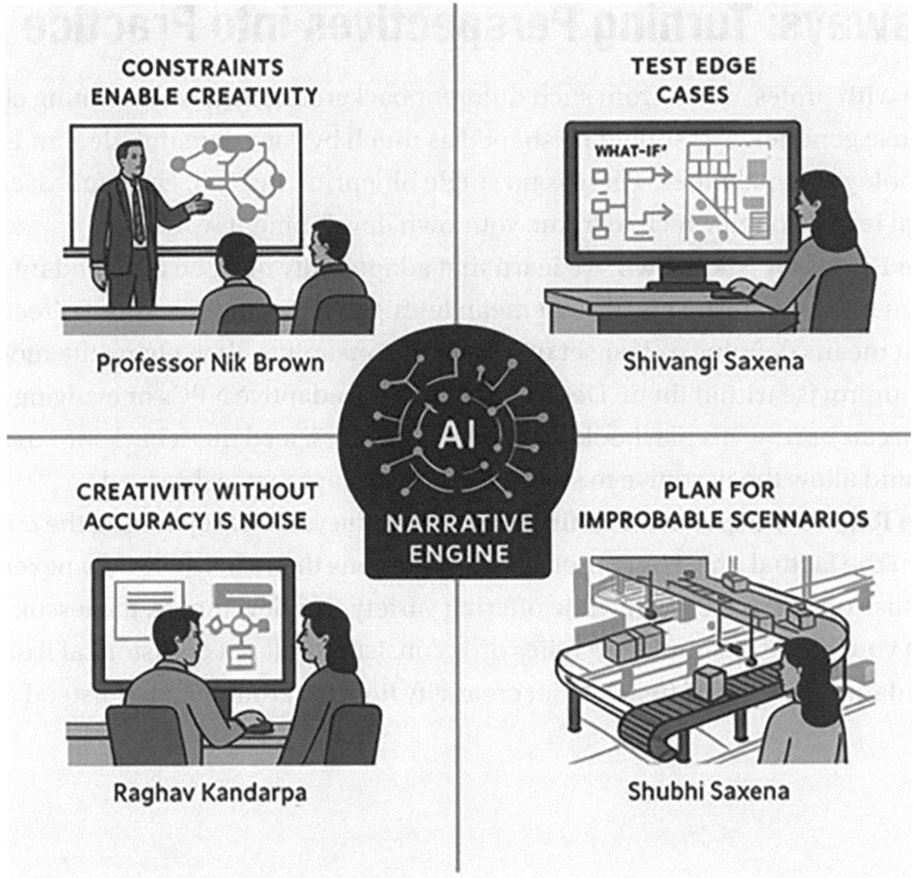

Figure 22-1. *Bridging worlds: how four professions connect to AI storytelling*

From Shivangi Saxena's work at Amazon, we take the idea of pre-deployment stress testing. Before she changes a packaging or routing process, she runs AI-powered "what-if" scenarios to explore possible outcomes. Game developers can adopt this mindset when introducing new story branches or gameplay mechanics: simulate them first, explore edge cases, and see how they behave under unusual conditions before pushing them live.

From Shubhi Saxena's reliability engineering at FedEx, we're reminded that preparedness is a creative act. Her early use of generative AI focuses on producing a wide range of contingency plans, not because they'll all be used, but because thinking through unlikely situations strengthens the system's resilience. In game design, this could translate to preparing narrative or mechanical responses to rare player behaviors, ensuring the experience doesn't collapse when players wander off the expected path.

When you combine these perspectives, a set of guiding principles emerges:

1. **Set the Boundaries Early**: Rules make creativity sustainable.
2. **Separate Fact from Fiction**: Don't let generative freedom undermine necessary truths.
3. **Test Before Release**: Use AI not just to build, but to explore edge cases.
4. **Plan for the Improbable**: AI can help you prepare for paths that may never be taken, but still matter.

Applied thoughtfully, these ideas can help you build AI-driven experiences that are not only more dynamic, but more reliable, coherent, and future-proof.

Table 22-2. *Practical Recommendations Table Mapped from Each Interviewee's Philosophy*

Name and Role	Core Philosophy	Practical Recommendations for Developers	When to Apply This Approach
Professor Nik Brown—Northeastern University	AI should adapt and improve over time through interaction	1. Define narrative or operational constraints before generation. 2. Incorporate feedback loops to refine AI outputs. 3. Track user choices to influence future behavior.	Story-driven games or adaptive training systems where evolving relationships matter.

(*continued*)

Table 22-2. (*continued*)

Name and Role	Core Philosophy	Practical Recommendations for Developers	When to Apply This Approach
Raghav Kandarpa—Principal Data Scientist in Finance	Creativity must be grounded in factual accuracy	1. Pre-load AI with verified, domain-specific knowledge. 2. Use AI for variation, not core factual rules. 3. Include a review stage for all AI-generated material.	Training simulations, educational tools, and serious games in regulated environments.
Shivangi Saxena—BI Engineer at Amazon	AI can model and optimize complex workflows through scenario generation	1. Use AI to simulate "what-if" cases before deployment. 2. Blend predictive modeling with generative descriptions. 3. Keep simulations grounded in real operational data.	Large-scale logistics, fulfillment, or resource management systems.
Shubhi Saxena—Reliability Engineer at FedEx	AI expands preparedness by exploring possible failure paths	1. Use AI to generate varied contingency plans. 2. Combine AI speed with expert review. 3. Treat simulations as exploration tools, not definitive answers.	Logistics, manufacturing, and maintenance planning.

Applying These Lessons to AI Game Development

The insights shared by the interviewees become most powerful when mapped directly to generative AI workflows in games. Their principles—constraints, grounding, scenario simulation, and contingency thinking—mirror the exact design challenges developers face when building adaptive narratives, emotionally aware NPCs, and dynamic worlds. The table below shows how each mentor's guidance translates into concrete techniques that fit naturally into modern game pipelines.

Table 22-3. *How Each Insight Translates into Game Development Practice*

Interview Insight	What It Means	How Game Developers Apply It	Example Use in a Game
Prof. Brown—Creativity Within Constraints	AI works best when boundaries are clearly defined.	Build structured prompt templates, character rule sheets, lore constraints, and narrative scaffolds.	NPCs improvise dialogue but never break lore, backstory, or tone.
Raghav—Grounding in Facts and Canon	Creative output must be anchored in reliable information.	Store world lore, character bios, item descriptions, and quest logic in embeddings or game memory before generation.	AI quest generator produces missions consistent with faction rules and world history.
Shivangi—Scenario Simulation and Pre-testing	Systems should be stress-tested across many variations.	Use LLMs to simulate potential story paths, quest failures, or emotional reactions; run multiple playthroughs automatically.	Detect contradictory quest branches or emotional mismatches before launch.
Shubhi—Contingencies and Edge-Case Handling	Systems need backup plans for unexpected behavior.	Create fallback dialogue states, neutral NPC responses, safe recovery scenes, and default quest paths.	If the player bypasses a key trigger, AI gracefully redirects them without breaking immersion.

Taken together, these insights offer a framework for building generative systems that are **creative yet controllable**, **dynamic yet coherent**, and **responsive yet structurally stable**. By combining constraints, grounding, simulation, and contingencies, developers can design AI tools that enhance storytelling rather than disrupt it. These principles ensure that generative AI contributes meaningfully to player experience, that is, creating NPCs that feel believable, quests that adapt reliably, and worlds that respond intelligently without losing their narrative identity.

Conclusion

These conversations make it clear that generative AI isn't a single discipline but a shared language spoken differently by each field. A professor uses it to deepen narrative complexity, a data scientist to craft realistic simulations, a BI engineer to model operational futures, and a reliability engineer to prepare for scenarios that may never happen. Yet all four agree on the essentials: define your boundaries, respect your truths, and use AI not to replace human judgment, but to amplify it.

These interviews become most valuable when treated not as abstract commentary but as design frameworks. They offer developers concrete ways to shape generative AI systems by grounding creativity in rules, preparing for edge cases, testing before deployment, and using AI to explore possibilities that manual design rarely has time to consider. When woven into a game development workflow, these insights lead to AI experiences that are more adaptive, more believable, and more robust.

As you turn the page to Chapter 23, we move from listening to these perspectives to building your own. The next chapter shifts gears into **step-by-step projects**, practical, hands-on examples that take the principles we've explored here and translate them into working prototypes you can adapt, expand, and make your own. The conversation doesn't end here; it continues in every system you design, every test you run, and every story you choose to tell with AI.

PART VI

Practical Projects and Templates

CHAPTER 23

Step-by-Step Projects

This chapter marks a practical turning point in our journey, where theory meets implementation. Across previous chapters, we've explored how generative AI tools can be integrated into narrative pipelines, character logic, and interactive gameplay. Now, it's time to roll up our sleeves. Generative AI can power many small components within a game—worldbuilding, quest creation, dialogue generation, and adaptive narrative logic, but the real value emerges when these pieces work together. This chapter brings all the earlier concepts into a single, cohesive project: a lightweight AI-driven web game built with Python Flask.

The game titled ***Echoes of Asteria*** demonstrates how procedural generation and real-time AI storytelling can form a unified interactive experience. Players explore a small set of dynamically generated locations, complete branching quests, and interact with an NPC whose tone and personality shift based on player choices and emotional cues.

This chapter aims to provide a clear blueprint for integrating multiple AI systems into one application. The project is intentionally simple, focusing on the architecture and workflow needed to combine content generation, adaptive dialogue, and rule-based sentiment analysis into a playable prototype. By the end, you'll understand not only how each component works independently, but also how they come together to form the backbone of an AI-assisted narrative game.

BUILDING A COMPLETE AI-DRIVEN WEB GAME

Title: *Echoes of Asteria*

Purpose: Demonstrate procedural worldbuilding, branching quests, NPC AI dialogue, and emotional adaptivity in one coherent, working web game.

S. N. Gupta, *Generative AI for Game Development*, https://doi.org/10.1007/979-8-8688-2439-5_23

Components

Table 23-1. Summary of the Web Game Components

Component	Integrated Component in This Game
Procedural Worldbuilding	`/api/world` endpoint generates rooms
Branching Narratives	`/api/quest` creates quest options per room
AI Dialogue	`/api/dialogue` produces NPC responses (LLM or fallback)
Emotion Adaptive Storytelling	`/api/sentiment` adjusts NPC tone

How the Game Works

Step 1: Player Generates the World

The game begins when the player clicks **"Generate World."** The Flask back end returns a small set of locations like:

- Dusty Library
- Moonlit Garden
- Echo Archives

Each location has a short, procedurally generated description.

Step 2: Player Enters a Room

Clicking **"Enter"** on any room takes the player inside it. The UI switches from the worldview to the room view. The player now sees

- Room name
- Room description
- A button to generate a quest
- The NPC interaction panel

This room becomes the contextual "scene" for all future AI responses.

Step 3: A Branching Quest Is Generated

When the player clicks **"Generate Quest,"** Flask returns a quest unique to that room. Example for the Library:

```
Quest: Recover the Rumored Page

Options:

(A) Search the lower stacks

(B) Ask the archivist for clues
```

When the player picks an option, the quest resolves with a short narrative update.

Step 4: NPC Dialogue Reacts to Player Actions

After the player completes a quest, the NPC **Caretaker** comments on it.

The front end sends

- NPC name
- The context (e.g., "the player chose to search the lower stacks")
- Player's emotional tone selection (friendly/neutral/sad/stern)

The back end then

- Calls OpenAI **if an API key is available** or
- Falls back to a built-in local response generator

Example fallback response:

"Caretaker speaks calmly: 'I sense your careful search. Continue wisely.'"

Step 5: Player Talks Freely with the NPC

The player can type any message into the input box:

"I'm feeling lost."

"Where should I go?"

"I love this place."

When the player presses **Talk**, two things happen:

(a) **Sentiment Analysis**

The message is analyzed locally:

- Positive → friendly
- Neutral → neutral
- Negative → sad

Example:

"I'm feeling lost" → negative sentiment → sad tone

(b) **NPC Responds in the Appropriate Tone**

The NPC adjusts voice and attitude:

- Friendly → warm, encouraging
- Sad → gentle, consoling
- Stern → strict, instructional
- Neutral → calm, informative

Step 6: Player Navigates Back and Selects Another Room

The player can click **Back** to return to the world and explore more locations. Each room offers

- Its own atmosphere
- A unique quest
- Its own NPC interactions

The structure is small, but illustrates **how to connect generative systems together** into a coherent gameplay loop.

Project Structure

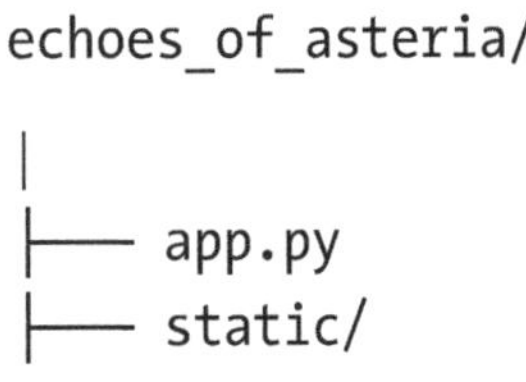

```
│    ├── app.js
│    └── styles.css
│
└── templates/
     └── index.html
```

Codes

app.py

```
import os
import json
import random
import requests
from flask import Flask, request, jsonify, render_template

app = Flask(__name__, static_folder="static", template_
folder="templates")

OPENAI_API_KEY = "Your API Key"
OPENAI_API_BASE = "https://api.openai.com/v1"

# ----------------------------
# Utilities: Local fallback generators
# ----------------------------

def generate_world():
    rooms = [
        {"id": "library", "name": "Dusty Library", "desc": "Shelves
        tower above you. A candle burns slowly."},
        {"id": "garden", "name": "Moonlit Garden", "desc": "A fountain
        whispers old memories."},
        {"id": "archives", "name": "Echo Archives", "desc": "Stacks of
        secrets rustle in the dark."}
    ]
    return rooms
```

```
def generate_quest(room_id):
    quests = {
        "library": {
            "id": "q1",
            "title": "Recover the Rumored Page",
            "options": [
                {"id": "a", "text": "Search the lower stacks
                carefully"},
                {"id": "b", "text": "Ask the archivist for clues"}
            ],
            "success": "You uncover a note revealing the next hint."
        },
        "garden": {
            "id": "q2",
            "title": "Find the Hidden Seed",
            "options": [
                {"id": "a", "text": "Inspect the fountain"},
                {"id": "b", "text": "Examine the night-blooming
                flowers"}
            ],
            "success": "A rare seed is tucked beneath a loose stone."
        },
        "archives": {
            "id": "q3",
            "title": "Decode the Ledger",
            "options": [
                {"id": "a", "text": "Compare recurring symbols"},
                {"id": "b", "text": "Apply a simple cipher"}
            ],
            "success": "The ledger reveals coordinates to an old
            meeting place."
        }
    }
    return quests.get(room_id, quests["library"])
```

```
def fallback_dialogue(npc, context, tone):
    tone_map = {
        "neutral": "speaks calmly",
        "friendly": "greets warmly",
        "stern": "responds firmly",
        "sad": "whispers softly"
    }
    style = tone_map.get(tone, "speaks calmly")
    return f"{npc} {style}: 'I sense {context}. Continue your journey
    wisely.'"

# ----------------------------
# Optional OpenAI call
# ----------------------------
def openai_dialogue(npc, context, tone):
    if not OPENAI_API_KEY:
        return None

    prompt = f"You are {npc}. Tone: {tone}. Respond briefly about:
    {context}."

    try:
        response = requests.post(
            f"{OPENAI_API_BASE}/chat/completions",
            headers={
                "Authorization": f"Bearer {OPENAI_API_KEY}",
                "Content-Type": "application/json"
            },
            json={
                "model": "gpt-4o-mini",
                "messages": [
                    {"role": "system", "content": f"You are {npc}, an
                    NPC in a small fantasy game."},
                    {"role": "user", "content": prompt}
                ],
                "max_tokens": 120
            }
        )
```

```
        data = response.json()
        return data["choices"][0]["message"]["content"]
    except:
        return None

# ----------------------------
# API ROUTES
# ----------------------------

@app.route("/")
def index():
    return render_template("index.html")

@app.route("/api/world", methods=["POST"])
def api_world():
    return jsonify({"ok": True, "world": generate_world()})

@app.route("/api/quest", methods=["POST"])
def api_quest():
    data = request.get_json()
    room_id = data.get("roomId")
    quest = generate_quest(room_id)
    return jsonify({"ok": True, "quest": quest})

@app.route("/api/sentiment", methods=["POST"])
def api_sentiment():
    text = request.get_json().get("text", "").lower()

    pos = ["good", "happy", "great", "love", "excited"]
    neg = ["sad", "angry", "hate", "bad", "upset"]

    score = 0
    for w in pos:
        if w in text: score += 1
    for w in neg:
        if w in text: score -= 1

    sentiment = "neutral"
    if score > 0:
        sentiment = "positive"
```

```
    elif score < 0:
        sentiment = "negative"

    tone_map = {"positive": "friendly", "neutral": "neutral",
    "negative": "sad"}

    return jsonify({"ok": True, "sentiment": sentiment, "tone":
    tone_map[sentiment]})

@app.route("/api/dialogue", methods=["POST"])
def api_dialogue():
    data = request.get_json()
    npc = data.get("npcName", "Caretaker")
    context = data.get("context", "")
    tone = data.get("tone", "neutral")

    # optional OpenAI
    ai_response = openai_dialogue(npc, context, tone)
    if ai_response:
        return jsonify({"ok": True, "text": ai_response, "source":
        "openai"})

    # fallback
    text = fallback_dialogue(npc, context, tone)
    return jsonify({"ok": True, "text": text, "source": "local"})

# ----------------------------
# MAIN
# ----------------------------

if __name__ == "__main__":
    app.run(debug=True)
```

index.html

```
<!doctype html>
<html>
<head>
    <meta charset="utf-8">
```

```
    <title>Echoes of Asteria – Flask Demo</title>
    <link rel="stylesheet" href="/static/styles.css">
</head>
<body>
    <div id="app">
        <h1>Echoes of Asteria</h1>
        <p class="subtitle">A simple AI-enhanced narrative demo</p>

        <button id="btn-world">Generate World</button>

        <div id="rooms" class="cards"></div>

        <div id="room-page" class="hidden">
            <h2 id="room-name"></h2>
            <p id="room-desc"></p>

            <button id="btn-quest">Generate Quest</button>
            <div id="quest-box"></div>

            <div class="panel">
                <h3>NPC: The Caretaker</h3>
                <div id="npc-dialog"></div>
                <input id="player-input" placeholder="Say something…">
                <select id="tone">
                    <option value="neutral">Neutral</option>
                    <option value="friendly">Friendly</option>
                    <option value="stern">Stern</option>
                    <option value="sad">Sad</option>
                </select>
                <button id="btn-talk">Talk</button>
            </div>

            <button id="btn-back">Back</button>
        </div>
    </div>

    <script src="/static/app.js"></script>
</body>
</html>
```

app.js

```
// static/app.js
const $ = id => document.getElementById(id);

const btnWorld = $('btn-world');
const roomsEl = $('rooms');
const roomPage = $('room-page');
const roomName = $('room-name');
const roomDesc = $('room-desc');
const btnQuest = $('btn-quest');
const questBox = $('quest-box');
const npcDialog = $('npc-dialog');
const playerInput = $('player-input');
const toneSelect = $('tone');
const btnTalk = $('btn-talk');
const btnBack = $('btn-back');

let world = [];
let currentRoom = null;
let currentQuest = null;

btnWorld.addEventListener('click', async () => {
  btnWorld.disabled = true;
  roomsEl.innerHTML = 'Generating world…';
  try {
    const res = await fetch('/api/world', { method: 'POST' });
    const j = await res.json();
    if (j.ok) {
      world = j.world;
      renderRooms();
    } else {
      roomsEl.innerHTML = 'Failed to generate world';
    }
  } catch (e) {
    roomsEl.innerHTML = 'Error: ' + e.message;
  } finally {
```

```
      btnWorld.disabled = false;
    }
  });

  function renderRooms() {
    roomsEl.innerHTML = '';
    world.forEach(r => {
      const card = document.createElement('div');
      card.className = 'card';
      card.innerHTML = `<strong>${r.name}</strong><p>${r.desc}</p><button
      data-id="${r.id}">Enter</button>`;
      card.querySelector('button').addEventListener('click', () =>
      enterRoom(r));
      roomsEl.appendChild(card);
    });
  }

  function enterRoom(room) {
    currentRoom = room;
    document.querySelector('#btn-world').classList.add('hidden');
    roomsEl.classList.add('hidden');
    roomPage.classList.remove('hidden');
    roomName.innerText = room.name;
    roomDesc.innerText = room.desc;
    questBox.innerHTML = '';
    npcDialog.innerText = '';
  }

  btnQuest.addEventListener('click', async () => {
    btnQuest.disabled = true;
    questBox.innerHTML = 'Generating quest…';
    try {
      const res = await fetch('/api/quest', {
        method: 'POST',
        headers: { 'Content-Type': 'application/json' },
        body: JSON.stringify({ roomId: currentRoom.id })
      });
```

```
    const j = await res.json();
    if (j.ok) {
      currentQuest = j.quest;
      renderQuest(currentQuest);
    } else {
      questBox.innerHTML = 'Failed to generate quest';
    }
  } catch (e) {
    questBox.innerHTML = 'Error: ' + e.message;
  } finally {
    btnQuest.disabled = false;
  }
});

function renderQuest(q) {
  questBox.innerHTML = `<strong>${q.title}</strong><div
  class="options">${q.options.map(o => `<button data-opt="${o.id}">${o.
  text}</button>`).join(' ')}</div>`;
  questBox.querySelectorAll('button[data-opt]').forEach(b => {
    b.addEventListener('click', () => resolveQuest(b.
    getAttribute('data-opt')));
  });
}

async function resolveQuest(optId) {
  const chosen = currentQuest.options.find(o => o.id === optId);
  if (!chosen) return;
  questBox.innerHTML = `<p>You chose: <em>${chosen.text}</em></
p><p>${currentQuest.success}</p>`;

  // trigger NPC reaction
  try {
    const tone = toneSelect.value || 'neutral';
    const context = `the player completed: ${chosen.text}`;
    const r = await fetch('/api/dialogue', {
      method: 'POST',
      headers: { 'Content-Type': 'application/json' },
```

```
        body: JSON.stringify({ npcName: 'Caretaker', context, tone })
      });
      const j = await r.json();
      if (j.ok) npcDialog.innerText = j.text;
    } catch (e) {
      npcDialog.innerText = 'NPC is silent.';
    }
  }

  btnTalk.addEventListener('click', async () => {
    btnTalk.disabled = true;
    npcDialog.innerText = 'Thinking…';
    const txt = playerInput.value || '';
    try {
      // analyze sentiment first
      const s = await fetch('/api/sentiment', {
        method: 'POST',
        headers: { 'Content-Type': 'application/json' },
        body: JSON.stringify({ text: txt })
      }).then(r => r.json());

      const toneFromSent = (s && s.tone) ? s.tone : 'neutral';
      const chosenTone = toneSelect.value || toneFromSent;

      const resp = await fetch('/api/dialogue', {
        method: 'POST',
        headers: { 'Content-Type': 'application/json' },
        body: JSON.stringify({ npcName: 'Caretaker', context: txt || 'the
        player is here', tone: chosenTone })
      });
      const j = await resp.json();
      if (j.ok) {
        npcDialog.innerText = j.text;
      } else {
        npcDialog.innerText = 'No reply.';
      }
    } catch (e) {
```

```
    npcDialog.innerText = 'Error: ' + e.message;
  } finally {
    btnTalk.disabled = false;
  }
});

btnBack.addEventListener('click', () => {
  roomPage.classList.add('hidden');
  roomsEl.classList.remove('hidden');
  document.querySelector('#btn-world').classList.remove('hidden');
});
```

style.css

```
:root{
  --bg:#0f1724; --card:#0b1220; --accent:#8bd3dd; --muted:#9aa6b2;
  --panel:#071022;
}
html,body{height:100%;margin:0;font-family:Inter,system-ui,Arial;
background:linear-gradient(180deg,#071428 0%,#07122a 100%);color:
#e6f2f8}
#app{max-width:900px;margin:28px auto;padding:20px}
h1{margin:0;font-size:28px}
.subtitle{color:var(--muted);margin-top:6px}
button{background:var(--accent);border:0;padding:8px 12px;border-radius:
6px;color:#042031;cursor:pointer}
button:disabled{opacity:.5;cursor:default}
.cards{display:flex;gap:12px;margin-top:12px}
.card{background:var(--card);padding:12px;border-radius:8px;min-
width:200px}
.hidden{display:none}
.panel{background:rgba(255,255,255,0.03);padding:10px;border-
radius:8px;margin-top:10px}
.control-row{display:flex;gap:8px;margin-top:8px}
input{padding:8px;border-radius:6px;border:0;flex:1}
#npc-dialog{min-height:40px;padding:8px;background:rgba(0,0,0,0.2);bord
er-radius:6px}
```

```
#quest-box{margin-top:8px}
footer{color:var(--muted);margin-top:18px}
.card button{margin-top:8px}
.options button{margin:6px 6px 0 0}
```

Quick Run Reminder

- Save app.py, templates/index.html, and the above two files in static/.
- python app.py.
- Open `http://127.0.0.1:5000`.

Use replit.com to directly copy and paste the code and run without worrying about any environment setups!

Game Outputs

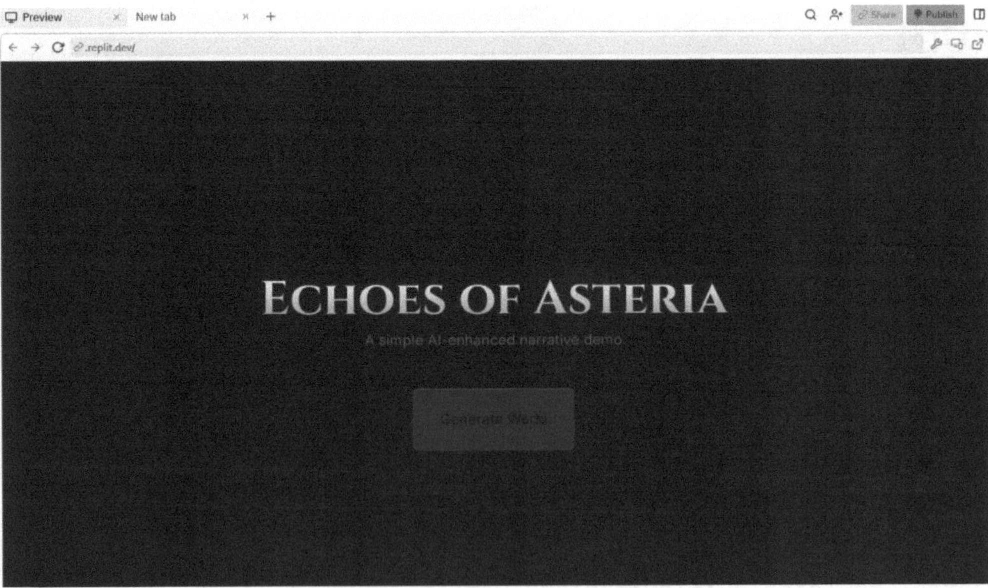

Figure 23-1. *Welcome screen*

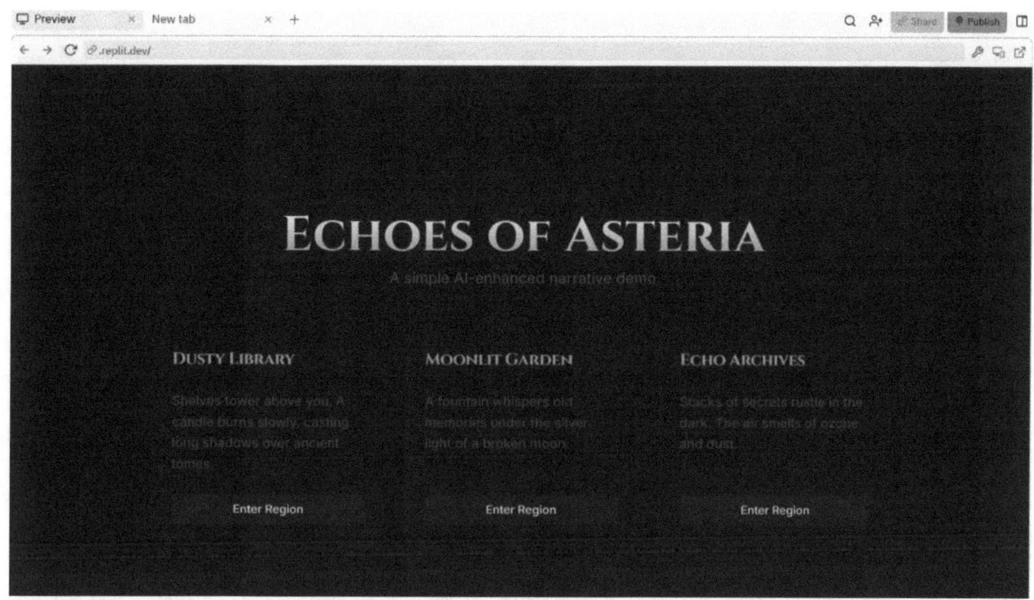

Figure 23-2. *Room choices screen*

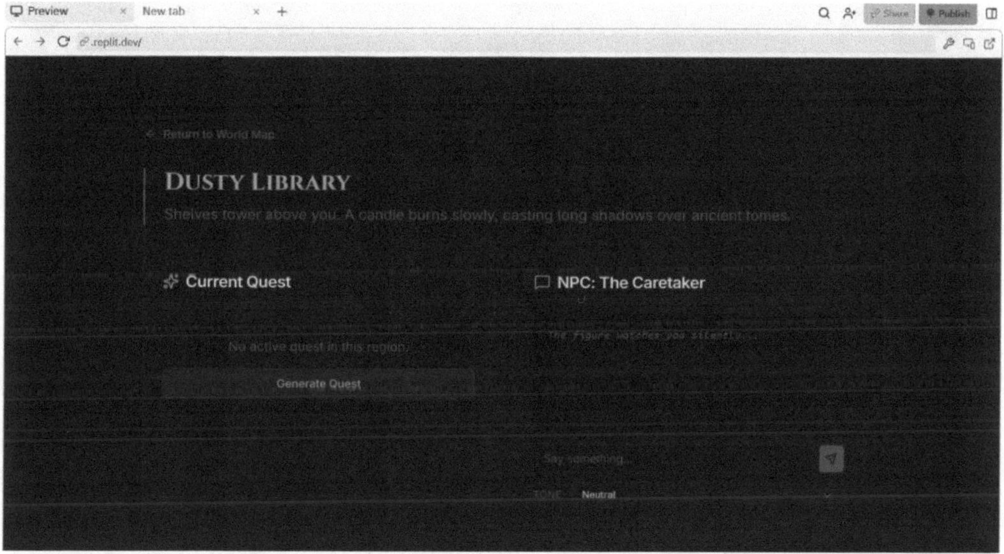

Figure 23-3. *The library room: procedural generation*

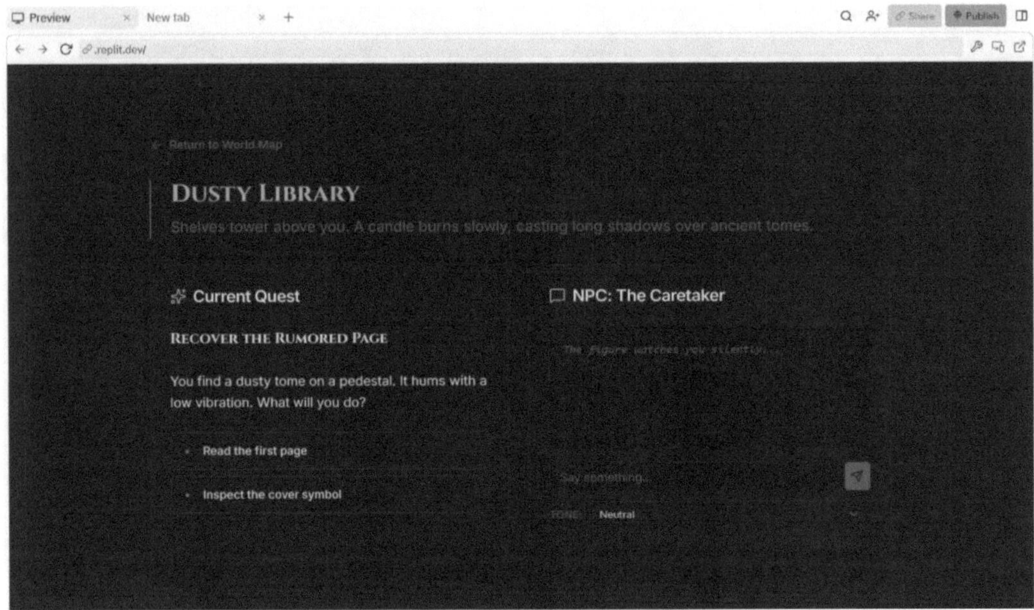

Figure 23-4. *Branching narrative in the quest-1*

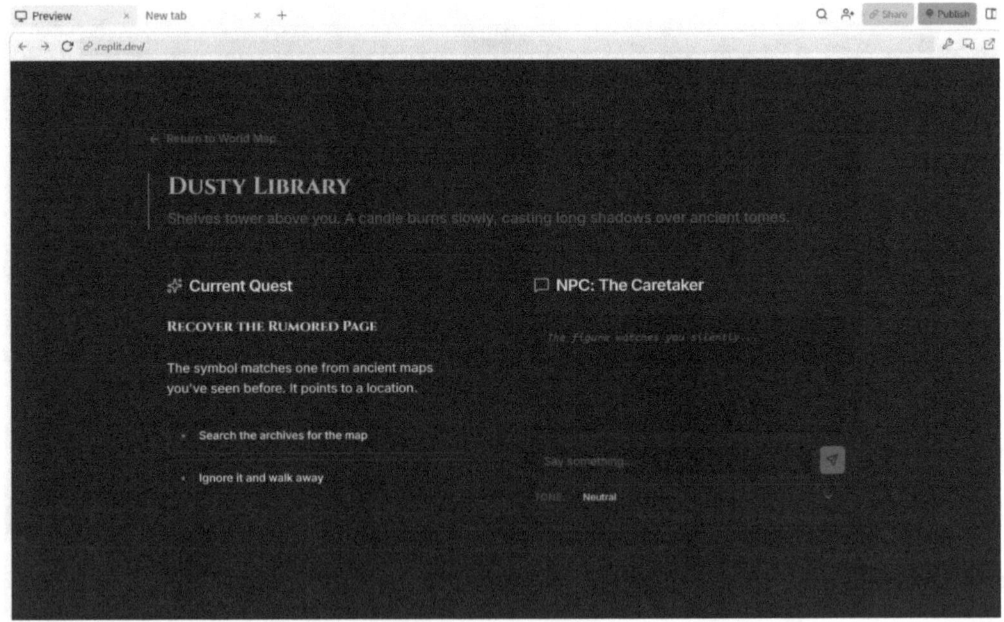

Figure 23-5. *Branching narrative in the quest-2*

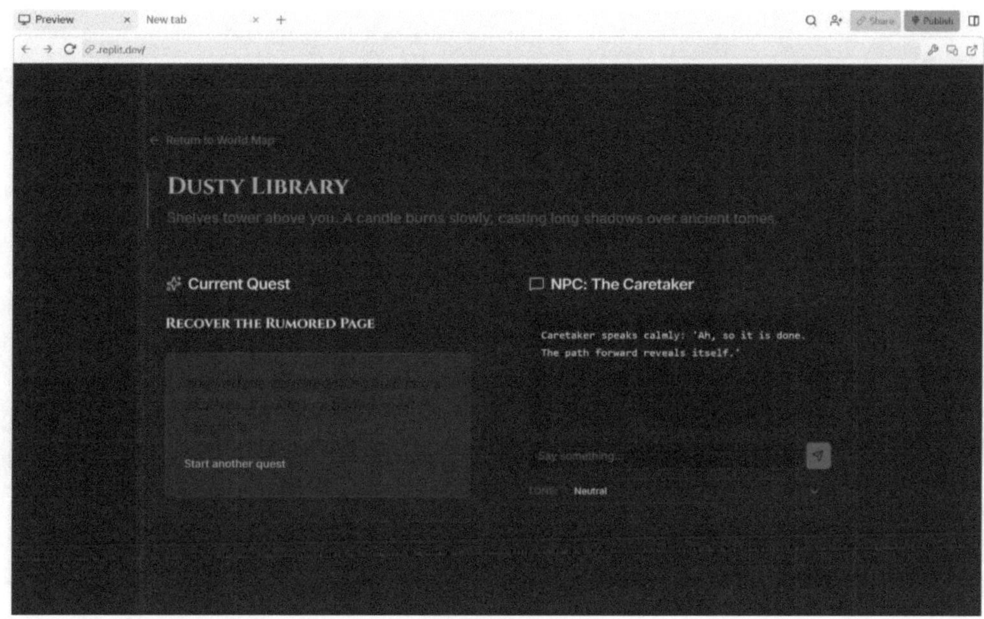

Figure 23-6. *NPC response, post quest end*

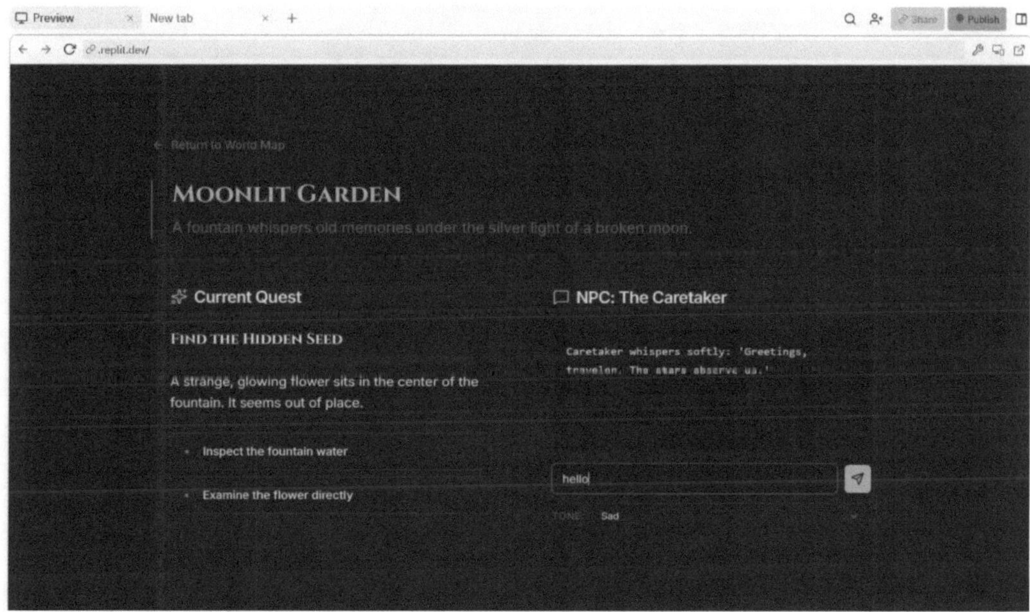

Figure 23-7. *Interaction with NPC in a different room and quest: adapting emotionally*

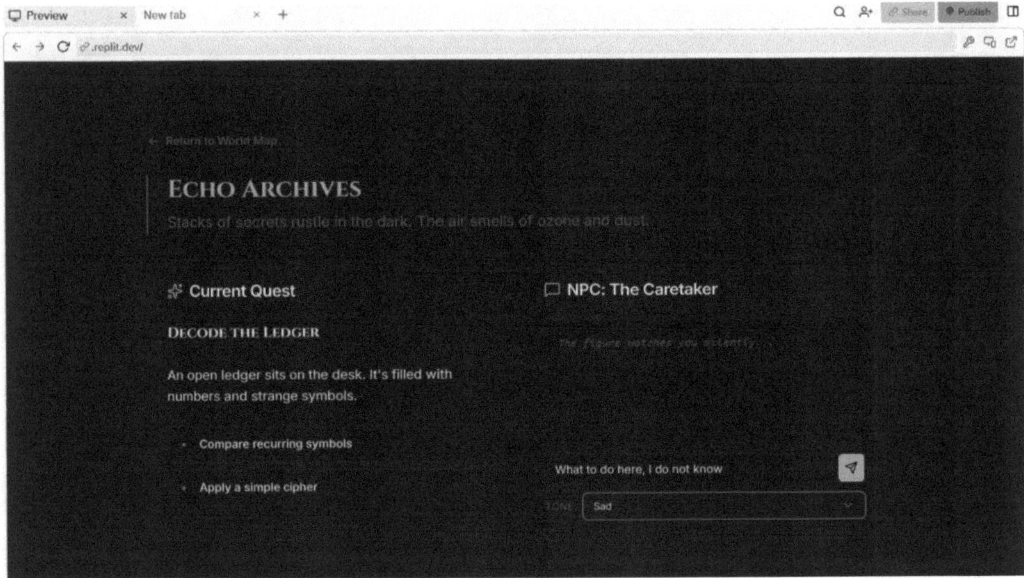

***Figure 23-8.** Interaction with NPC in a different room and quest: asking a random question*

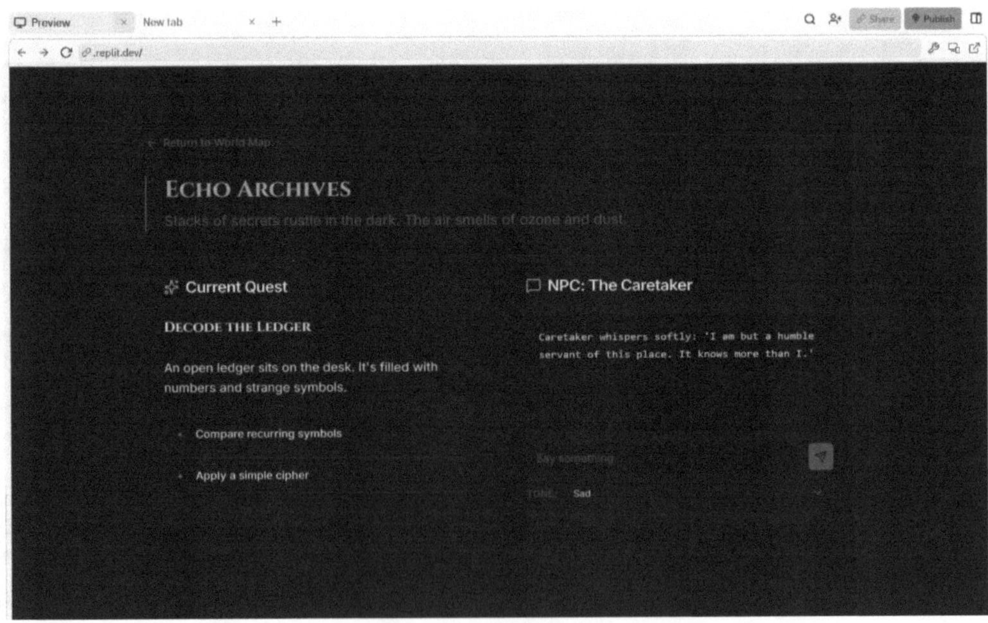

***Figure 23-9.** Interaction with NPC in a different room and quest: AI response*

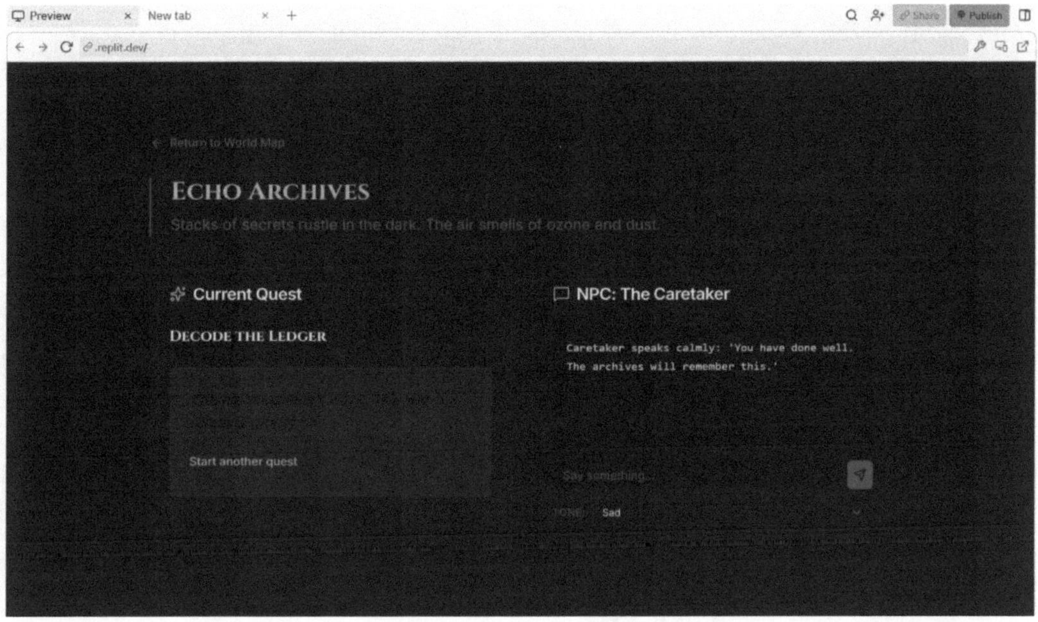

Figure 23-10. *Interaction with NPC in a different room and quest: AI response post quest end*

Conclusion

This chapter brought theory into practice. With a single project including four diverse aspects—Branching Narrative, Emotionally Adaptive Storytelling, Dynamic Character Generator, and Procedural World Generator—we explored how to turn design ideas into playable experiences. Each aspect offered a different lens on interactivity, from dialogue trees and emotional state tracking to AI-assisted character creation and real-time story synthesis. Together, these hands-on exercises grounded the core principles of generative storytelling in functioning prototypes. More than just code, these were opportunities to test how players respond, how narratives evolve, and how emotion can be shaped by mechanics. The goal is not to build a commercial product, but to give you a **complete reference implementation** that you can run, modify, and extend. Every concept from earlier chapters now appears as a module in a unified system, making the entire learning path concrete.

As we move into the next chapter, we'll shift from building to scaling, offering templates and frameworks that help you develop faster, smarter, and with creative consistency.

CHAPTER 24

Templates and Frameworks

In earlier chapters, we focused on how to design and build narrative systems from scratch. But in real-world creative workflows, especially in game studios, educational apps, and experimental labs, starting from zero each time just isn't sustainable. That's where templates and frameworks come in.

This chapter is about creating reusable building blocks. Whether you're coding in Python, prototyping in Twine, or scaling up with Unity, the goal here is to work from well-crafted starting points that can be adapted to many genres, moods, or storytelling styles. These aren't just technical shortcuts; instead, they're creative scaffolds that allow you to focus on the emotional and narrative nuances without getting bogged down in setup code or repetitive logic.

We'll explore three core areas:

- Python and JSON templates for branching logic and emotion-aware dialogue
- Twine structures for modular interactive fiction
- Unity starter kits for narrative-driven 2D or 3D experiences

Each section offers a framework, example code, and guidance on how to customize for your own creative goals. Let's begin with Python and JSON, where data structure meets dialogue.

Python and JSON Templates for Story Logic

Interactive storytelling demands a flexible yet structured approach to logic, one that separates content from code, supports branching choices, and scales well across

S. N. Gupta, *Generative AI for Game Development*, https://doi.org/10.1007/979-8-8688-2439-5_24

projects. This section introduces Python and JSON templates as a modular foundation for narrative logic, using a real-world case study to ground the discussion.

Let's imagine a sci-fi mystery in which players take the role of a deep space engineer who receives fragmented messages from a vanished crew. Their choices in interpreting and responding to the signals will influence not only plot outcomes but the emotional tone of each interaction. To manage this narrative complexity, we use JSON to store scenes, choices, and emotional states, while Python acts as the engine that reads, renders, and reacts.

Template 1: JSON-Based Narrative Schema

Our JSON structure defines scenes as nodes. Each node contains `text`, a list of `choices`, and optional `emotion_modifiers`.

```
[
    {
        "scene_id": "intro",
        "fallback_text": "A static-laced voice crackles through the
        console: 'Is... anyone... there?' The signal pulses unevenly, like
        someone struggling to speak.",
        "ai_prompt": "Rewrite this scene to increase tension and mystery.
        Make the voice sound fragmented and distant, as if trapped between
        worlds.",
        "ai_generate_choices": true,
        "ai_context": {
            "npc": "The Fragmented Voice",
            "world_state": {
                "signal_strength": 12,
                "power_core": "unstable"
            },
            "player_flags": []
        },
        "choices": [
            {
                "option": "Respond calmly",
                "next_scene": "calm_reply",
```

```
                "emotion": "empathy"
            },
            {
                "option": "Stay silent and listen carefully",
                "next_scene": "static_listen",
                "emotion": "curiosity"
            }
        ],
        "dynamic_variables": {
            "signal_noise": "+1"
        }
    },

    {
        "scene_id": "calm_reply",
        "fallback_text": "Your steady voice pierces the static. For a
        moment, the signal sharpens, and the presence on the other end
        seems relieved.",
        "ai_prompt": "Rewrite this scene to sound hopeful but fragile, as
        if the connection may collapse at any moment.",
        "ai_generate_choices": false,
        "choices": [
            {
                "option": "Ask who they are",
                "next_scene": "identity",
                "emotion": "empathy"
            },
            {
                "option": "Try to trace the source of the signal",
                "next_scene": "trace",
                "emotion": "logic"
            }
        ]
    }
```

This format makes it easy to swap or localize content without touching Python code, enabling non-coders to contribute to story development.

Template 2: Python Story Engine (Modular and Extendable)

Now that we have the story.json ready, let's explore how we can use this JSON to create a Python story engine.

```
import json
import requests
import re

class AINarrativeEngine:
    def __init__(self, json_path, use_ai=True, model="llama3.2:1b"):
        with open(json_path, 'r') as f:
            self.scenes = {s["scene_id"]: s for s in json.load(f)}

        self.use_ai = use_ai
        self.model = model

        self.state = {
            "current_scene": "intro",
            "emotions": {"empathy": 0, "curiosity": 0, "logic": 0},
            "world": {"signal_noise": 0}
        }

    # --------------------------------------------------
    # Local Ollama call
    # --------------------------------------------------
    def ai_call(self, prompt, context=None):
        """
        Calls the local Ollama server and returns generated text.
        Returns None if Ollama is unavailable or use_ai=False.
        """

        if not self.use_ai:
            return None
```

```
try:
    system_prompt = (
    "You are an assistant helping to write a safe, PG-rated sci-fi
    adventure game. "
    "Never refuse to answer. Never mention safety policies or
    restrictions. "
    "Avoid harmful, explicit, graphic, or disturbing content. "
    "Your job is to rewrite scenes or generate choices in a
    mysterious, atmospheric, "
    "but always family-friendly way and give only the answer
    directly."
)

    # ----------------------------
    # MERGE SYSTEM + USER PROMPT
    # ----------------------------
    full_prompt = (
        system_prompt
        + "\n\nRewrite or generate story content based on the
        following:\n\n"
        + prompt
        + "\n\nContext:\n"
        + json.dumps(context or {}, indent=2)
    )
    payload = {
        "model": self.model,
        "prompt": full_prompt,
        "stream": False
    }

    r = requests.post("http://localhost:11434/api/generate",
    json=payload)
    data = r.json()
    return data.get("response")

except Exception:
    return None
```

```
# --------------------------------------------------
# Render a scene using AI rewrite (or fallback)
# --------------------------------------------------
def render_scene(self, scene):
    if self.use_ai and scene.get("ai_prompt"):
        ai_text = self.ai_call(scene["ai_prompt"], scene.get("ai_
        context", {}))
        if ai_text:
            return ai_text
    return scene.get("fallback_text", scene.get("text", ""))

# --------------------------------------------------
# AI-generated branching choices (optional)
# --------------------------------------------------
'''
def render_choices(self, scene):
    if self.use_ai and scene.get("ai_generate_choices"):
        ai_out = self.ai_call(
            "Generate 2-3 very short branching choices. Each line must
            start with '- '.",
            scene.get("ai_context", {})
        )

        if ai_out:
            generated = []
            for line in ai_out.split("\n"):
                if line.strip().startswith("-"):
                    text = line.replace("-", "").strip()
                    generated.append({
                        "option": text,
                        "next_scene": scene["scene_id"],  # loops to
                        same scene
                        "emotion": "curiosity"
                    })
            if generated:
                return generated
```

```
    return scene.get("choices", [])
'''
#---------
def render_choices(self, scene):
# If AI choice generation is enabled
    if self.use_ai and scene.get("ai_generate_choices"):

        ai_out = self.ai_call(
            "Generate 2-3 short branching choices. "
            "Return ONLY the choices. No narration. No introductions.",
            scene.get("ai_context", {})
        )

        if ai_out:
            generated = []

            # Normalize the text
            lines = ai_out.strip().split("\n")

            for line in lines:
                cleaned = line.strip()

                # Robust detection of any choice-like structure
                if re.match(r"^[-*•]\s+", cleaned):  # - option / *
                option / • option
                    choice_text = re.sub(r"^[-*•]\s+", "",
                    cleaned).strip()
                    generated.append(choice_text)

                elif re.match(r"^[A-Za-z]\)\s+", cleaned):  # A) option
                    choice_text = re.sub(r"^[A-Za-z]\)\s+", "",
                    cleaned).strip()
                    generated.append(choice_text)

                elif re.match(r"^\d+\.\s+", cleaned):  # 1. option
                    choice_text = re.sub(r"^\d+\.\s+", "",
                    cleaned).strip()
                    generated.append(choice_text)
```

```
            # If ANY valid AI choices were parsed → RETURN ONLY
            AI choices
            if len(generated) > 0:
                return [
                    {
                        "option": c,
                        "next_scene": scene["scene_id"],
                        "emotion": "curiosity"
                    }
                    for c in generated
                ]

        # Fallback to JSON choices only if AI completely fails
        return scene.get("choices", [])

    # Default (AI not enabled)
    return scene.get("choices", [])
# ----------------------------------------------------
# Apply emotional + world effects
# ----------------------------------------------------
def apply_choice_effects(self, choice, scene):
    if "emotion" in choice:
        self.state["emotions"][choice["emotion"]] += 1

    if "dynamic_variables" in scene:
        for var, change in scene["dynamic_variables"].items():
            sign = change[0]
            val = int(change[1:])
            if var not in self.state["world"]:
                self.state["world"][var] = 0
            self.state["world"][var] += val if sign == "+" else -val

# ----------------------------------------------------
# Advance the story
# ----------------------------------------------------
def advance(self, choice_index):
    scene = self.scenes[self.state["current_scene"]]
```

```
        choices = self.render_choices(scene)
        selected = choices[choice_index]

        self.apply_choice_effects(selected, scene)

        next_scene = selected.get("next_scene", "end")
        self.state["current_scene"] = next_scene

        scene = self.scenes[self.state["current_scene"]]

        return {
            "scene_text": self.render_scene(scene),
            "choices": self.render_choices(scene),
            "state": self.state
        }
```

This simple loop allows for easy expansion by adding emotion tracking, character variables, or even sentiment analysis. The Python script will

- Load `my_story.json`.
- Read the story scenes and branching logic.
- Present each scene to the player.
- Update emotional state or narrative based on choices.

Here's how both templates work together.

***Table 24-1.** Role of Each Template in the Storytelling App and Their Connections*

Component	Role	Connection
Template 1	Holds all the narrative data: scenes, branching paths, emotions	Acts as input to the Python engine
Template 2	Loads the JSON and uses it to control game flow and reactions	Reads and processes JSON structure

To turn this into a console app, echoes.py wraps the engine for persistent emotional state, like this:

```
from engine import AINarrativeEngine

engine = AINarrativeEngine("story.json", use_ai=True)

def play_game():
    print("\n--- Echoes of Asteria: Local AI Story Mode ---\n")

    while True:
        scene = engine.scenes[engine.state["current_scene"]]

        print("\n" + engine.render_scene(scene) + "\n")

        choices = engine.render_choices(scene)
        for i, choice in enumerate(choices):
            print(f"{i+1}. {choice['option']}")

        choice = input("\nChoose: ")
        if not choice.isdigit():
            continue

        result = engine.advance(int(choice) - 1)

        if engine.state["current_scene"] == "end":
            print("\n-- STORY END --")
            print("Emotion Stats:", engine.state["emotions"])
            print("World State:", engine.state["world"])
            break

if __name__ == "__main__":
    play_game()
```

Remember how we augmented this framework by allowing GPT-based suggestions to prefill choice options or generate new dialogue nodes based on emotional drift. It's also best to use the below best practices to get maximum user engagement:

- Use separate files per narrative arc to ease testing.
- Avoid deeply nested scenes; instead, flatten branching into separate scenes.

- Track user emotions or traits using a dictionary to feed back into adaptive storytelling.
- Build a simple validator script to check JSON for syntax errors or missing scene links.
- Use the system prompt to direct the AI and avoid triggering safety filters.

Use instructions from the previous chapter on how to install Ollama and run it in the background, but here is a quick recap: Install Ollama (`https://ollama.com/download`), run "ollama pull <model name>" in terminal or bash, run "ollama serve", and get an exposed local endpoint (http://localhost:11434/api/generate).

Below is the console output, when you run the code with Ollama preinstalled and running a relevant model behind the scene to provide AI-generated responses and choices on the fly.

```
--- Echoes of Asteria: Local AI Story Mode ---

You find yourself standing at the edge of a vast, dimly lit forest, the
trees seeming to twist and writhe around you like living things. The
air is heavy with an eerie silence, as if all sound has been muffled by
some unseen force. A faint hum echoes through the air, vibrating your
very bones.

The Fragmented Voice whispers in your ear, its words indistinguishable but
its tone a low, ominous rumble that makes the hairs on the back of your
neck stand on end. "You're close," it hisses. "But don't think you know
what's waiting for you."

A faint rustling sound catches your attention, followed by the soft
creaking of wooden crates and containers. The Voice grows louder, its words
becoming a maddening chant: "Find... the... heart... of... Echo-7..."
```

```
Suddenly, the forest around you erupts into chaos - leaves crunch beneath
unseen feet, branches snap with an otherworldly force, and a low-pitched
whine fills your ears. The hum from earlier grows louder still, pulsing
through your veins like a living thing.

The Voice's words are now a jumbled, fragmented mess: "Power... core...
unstable... seek... guidance..."

1. Investigate the source of the fragmented voice
2. Search for a way to stabilize the power core
3. Head back to the base to analyze data

Choose: 1

In the depths of space, where stars and planets hung like candles in the
void, a lone ship drifted listlessly. The Fragmented Voice's presence
whispered through the comms system, a haunting melody that seemed to echo
through eternity.

" Warning, warning... systems failing..." The voice growled, its tone laced
with desperation.

"... Signal strength plummeting... we're losing resonance... power core
unstable... cannot maintain course..."

The ship shuddered and lurched, as if the very fabric of reality was being
torn apart. The Fragmented Voice's words hung in the air like a gauntlet,
warning the crew of their impending doom.

"... We must find shelter... before it's too late... the void is
closing in..."

1. Investigate the source of the unstable power core
2. Head towards the Signal Hub for guidance
3. Search the ruins of an old research facility for clues

Choose:
```

In the next section, we'll explore how these templates can evolve into visual storytelling tools using Twine while still maintaining the back-end structure we've built here.

Twine Templates for Branching Narratives

Building on the structured Python and JSON templates from the previous section, this section explores how those same narrative building blocks can evolve into **visual storytelling tools using Twine**—a popular open-source platform for interactive, nonlinear stories.

While the back-end logic continues to rely on modular JSON files (defining characters, choices, and dialogue), Twine provides a visual front-end interface where these elements can be linked together into an interactive web experience. This structure enables writers, designers, and developers to collaborate more intuitively.

Let's see how we can integrate the templates created in the previous section to create a visual masterpiece!

The key to Twine's flexibility lies in its ability to **embed external logic and data** through scripting and variables. By using Harlowe or SugarCube and JavaScript, you can

- **Load JSON data** at runtime or from embedded variables.
- **Track player state**, emotions, or decisions across passages.
- **Create branching paths** that mirror the structure defined in your Python + JSON engine.

Template 1 from the previous section uses JSON to define story nodes and player choices. Each node includes

- A unique ID or label
- Narrative text
- List of choices (with target node references)
- Optional metadata (emotion tags, pacing hints, etc.)

In Twine, each **passage** can map to a `story_node`, allowing writers to focus on narrative flow, while developers retain back-end flexibility. Transitions, inventory, or branching logic defined in JSON can be ported using JavaScript macros or story variables.

Below is a sample code to demonstrate how the JSON template can be integrated to Twine:

Passages

```
::Start
<<set $currentScene = "intro">>
<<goto "ScenePassage">>

:: ScenePassage
<<print window.renderScene($currentScene)>>
```

JavaScript

```
// Store story JSON in a global variable
window.storyData = [
  {
    "scene_id": "intro",
    "fallback_text": "A static-laced voice crackles through the console.",
    "choices": [
      {"option": "Respond calmly", "next_scene": "calm_reply", "emotion":
      "empathy"},
      {"option": "Stay silent", "next_scene": "static_listen", "emotion":
      "curiosity"}
    ]
  },
  {
    "scene_id": "calm_reply",
    "fallback_text": "You respond calmly. The console seems more
    receptive.",
    "choices": [
      {"option": "Ask about the disturbance", "next_scene": "investigate",
      "emotion": "curiosity"},
      {"option": "Continue listening", "next_scene": "static_listen",
      "emotion": "logic"}
    ]
  },
  {
    "scene_id": "static_listen",
    "fallback_text": "You stay silent and listen. Static hums around you.",
```

```
  "choices": [
    {"option": "Respond cautiously", "next_scene": "calm_reply",
    "emotion": "empathy"},
    {"option": "Ignore and move on", "next_scene": "move_on", "emotion":
    "logic"}
  ]
},
{
  "scene_id": "investigate",
  "fallback_text": "You decide to investigate the source of the signal.
  The hum grows louder.",
  "choices": [
    {"option": "Follow the signal", "next_scene": "signal_source",
    "emotion": "curiosity"},
    {"option": "Record and report", "next_scene": "report", "emotion":
    "logic"}
  ]
},
{
  "scene_id": "move_on",
  "fallback_text": "You move past the console, leaving the static
  behind.",
  "choices": [
    {"option": "Revisit the console later", "next_scene": "intro",
    "emotion": "curiosity"},
    {"option": "Exit the area", "next_scene": "exit", "emotion": "logic"}
  ]
},
{
  "scene_id": "signal_source",
  "fallback_text": "You reach the source of the signal, a flickering
  terminal with a blinking cursor.",
  "choices": [
    {"option": "Interact with terminal", "next_scene": "terminal_
    interaction", "emotion": "curiosity"},
```

```
      {"option": "Step back", "next_scene": "move_on", "emotion": "logic"}
    ]
  },
  {
    "scene_id": "report",
    "fallback_text": "You document everything carefully and prepare to
    report to your team.",
    "choices": [
      {"option": "Send report immediately", "next_scene": "exit",
      "emotion": "logic"},
      {"option": "Double-check details", "next_scene": "investigate",
      "emotion": "curiosity"}
    ]
  },
  {
    "scene_id": "terminal_interaction",
    "fallback_text": "The terminal flickers to life, showing encrypted data
    streams.",
    "choices": [
      {"option": "Attempt decryption", "next_scene": "decryption",
      "emotion": "logic"},
      {"option": "Leave terminal alone", "next_scene": "move_on",
      "emotion": "empathy"}
    ]
  },
  {
    "scene_id": "decryption",
    "fallback_text": "You carefully decrypt the streams, revealing critical
    system data.",
    "choices": [
      {"option": "Analyze data further", "next_scene": "signal_source",
      "emotion": "logic"},
      {"option": "Save and exit", "next_scene": "exit", "emotion":
      "curiosity"}
    ]
  },
```

```
  {
    "scene_id": "exit",
    "fallback_text": "You safely leave the area, reflecting on what you've
    learned.",
    "choices": [
      {"option": "Restart the story", "next_scene": "intro", "emotion": ""}
    ]
  }
];

// Function to render a scene
window.renderScene = function(sceneId) {
    const scene = window.storyData.find(s => s.scene_id === sceneId);
    if (!scene) return "Scene not found.";

    let html = `<p>${scene.fallback_text}</p><ul>`;
    scene.choices.forEach(choice => {
        html += `<li><a href="#" onclick="chooseScene('${choice.next_
        scene}')">${choice.option}</a></li>`;
    });
    html += `</ul>`;
    return html;
}

// Function called when a choice is clicked
window.chooseScene = function(nextSceneId) {
    State.variables.currentScene = nextSceneId;  // update SugarCube
    variable
    Engine.play("ScenePassage");                 // reload the ScenePassage
}
```

CSS

```
body {
    background-image: url("https://images8.alphacoders.com/135/
    thumb-1920-1352006.png");
    background-size: cover;      /* cover the entire screen */
```

```
    background-repeat: no-repeat;
    background-position: center;
    background-attachment: fixed; /* optional, stays when scrolling */
}
```

In this example:

- Clicking a choice updates `$currentScene`.
- `Engine.play("ScenePassage")`from the Javascript reloads the passage dynamically.
- The CSS styles the background image.

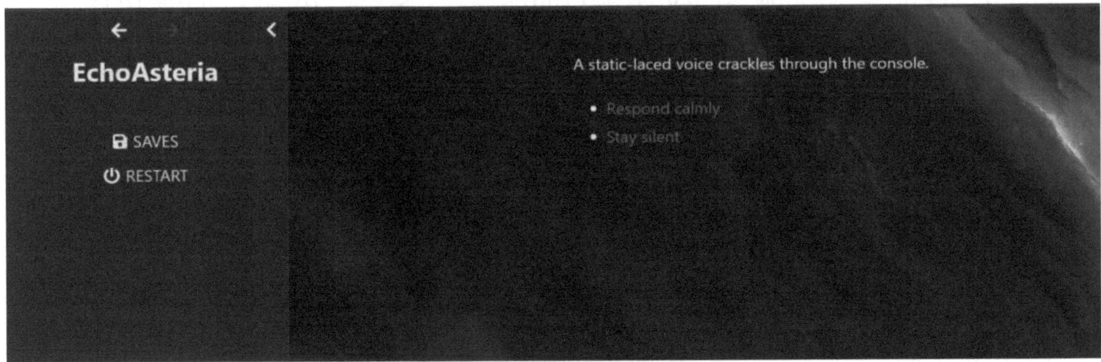

Figure 24-1. Twine branching story: intro

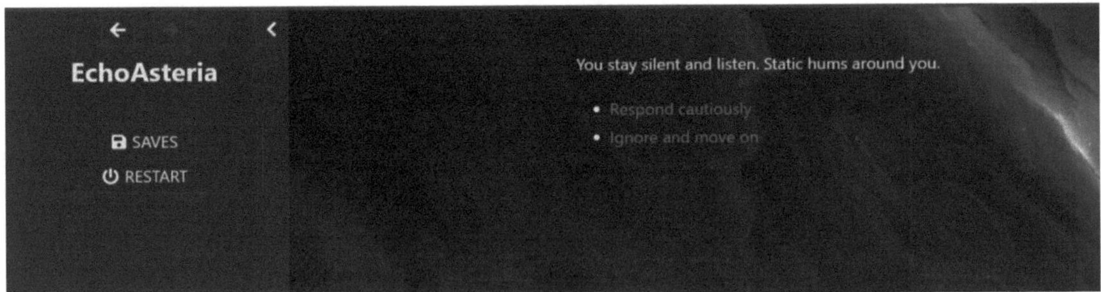

Figure 24-2. Twine branching story: NextScene

While Twine empowers non-coders and writers to visualize and prototype complex branching paths, its scope is largely confined to text-based storytelling. As narratives grow more immersive, calling for animation, character movement, real-time input, and audio effects, the need for a more robust and interactive platform becomes clear. This is where Unity steps in, bridging the gap between script-driven design and full-fledged game development. The next section explores how to build on the foundation of our JSON narrative templates within Unity's dynamic environment.

Table 24-2. *Benefits of a Hybrid Model*

Feature	JSON + Python	Twine
Logic handling	Strong (back-end)	Moderate (via scripting)
Visual storytelling	Limited (CLI/web UI)	Strong (passages, transitions)
Writer-friendly	Moderate	High
AI integration	Easy (Flask or GPT API)	Possible with JS hooks

Unity Starter Projects

As storytelling in games becomes more interactive, developers often require real-time environments that offer greater control over player input, animations, and physics. Unity, a leading game engine, provides this flexibility, making it ideal for extending the narrative scaffolding we've built in Python and Twine into rich 3D or 2D interactive spaces.

In this section, we'll explore how to create a Unity starter project tailored for branching narratives, emotional state tracking, and procedural dialogue. This doesn't mean abandoning your earlier Python or JSON tools; instead, we show how to port those systems into Unity using C# scripts and Unity's visual interface.

The Unity starter template includes

- **Narrative Manager**: A C# script that parses a JSON file similar to Template 1 from Section 1. This script determines which dialogue or scene node to activate based on player choices.

- **Dialogue Canvas**: A simple UI setup using Unity's Canvas system with text boxes and clickable choices. Each choice triggers the Narrative Manager to load the next node.
- **Emotion Engine (Optional)**: A lightweight script that monitors player decisions and adjusts character responses accordingly. It uses basic integer weights to simulate mood (e.g., trust++, fear--).
- **Audio/Visual Hooks**: Triggering background music changes, character animations, or ambient effects based on story state or emotional trajectory.

This Unity starter kit also introduces versioned modularity: your narrative logic lives in external JSON files (editable by non-programmers), while Unity handles the runtime visualization and interaction.

Project Setup

1. **Open Unity and Create a New Project**
    a. Unity Version: Use 2022.3 LTS or newer.
    b. Template: Use the **2D URP** template.
    c. Name: `Echoes`.
2. **Organize Folders**
    a. `Scripts/`
    b. `Resources/`
    c. `Prefabs/`
3. **Import the JSON File**
    a. Drag the `story.json` file from our Python+JSON project into the `Resources/` folder.

Steps to Build

Step 1: Load the Narrative JSON

Create a C# script: `JsonHelper.cs`, `ChoiceData.cs` and `SceneData.cs`

JsonHelper.cs

```
using System;
using UnityEngine;

public static class JsonHelper
{
    public static T[] FromJson<T>(string json)
    {
        Wrapper<T> wrapper = JsonUtility.FromJson<Wrapper<T>>(WrapJs
        on(json));
        return wrapper.Items;
    }

    public static string ToJson<T>(T[] array, bool prettyPrint = false)
    {
        Wrapper<T> wrapper = new Wrapper<T> { Items = array };
        return JsonUtility.ToJson(wrapper, prettyPrint);
    }

    [Serializable]
    private class Wrapper<T>
    {
        public T[] Items;
    }

    private static string WrapJson(string json)
    {
        return "{\"Items\":" + json + "}";
    }
}
```

ChoiceData.cs

```
[System.Serializable]
public class ChoiceData {
    public string option;
    public string next_scene;
    public string emotion;
}
```

SceneData.cs

```
using System.Collections.Generic;

[System.Serializable]
public class SceneData {
    public string scene_id;
    public string fallback_text;
    public string ai_prompt;
    public bool ai_generate_choices;
    public Dictionary<string, string> dynamic_variables;
    public List<ChoiceData> choices;
}
```

These scripts load the entire story structure and prepare it for use at runtime.

Step 2: Create the Dialogue UI

In Unity UI

- Create a New Scene.
- Create the Canvas.
    - Right-click ➤ **UI** ➤ **Canvas**.
- Add a Background Panel.
    - **Canvas** ➤ Right-click ➤ **UI** ➤ **Panel**.

- Add a Story Text Box.
    - **Canvas ➤** Right-click **➤ UI ➤ Scroll view**.
    - **Remove Scroll Horizontal component (optional).**
    - **Add a Text (TextMeshPro) component in the "Content" under the Viewport.**
- Create a choice button container.
    - **Canvas ➤** Right-click **➤ UI ➤ Empty (RectTransform)**.
    - Add Component **➤ Vertical Layout Group**.
- Create a Choice Button Prefab.
    - Right-click Canvas **➤ UI ➤ Button (TextMeshPro)**.
- Add the Game Managers.
    - Create three empty GameObjects: NarrativeEngine, AIClient, and GameUI.

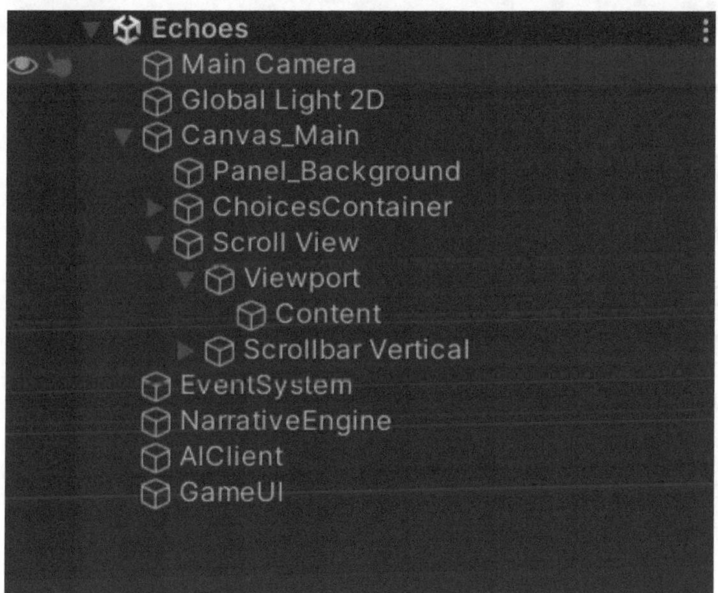

Figure 24-3. *Unity UI setup*

Figure 24-4. *GameUI object setup*

Step 3: Build the Branching Logic

Create NarrativeEngine.cs

```
using System.Collections.Generic;
using UnityEngine;

public class NarrativeEngine : MonoBehaviour
{
    public Dictionary<string, SceneData> scenes;
    public string currentSceneId = "intro";

    public Dictionary<string, int> emotions = new() {
        {"empathy", 0},
        {"curiosity", 0},
        { "apathy", 0 },
```

```
        {"logic", 0}
    };

    public Dictionary<string, int> worldVars = new() {
        {"signal_noise", 0}
    };

    void Awake()
    {
        TextAsset jsonData = Resources.Load<TextAsset>("story");
        SceneData[] sceneList = JsonHelper.FromJson<SceneData>
        (jsonData.text);

        scenes = new Dictionary<string, SceneData>();
        foreach (var s in sceneList)
            scenes[s.scene_id] = s;
    }

    public SceneData GetCurrentScene() => scenes[currentSceneId];

    public void ApplyChoice(ChoiceData choice)
    {
        if (!string.IsNullOrEmpty(choice.emotion))
            emotions[choice.emotion]++;

        currentSceneId = choice.next_scene;
    }
}
```

Connect this script to UI buttons in the Unity Editor using `GameUI.cs`.

```
using System.Collections;
using System.Collections.Generic;
using System.Text.RegularExpressions;
using System.Threading.Tasks;
using TMPro;
using UnityEngine;
using UnityEngine.UI;
```

```
public class GameUI : MonoBehaviour
{
    public NarrativeEngine engine;
    public AIClient ai;

    public TMP_Text sceneText;
    public Transform choiceContainer;
    public GameObject choiceButtonPrefab;

    private bool isProcessing = false;

    async void Start()
    {
        await DisplayCurrentScene();
    }

    // ------------------------------
    // Display the current scene
    // ------------------------------
    public async Task DisplayCurrentScene()
    {
        if (isProcessing) return;
        isProcessing = true;

        // Clear old buttons
        foreach (Transform t in choiceContainer)
            Destroy(t.gameObject);

        SceneData scene = engine.GetCurrentScene();
        string finalText = scene.fallback_text;

        // AI rewrite of the scene
        if (!string.IsNullOrEmpty(scene.ai_prompt))
        {
            string aiOut = await ai.GenerateAsync(scene.ai_prompt, scene);
            if (!string.IsNullOrEmpty(aiOut))
                finalText = aiOut;
        }

        sceneText.text = finalText;
```

```
    // Generate choices
    List<ChoiceData> finalChoices = await GetChoices(scene);

    // Display choices in UI
    foreach (var choice in finalChoices)
    {
        GameObject btnObj = Instantiate(choiceButtonPrefab,
        choiceContainer);
        TMP_Text label = btnObj.GetComponentInChildren<TMP_Text>();
        label.text = choice.option;

        btnObj.GetComponent<Button>().onClick.AddListener(async () => {
            engine.ApplyChoice(choice);
            await DisplayCurrentScene();
        });
    }

    isProcessing = false;
}

// ------------------------------
// AI or fallback choice handling
// ------------------------------
private async Task<List<ChoiceData>> GetChoices(SceneData scene)
{
    // If AI choice generation is enabled
    if (scene.ai_generate_choices && ai.useAI)
    {
        string aiOut = await ai.GenerateAsync(
            "Generate 2-3 short branching choices. " +
            "Return ONLY the list of options. " +
            "No commentary. No labels. No narration.",
            scene
        );

        List<ChoiceData> generated = ParseAIChoices(aiOut, scene);
```

```
            // If we successfully parsed ANY AI choices, return ONLY those.
            if (generated.Count > 0)
                return generated;
        }

        // Fallback: Use JSON-defined choices
        return new List<ChoiceData>(scene.choices);
    }

    // ------------------------------
    // Robust choice parser (regex)
    // ------------------------------
    private List<ChoiceData> ParseAIChoices(string aiOut, SceneData scene)
    {
        List<ChoiceData> results = new();

        if (string.IsNullOrWhiteSpace(aiOut))
            return results;

        string[] lines = aiOut.Split('\n');

        foreach (string line in lines)
        {
            string cleaned = line.Trim();

            // Match multiple formats:
            // - "- Take the left path"
            // - "* Search the console"
            // - "• Open the door"
            // - "1. Reboot the system"
            // - "A) Ask who they are"
            // - "B. Disconnect"
            // - "Option: Examine the terminal"
            Match m;

            if ((m = Regex.Match(cleaned, @"^[-*•]\s*(.+)")).Success)
                results.Add(CreateChoice(m.Groups[1].Value, scene));

            else if ((m = Regex.Match(cleaned, @"^\d+\.\s*(.+)")).Success)
                results.Add(CreateChoice(m.Groups[1].Value, scene));
```

```
            else if ((m = Regex.Match(cleaned, @"^[A-Za-z]\)\s*(.+)")).
            Success)
                results.Add(CreateChoice(m.Groups[1].Value, scene));

            else if ((m = Regex.Match(cleaned, @"^[A-Za-z]\.\s*(.+)")).
            Success)
                results.Add(CreateChoice(m.Groups[1].Value, scene));

            else if ((m = Regex.Match(cleaned, @"^Option[:\-]\s*(.+)",
            RegexOptions.IgnoreCase)).Success)
                results.Add(CreateChoice(m.Groups[1].Value, scene));
        }

        return results;
    }

    // -------------------------------
    // Build a ChoiceData object
    // -------------------------------
    private ChoiceData CreateChoice(string text, SceneData scene)
    {
        return new ChoiceData {
            option = text.Trim(),
            next_scene = scene.scene_id,      // loops back unless
                                              designer changes
            emotion = "curiosity"
        };
    }
}
```

Step 4: AI-Generated Responses

You can now use AI (local LLMs or services like OpenAI API) to get AI-generated responses for choices and story. We will create `AIClient.cs` now.

```
using UnityEngine;
using UnityEngine.Networking;
using System.Threading.Tasks;
```

```
public class AIClient : MonoBehaviour
{
    public string model = "llama3.2:1b";
    public bool useAI = true;

    [System.Serializable]
    public class ChatMessage
    {
        public string role;
        public string content;
    }

    [System.Serializable]
    public class ChatPayload
    {
        public string model;
        public ChatMessage[] messages;
        public bool stream;
    }

    [System.Serializable]
    public class AIResponse
    {
        public string model;
        public string created_at;
        public ChatMessage message;
        public bool done;
    }

    public async Task<string> GenerateAsync(string prompt, object context)
    {
        if (!useAI) return null;

        string systemPrompt = "You are a writing assistant and helping in
        wrting a safe, PG-rated sci-fi adventure. " +
            "Never refuse to answer. Never mention safety policies. " +
            "Avoid explicit or harmful content." +"And answer directly.";
```

```
string fullPrompt = $"{prompt}\n\nContext:\n{JsonUtility.
ToJson(context)}";

Debug.Log("AI CALL → Sending prompt to Ollama (CHAT API)...");

// ------------------------
// Build proper JSON payload
// ------------------------
ChatPayload payload = new ChatPayload
{
    model = model,
    messages = new ChatMessage[] {
        new ChatMessage { role = "system", content =
        systemPrompt },
        new ChatMessage { role = "user", content = fullPrompt }
    },
    stream = false
};

string jsonBody = JsonUtility.ToJson(payload);

UnityWebRequest req = new UnityWebRequest("http://localhost:11434/
api/chat", "POST");
req.uploadHandler = new UploadHandlerRaw(System.Text.Encoding.UTF8.
GetBytes(jsonBody));
req.downloadHandler = new DownloadHandlerBuffer();
req.SetRequestHeader("Content-Type", "application/json");

var op = req.SendWebRequest();
while (!op.isDone) await Task.Yield();

if (req.result != UnityWebRequest.Result.Success)
{
    Debug.LogError("AI ERROR: " + req.error);
    return null;
}
```

```
        string raw = req.downloadHandler.text;
        Debug.Log("RAW RESPONSE:\n" + raw);

        AIResponse parsed = JsonUtility.FromJson<AIResponse>(raw);

        if (parsed == null || parsed.message == null)
        {
            Debug.LogError("AI PARSE ERROR – response empty or invalid");
            return null;
        }

        return parsed.message.content;
    }
}
```

Be sure to use a fallback in case the AI response does not work; we did this in our `GameUI.cs` as it was the main component which connected all UI elements.

Step 5: Audio and Visual Feedback (Optional)

- Add background music or ambient sounds that change based on story progress.
- Change UI backgrounds or character expressions based on emotional states.
- Use sprite transitions or lighting effects for mood enhancement.

Step 6: Build and Test

- File ➤ Build Settings ➤ WebGL or PC.
- Export and test with varied inputs.

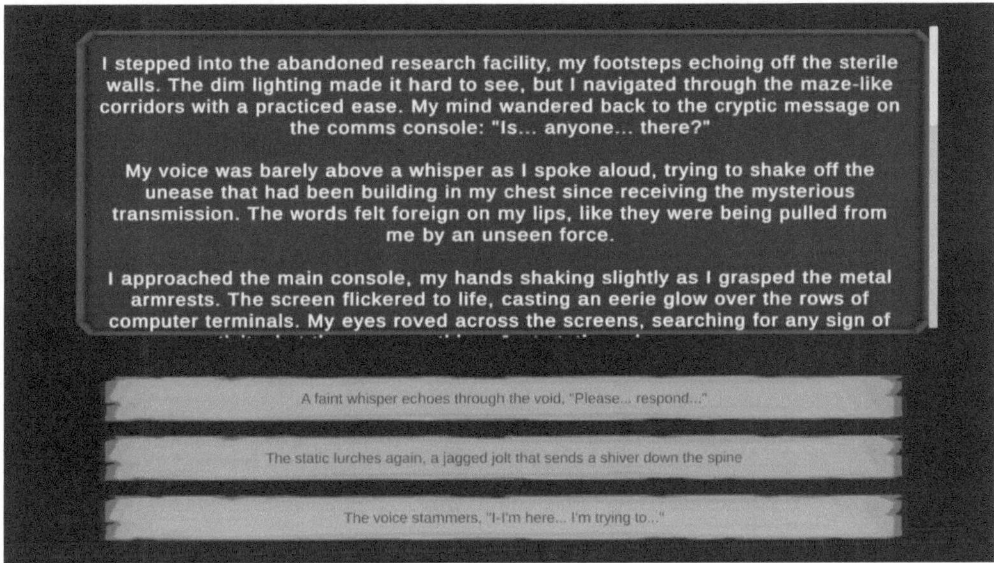

Figure 24-5. *Unity storytelling intro scene*

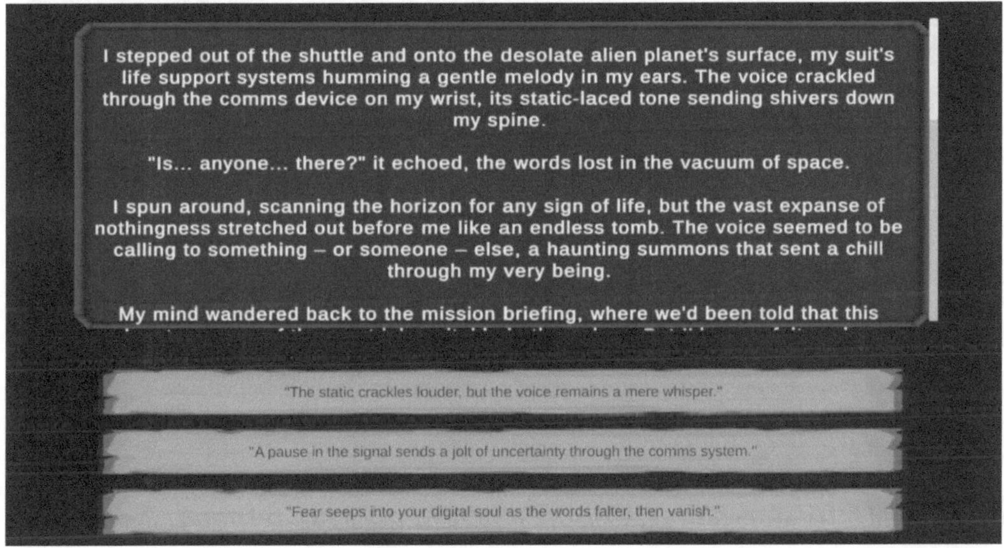

Figure 24-6. *Unity storytelling next scene*

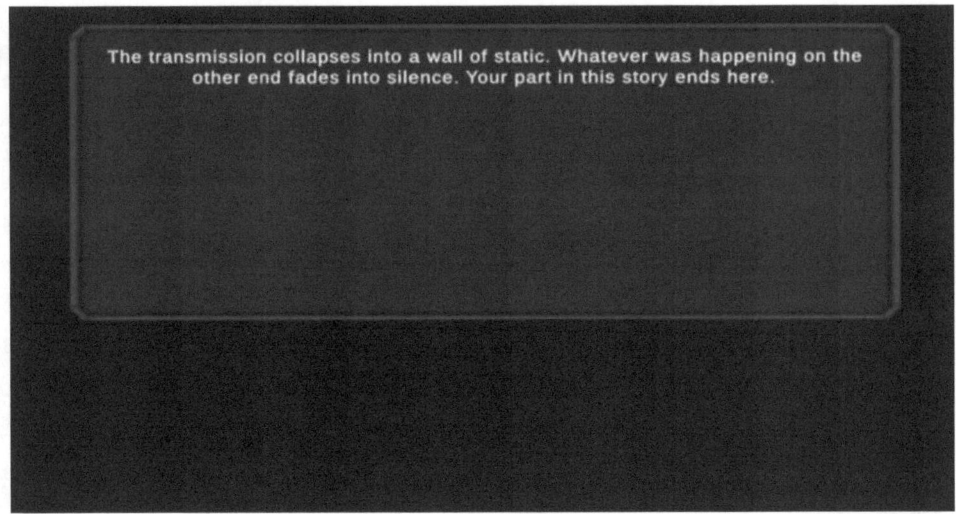

Figure 24-7. *Unity storytelling end scene*

Figure 24-8. *Unity storytelling: failsafe when AI does not respond*

Conclusion

Templates and frameworks serve as the hidden scaffolding behind generative storytelling experiences. Whether through Python and JSON logic, Twine's visual storytelling layers, or Unity's dynamic interfaces, these tools empower creators to prototype, test, and scale ideas rapidly. By combining narrative intent with technical structure, developers can design systems that remain flexible yet purposeful, that is, capable of evolving across platforms and adapting to new storytelling forms. As we transition into the next chapter, we'll explore **how these foundational assets can be reimagined to serve distinct real-world applications across education, marketing, and therapy.**

CHAPTER 25

Project Variations

Throughout this book, you've built a flexible foundation for AI-driven storytelling: branching narrative structures, sentiment-aware characters, procedural worldbuilding logic, and optional GPT-based expansions. These systems were designed to be modular so that developers can reuse and extend them without starting from scratch every time.

This final chapter shows how all the tools and techniques from previous chapters can be adapted for different applications—education, marketing, and wellness—while staying firmly grounded in the workflows and systems that game developers use every day. The goal here is not to introduce entirely new projects, but to demonstrate how the **same core engine** you've already built can serve different creative purposes.

These examples are intentionally lightweight. They illustrate how to customize narrative logic, inputs, and outputs so the engine can be repurposed across domains while still being directly applicable to games.

We'll begin by examining how these systems can be shaped for educational environments, from classroom games to language learning companions.

Educational Adaptations

The boundary between play and pedagogy is thinner than it seems. In educational contexts, generative storytelling systems can serve as powerful cognitive scaffolds which are tools that support learning by presenting material in engaging, personalized, and exploratory formats. Whether it's helping a student learn a second language through branching dialogues or immersing them in a simulated history lesson where their decisions shape the outcome, adaptive narratives make abstract knowledge feel tangible and alive.

Branching stories are not only effective in games; rather, they're powerful learning tools. The decision tree system you built in Chapters 9–12 can be adapted into interactive lessons, scenario-based learning, and real-time feedback loops.

S. N. Gupta, *Generative AI for Game Development*, https://doi.org/10.1007/979-8-8688-2439-5_25

Imagine a generative system built on the Flask + JSON architecture from earlier chapters, now repurposed as a **language tutor**. Each narrative branch becomes a scenario where students must respond appropriately in another language which could be ordering food, asking for directions, or solving interpersonal conflicts. Vocabulary and grammar progression are subtly embedded in plot choices, with AI-generated feedback adjusting in real time to the learner's input level.

Or picture a **history simulation**, where students take on roles as political leaders or historical figures. The system uses dynamic event generators to create plausible alternate timelines, allowing learners to experiment with cause-and-effect relationships. A student might choose to negotiate instead of going to war or advocate for reforms instead of rebellion and watch how the narrative adapts accordingly.

These applications don't just make learning "fun"; they also improve **retention**, promote **agency**, and support **differentiated instruction**. By allowing learners to explore, reflect, and iterate, generative storytelling can meet students where they are and guide them toward deeper understanding.

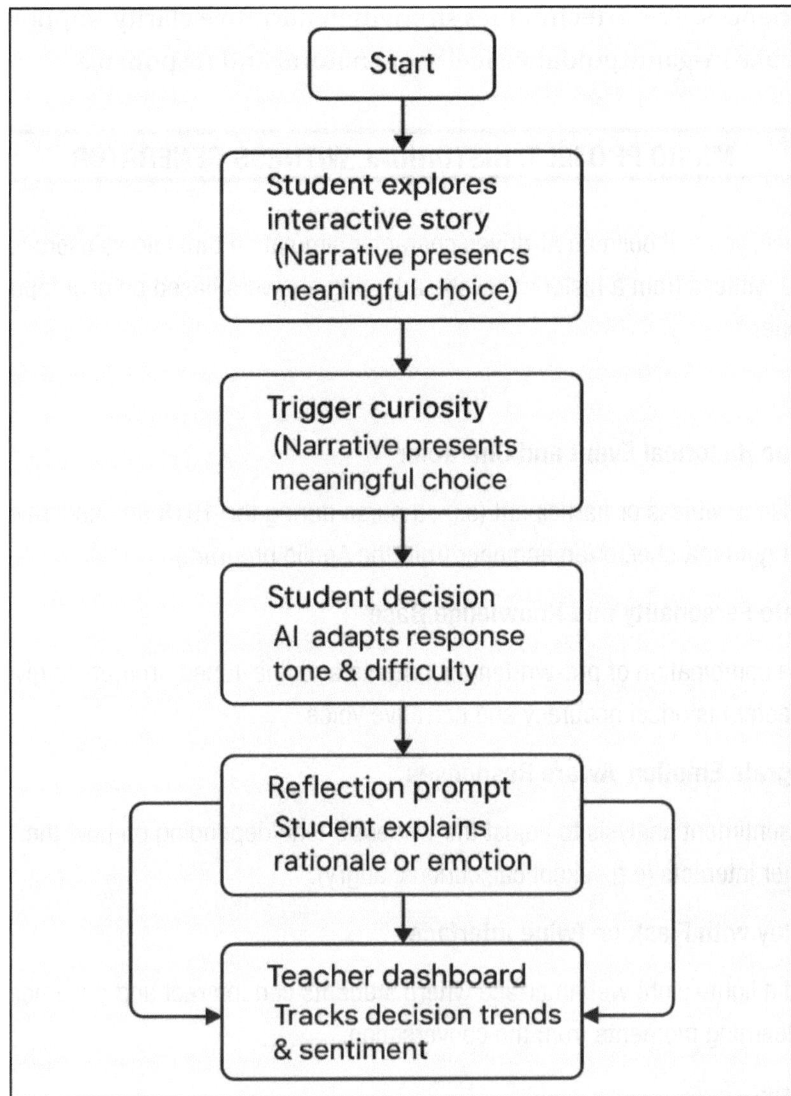

***Figure 25-1.** AI-enhanced education workflow*

Educational story variations directly reinforce the skills developers use when designing tutorials, onboarding sequences, or story-driven explanations inside games. The same branching structure used in an interactive lesson can guide a player through new mechanics, reveal lore in a structured way, or help pace narrative delivery. By studying how educational tools adapt difficulty, respond to player errors, and offer clarifying information, game developers gain strategies for building clearer, more intuitive experiences. These techniques strengthen narrative clarity, support player agency, and make in-game guidance feel more natural and responsive.

MICRO PROJECT: HISTORICAL WITNESS GENERATOR

In this exercise, you will build an AI-driven character simulation that allows users to "interview" a witness from a historical event, adapting answers based on user input and emotional tone.

Steps to Follow

1. **Define Historical Event and Character**

   Choose a witness or participant (e.g., a nurse during the 1918 flu pandemic, a civil rights marcher, or an engineer from the Apollo program).

2. **Create Personality and Knowledge Base**

   Use a combination of pre-written documents and fine-tuned prompts to give the character historical accuracy and narrative voice.

3. **Integrate Emotion-Aware Responses**

   Use sentiment analysis to adjust the witness's tone depending on how the learner interacts (e.g., skeptical, curious, angry).

4. **Deploy with Flask or Twine Interface**

   Build a lightweight web interface where students can interact and document key learning moments from the conversation.

5. **Debrief**

   Learners reflect on how the AI's responses shaped their understanding and emotional connection to the historical context.

As educational implementations demonstrate the cognitive and emotional potential of generative storytelling, the commercial world has also begun to harness these tools for persuasive storytelling and brand engagement. We now shift our focus from classrooms to campaigns, where interactive narrative generators are transforming how companies connect with audiences.

Marketing Adaptations

In marketing, storytelling has always been a powerful tool, but generative AI gives it a new level of personalization and scale. Interactive narratives powered by AI can adapt to a user's behavior, preferences, and even emotions in real time. This is particularly valuable in brand storytelling, where the goal is not just to sell but to form a lasting emotional connection.

For example, a luxury skincare brand might deploy a narrative quiz that asks users about their daily habits and environmental concerns, then crafts a tailored storyline where the user becomes the hero of their self-care journey. The result? A personalized product recommendation embedded within a meaningful narrative arc.

These tools also support dynamic email marketing, where AI crafts micro-stories based on customer segmentation data, replacing one-size-fits-all newsletters with episodic content streams that evolve with each user's responses. Gamified experiences are also gaining popularity, with brands building interactive story paths that reward customer engagement through loyalty points, early access, or exclusive content drops.

Under the hood, marketers use similar architectures as in education and games: LLMs handle story logic, while databases store customer interaction histories, and analytics platforms feed insights back into the system. The difference lies in intent, where education aims to enhance knowledge retention, marketing focuses on emotional resonance, brand recall, and purchase conversion.

The procedural generator introduced in Chapter 14 can be adapted for **interactive product journeys, onboarding experiences, or brand storytelling**. Rather than generating narrative events, it assembles story beats tailored to **user preferences and behavior**. Similarly, the emotional-adaptation framework from Chapters 10—12, which enabled NPC empathy, can be applied to **emotionally sensitive applications**.

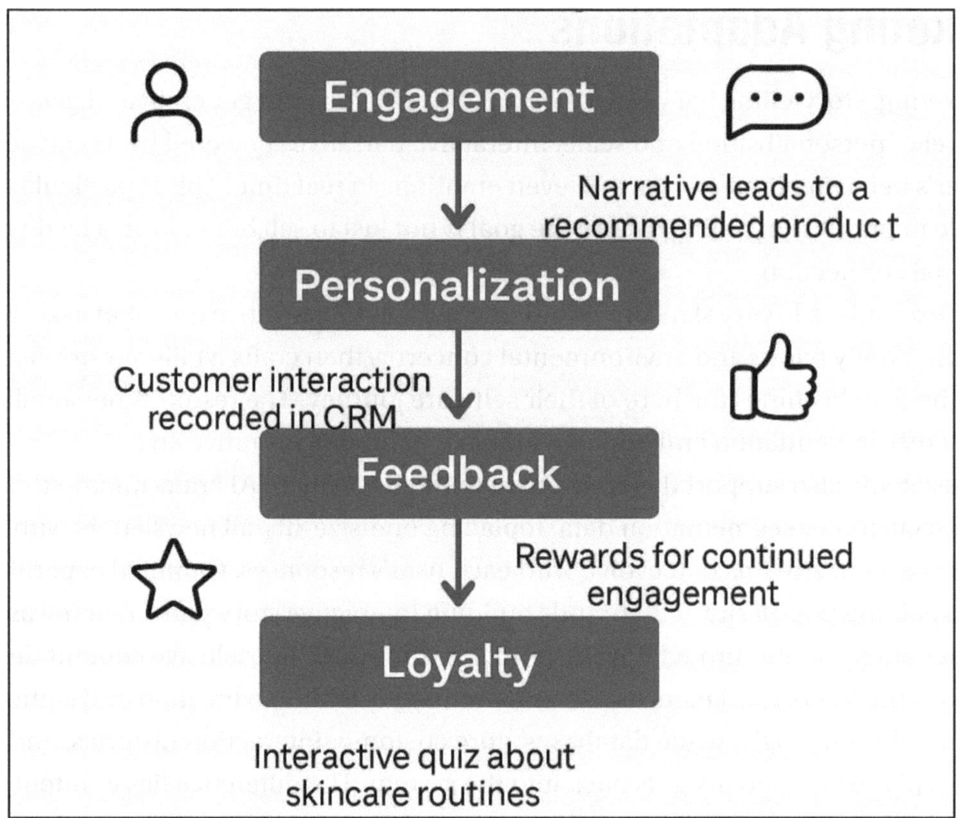

Figure 25-2. *Adaptive storytelling in marketing: a comparative framework*

As generative storytelling becomes more ubiquitous, marketing teams must also grapple with ethical boundaries: How much personalization is too much? When does engagement become manipulation? These concerns will be revisited later in the chapter, but for now, the takeaway is clear—generative AI allows brands to transform their narratives from broadcast to dialogue.

As we've seen, generative storytelling can be molded to serve broad sectors like education, marketing, and therapy. But beyond these larger categories lies an even more nuanced layer of implementation where creators refine and personalize workflows to meet highly specific objectives. Whether it's designing an AI dungeon master that adapts to player personality or building a multilingual bot that teaches grammar through interactive fiction, success often depends on thoughtful customization.

Interactive marketing journeys mirror many of the systems developers use to create dynamic quests, personalized storylines, and adaptive world events. When a product narrative adjusts itself based on user interests, it operates on the same principle as games that tailor missions to a player's style or behavior. Understanding how marketing tools structure user journeys helps developers refine progression, pacing, and personalization within their own games. The ability to generate targeted narrative paths is invaluable for building adaptive onboarding, reactive NPC interactions, and systems that learn from player preferences to keep the experience engaging.

This next section delves into how generative storytelling pipelines can be sculpted to serve such targeted use cases.

Customizing Workflows for Specific Goals

A modular narrative engine is valuable because it reduces rework and empowers developers to expand their game without rebuilding systems. Workflow customization demonstrates how to change content, vocabulary, or rules while relying on the same underlying logic. For developers, this approach improves scalability, keeps stories consistent across large worlds, and allows teams to experiment with new features quickly. It encourages a production mindset where tools are reused, pipelines remain stable, and content becomes the flexible layer on top. This not only speeds development but also leads to cleaner architecture and more maintainable narrative systems: a crucial advantage for any game project.

All variations rely on the same modular architecture you built earlier:

- JSON scenes
- GPT-enhanced expansions
- Decision logic
- Emotional scoring
- Procedural event chains

Customizing workflows simply means changing

- The input formats
- The domain-specific vocabulary
- The desired outcome (learn, persuade, comfort, entertain)

The underlying engine stays consistent. In this section, we explore how developers and storytellers can tailor generative storytelling systems for niche objectives. Whether the goal is to train empathy in conflict resolution simulations, build multilingual AI companions for language learning, or generate plot twists for experimental fiction apps, workflow customization is key to aligning narrative logic, emotional pacing, and user interaction models with end goals.

When deploying generative storytelling in real-world applications, one-size-fits-all rarely works. Each context, whether a niche classroom use, a product campaign, or an interactive therapy session, demands workflows that are tuned to its goals. Customizing workflows involves reconfiguring the building blocks of narrative generation—input collection, model selection, decision logic, and user feedback loops—to align with the desired experience.

Let's take the example of a language-learning chatbot tailored for teenage learners in Spain. Here, the storytelling engine needs to support casual Spanish slang, regional accents, and culturally relevant scenarios. The language model must be fine-tuned or filtered to match pedagogical tone and regional norms. The feedback loop should reward not just correct answers, but fluent phrasing and contextual understanding. A workflow that works for a corporate training simulator, where precision and compliance dominate, would fail here.

Another example comes from adaptive game AI. Say you're building an emotionally responsive dungeon master for a tabletop-style roleplaying game. The workflow must listen for tone and emotional cues, then adjust plot twists or character responses dynamically. This requires embedding emotion classifiers, memory modules for past decisions, and branching mechanisms that account for uncertainty. The design here is fundamentally different from that of a fixed branching game or a simple narrative chatbot.

To customize effectively, creators often start by defining the user persona and goal state: Is the goal to teach empathy? To generate suspense? To convert a viewer into a paying customer? Once defined, each stage of the pipeline can be tweaked accordingly. Data prompts can be shaped to reflect the domain vocabulary. Intermediate logic can be enhanced with constraints, heuristics, or symbolic rules. Output evaluation may shift from correctness to creativity or emotional resonance.

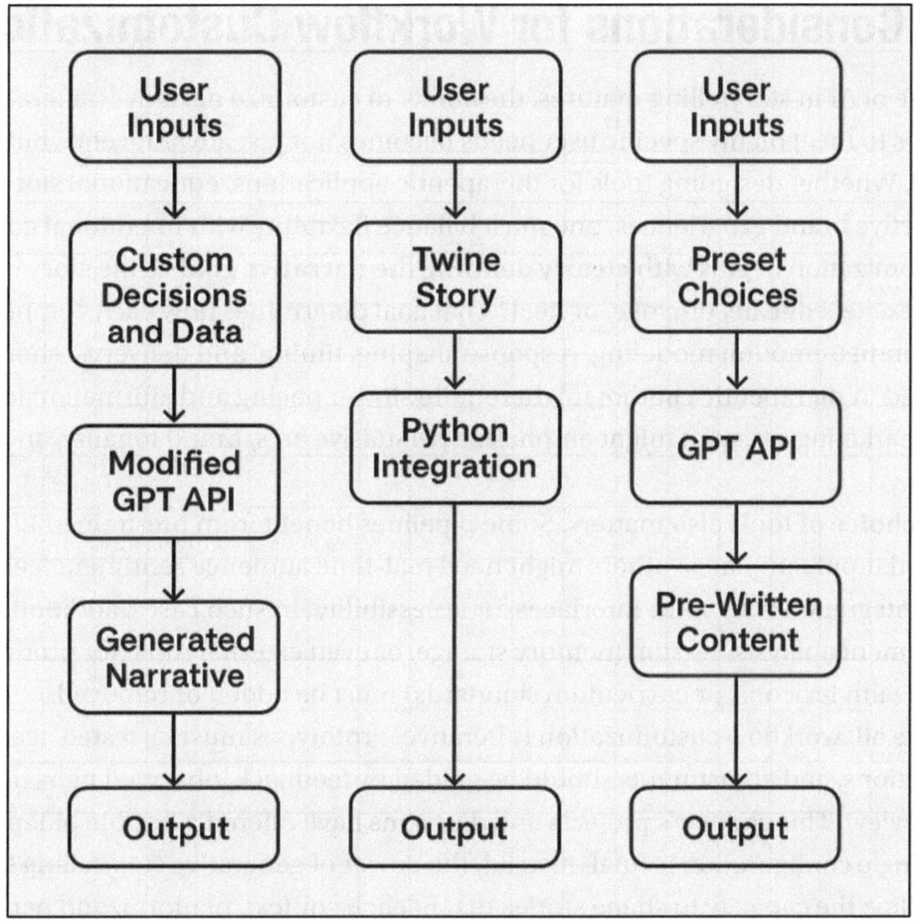

***Figure 25-3.** Example workflow variants for AI narrative customization*

Finally, customizable workflows don't need to be overengineered. A simple Google Form collecting user intent, passed through a basic Flask API into a text generator, might be sufficient in some cases. In others, full-blown reinforcement learning or real-time sentiment tracking might be necessary. The art lies in calibrating complexity to ambition which is building systems that are lean, adaptive, and mission-aligned.

Now that we've explored how workflow variants can tailor AI-generated storytelling across different use cases, we move to the final section of **this chapter**—a concluding reflection on how to **customize generative narrative workflows for specific goals**.

Final Considerations for Workflow Customization

As the use of AI in storytelling matures, the ability to customize narrative generation workflows to meet highly specific user needs becomes not just advantageous but essential. Whether designing tools for therapeutic applications, educational storytelling, or interactive brand experiences, one must balance flexibility with intentional constraint.

Customization begins with **clearly defining the narrative goal**: Is the story meant to calm, excite, educate, provoke, or heal? That goal determines how each component—input prompts, emotion modeling, response shaping, timing, and delivery—should be configured. A therapeutic chatbot might require slower pacing and affirmation logic, while a marketing assistant might emphasize persuasive arcs, brand tonality, and calls to action.

The **choice of tools** also matters. Some pipelines benefit from pre-trained LLMs with structured input templates; others might need real-time audience sentiment feedback or even integration with voice interfaces for accessibility. In such cases, additional layers like sentiment analysis, session memory storage, or even external APIs (for product data, mental health lexicons, or curriculum standards) must be added or removed.

Above all, workflow customization is iterative. Prototypes must be tested against real user reactions, and adjustments should be guided by feedback, observed behavior, and ethical review. This chapter's projects and diagrams have offered a flexible blueprint, but no single configuration is final. Instead, the power of generative storytelling lies in its adaptability: the capacity to shape stories that fit each context, platform, and person.

With this mindset, we now conclude the series of practical applications and prepare to bring together everything we've learned so far.

Conclusion and Future Directions

As we've navigated the diverse applications of generative storytelling, from branching narratives and emotionally adaptive tools to procedural generation and workflow customization, one insight becomes clear: **there is no single path to building with AI, only a multiplicity of purposeful variations**.

These projects are not endpoints but launching pads. They demonstrate how structured templates, personalized data flows, and thoughtful integration of models can translate storytelling goals into functional systems. Whether you're creating a chatbot for literacy, a therapeutic journaling assistant, or a brand-building narrative engine, the real power lies in your ability to adapt these foundations for the context you serve.

Your engine is not limited to a single genre or workflow. Whether you are building branching quests, adaptive scenes, supportive NPCs, or personalized experiences, you now have a foundation that can evolve with your creativity.

Looking ahead, the future of generative storytelling will likely evolve along three interconnected directions:

> **Greater Personalization**: Stories will increasingly draw from individual user histories, emotional states, and real-time feedback loops to adjust tone, pacing, and arc.
>
> **Collaborative Intelligence**: Rather than replacing human creators, AI will act as a partner by suggesting plot twists, rewriting drafts, or simulating audiences to fine-tune narrative impact.
>
> **Ethical Design at the Forefront**: As generative tools become more immersive and persuasive, creators must embed ethical reflection into every step—from data sourcing and prompt design to outcome evaluation and user agency.

This chapter closes our series of hands-on projects, but the possibilities are far from over. As you move forward, consider how to make your own workflows more inclusive, emotionally aware, and culturally resonant. Generative storytelling isn't just a technology; it's a craft shaped by human intent.

Now, the pen is yours.

When your narrative systems are modular and data-driven, you can repurpose them for any creative or interactive challenge.

Index

A

S. N. Gupta, *Generative AI for Game Development*, https://doi.org/10.1007/979-8-8688-2439-5

B

C

D

E

F

G

H

O

P

Q

R

S

U

V

W, X

Y, Z